Saeculum

Saeculum
Defining Historical Eras in Ancient Roman Thought

PAUL HAY

University of Texas Press
Austin

This book has been supported by an endowment dedicated to classics and the ancient world and funded by the Areté Foundation; the Gladys Krieble Delmas Foundation; the Dougherty Foundation; the James R. Dougherty, Jr. Foundation; the Rachael and Ben Vaughan Foundation; and the National Endowment for the Humanities.

Copyright © 2023 by the University of Texas Press
All rights reserved
Printed in the United States of America
First edition, 2023

Requests for permission to reproduce material from this work should be sent to:

Permissions
University of Texas Press
P.O. Box 7819
Austin, TX 78713–7819
utpress.utexas.edu/rp-form

♾ The paper used in this book meets the minimum requirements of ANSI/ NISO Z39.48–1992 (R1997) (Permanence of Paper).

LIBRARY OF CONGRESS CATALOGING-IN-PUBLICATION DATA

Names: Hay, Paul (Paul Jerome), author.
Title: Saeculum : defining historical eras in ancient Roman thought / Paul Hay.
Description: First edition. | Austin : University of Texas Press, 2023. | Includes bibliographical references and index.
Identifiers: LCCN 2022034827 (print) | LCCN 2022034828 (ebook)
ISBN 978-1-4773-2739-5 (hardcover)
ISBN 978-1-4773-2740-1 (adobe pdf)
ISBN 978-1-4773-2741-8 (epub)
Subjects: LCSH: History—Periodization. | Historiography. | Rome—History—Periodization. | Rome—Historiography.
Classification: LCC DG205 .H39 2023 (print) | LCC DG205 (ebook) | DDC 937/.01—dc23/eng/20220816
LC record available at https://lccn.loc.gov/2022034827
LC ebook record available at https://lccn.loc.gov/2022034828

doi:10.7560/327395

Contents

Acknowledgments   *vii*

Introduction
A New Order of the Ages   *1*

1   Omen History
Sulla and the Etruscans on Periodization   *17*

2   Eternal Returns
Cataclysmic Destruction in Greek and Roman Thought   *40*

3   Inflection Points
Progress and Decline Narratives with Periodization   *70*

4   Beyond the Metallic Ages
Technical Histories and Culture Heroes   *83*

5   Acting Your Age
Periodization in Roman Politics after Sulla   *108*

6   Pyramids and Fish Wrappers
Roman Literary Periodization   *135*

Conclusion
Spaces after Periods   *163*

Notes   *171*

Bibliography   *217*

General Index   *237*

Index Locorum   *253*

Acknowledgments

This book is based on graduate work completed in 2017 at the University of Texas at Austin. I would first like to thank my supervisor, Andrew Riggsby, whose knowledgeable feedback, sage professional advice, and generous guidance helped shape this project over many years while simultaneously shaping me as a scholar.

I would also like to thank the other members of the University of Texas at Austin faculty who were instrumental in assisting my research and encouraging my progress: Karl Galinsky, Ayelet Haimson Lushkov, and Penelope Davies, as well as Molly Pasco-Pranger from the University of Mississippi. I am grateful for the incisive comments from Victoria Pagán and the other anonymous readers for the University of Texas Press. Amy Lather, Jacqueline Dibiasie-Sammons, and Chuck Oughton read early drafts of several chapters and offered encouragement, which I truly appreciated. Several of my colleagues at Case Western Reserve University heard parts of this project and fostered its completion with comments and support; I humbly thank Paul Iversen, Rachel Sternberg, Timothy Wutrich, and Peter Knox. The enthusiastic support of my colleague Janice Siegel at Hampden-Sydney College helped push the book to the finish line. Many others contributed along the way in some form or another, for which I am deeply thankful. All remaining errors in the text are, of course, my own.

Portions of this book, primarily chapter 1, appeared in earlier form as "Saecular Discourse: Qualitative Periodization in First-Century BCE Rome" in *The Alternative Augustan Age* (2019, Oxford University Press). I would like to thank Kit Morrell, Josiah Osgood, and Kathryn Welch, as well as Stefan Vranka at OUP, for their kind permission to include a revised version of that text in this volume. Early drafts of various parts of this book were delivered as papers at the 2017 Society for Classical Studies Annual Meeting in Toronto and the 2018 Classical Association of the Middle West and South (Southern Section) Biennial Meeting in Winston-Salem; I benefited greatly from the helpful questions and comments of the attendees at both events. I would especially like to thank the editorial staff at the University of Texas Press, in particular Jim Burr and Robert Kimzey for their extensive guidance, as well as Kerri Cox Sullivan and Suzanne Rebillard for their indefatigable copyediting and proof-reading prowess. I would also like to thank Michael Hendry for compiling the indices.

Finally, I would like to thank my immeasurably supportive family, who made everything possible: Mom and Dad, John and Jessica, Kathy and Hans, and all the rest.

Saeculum

Introduction

A New Order of the Ages

An apocryphal quotation, most often attributed to historian Arnold J. Toynbee, declares that "history is just one damn thing after another." Of course, one form of transmitting historical data, the "chronicle," simply is, in fact, a list of one thing after another as each occurred. When we speak of history, or perhaps more specifically of historiography, however, we do not imagine mere lists of events in chronological order, but instead we expect more sophisticated explanations of events organized so as to convey causality and purpose. History is not the aggregate of atomized episodes, but a process of organizing those episodes into a coherent whole. This process is an intellectual activity requiring a degree of historical cognition, by which I mean an awareness of some kind of organization that will make sense to a given audience. In this volume, I recover an ancient mode of chronological discourse, little acknowledged previously, by which Romans created history.

The creation of a history is different than the mere accounting of facts in chronological order. Historiography inevitably seeks to apply a degree of coherence to the events one has chosen to describe, and by so doing it artificially creates a comprehensible, unified sequence of events; in other words, to create history is to narrativize a chosen set of events. The emphasis on the narrative underpinning of any claimed account of history was a career-long focus of the philosopher of history Hayden White, perhaps most famously articulated in his 1973 book *Metahistory: The Historical Imagination in Nineteenth-Century Europe* and explored more fully in his 1987 essay collection *The Content of the Form: Narrative Discourse and Historical Representation*. While White's elaborate system of typologies is not germane to my project, I share

2 | *Saeculum*

with him an insistence on the artificiality of any cognitive organization of time into history. As he writes, the "value attached to narrativity in the representation of real events arises out of a desire to have real events display the coherence, integrity, fullness, and closure of an image of life that is and can only be imaginary."[1] What I focus on in this study is one specific mechanism through which the Romans acted on this desire; my interest is in the discursive framework with which the Romans attempted to narrativize events in order to craft histories, whether of their civilization, of their city, of their literature, of their moral development, or of any other chosen focus. This mechanism is, ultimately, a variation on the process of periodization.

Periodization, generally speaking, is the categorization of the past into quantitatively discrete units of time (i.e., periods) with unifying characteristics.[2] By breaking down the timeline into coherent time units, periodization provides an artificial, yet comprehensible, framework through which we can try to understand individual events in context. Thus the ultimately fictive process of periodization has a genuine utility to it, providing thinkers with more digestible units with which to narrativize history.

A historical narrative can take many shapes. Linear narratives can be teleological, aiming at a particular endpoint (such as Fukuyama's well-known "end of history," in which Western liberal democracy is the *telos* of modern political development) or just moving in a general direction ("progress" or "decline"). Historical narratives can be circular, in which the same general trends recur endlessly in the same order; they can be parabolic, as in a "rise and fall" (such as Thomas Cole's "The Course of Empire" series of paintings) or its opposite; they can be sinusoidal, perpetually wavering back and forth between trends in a never-ending pendulum movement. Sometimes historians appeal to metaphors such as the body–state analogy, in which the growth and development of a state matches the phases of maturation in a human body, from childhood to senescence. Polybius (6.51.4) famously described a historical anacyclosis in which governments continually move through three phases of political organization, each beginning in a positive version but devolving into a negative version. (As we will see, this model retained a degree of influence in first-century BCE Rome.) Periodization can thus provide the building blocks for all these narrative arcs, with the historical timeline having been organized into discrete units; it is a mode of structuring history for the purpose of creating narrative.

Of course, exactly how useful any periodized timeline may be will vary, and there are perils to this sort of narrativization of history given the fundamental arbitrariness of the activity. Eviatar Zerubavel has written extensively about the sociology of time, and in his 2003 book *Time Maps: Collective Memory and the Social Shape of the Past*, he summarizes the intellectual dangers of periodization: one must inflate the differences between two chronologically close events that occupy two different periods, and likewise one must exaggerate the similarities of events within the same period even if they may be hundreds or thousands of years apart. Having selected the particular qualitative characteristics of one's chosen period (its "identity"), one must "lump together" events that, from many other perspectives, seem decidedly unrelated. For Zerubavel, particular episodes become remembered as marking the end of one period and the beginning of another because "they are collectively perceived as having involved significant identity transformations."[3] The identities of the periods constitute the narrative that is created by the historian, and "the temporal breaks we envision between supposedly distinct historical 'periods' help articulate mental discontinuities between supposedly distinct cultural, political, and moral identities."[4]

Despite the basic arbitrariness of periodization in general, one nonetheless notices that certain periodized timelines (and, inherently, periodized narratives of history) are entrenched within various cultures. In Zerubavel's words, this is a product of social forces: "Any system of periodization is thus inevitably social, since our ability to envision the historical watersheds separating one conventional 'period' from another is basically a product of being socialized into specific *traditions* of carving the past."[5] What Zerubavel leaves less analyzed, though, are the structural forces (generally top–down) that help certain periodized timelines become more socially widespread than others. Throughout this book, I direct my focus toward the originators and producers of Roman periodization systems and hypothesize the rationales behind their chosen systems.

Roman examples of periodization occur less frequently than one would perhaps expect. The Romans never seem to have talked about centuries or decades as units with any sort of qualitative identity.[6] Consular years, although used frequently as chronological markers,

4 | *Saeculum*

are never referred to with any sort of qualitative identity (as Americans might talk about the "Reagan years"). When the Romans discussed their early kings, they never gave attributes to specific regnal periods, and even during the Empire the Romans devoted little energy to describing emperors' reigns as distinct temporal units.[7] Despite their attention to calendars and *fasti*, the Romans never utilized their *formal* chronographical terminology to set up qualitatively defined periods from them. Most provocatively, Nicholas Purcell has asserted that the erection of the Capitoline temple was understood even decades later as a chronological marker from which dating could occur (as if inaugurating a new era of time).[8] It is true that the Romans knew of the concept of periodization well before the first century BCE, but the specific form of periodization that saecular discourse encouraged—qualitative, discrete, and multiple eras—was an innovation of the last century of the Republic.

The Romans' experiments with periodization largely began during the first century BCE, through the adaptation of not chronographical but divinatory language. The use of periodization by the Roman intellectual community has, to date, received limited scholarly attention.[9] The most sustained overview of the Roman periodizing habit is found in the relevant chapters of G. W. Trompf's 1979 volume *The Idea of Historical Recurrence in Western Thought*. For Trompf, the Romans' periodized systems are largely influenced by the anacyclosis of Polybius, itself a vaguely periodized and cyclical timeline of political organizations. But Trompf distinguishes only two forms of Roman historical consciousness during the first century BCE: political narratives (which need not even be periodized, but could simply be a general moral decline) and "Age theory," roughly corresponding to the metallic age mythology first seen in Hesiod's *Works and Days*. I argue throughout this book for a more robust Roman use of periodization to organize history, both past and future. More recently, Denis Feeney's 2007 book *Caesar's Calendar: Ancient Time and the Beginnings of History* stimulated a fresh interest, among scholars of both Roman literature and Roman history, in the pervasive cultural consequences of Julius Caesar's calendar reform (and the larger pattern of technical knowledge moving out of the hands of elites and into a non-elite expert class). Feeney's volume pointed the way toward a greater exploration of time discourse within the first century BCE, which I have taken up with this monograph.

Two other recent studies have also approached the idea of periodization in antiquity in ways that usefully complement my own research. Many scholars have noted affinities between the Augustan regime and earlier Hellenistic kingships, and Paul J. Kosmin's 2018 book *Time and Its Adversaries in the Seleucid Empire* has shown that the Seleucids were experimenting with political propaganda that involved dividing history into epochs (with resistance in the form of alternative historical timelines). Similarly, Trevor Luke's 2014 book *Ushering in a New Republic: Theologies of Arrival at Rome in the First Century BCE* draws a connection between the new vocabularies of time at Rome in the first century BCE (as a result not just of the reforms identified by Feeney but also of various other strands in Republican thought and ritual) and the anthropological concept of the "culture hero," asserting like I do that Sulla's contribution to later Roman behavior was immensely significant. What I hope to contribute to these scholarly discussions about first-century BCE Roman thought is the idea that the Romans developed and eventually instituted the concept of periodization, and did so in a culturally characteristic way.

The form of periodization most often used by the Romans during the first century BCE is based on the concept of the *saeculum*. A *saeculum* was a unit of time in Etruscan divinatory ritual that marked the "lifetime" of a particular town or civilization, but the Romans adapted this concept to refer to an "age" or "era" in the cosmic timeline of events in a particular historical focus.[10] This Roman form of periodization organized both past events and future events (a vestige of the divinatory origin) into *saecula*, and because these timelines are so strongly narratological in nature, I refer throughout this book to this method of periodization as "saecular discourse" or "saecularity." Saecularity is a discursive mode; it is a way of talking about history that, through its own language, constitutes a narrative structure for that history, even if not explicitly laid out as such. Thus, saecularity is also inevitably a way of thinking about history, or indeed of perceiving history itself; it is a piece of "cognitive software" that emerges in the Roman intellectual world during the first century BCE. Of course, saecular discourse is not only a cognitive concept, but also a cultural one: its emergence in Rome happens within a set of previous cultural contexts, and its deployment throughout the first century BCE occurred as Roman thinkers pursued particular intellectual goals within their communities. My approach to periodization in this

6 | *Saeculum*

book, then, balances questions of what the Romans are saying in the saecular mode *and* what they hope to achieve by saying it in that mode.

From its roots in the first century BCE, periodization gained increasing cultural cachet at Rome until the rise of Christianity, at which point it broke off into various directions. Due to both the size constraints of this work and because of further developments in the Neronian period and beyond (including millenarianism and the chiliastic movements of Christian Rome which began to emerge at this time), I have limited the temporal scope of this project to the period from roughly 88 BCE to the end of the reign of Augustus in 14 CE. Brief analyses of texts before and slightly after this range appear, but I am largely interested in the first century BCE and the intellectual developments therein. From a geographical standpoint, my focus is mostly within the city of Rome, although relevant examples from the provinces also appear. My evidence comes chiefly from Roman literature, but I discuss saecular discourse in epigraphic sources, in cult practice, and in other elements of ancient material culture.[11]

After the death of Augustus, senate members competed with each other to offer up lavish honors to grant the deceased *princeps*. Some senators proposed that his funeral procession should pass through the triumphal gate, or that the name "August" should be transferred to September because he was born in September. One unnamed senator suggested (unsuccessfully, it seems) that the entire span of time that marked the life of Augustus should be named the *"saeculum Augustum"* and entered as such in the *Fasti*.[12]

This is a peculiar anecdote (and possibly apocryphal, although there is no good reason to reject it out of hand). It tells us that by 14 CE the technical term *saeculum* was familiar enough among the senators and, presumably, the Roman people that passing such a resolution would be meaningful (and would confer honor not only on Augustus but on the unnamed senator who proposed it).[13] This term originally had a connection with human lifespans,[14] so the designation of Augustus's entire life as the *"saeculum Augustum"* bears a certain technical accuracy. The peculiar aspect of the proposition is that it would honor many years of the Augustan Age which occurred before Augustus was known for anything (or even named Augustus); the senate would be paying respect not only to the decades of his reign as *princeps* but also to the messy decades leading up to them. It is also an honor unlikely to be offered to Augustus's successor Tiberius at his death, because his own lifetime overlapped with that of Augustus; it is ambiguous what the impact of the honor would be if the same years could be part of two different named *saecula*. Moreover, this proposition would seem to be a bit of a faux pas: Augustus had taken pains to "re-calculate" that *saeculum* by which Ludi Saeculares were organized before putting on his games in 17 BCE (perhaps for many Romans the first time they became familiar with the term), setting it at 110 years instead of the customary 100.[15] For the senate then to declare a new *saeculum*, totally detached from the usual sequence, and set at a little under 76 years, would seem to expose the whole system as suspiciously arbitrary and thus taint Augustus's celebration of those games. Clearly, for these risks and concerns to have been ignored,[16] the proposed honor of an eponymous *saeculum* must have conveyed great prestige and significance to the Romans. What do we make of the *saeculum*?

The term *saeculum* has a broad lexical range. Often it represents a generation of people, whether in one single family or line, or in the general population more broadly. Similarly, it can refer to a period of time roughly corresponding to an average human lifetime (or a particular person's lifetime, as it does in the proposed Augustan *saeculum*). It also is frequently used by prose authors to indicate a period of 100 years (as in the modern term "century"). But perhaps the most important use of the term *saeculum* is in reference to divisions of history, commonly those metallic ages whose literary history can be traced back to Hesiod's *Works and Days*.[17] This cosmic use of *saeculum* comes from the vocabulary of Etruscan divinatory theory and practice, in which civilizations have a set amount of *saecula* before their destruction.[18]

As should be obvious from these shifting definitions, the concept of the *saeculum* is malleable. Over the course of the first century BCE, Roman writers and other figures use this concept in a variety of contexts and for a variety of purposes, experimenting with its meaning and pushing it in new directions. What initially begins as an idea about temporality, focused around the specific term *saeculum*, eventually grows to become an entire discursive language, absorbing not just other terms (*aetas, aevum, tempus*) but also related concepts from the anthropological sphere (culture heroes, Metallic Age mythology) and the philosophical realm (palingenesis, ekpyrosis). Thus we might say that the concept of the *saeculum* (as Sulla received it from the Etruscans) evolved into the process of saecularity (as the Roman intelligentsia received it from Sulla). As a result of this persistent innovation, the body of literature engaging with the *saeculum* concept develops a new mode of describing time and history, which manifests as the Roman invention of periodization. This discursive mode is "saecularity."

Saecularity is, in short, a way to narrativize history; it is a discourse that creates a larger framework for all historical events by organizing history into discrete units with qualitative characteristics. For example, when modern American historians refer to the "Atomic Age," they envision a period of time beginning with the Trinity test bomb in 1945 and ending with the fall of the Soviet Union in 1991.[19] This period is marked by the existence of nuclear technology (for bombs as well as for benign energy purposes) and the ongoing possibility of nuclear war, with attendant changes in world politics and social movements. The actual realities of the history of nuclear technology (e.g., nuclear chain reactions that were created before the Trinity test, as well as the continuing proliferation of nuclear technology post-USSR) are not necessarily important here; instead, the discourse of saecularity creates a simpler version of the past (or present) by imagining one period with largely uniform characteristics and a limited focus. The Atomic Age becomes "defined," then, by such qualities as optimism about nuclear power's role as a solution to energy crises, as well as public anxiety about nuclear war; looming thermonuclear devastation is not, in this narrative, a feature of the period before 1945 nor of the period after 1991.

Similarly, we could divide the history of British literature into multiple eras marked by particular aesthetic sensibilities, creating a narrative for the development of literary taste: the outward-looking formality of Neoclassicism is countered by the individual-centered emotion of Romanticism, which in turn gives way to the more detached Victorianism, and so forth. These eras are not quantitatively defined (as would be "eighteenth-century literature," "nineteenth-century literature," etc.) but instead are organized based on the qualitative characteristics of their literature.

This kind of historical schematization was also present in ancient thought. Examples of such "qualitative characteristics" in the ancient world could be the existence of phenomena like sea travel, or differing tastes in metallurgy, or the variety of standards of luxury. As I define the term, "saecularity" is a mode of thought through which one perceives and organizes history into distinct time-units defined by such qualitative characteristics, creating a broader historical narrative—a meaningful shape for the historical timeline. (Thus, saecularity represents a version of periodization, and while the Romans were not natural periodizers,[20] saecularity was their most common form of the practice.) The time-units of saecular discourse (which I refer to throughout this project as *saecula* even if that particular Latin word is not used in the context) tend to have discrete, finite lengths as well as markers for their beginnings and endings. Saecularity gives individual *saecula*, and the transitions between *saecula*, a real and intelligible importance for human history, because the organization of these time-units forms a cosmic narrative, and thus one's description of the sequence of *saecula* becomes how one describes the total human experience.

The discourse of saecularity is marked by a set of features used by authors and artists to convey these qualitatively defined time-units. The bulk of the evidence for this intellectual trend lies in written language. Commonly, the word *saeculum* will be used to refer to these time-units, although (as is demonstrated above) that word has several uses, not all of which relate to saecularity. Other words are also sometimes used instead, primarily *aetas, aevum, lustrum*,[21] and *tempus*.[22] Obviously, not every example of these terms invokes saecular discourse, since they appear in a number of formulaic phrases regarding time, but the words do appear throughout the literature of the first century BCE in certain contexts to refer to chronological schematization.[23]

In addition to this terminology, various mythological figures and imagery commonly invoke saecular discourse. The great flood associated with Deucalion and Pyrrha is a frequent image for saecularity, as it conveys the transition between two totally different eras: in one interpretation of that cataclysm, all humans beings post-flood lack any relation to those who lived pre-flood (except for the human descendants of Deucalion and Pyrrha themselves).[24] Similarly, the fiery destruction caused by Phaethon's ill-fated ride and his subsequent destruction at the hands of Jupiter (often imagined or recast by classical authors as a massive natural disaster) represents another cataclysmic event that can separate epochs of human history.[25] Practitioners of the discourse of saecularity also deploy in many instances the figure of the "culture hero," a quasi-mythological personage whose discovery or invention changes the course of human history. The culture hero thus is capable of bringing about a new *saeculum*

10 | *Saeculum*

through this discovery; the culture hero's invention is so important that it completely alters the fundamental characteristics of the age. One of the paradigmatic culture heroes for classical mythology, Prometheus, is often an element of saecular discourse.[26] Many others, however, are left unnamed, since their inventions are the crucial aspect as it relates to saecularity. These mythological figures, along with the time terminology of qualitatively characterized eras, make up the expressive vocabulary of saecularity.

The discourse of saecularity is a useful mode of thought for a wide variety of intellectual areas. One benefit it provides is a different way to express ideas about the future, which in ancient thought is often limited. Frequently, ancient writers do not imagine a future that is in any meaningful way different from the present.[27] Saecularity provides a language that addresses this feature of ancient thought; one can simply posit a new *saeculum* that will take place in the future, a time-unit qualitatively different from the present. Moreover, saecularity allows one to describe multiple futures, simply by conceiving of a sequence of *saecula* that are still to come. This is crucial for poets who are very concerned about posterity and their own poetic immortality; gestures toward periodization destabilize the notion of a fixed permanent fame. Alternatively, such poets can imagine a future where their works are venerated even if their contemporary fame is meager, providing a way to save face while also attacking more successful rivals.

Saecularity influences Roman expressions not just of the future but also of the past. Roman authors could situate themselves as connected to (or disconnected from) past world events through periodization. They could depict historical incidents as occurring in a different *saeculum* from the present, or they could show events and people from earlier *saecula* as being analogous with contemporary events and people. Periodization also gives a model for describing a seemingly continuous history (e.g., the history of the Roman state) with multiple breaks in the line. This model had sociopolitical appeal; for example, it allowed late first-century BCE figures to show that the Augustan government's relationship with the Republican past (a crucial matter for regularizing the rule of Rome's first *princeps*) could contain elements of both rupture and continuity. The religious overtones of the term *saeculum*, drawn from Etruscan divinatory language, should not be ignored, since saecularity always, at some level, suggests cosmic order and/or divine assent. This is true even though one's saecular model could be "universal" (applying to the entire world) or just localized (relevant only at Rome, for example, or only in one limited realm); parallel sequences are not impossible.[28] Most importantly, the discourse of saecularity allows its practitioner to create a complex narrative for all of history—*not* simply a progress or decline narrative. By dividing human history into *saecula*, one can depict a parabolic arc (such as a Rise and Fall narrative, or a Downfall and Redemption), or a circular model of history, or a pendulum's swing. These extra shapes lend extra levels of sophistication to the worldviews of first-century BCE Romans and expand the possible depictions (and directions) of human history.

Another consequence of using a saecular model is that the transitional moment between two *saecula* (a moment that philosophers termed "metakosmesis") gains increased significance. For those imagining a saecular world history with cosmic importance, these transitions were often accompanied by fantastic omens. But any saecular model will emphasize the people or actions that caused history to move from one *saeculum* to another, and thus talking about such people or actions within saecular discourse increases their historical import: they are not merely worthy of recollection but in fact totally altered the historical timeline. These metakosmetic events are often propelled by the actions of culture heroes, whose introductions of innovative practices change the course of human history. Saecular discourse emphasizes the role of culture heroes by sharpening the focus on their actions as a metonym for an entire era of time.[29] (For example, many important events occurred during the years 1945–1991, but Oppenheimer's work on the Manhattan Project makes him the inaugurator of the Atomic Age.) Metakosmetic events can also be natural disasters such as floods (Deucalion's flood, Ogyges's flood, etc.) or other cataclysms that eliminate some element of the *saeculum* that preceded them (such as the existence of advanced human civilization). Romans could look forward to (or fear) a coming metakosmesis as a way to comment on their own times, or they could designate some aspect of the recent past as the dawning of a new *saeculum* and thus give it a metakosmetic emphasis.

Because of the utility of saecular discourse in the intellectual realm, the first century BCE eventually saw the emergence of periodization in many areas of thought, not just mythological imagery in poetry. Saecular discourse informs Roman discussions on politics (contemporary and earlier), history (Roman and otherwise),

12 | *Saeculum*

philosophy, and most prominently, morality. This wide range of applications demonstrates periodization's broad sociocultural appeal. (Indeed, saecular discourse became such a popular discursive mode that it appears in writings on such obscure topics as the development of fishponds,[30] among others.) But saecularity made its deepest mark in the language of the sociopolitical world of the Augustan period and of artistic, particularly literary, progress. While the mythology of the Metallic Ages (as first seen in Hesiod) is perhaps the most familiar of the applications of saecular discourse during this time, its appeal is not the genesis for the explosion of saecularity, but in fact is just a symptom of a trend that began decades earlier. Indeed, far from being just some literary game for the world of learned poetry, the rhetoric of periodization was a prominent intellectual tool for many first-century BCE Roman thinkers.

The structure of this book emphasizes both the contributing factors in the development of saecular discourse and also the cultural products that this mode of discourse created. In the first chapter, I argue that Sulla introduced the concept of a qualitatively defined *saeculum* to Rome after the omen that signaled the new Etruscan *saeculum* in 88 BCE. The term *saeculum* has its roots in the divinatory language of the Etruscan culture, which we know of chiefly through later sources (who require diachronically minded interpretation). But at a basic ontological level, the term *saeculum* as understood by the Romans of the first century BCE differed strongly from its original use as a term of Etruscan lore. Evidence from the surviving fragments of Sulla's memoirs, as well as the details of Sulla's political career (especially as dictator of Rome), strongly suggests an awareness of the Etruscan lore surrounding his life and, moreover, a deployment of this language for his own self-glorification. It was Sulla's exploitation of Etruscan divinatory practice, from which comes the term *saeculum*, that demonstrated the possibilities of periodization as a tool of political propaganda. Sulla presented himself as an epochal figure in Roman history: a "man of the *saeculum*" (a term I borrow from Luke [2014]) whose arrival in Roman politics would herald the advent of a new era of peace and security for the Republic. Through this exploitation of Etruscan divinatory practice, Sulla subtly transformed the *saeculum* into a qualitatively defined period characterized by his own actions and presence, and thus demonstrated the possibility of saecular discourse as a mode for shaping Roman history. The effect of this change was so profound that, for example, by the second century CE, Plutarch could not imagine the concept of the *saeculum* without each period being defined qualitatively.

Sulla's innovation added a new mechanism for Romans to describe history, but the discourse of saecularity would continue to be molded by the influence of other factors, primarily Greek philosophy. In chapter 2, I consider various elements of Greek philosophy that shaped Roman use and understanding of periodization during the first century BCE. Certain philosophical schools had already discussed the possibility of massive ruptures in the linear trajectory of history: the Stoic "ekpyrosis," the reincarnation of the same soul in different bodies (metempsychosis), and Epicurean infinite reassembly of atoms in the same structure (palingenesis), all of which offered concepts conducive to explaining the temporal consequences of periodization through variations on eternal recurrence. Wedded to the Etruscan concept of the *saeculum*, these ideas (at their broadest conceptual level) helped negotiate the tension between uniformity and novelty inherent in saecularity. Plato's and Aristotle's hypothesized catastrophic disasters nevertheless have survivors, traces of the pre-catastrophe period who can survive into the next phase. These cataclysmic events, which often take the form of plausible natural disasters, mark the transition from one *saeculum* to another (metakosmesis through annihilation). I contend that the Romans begin to use the mythological figures associated with such events, mainly Deucalion and Phaethon, as a shorthand for any sort of saecular transition, such that these two otherwise unrelated figures become, by the first century CE, cognitively linked in the Roman mind. The destruction of civilization also plays a major role in Roman thought in the descriptions of a "post-Roman world," literary evocations of a future *saeculum* after Rome has been destroyed. I show how these earlier philosophical suggestions are deployed via the language of periodization to articulate anxieties about the possibility that, despite the Principate's insistence otherwise, Rome might not survive forever. Thus, I situate the first-century BCE experimentation with the *saeculum* within a longer history of Hellenistic philosophy in Roman intellectual circles.

My explorations into Greek philosophy's influence on Roman saecularity reveal some of the ways that Romans use this discursive mode in order to discuss various kinds of Roman histories. In the

14 | *Saeculum*

remaining chapters, I make a more expansive claim for applications of saecular discourse in Roman thought. First I begin, in chapter 3, with an examination of progress and decline narratives in the Roman intellectual world. The concepts of historical progress and historical decline were already fundamental ideas in antiquity long before the end of the Roman Republic. The new discursive mode of periodization allowed for a more sophisticated articulation of progress or decline in any given realm by introducing meaningful inflection points, that is, significant historical moments when one stage gave way to another in the ongoing process of progress or decline. This expansion of the discourse meant that credit or blame could be spread to a wider group of people or events. For example, while Romans had long enjoyed the use of moral decline narratives, their traditionalist moral declines were overly simplistic; saecular discourse allowed the narrative to progress in stages, and it let authors pick particular moments and agents to bring about the shift into a new age. Assertions of cultural progress came less naturally to the conservative Romans, but Cicero provides us with an example of a progress narrative about religious credulity in a passage from his *De republica*; I show that Cicero applies the discourse of saecular organization while describing the increasing stages of religious skepticism in Roman history. The introduction of periodization to the Roman intellectual world resulted in an energized use of progress and decline narratives because of the increased ability to articulate meaningful nuances through saecular discourse.

The mythology of the metallic ages is the most common area of classical scholarship for discussions of the *saeculum* and Roman discussion of historical ages, but the unfortunate consequence of this scholarly focus is that almost no attention has been paid to parallel but distinct developments in saecular narratives that the language of periodization gave the Romans. In chapter 4 I demonstrate the parallel notion of the "technical history," a periodized narrative of the development of a particular skill or cultural practice, which flourished alongside metallic age narratives as a counterexample of saecular discourse in action. Technical histories, found in authors ranging from the poet Propertius to the medical writer Celsus, also emphasize the importance within periodization of the culture hero, a quasi-mythological personage whose discovery or invention changes the course of human history. The culture hero thus is capable of bringing about a new *saeculum* through this discovery; the culture hero's invention is so important that it completely alters the fundamental characteristics of the age. Two of the paradigmatic culture heroes for classical mythology, Prometheus and Hercules, were often elements of Roman saecular discourse in the first century BCE, as we will see in this chapter and the following one. While the Metallic Ages mythology was prevalent within Roman poetry, it existed alongside other saecular articulations of temporality.

In chapter 5, I examine the use of saecular discourse in the Roman political world after Sulla. Although it was Sulla who first exposed the power of periodization as a political tool, the decades after his death saw virtually no deployment of such language. Only later did Cicero (on behalf of Pompey and, later, himself), Messalla Corvinus, and Agrippa use the vocabulary of the culture hero in order to suggest the coming of a new political age at Rome. But the most familiar beneficiary of periodization in the Roman political sphere was Octavian (later to be known as Augustus). Augustus and his Principate are indelibly linked to the concept of the Roman *saeculum* through the various declarations of a new Golden Age that can be read not only in imperial iconography but also in the poetry of Augustus's reign. I examine three historical "objects" most closely associated with the saecular historicizing of Augustus and show how, in light of the expansive intellectual exploration of periodization throughout the first century, these objects offer more ambiguous support than has been previously understood: the Ludi Saeculares, the myths of Augustus's birth, and the Palatine Hill complex. These case studies reveal the multifaceted ways in which periodization furthered the goals of the Augustan government; saecular discourse had various contours (beyond Golden Age rhetoric) that aligned, or could be made to align, with Augustan politics.

I proceed in the final chapter to focus on one particular form of the technical history more complex than the others: literary history. A growing awareness that Roman literary history could also be conceived of in terms of literary *saecula*, literary ages analogous to the ages of human history, gave Roman writers a new way to situate themselves within the ongoing dialectic of Roman literature by historicizing developments within genres or aesthetic movements. I argue that through an organization of literary history into qualitatively defined periods, Romans could explain away their current lack of success, or the popularity of their literary rivals, by depicting it as the result of the aesthetic tastes of the current *saeculum*, which would

16 | *Saeculum*

soon give way to the new tastes of a new age. The Bibliotheca, the library constructed on the Palatine Hill by Augustus, existed as a physical nexus for the political and literary discourse on saecularity, and the existence of a quasi-national library with both Greek and Latin collections could cause Roman writers to reflect on cultural periodization in the broadest sense: the rise and fall of Greek letters had led to the rise of Latin literature, currently reaching its peak. The construction of the Bibliotheca both reacted to and pushed forward the national conversation on literary saecular discourse.

What I hope to show, with this range of examples of periodization, in a variety of different intellectual venues and generic forms, is that this mode of discourse profoundly affected the development of the Roman understanding and articulation of temporality during the first century BCE. We can see that in the century after Sulla, periodization became a prominent tool for understanding various topics of Roman sociopolitical thought, from contemporary morality to literary history, from commentary on the Augustan government to applications of the trope of the Golden Age. Its reach extends not simply to the literature of the time but also to public ritual and monumental architecture, and Augustan poets participated in the national conversation alongside scholars, historians, and political figures. This study of Roman saecular discourse recovers an important facet of the Roman historical consciousness during a time of great sociopolitical upheaval and has consequences for our understanding of Roman historical claims in much of the literature and political activity of the first century BCE.

1 | Omen History
Sulla and the Etruscans on Periodization

The term *"saeculum,"* and the chronological concept attached to that term, came to the Romans from the realm of Etruscan divination. If we wish to understand how the Romans acquired this Etruscan concept, it may be discouraging to discover that our two major sources for the Etruscan *saeculum* doctrine, Plutarch and Censorinus, wrote well after the first century BCE. However, it is not through antiquarian evidence that we can recover the origin of periodization at Rome, but through the behavior of one of its most infamous dictators: Lucius Cornelius Sulla. Sulla's activities during the 80s BCE transformed the city of Rome at all levels: the political, the sociocultural, and even the architectural. But Sulla made no attempt to hide this revolutionary activity; rather, he publicly asserted that this transformation was part of a divine plan, according to which he had been chosen to lead Rome into a new period of history.

The career of Sulla thus provides the first significant instance of periodization in the mainstream Roman intellectual world. As I outline below, Sulla's revolutionary changes to Roman culture included a new way of understanding Roman temporality which proved to be influential among the Roman intellectual community (long after Sulla's career and life had ended). More specifically, Sulla's program of self-presentation enhanced his claims of divine approval by adopting the discourse of periodization: Sulla depicted himself as the inaugurator of a new era, a Sullan Age that would bring about a sense of renewal at Rome. This innovative decision to organize Roman history around himself likely introduced many Romans to the possibilities of saecular discourse and spurred this

18 | *Saeculum*

intellectual trend to greater prominence throughout the first century BCE.

Sulla and the New Era

Lucius Cornelius Sulla (138–78 BCE) was born into a patrician family and received an extensive education, becoming fluent in Greek and acquiring a taste for the dramatic arts. Elected as quaestor to serve under Marius in the Jugurthine War, Sulla first made his name by persuading Bocchus, the king of Mauretania, to betray Jugurtha and hand him over to himself. Because of the publicity around this action, Sulla was able to leverage his standing and take exceptional credit for the Roman success in the war. Sulla rose up the *cursus honorum* in the following decades with more military accomplishments, including a long governorship in the Greek East. As a result of his victories throughout Italy during the Social War (91–88 BCE), Sulla ran for the consulship and won in 88 BCE, but after his command in the Mithridatic War was absorbed by Marius, Sulla marched on the city of Rome and reclaimed his authority by force. Sulla's war against Mithridates was generally successful (and included the sack of Athens) but ultimately inconclusive by the time Sulla returned to Rome in 83 BCE. With his political enemies waiting to attack him, Sulla was forced to march on Rome a second time and defeat his foes in battle. The subsequent civic chaos led to Sulla's election as dictator in 81 BCE, during which period of rule he enacted both an ambitious building program and a series of bloody proscriptions against his enemies and their families which would be remembered later as a major atrocity in Roman history. Upon the completion of his dictatorial activities and a second consulship, Sulla retired to the country and supposedly spent his remaining days in luxury before his death in 78 BCE.

Our evidence for Sulla's rhetoric of periodization lies primarily in the form of his memoirs,[1] a work in twenty-two books that survives only in fragments and was allegedly composed up until his death in 78 BCE.[2] While I will concede that some of the saecular anecdotes from this work may only have been first publicized in the memoirs themselves, I find it likely that Sulla's self-presentation as a man of saecular significance began years earlier, probably as soon as each major incident (such as omens) occurred.[3] Given the earlier

Omen History | 19

numismatic and epigraphic evidence for Sulla's saecular "image management," we can expect that Sulla surely did not wait until the composition of his memoirs to promote his purported blessings from heaven. Thus, it is likely that Sulla's use of periodization to describe himself and his achievements was an ongoing process that extended throughout his career until his death.

Sulla's life (at least within the memoirs, if not also in reality) was marked by several conspicuous prodigies. An omen occurred at Laverna in 90 BCE,[4] before Sulla set out from Rome as a commander in the Social War and thus during the period when commanders would look for signs of divine approval before departure.[5] At Laverna, a chasm opened up in the earth and belched forth flames to the sky;

εἰπεῖν δὴ καὶ τοὺς μάντεις ὡς ἀνὴρ ἀγαθὸς ὄψει διάφορος καὶ περιττὸς ἄρξας ἀπαλλάξει τῇ πόλει ταραχὰς τὰς παρούσας. τοῦτον δὲ αὐτὸν εἶναί φησιν ὁ Σύλλας· τῆς μὲν γὰρ ὄψεως ἴδιον εἶναι τὸ περὶ τὴν κόμην χρυσωπόν, ἀρετὴν δὲ οὐκ αἰσχύνεσθαι μαρτυρῶν ἑαυτῷ μετὰ πράξεις καλὰς οὕτω καὶ μεγάλας. (Plutarch, Sull. 6.7)

Whereupon the soothsayers declared that a brave man, of rare courage and surpassing appearance, was to take the government in hand and free the city from its present troubles. And Sulla says that he himself was this man, for his golden head of hair gave him a singular appearance, and as for bravery, he was not ashamed to testify in his own behalf, after such great and noble deeds as he had performed.[6]

As Ramage writes, "Self-eulogy is clearly at work here . . . and Sulla indulges in it without apology."[7] This is certainly true, but there is more to the anecdote, given its placement within the memoirs. Luke has plausibly argued, based on the reconstruction by Lewis of the structure of the work as a whole, that the Lavernan prodigy would have appeared in the introductory material of book 1 of the memoirs, in the dedication to Lucullus.[8] Such an early appearance in the lengthy work sets a tone for Sulla's memoirs, suggesting that we read the events of his life (e.g., his dictatorship) in light of this omen. With the close proximity of Laverna to the site of the Battle of the Colline Gate, where Sulla later defeated the Samnites (the last holdouts from the Social War) in 82 BCE and earned a triumph, the prodigy then

20 | *Saeculum*

serves in the memoirs as a divine approval of Sulla's subsequent take-
over of Rome following that battle.

The prodigy at Laverna was preceded by another event in 95 BCE
when Sulla was acting as governor in Cilicia. Plutarch describes Sulla's interaction with a Chaldean seer:

> ἱστορεῖται δέ τις ἀνὴρ τῶν μετὰ Ὀροβάζου καταβεβηκότων,
> Χαλδαῖος, εἰς τὸ τοῦ Σύλλα πρόσωπον ἀπιδὼν καὶ ταῖς
> κινήσεσι τῆς τε διανοίας καὶ τοῦ σώματος οὐ παρέργως
> ἐπιστήσας, ἀλλὰ πρὸς τὰς τῆς τέχνης ὑποθέσεις τὴν φύσιν
> ἐπισκεψάμενος, εἰπεῖν ὡς ἀναγκαῖον εἴη τοῦτον τὸν ἄνδρα
> μέγιστον γενέσθαι, θαυμάζειν δὲ καὶ νῦν πῶς ἀνέχεται μὴ
> πρῶτος ὢν ἁπάντων. (Plutarch, *Sull.* 5.5–6)

> It is also recorded that a certain man in the retinue of Oroba-
> zus, a Chaldaean, after looking Sulla intently in the face, and
> studying carefully the movements of his mind and body, and
> investigating his nature according to the principles of his pecu-
> liar art, declared that this man must of necessity become the
> greatest in the world, and that even now the wonder was that
> he consented not to be first of all men.[9]

While Plutarch does not directly attribute this story to Sulla's
memoirs, they are the likely source for his description.[10] On its own,
this anecdote simply makes Sulla look important, a superlative figure
in world history. But as part of Sulla's larger program of self-serving
prodigies and supernatural events, it contributes to the depiction of
Sulla as a singular individual destined to lead Rome unilaterally—
perhaps bringing about a qualitatively different period in Roman
history.[11]

With these earlier events in mind, we come to the events of
88 BCE. This was a watershed year in Roman history, as it saw the
end of the first wave of the Social War, the election of Sulla as consul, and the first time an active general ever led a march on the city
of Rome. Plutarch describes a series of peculiar omens that marked
this year (*Sull.* 7), with the most significant being the following:

> τὸ δὲ πάντων μέγιστον, ἐξ ἀνεφέλου καὶ διαίθρου τοῦ
> περιέχοντος ἤχησε φωνὴ σάλπιγγος ὀξὺν ἀποτείνουσα καὶ
> θρηνώδη φθόγγον, ὥστε πάντας ἔκφρονας γενέσθαι καὶ

Omen History | 21

καταπτῆξαι διὰ τὸ μέγεθος. Τυρρηνῶν δὲ οἱ λόγιοι μεταβολὴν ἑτέρου γένους ἀπεφαίνοντο καὶ μετακόσμησιν ἀποσημαίνειν τὸ τέρας. (Plutarch, *Sull.* 7.3)

But most important of all, out of a cloudless and clear air there rang out the voice of a trumpet, prolonging a shrill and dismal note, so that all were amazed and terrified at its loudness. The Tuscan wise men declared that the prodigy foretokened a change of conditions and the advent of a new age.[12]

Plutarch continues on at this point into a digression on the specifics of the Etruscan system of *saecula*, which will require further analysis below, but for now the crucial information from this passage is the occurrence of a prodigy which many people knew about. Furthermore, Plutarch goes on to say that the senate held a session in the temple of Bellona to discuss this prodigy with the Etruscan soothsayers, thus establishing that the declaration of a new age was known in the Roman political world.[13] A reader of Sulla's memoirs is then invited to draw connections between the Lavernan prodigy of 90 BCE (predicting a sole ruler would save Rome), this transition in *saecula* in 88 BCE (bringing about a new age), and the unprecedented actions of Sulla in that year. Indeed, Luke argues that Sulla desired the Lavernan prodigy to be interpreted by his readers in light of the omens from 88 BCE and the related Social War disturbances (such as the fallout at Rome between Marian and Cinnan partisans and Sulla), including the announcement of a new *saeculum*, and that these connections would have been publicized by Sulla in the 80s, perhaps as early as 88 BCE.[14] Sulla, preordained by the gods to bring about the new *saeculum*, would rule over Rome and favorably transform Roman life and culture.

Beyond Sulla's self-presentation in real life, what did he say about this saecular metakosmesis in his memoirs? It seems more than likely that Sulla wrote about this event, and probably also described the Etruscan system of *saecula* in detail, as well. Sulla was especially interested in omens, prodigies, and the supernatural, as the surviving fragments of his memoirs show, so his failure to mention such an event (especially one that received senatorial attention) would be uncharacteristic and inopportune. Also, having composed twenty-two books of memoirs, Sulla had plenty of room for such digressions.[15] Moreover, in these end-of-career memoirs, Sulla would have

22 | *Saeculum*

used any justification for his earlier actions and preservation of his stature, be it practical or supernatural; Lewis points out that as a result of the dismantling of Sulla's reforms (and legacy) after his retirement, he would have been in a position by the time of the composition of the memoirs to feel the need "to reassert his *dignitas* and *auctoritas*, the validity of his own position, the value of his settlement and his readiness and capacity to defend it."[16] This defensive attitude likely led to an account of his life full of frequent moments of self-glorification.[17]

While Plutarch does not cite Sulla in his description of this episode, that absence of a citation certainly does not preclude the possibility that Sulla is his source.[18] Balsdon noted nine passages in Plutarch's *Sulla*, "all to do with the supernatural and the miraculous, where it seems certain that Plutarch was drawing his material directly from Sulla's book."[19] And Bates points out that many stories in the biography (e.g., the Chaldean seer episode) are so dependent on Sulla's perspective that they must have come from the memoirs even though Plutarch does not directly cite it.[20] While Plutarch may have exerted a stronger presence in the written explanation of the Etruscan *saeculum* doctrine as we receive it (as I will explain below), it is very likely that Sulla described and explained the omen of 88 BCE in his memoirs.[21]

Sulla Makes History

In his memoirs, Sulla embraced the rhetoric of periodization as part of his self-presentation as a singular, epoch-making Roman, but this attitude was not confined to his writings. We can find evidence of saecular discourse as a foundation for his propaganda in various other physical media. Most explicitly, a surviving inscription in Asia shows the introduction of a "Sullan era" in 85/84 BCE for the counting of time, as Hellenistic kings (and, after Sulla, Roman leaders) sometimes implemented.[22] Flower also notes the many other eras he inaugurated throughout Italy, including the *Fasti Ostienses*.[23] This calendar reform reflects a sense of Sulla "bringing about a new age" at the most basic level of chronological organization.

Numismatic examples also suggest a broader Sullan approach to self-referential periodization. As Crawford aptly describes, production of coinage in the 80s BCE occurred at a massive scale (especially in light of the decreased production of the 90s) and regularly featured references to contemporary events, thus providing us with valuable evidence for the larger Sullan program of self-presentation.[24] In 82 BCE Sullan moneyers issued a coin[25] with Janus on the obverse and the prow of a ship on the reverse, apparently an allusion to the story of Saturn sailing to Latium, and being welcomed by Janus, to bring about the Golden Age.[26] While this iconography is very common in Republican coinage of the third and second centuries BCE, in this particular example Sulla has placed his name (and title as *Imperator*) around the prow of the ship. As Ramage writes, "The message is clear: Sulla as the holder of legitimate power, the *imperium*, is bringing a new Golden Age to Rome, an age based in peace as the earlier one had been. The appearance of Sulla's name above the prow underlines the fact that he has replaced Saturn as master of the ship."[27] Even if this particular numismatic imagery lacks a saecular reference, the sheer volume of production of coin types such as this with iconography recalling traditional Republican types from the second century (often with a Roma head on the obverse) helped Sulla identify his cause with the *res publica* and his epochal restoration of it.[28]

One further element of the "Sullan revolution" of the late 80s BCE that contributes to the larger saecular program (through an insistence on Sullan innovation, or re-foundation) is Sulla's extensive building activity.[29] Most important are the many renovations Sulla made to the Forum Romanum and the adjacent parts of the Capitoline. The significance of these works cannot be overstated, as the Forum Romanum was a nexus of sociopolitical action in the city and allowed for the greatest impact of Sulla's building projects on the Roman people.[30] These changes to the cityscape may have been associated with Sulla's other social and political reforms as part of the broader Sullan revolution.[31]

Sulla's activity in the Forum Romanum was manifold.[32] Sulla tore down the rostra and built a new one that was higher and oriented differently than the previous version. Given the rostra's symbolic significance as a site for popular orations and other civic activity, Sulla's rebuilding could enhance his claims to have ushered in a new era of Roman history (a new rostra for a new Rome). Next to the new rostra, Sulla erected a monumental equestrian statue of himself (bearing the title SULLA FELIX).[33] This was, supposedly, the first gilded statue in Rome in centuries,[34] and it

24 | *Saeculum*

was "an eye-catching monument."[35] Sulla deemed it important enough to place it on gold coinage, for which the legend would suggest that the dedication on the statute included both FELIX and DICTATOR.[36] Ramage makes much of this statue, noting that "at the center of Roman political activity and power was an impressive reminder of the charismatic leader who had brought about the present felicitous state of affairs."[37] Further, the statue "served as a symbol of the new *Saeculum Sullanum*."[38] The novelty of a gilded statue, combined with its inscription and its placement in an area so loaded with traditional Republican memory, must have contributed strongly to the feeling that Sulla, with the approval of the gods, had brought a new era (though an era not without some continuity with the past) to the city of Rome.

In addition to his work on the rostra, Sulla repaved the area around it, including the Comitium, which also served to elevate the area slightly. On its face, this action is seemingly innocuous, and probably a much-needed fix to an old, worn pavement. A slightly different effect might have been understood in consideration of the fact that the Forum was "the place where some of the more gruesome displays of the Proscriptions were put on."[39] The pavement of the streets of the Forum Romanum would have been, quite literally, drenched in the blood of untold numbers of Romans during Sulla's proscriptions, and for Romans who had survived the horrors of that time, they may have had difficulty looking at that pavement without recalling certain atrocities committed on it and pools of blood left upon it.[40] Sulla's repaving, then, might actually be interpreted as a sort of historical whitewash; his new era would eliminate the traces of his own controversial actions in the previous era.[41]

Sulla also demolished the Curia Hostilia and replaced it, in a slightly different orientation, with a bigger building (probably called the Curia Cornelia). Since Sulla had expanded the senate from three hundred to six hundred members, he needed a new Sullan senate house to accommodate this Sullan senate. Moreover, his fundamentally new senate (largely stocked with handpicked partisans from the equestrian class who had fought alongside him) now had a visually new complement with this new Curia in the Forum Romanum. In the process of completing the new Curia, Sulla was required to tear down a long-standing statue of Pythagoras (per Pliny, *HN* 34.26); given the saecular resonances of that historical personage (on whom see more in chapter 2), it is possible that Sulla intended this move to be interpreted all the more as an indication of the arrival of a new epoch.

A fire that had broken out on the Capitoline in 83 BCE, near the Forum Romanum, had damaged several buildings in that area. Most significant of all of these was the destruction of the Temple of Jupiter Optimus Maximus (which still had not been refurbished by the time Sulla marched in his triumph along its ruins in 81 BCE). Luke considers this destruction "one of the key calamities of the civil war that inspired fear that Rome might possibly come to an end"; this eschatological connotation comes from the fact that "the loss of the temple of Rome's patron deity, a structure that was built at the beginning of the Republic, could easily be taken as an omen of the Republic's end and Rome's fall."[42] Furthermore, the fact that it was destroyed not by an earthquake or an attack by an enemy but by fire would likely have recalled, for many Romans, the Stoic concept of the periodic conflagration that brought up the destruction of the universe (about which see much more in chapter 2).

Naturally, if the temple's destruction could portend a Roman end, its reconstruction could be seen as a marker of a new beginning at Rome, and Sulla fervently sought to be the man to rebuild it (although we know that he was only able to make plans before retirement and death ended his efforts). We do know that he had intended to use columns taken from the Temple of Olympian Zeus (or some reconstruction project for it) at Athens to help rebuilt the Temple of Jupiter Optimus Maximus,[43] but these plans never materialized. Lost in the destruction of the temple in 83 BCE were the Sibylline Books, so when Sulla increased the number of the college of priests in charge of these books to fifteen (thereafter referred to as "*XVviri*"), he also tasked them with reconstructing the books by seeking out privately owned excerpts (a move later requiring Augustus to charge his own *XVviri* with deleting false inclusions from the official books).[44] Given the connection between the saecular prophecy of 88 BCE that Sulla promoted and the saecular prophecies attributed to the Sibylline Books (and the related oracular utterances floating around the Roman intellectual community), Sulla no doubt wanted to ensure that his new era preserved the material conferring religious authority on his self-presentation.[45]

Sulla did not live to see the reconstruction of the Temple of Jupiter Optimus Maximus. Likewise, Sulla ordered but did not actually execute the erection of a so-called Tabularium (its purpose still unclear) facing the Forum Romanum as a visual backdrop behind the rostra, affecting the public's view of the Capitoline.[46] Unlike the sternly traditional Temple of Jupiter, this "Tabularium" would have been a markedly Sullan structure for all to see: Tucci writes, "The Capitoline Temple . . . was rebuilt upon the same foundations and with the same plan as the temple of 509 BC, and was rather anachronistic; the 'Tabularium,' on the other hand, was innovative from a technological and architectural point of view."[47] Much like his gilded statue, the "Tabularium" would have inserted a blunt visual reminder of Sulla's presence in the new era of the Forum Romanum. We know that the completed structure actually surrounded the old Temple of Veiovis; Tucci notes that this "Tabularium," whatever its purpose, was "indifferent to pre-existing buildings."[48] The visual effect was to impose the architectural signature of Sulla within this traditional Republican space.

Sulla's building plans in the Forum Romanum and on the Capitoline were nothing short of transformative. It is at this time that "the drive to assert the power of a single political leader reached new heights," and with Sulla's extensive renovations here, "the aristocratic consensus of display was doomed, and the way was paved for the dissolution of the Forum Romanum as stage for the Roman hereditary elite in the age of Caesar and Augustus."[49] Elsewhere in Rome, Sulla's program of self-promotion as a figure bringing saecular change to Rome was enacted for all to see. Sulla's enlargement of the pomerium, the first time this had happened in Rome since (allegedly) the reign of Servius Tullius, contributed to Sulla's self-presentation as a second founder of Rome.[50] By altering the boundaries of the city, Sulla was effectively restarting Roman history, which may have led to the next generation's insulting comment that Sulla was "iste Romulus."[51] (Even his retirement, as Flower speculates, could have been a political performance intended to make Sulla look like a Solon-esque "Lawgiver" figure, a softer version of the saecular culture hero.[52]) These changes to the cityscape may have been associated with Sulla's other social and political reforms.[53]

The mythical figure Sulla sought to identify with the most, however, was Hercules.[54] During the 80s BCE, Sulla rebuilt the Temple of Hercules Custos near the Circus Flaminius, set up a Hercules Sullanus (either a shrine or a statue) on the Esquiline, and built or rebuilt sanctuaries for Hercules at Tibur and near Sulmo.[55] The overall effect of such building "suggests that the Dictator not only felt, but was even promoting a special relationship between himself and the god."[56] Sulla also at one point publicly dedicated one-tenth of his possession to Hercules as a thanks offering;[57] this act occurred during public banquets at which Sulla evidently made his association with Hercules evident through statuary or other means.[58] More significantly, a coin type appeared in 80 BCE whose reverse image was Hercules strangling the Nemean Lion, thus depicting Hercules in his role as a culture hero, the "mythological prototype of a hero whose virtues and labors brought salvation to mankind."[59] Sulla, "the type suggests, is such a savior."[60] The concept of the culture hero, a figure providing some benefaction to the world or ridding it of some dangerous evil, often was used in antiquity to articulate the change from one historical *saeculum* to the next, as I discuss in chapter 4. It is telling, then, that Sulla began to cultivate the connection to Hercules in 88 BCE, the year of the Etruscan omen about the introduction of a new *saeculum*.[61]

Despite the scattered evidence, it is reasonably clear that Sulla adopted the mode of periodization as a way to present himself and his actions as part of a divinely authorized revolution to save Rome from its lapse into chaos. Sulla attempted to legitimize his political and military tactics, and his many domestic reforms, by depicting himself as a man destined to lead a new period of Roman history, for which the new Etruscan *saeculum* starting in 88 BCE served as a convenient complement. His reforms at Rome "came in a radical political moment in 81, presented as a coherent system with Sulla as the author bringing forth a new 'age.'"[62] Out of the chaos of the civil conflicts of the early first century BCE, Sulla's adoption and adaptation of saecular discourse brought about "the creation of a broadly formulated and clearly articulated conception of the charismatic individual leader as the divinely chosen conqueror, whose victories in the field were proof of his extraordinary gifts and of the divine sanction of his political order."[63] Ramage speaks of a Sullan system of propaganda, "surprisingly complete, based firmly in Roman values, appearing in all the media, and covering most of the Empire. . . . This system was to serve as a prototype for Imperial propaganda."[64] Periodization lies at the heart of this system, and Sulla used saecular discourse in "a conscious effort on his part to convey his image to the whole world, East and West alike."[65] The stage had been set for future Roman autocrats: "Sullan propaganda is a profoundly significant forerunner of the imperial image of the emperor as saviour

28 | *Saeculum*

of the commonwealth and earthly incarnation of specific Virtues."[66] For Sulla, a qualitatively distinct era of Roman history, and even of world history, began with his career.

Sullan Era, Etruscan *Saeculum*

The career of Sulla provides the first significant instance of periodizing rhetoric in the mainstream Roman intellectual world, but what was the version of the Etruscan saecular doctrine as Sulla understood it? As I wrote earlier, Plutarch notes several omens that marked the career of Sulla, including the 88 BCE omen that a change from one *saeculum* to another had taken place. The following passage provides a full excerpt of Plutarch's description of that omen, including an interpretation of the *saeculum* system as Plutarch knew it:

τὸ δὲ πάντων μέγιστον, ἐξ ἀνεφέλου καὶ διαίθρου τοῦ περιέχοντος ἤχησε φωνὴ σάλπιγγος ὀξὺν ἀποτείνουσα καὶ θρηνώδη φθόγγον, ὥστε πάντας ἔκφρονας γενέσθαι καὶ καταπτῆξαι διὰ τὸ μέγεθος. Τυρρηνῶν δὲ οἱ λόγιοι μεταβολὴν ἑτέρου γένους ἀπεφαίνοντο καὶ μετακόσμησιν ἀποσημαίνειν τὸ τέρας. εἶναι μὲν γὰρ ὀκτὼ τὰ σύμπαντα γένη, διαφέροντα τοῖς βίοις καὶ τοῖς ἤθεσιν ἀλλήλων, ἑκάστῳ δὲ ἀφωρίσθαι χρόνων ἀριθμὸν ὑπὸ τοῦ θεοῦ συμπεραινόμενον ἐνιαυτοῦ μεγάλου περιόδῳ. καὶ ὅταν αὕτη σχῇ τέλος, ἑτέρας ἐνισταμένης κινεῖσθαί τι σημεῖον ἐκ γῆς ἢ οὐρανοῦ θαυμάσιον, ὡς δῆλον εἶναι τοῖς πεφροντικόσι τὰ τοιαῦτα καὶ μεμαθηκόσιν εὐθὺς ὅτι καὶ τρόποις ἄλλοις καὶ βίοις ἄνθρωποι χρώμενοι γεγόνασι, καὶ θεοῖς ἧττον ἢ μᾶλλον τῶν προτέρων μέλοντες. τά τε γὰρ ἄλλα φασὶν ἐν τῇ τῶν γενῶν ἀμείψει λαμβάνειν μεγάλας καινοτομίας, καὶ τὴν μαντικὴν ποτὲ μὲν αὔξεσθαι τῇ τιμῇ καὶ κατατυγχάνειν ταῖς προαγορεύσεσι, καθαρὰ καὶ φανερὰ σημεῖα τοῦ δαιμονίου προπέμποντος, αὖθις δ' ἐν ἑτέρῳ γένει ταπεινὰ πράττειν, αὐτοσχέδιον οὖσαν τὰ πολλὰ καὶ δι' ἀμυδρῶν καὶ σκοτεινῶν ὀργάνων τοῦ μέλλοντος ἁπτομένην. ταῦτα μὲν οὖν οἱ λογιώτατοι Τυρρηνῶν καὶ πλέον τι τῶν ἄλλων εἰδέναι δοκοῦντες ἐμυθολόγουν. (Plutarch, *Sull.* 7.3–5)

But most important of all, out of a cloudless and clear air there rang out the voice of a trumpet, prolonging a shrill and dismal note, so that all were amazed and terrified at its loudness. The Tuscan wise men declared that the prodigy foretokened a change of conditions and the advent of a new age. For according to them there are eight ages in all, differing from one another in the lives and customs of men, and to each of these God has appointed a definite number of times and seasons, which is completed by the circuit of a great year. And whenever this circuit has run out, and another begins, some wonderful sign is sent from earth or heaven, so that it is at once clear to those who have studied such subjects and are versed in them, that men of other habits and modes of life have come into the world, who are either more or less of concern to the gods than their predecessors were. All things, they say, undergo great changes, as one again succeeds another, and especially the art of divination; at one period it rises in esteem and is successful in its predictions, because manifest and genuine signs are sent forth from the Deity; and again, in another age, it is in small repute, being off-hand, for the most part, and seeking to grasp the future by means of faint and blind senses. Such, at any rate, was the tale told by the wisest of the Tuscans, who were thought to know much more about it than the rest.[67]

Plutarch's digression in this passage on the specifics of the Etruscan system of *saecula* may reflect the same understanding that Sulla had at the time, and the possibility even exists that Plutarch derives his interpretation from writing that appears in his source (which is almost certainly Sulla's memoirs). On the other hand, almost two hundred years of development and discussion stood between Plutarch, writing in 115 CE, and Sulla, writing in 78 BCE, so the possibility also exists that the two men imagined two different systems.[68]

We possess another, earlier account of the Etruscan saecular doctrine, composed by Varro in the middle of the first century BCE, although it is preserved in the *De die natali* of Censorinus from 238 CE.[69] Censorinus composed this scholarly treatise on time and its organizing principles through liberal citations of earlier writers. In the following passage, he explains the Etruscan saecular doctrine and quotes Varro on some specifics:

30 | *Saeculum*

Sed licet veritas in obscuro latet, tamen in unaquaque civitate quae sint naturalia saecula, rituales Etruscorum libri videntur docere, in quis scriptum esse fertur initia sic poni saeculorum: quo die urbes adque civitates constituerentur, de his, qui eo die nati essent, eum, qui diutissime vixisset, die mortis suis primi saeculi modulum finire, eoque die qui essent reliqui in civitate, de his rursum eius mortem, qui longissimam egisset aetatem, finem esse saeculi secundi. Sic deinceps tempus reliquorum terminari. Sed ea quod ignorarent homines, portenta mitti divinitus, quibus admonerentur, unumquodque saeculum esse finitum. Haec portenta Etrusci pro haruspicii disciplinaeque suae peritia diligenter observata in libros rettulerunt. Quare in Tuscis historiis, quae octavo eorum saeculo scriptae sunt, ut Varro testatur, et quot numero saecula ei genti data sint, et transactorum singula quanta fuerint quibusve ostentis eorum exitus designati sint, continetur. Itaque scriptum est quattuor prima saecula annorum fuisse centenum,[70] quintum centum viginti trium, sextum undeviginti et centum, septimum totidem, octavum tum demum agi, nonum et decimum superesse, quibus transactis finem fore nominis Etrusci. (*DN* 17.5–6)

Although the truth lies hidden in darkness, nevertheless the ritual books of the Etruscans seem to teach what the natural ages are in each society, in which they say it is written that the beginning of each Age is determined as follows. Starting from the day on which the particular cities and states were founded, out of those who were born on that day, the day of death of the one who lived the longest marks the end of the First Age. Next, out of those who were alive in the state on *that* day, in turn the day of death of the person who lived the longest is the end of the Second Age, and so the duration of the rest of the Ages is marked off. But due to human ignorance, certain portents are sent by the gods to show when each age is over. The Etruscans, who have experience in their special science of reading omens, watched for these portents diligently and entered them in books. So the Etruscan Chronicles, which were written in their Eighth Age, as Varro tells us, contain not only how many Ages were given to that people, but also how long each of the past Ages was, and what signs marked their ends. And so it is written that the first four Ages were 105 years long; the Fifth was 123 years; the Sixth and Seventh were 119 years; the Eighth Age was still going on; the Ninth and Tenth remained; and after these were over would come the end of the Etruscan name.[71]

Crucially, as Hall points out, Censorinus specifically cites the "ritual books of the Etruscans" as his authority for the basic explanation of the saecular doctrine (possibly indicating that he had consulted them himself), and only quotes Varro for the specific details of the Etruscans' own data.[72] Whether Censorinus accessed the ritual books of the Etruscans directly or only through Varro, nevertheless they appear to form his ultimate source for this material. And while the *Tuscae historiae* were written in the eighth *saeculum* (i.e., the second century BCE), these ritual books were presumably much older (and thus their material is less likely to be distorted by later interpolations).

This lengthy passage is a rich source of information about the Etruscan saecular doctrine. Each *urbs* or *civitas* would last for a finite length of time, measured in a series of *saecula*. The Etruscan *saeculum* was calculated in such a way that the death of the oldest living person born on the day of the city's founding signaled the end of the first *saeculum*. Among the surviving members at that point, whoever lived the longest would mark the end of the second *saeculum* with his death, and so on. Therefore, no citizen born in, for example, Saeculum 2 was alive in Saeculum 4. Evidently, no one was keeping track of who the oldest man in town was, so portents, which diviners could interpret, marked the transition from one *saecula* to another, and the Etruscans recorded these omens for future reference (to keep track of each town's impending doom). The *Tuscae historiae*, which Varro read, included how many *saecula* the entire Etruscan civilization was going to last (ten total), as well as when each began and ended, and with what portents the transitions were indicated.

It is important to note here what this passage does *not* say, as well. It does not say how the Etruscans arrived at the number 10 for the number of *saecula* they would receive—presumably through some manner of divination.[73] Nor does it say anything about each *saeculum* having any particular qualitative characteristics. And, perhaps most importantly, this only tells us how the Etruscans calculated their own *saecula*; it does not say anything specifically about Roman practice.[74]

32 | *Saeculum*

(We will see in chapter 5 the difficulty of calculating when to expect celebrations of the Ludi Saeculares.)

To what extent can we trust Censorinus as a faithful transmitter of the facts of the doctrine of the *saeculum*, especially of Varro's material? Cornell notes that "the passage in question is not strictly speaking a 'fragment' of Varro at all, because it does not reproduce Varro's exact words," and thus it is possible that the description of the Etruscan doctrine is refracted through the perspective of Censorinus (or reflects his own scholarship, as posited by Hall), and so because of that, there "must be a chance that Censorinus misunderstood what he had read in Varro."[75] Opinions of Censorinus as a scholar differ,[76] but it seems reasonable to suggest that he does not veer too far from his originals. Given his extensive use of Varro throughout his work, Censorinus likely preserves a first-century BCE perspective.[77]

Varro's credibility is sometimes also questioned, particularly regarding etymology,[78] but cultural scholarship such as in this passage allowed him to consult native informants and experts for Etruscan material, as well as the contents of the *Tuscae historiae*. Cornell has accepted the authenticity of Varro's research and analyzes it in connection with previously known facts about Etruscan record-keeping.[79] He believes there is a strong possibility that the *Tuscae historiae* were arranged within a framework of *saecula* and perhaps used the chronological system of *saecula* in a manner similar to a Greek time-unit, the Olympiad, and "in view of the religious character of the concept of *saecula*, it would seem that the business of recording time was supervised by priests."[80] Indeed, "many of the local Etruscan traditions known to us, including the theory of *saecula* attributed by Varro to *Tuscae historiae*, are closely connected by their strong religious emphasis with the tradition of the *Etrusca disciplina*."[81] The pertinent question, though, is whether the Varronian description of the Etruscan saecular doctrine matches Sulla's understanding of it when promoting historical periodization in his career (decades before Varro's composition).

Plutarch's account, which may or may not have drawn information from Sulla's memoirs, contains several departures from the Varronian version. In the Plutarch version there are eight ages, not ten, and it is unclear whether the ages are local (i.e., each city or state gets its own series of *saecula*) or global.[82] The ages have characteristics connected to each *ethos* of the people, evidently their social customs and/or moral standards, one of which is "how much people respect divination" (although this seems to be based on "how good a job the diviners do," also a characteristic of an age). Portents declare the transition between ages, which only the prophets can understand; there is no connection to the lifetimes of long-lived people and no way to calculate an age. An age can be better or worse than the one preceding it, but there is no general direction that they are all going; it is not as though each age gets worse and worse. Also, Plutarch does not provide any data from the Etruscans' records regarding their own *saecula*, which in Plutarch's mind may apply to the whole world.

We must account for these discrepancies. Varro, a polymath who did research and read earlier material, would have likely included some of these Plutarchan details if Sulla had written them in his memoirs (though Censorinus might have left it out). On the other hand, if Plutarch performed any of his own antiquarian research beyond what Sulla wrote, it might explain the lack of an explicit citation in that section of the biography. Plutarch's assertion that each *saeculum* has particular characteristics seems to be influenced by the evolution of the term in the first-century BCE Roman world, and his claim that there are eight ages is surely an error (since Varro was already writing in the presumptive ninth age, after the portents of 88 BCE).[83] Plutarch's lack of technical specificity and addition of qualitative characteristics, then, can be explained by the evolution of saecular discourse in the first century BCE. Through his retrojection of developments in Roman periodization back to its origins as Etruscan religious practice, Plutarch in fact reflects the growth of qualitative periodization as a mode of organizing history.

The version of the Etruscan saecular doctrine set forth by Varro and Censorinus reflects the closest analogue to the version of the doctrine as Sulla knew and understood it.[84] However, Sulla's innovation was to attach himself to the new *saeculum* he described for Roman history. If the account of the Etruscan saecular doctrine set forth by Censorinus (and his source, Varro) best reflects the Roman understanding of the doctrine as it existed in the early first century BCE, then Sulla provides a bridge between that version and the one Plutarch describes, in which each *saeculum* has particular characteristics. The Etruscan doctrine had already made a connection between a *saeculum* and the lifetime of one man, since each *saeculum* ended with the death of the oldest living person alive at the last metakosmesis. While nothing needed to be special about this person (beyond longevity), Sulla depicted himself as the "man of the *saeculum*"

34 | Saeculum

whose rule at Rome caused the new era of peace to occur. Through this transition, the *saeculum* became a term denoting a qualitatively defined period. The Sullan saecular model preserves the idea of *saecula* occurring in a set sequence, divinely preordained, for which there are clear metakosmetic moments (and attendant prodigies), but his deviation from the Etruscan original is the idea that each *saeculum* is defined qualitatively and not simply quantitatively. His innovation was to transform the *saeculum* from an Etruscan technical term into a new Roman way to talk about history in qualitative periods, as Plutarch later received it. It is on this model that the subsequent adaptations of the Roman intellectual community during the first century BCE are based.

From Etruria to Rome

So far the only sources for the Etruscan saecular doctrine examined here are Romans and Greeks who may be refracting the original Etruscan source material through foreign biases. But modern scholars may possess material evidence for Etruscan practice. A votive pit in a monumental complex found at Pian di Civita at Tarquinia and datable to about 700 BCE contained two bronze objects, including a trumpet-like musical instrument, that were folded three times.[85] Van der Meer notes that "broken, bent or folded objects may indicate earmarking and a rite of passage, the end and beginning of a new era," and that some scholars have interpreted the items as ceremonial or religious in nature.[86] Intriguingly, a trumpet-like noise is a common omen in Roman accounts, and Plutarch's description of the metakosmesis of 88 BCE included a trumpet blast from the sky. These material findings may lend some credence to the scholarship of Varro, Plutarch, and Censorinus.[87]

One other potential Etruscan source of engagement with saecular doctrine is the Prophecy of Vegoia, a text purporting to be a prophecy from the semi-mythical Etruscan figure Vegoia. Most scholars take the Prophecy of Vegoia to be an early first-century BCE translation from Etruscan into Latin.[88] The text reads:

> Idem Vegoiae Arrunti Veltymno. Scias mare ex aethera remotum. Cum autem Juppiter terram Aetruriae sibi vindicavit,

constituit iussitque metiri campos signarique agros. Sciens hominum avaritiam vel terrenum cupidinem, terminis omnia scita esse voluit. Quos quandoque quis ob avaritiam prope novissimi octavi saeculi data sibi homines malo dolo violabunt contingentque atque movebunt. Sed qui contigerit moveritque, possessionem promovendo suam, alterius minuendo, ob hoc scelus damnabitur a diis. Si servi faciant, dominio mutabuntur in deterius. Sed si conscientia dominica fiet, caelerius dominus extirpabitur, gensque eius omnis interiet. Motores autem pessimis morbis et vulneribus efficientur membrisque suis debililabuntur. Tum etiam terra a tempestatibus vel turbinibus plerumque labe movebitur, fructus saepe ledentur decutienturque imbribus atque grandine, caniculis interient, robigine occidentur. Multae dissensiones in populo. Fieri haec scitote, cum talia scelera committuntur. Propterea neque fallax neque bilinguis sis. Disciplinam pone in corde tuo.

(Prophecy) of Vegoia, to Arruns Veltymnus: "Know that the sea was separated from the sky. But when Jupiter claimed the land of Aetruria for himself, he established and ordered that the fields be measured and the croplands delimited. Knowing the greed of men and their lust for land, he wanted everything proper concerning boundaries. And at some time, around the end of the eighth *saeculum*, someone will violate them on account of greed by means of evil trickery and will touch them and move them. [. . .] But whoever shall have touched and moved them, increasing his own property and diminishing that of another, on account of this crime he will be damned by the gods. If slaves should do it, there will be a change for the worse in status. But if the deed is done with the master's consent, very quickly the master will be uprooted and all of his family will perish. The ones who move [the boundaries] will be afflicted by the worst diseases and wounds, and they will feel a weakness in their limbs. Then also the earth will be moved by storms and whirlwinds with frequent destruction, crops often will be injured and will be knocked down by rain and hail, they will perish in the summer heat, they will be felled by mildew. There will be much dissension among people. Know that these things will be done when such crimes are

36 | *Saeculum*

committed. Wherefore be not false or double-tongued. Keep this teaching in your heart."[89]

Here we find an Etruscan prophecy about political tensions combined with meteorological destruction, all connected to the transition from one *saeculum* to the next. Luke sees the Prophecy of Vegoia as part of the larger matrix of omens and supernatural material that circulated during the Social War, since it "addresses Italian anxieties concerning property rights, a prevalent concern in the relations between Rome and the Italians since the time of the Gracchi," and because the Prophecy "looked forward to the imminent end of the *saeculum*," it "was probably circulated before 88 BCE and thus forms part of the context in which Plutarch, following Sulla, placed the declaration of the new *saeculum*'s advent."[90] If the Prophecy of Vegoia is an authentic Etruscan text and evidence of how Etruscans understood their *saeculum* system, then Sulla's articulation of periodization was likely based on some combination of the depictions of the saecular doctrines in the Plutarch account and in the Varro/Censorinus account.

After Sulla, the discourse of periodization exploded in the Roman world, as subsequent Romans adapted and experimented with periodization. Obviously, I have selected Sulla as an important marker in the intellectual history of this temporal concept, which implies that I see Sulla's contribution to its history as so important as to merit special mention in this way (even though the very notion of periodization was not completely unknown to previous Romans and even though we can find some traces of this kind of language or thinking in Roman affairs before Sulla's rise). No ancient source actually declares Sulla unique in this regard, nor does anyone explicitly attribute their use of periodization language to an innovation by Sulla. But what is at stake here is an explanation for an intellectual trend that is apparent to us even with the survival of only a fraction of the writings of the first century BCE: an explosion of Roman interest in temporality and in the concept of a historical consciousness marked by qualitatively defined eras rather than a smooth, linear accumulation of dates or general forces.

This broad acceptance of saecular discourse, however, is not altogether obvious or expected. Beyond the esoteric nature of the saecular doctrine, the negative attitude of some Romans toward Etruscan culture would seem to be an impediment to its adoption by the Roman intelligentsia.[91] How did this one esoteric aspect of Etruscan culture permeate Roman intellectual life? Within aristocratic Roman political competition, emulation of successful figures was a common strategy, and Sulla was in many ways a tremendous success. Rosenblitt identifies a turning point in Roman political discourse after Sulla's reign, which she calls "hostile politics," whereby elites emphasized the declaration of their political foes as enemies of the state and held overt celebrations of civil war victories and obtaining spoils.[92] Sulla's individual contributions to this shift in the language of Roman politics do not necessarily need to be dominant. But Rosenblitt also identifies a rise among the successful autocrats of the first century BCE in appeals to stability over concerns for justice and *mos maiorum*; "when previously accepted government or governmental forms lose legitimacy, both violent change and novel legitimating ideologies become possible."[93] The "novel legitimating ideology" that could best explain some of these nascent intellectual trends is saecular periodization.[94]

Moreover, Sulla was something of an aristocratic cultural trendsetter: as just one example, Balsdon writes that by giving his children the *praenomina* Faustus and Fausta, Sulla "started a fashion" among the aristocracy of Rome in the late Republic and Imperial family for using *praenomina* that were either archaic or usually only *cognomina*.[95] Sulla's deep interest in the supernatural and exotic, particularly when it applied to himself (such as in coining the moniker Epaphroditos), took a central role in his own self-presentation, so if anyone could bring Etruscan divinatory terminology into the Roman mainstream, it would have been Sulla.[96] After Sulla's example, the utility of this language of periodization grew clear to the Roman intellectual community, and the Romans began to develop this historicizing mode into a robust tool for organizing history.[97]

I realize that by crediting Sulla with the innovation of saecular discourse at a particular moment in Roman history, I am opening myself up to the criticism that I have fallen prey to the very same biases that dominated Roman thought on technical progress: just as the Romans were obsessed with positing a *primus inventor* for every cultural practice, I have given special weight to the contributions of Sulla toward the development of this intellectual trend. And by asserting that qualitative periodization "begins" during the reign of Sulla at Rome, I am deploying the same kind of saecular discursive mode that I am identifying within the Roman world. I will concede

38 | *Saeculum*

that I have placed Sulla in a particularly prominent role in the narrative of this historical development, but I am also willing to declare that the kind of shift in temporality that I identify in the first century BCE would likely only have occurred if a single powerful personage set it into motion or a single momentous episode took place that influenced the wider culture. The disastrous instability of 88 BCE, and the prominence of Sulla as an individual in Roman politics, certainly fit the bill. The scholarly conversation on this issue may someday offer up alternative explanations, but for now I am confident that Sulla should receive the credit I give him here.

I will also note, however, that broader interest in Etruscan culture and religion, independent of the influence of Sulla, may be both a cause and an effect of the growing interest in periodization in the first century BCE. Many Roman writers, most prominently Vergil, had Etruscan origins, as did his champion and friend Maecenas. We know of Etruscan experts at Rome in the late Republic such as Julius Aquila, Caecina, and Tarquitius Priscus,[98] to say nothing of polymaths like Varro and Nigidius Figulus who covered Etruscan topics.[99] (The rise of Neo-Pythagoreanism, discussed in chapter 2, is also related to this interest.) Because of this general Roman interest in Etruscan culture, we need not assume that Sulla himself was the source of all future experiments with periodization, and Sulla need not be the only means by which Romans learned about Etruscan culture.[100]

Over the course of the hundred years after Sulla's death, Roman thinkers and artists added elements of other intellectual approaches to time and history (including philosophical ideologies ostensibly hostile to Etruscan supernaturalism), adapting saecular discourse to their needs and expanding its range of use. The language of qualitative periodization is largely absent from Roman politics in the first few decades after Sulla; perhaps the negative reputation Sulla received after his death led Roman political figures to try to avoid any connections to the dictator, or perhaps it seemed silly to claim yet another new era so soon after Sulla had successfully declared his own. Instead, saecular discourse emerged in the first century BCE as a way to periodize Roman (or human) history, but with greater sophistication. Sulla never fully articulated a division of all Roman history into distinct periods, with his own at the end; based on the evidence we have, it seems that he only ever proclaimed a past age and present new age. Future users of the rhetoric of periodization realized that multiple periods, including the possibility of ones that occurred later than the present, would give a much more nuanced or rhetorically effective arc of history. Its practitioners also used a wider range of criteria to divide the history of the Republic into periods; more could be done than simply to choose a powerful figurehead for every period. Indeed, Roman scholars and writers were deploying saecular discourse for various intellectual assertions long after Sulla's legislation was canceled and his "era" swept into the dustbin of Roman history.

2 | Eternal Returns

Cataclysmic Destruction in Greek and Roman Thought

Sulla's popularization of the Etruscan divinatory language of the *saeculum* may have been the seed that would soon flourish as the rise of saecular discourse, but widespread Roman interest in the various schools of Greek philosophy was the fertile soil into which he planted it. It is clear that philosophical ideas from the east had made their way to Rome long before the infamous "expulsion of the philosophers" episode in 155 BCE during which Cato the Elder reeled in horror at the publicly delivered sophistry of Carneades. The Roman intelligentsia was energized by the presence not only of Greek ideas but of Greek philosophers themselves in the first century BCE before, during, and after the rise of Sulla and his promulgation of saecular periodization; moreover, interest in Greek philosophy was not solely the pursuit of eccentric Roman elites with leisure time, but was fairly widespread throughout the Roman intellectual community.[1]

In this chapter, I will examine a selection of concepts familiar to Greek philosophy and evaluate their influence on the development of periodization in first-century BCE Rome. Their particular contribution to the changing Roman sense of temporality centers on the notion of cataclysmic change.[2] At the level of the individual human being, this cataclysm is death; the possibility of life after death, in the form of metempsychosis (transfer of the soul from one body to another, often associated with Pythagoreanism) or palingenesis (the spontaneous reassembly of all one's constituent atoms into the identical configuration, an Epicurean concept) could engender a profound change in the meaning of a "lifetime." Humans could have lifetimes, but cities and states could as well, so at the level of a civilization, we also see the Stoic doctrine of ekpyrosis (universal conflagration) and the more modest imagery of social collapse articulated by the Academic and Peripatetic schools. These Greek philosophical notions all contributed to the evolution of Roman saecular temporality, and they affected Roman cognition of the saecular timeline they now conceived of and described; owing to this influence, we will see that certain mythological figures (Phaethon plus Deucalion and Pyrrha) began to be grouped together in the Roman mind due to their saecular connotations.

Metempsychosis, the transfer of souls from one body to another (be it human, animal, plant, or even bean), was promulgated by several Greek philosophers (Presocratic and later), perhaps most famously by Plato in the Myth of Er. But the name most often attached to it in later Roman thought is Pythagoras.[3] Metempsychosis was understood by the first-century BCE Romans to be an aspect of what they believed was a unified school of thought called "Pythagoreanism,"[4] and was used to explain the other commonly cited aspect of Pythagoreanism, its emphasis on vegetarianism.[5] Pythagorean influence on Roman thought actually predates its influence on saecularity, since by the early second century, Pythagorean elements had appeared in several works; farce and mime make references to metempsychosis, suggesting that the Roman public was aware of this aspect of Pythagoreanism.[6] Perhaps most prominent among these early Roman writers was Ennius, who famously declared himself to be the reincarnated Homer.[7] Because of the insistence on this Roman connection between metempsychosis and Pythagoreanism, I treat it as such in the development of saecularity in the period following Sulla at Rome, although we find versions of metempsychosis in the works of several Greek philosophers.

Given the cultural relevance of Pythagoreanism, it is likely that the influence of metempsychosis on saecularity would have been widespread.[8] "Neopythagoreanism," an alleged update of the original doctrine, emerged in the late second and first centuries BCE; one of its more notable adherents was Nigidius Figulus, the Roman scholar of Etruscan culture. It was Nigidius Figulus who published in his *De diis* an esoteric declaration that human history could be divided into periods, each ruled by a specific god, with the final "Age of Apollo" looming.[9] Whether this saecular prophecy was related to his Neopythagorean associations is unclear, however. Awareness of Pythagoreanism flourished at Rome during the first century BCE,

42 | *Saeculum*

but scholars disagree whether, as Cicero claims (*Timaeus* 1), this amounted to a complete revival or if this period simply saw a much greater interest in Pythagoreanism and a willingness to self-identify as a Pythagorean (as was done by the Augustan philosopher Quintus Sextius).[10]

Examples of Pythagorean influence can be found throughout Augustan literature. For example, the discourse by Anchises on the soul in the underworld scene of *Aeneid* 6 contains Pythagorean ideas strained through later Platonic meditations.[11] In a more direct connection between the philosopher and saecular discourse, Ovid shows a Pythagorean influence, naturally, in his long speech by Pythagoras at the beginning of *Metamorphoses* 15.[12] Notably, in multiple places during the long speech, particularly with reference to the Metallic Age myth,[13] Ovid applies the lexicon of saecularity, suggesting that he found Pythagoreanism and saecular discourse compatible. The persistence in Rome of the legend of Numa's education under Pythagoras may also reflect how the philosophical ideas connected to Pythagoras had permeated the Roman intellectual mainstream throughout the first century BCE.[14] As a consequence, Pythagorean metempsychosis was deployed by Romans as an apparatus for the evolution of saecular discourse.

A useful example of the Roman adoption of metempsychosis into saecular discourse is provided by [Tibullus]'s *Panegyric to Messalla*, typically dated to roughly 30 BCE.[15] At the conclusion of the poem (4.1.190–211), the poet declares his eternal allegiance to Messalla and promises to write him flattering verses forever. For the poet, this sentiment is not chosen lightly: he literally declares that his celebration of Messalla in verse will not be stopped by his death (203). After several other lifetimes spent in the bodies of animals (206–209), a distant age (*longa aetas*, 210) will receive him as a human (209), and he will then return to writing more laudatory verses for Messalla (211).[16] Each creature that the poet's soul inhabits is an *aetas* in the history of that soul, and some distant *aetas* will see that soul eventually return to a human body. Thus [Tibullus] has taken the concept of the finite saecular history of a *civitas*, as Sulla and the Etruscans used it, and changed it into a saecular "history" of his eternal soul, which occupies a different body in each *saeculum* of its history.

The process of metempsychosis parallels the division of history into *saecula* in that it provides a "history" of a soul, and organizes that history into discrete units (i.e., individual lives). Since the

Etruscan *saeculum* is calculated based on a person's lifetime (and is, in a broader sense, related to the span of human life),[17] the comparison between *saecula* and distinct lifetimes is all the more apt. In fact, Diogenes Laertius (8.4–5) even recorded the history of Pythagoras's own soul, tracking every person it had inhabited through Pythagoras himself. Furthermore, metempsychosis allows for the possibility that one person is the reincarnation of a person of an earlier age; Pythagoras himself had a counterpart from the Heroic Age, the Trojan Euphorbus. And one ancient source claimed that Pythagorean metempsychosis was related to the idea that "what happens happens again at some time according to certain cycles," further suggesting a link between metempsychosis and saecularity in this articulation of the cyclicality of time.[18] Metempsychosis alters the temporal scheme associated with the human lifetime by changing it from something linear to something cyclical and periodic.

In the *Panegyric to Messalla*, [Tibullus] neatly encapsulates the resonance between ages and lifetimes that metempsychosis demonstrates. The poem shows that the focus of the saecular mode can be more limited temporally than a city or a civilization; moreover, the connection to metempsychosis emphasizes the enduring sameness of the spirit of each *saeculum* despite the outward change in appearance in the host body from *saeculum* to *saeculum*. The concept of metempsychosis provides an intellectual basis for the idea that the identity of one's focus (be it a civilization or any other entity) is fundamentally preserved even if profound qualitative characteristics have changed from age to age, which underlies all saecular discourse.

Another similar concept in Greek philosophy from which Romans drew in their experiments with saecularity is the (generally Epicurean) idea of palingenesis, the process by which one's atoms randomly return again in the future to the same order they occupy in the present (a version of eternal recurrence). In the Epicurean physical model, both time and space are infinite, and there are also an infinite number of indivisible atoms in the universe, all of which are constantly in motion. The universe and everything in it (i.e., its atoms) are eternal and cannot be destroyed. Combining those Epicurean rules of physics, one must conclude that any arrangement of atoms (e.g., the arrangement of atoms that makes up the specific person "Socrates") will and in fact must occur an infinite number of times in the future and in an infinite number of places, and must have already occurred an infinite number of times in the past, and

44 | *Saeculum*

must exist in an infinite number of places at the very present.[19] Thus the arrangement of atoms we call "Socrates" will return again someday, and this phenomenon of endlessly repeating atomic reassembly is called palingenesis.

An essential Epicurean question is whether this identical arrangement of atoms (which includes the soul, since it is also made up of atoms) is our same "Socrates" or some sort of other person. In other words, does the discontinuity created by palingenesis (i.e., the gulf of years separating one arrangement of "Socrates" from another) mean that the identity of the two arrangements is different, even if, at an atomic level, they are identical? Or will "Socrates" really live again after death? A Vatican Saying, preserving the original words of Epicurus, insists that (as the saying goes) you only live once, suggesting (if this is a dogmatic point rather than a mere aphorism) that each "Socrates" is a different person.[20] And Pseudo-Justin, a later Christian author, claims that Epicurus himself says that the process of palingenesis does happen (*De resurrectione* 6), so Epicurus must have addressed the issue directly in his own writings.[21]

This earlier Epicurean discussion of palingenesis affected later Roman saecular discourse,[22] especially the debate by Lucretius about this Epicurean issue.[23] At 3.670–678, Lucretius argues against the possibility of reincarnation by noting that since we cannot remember anything from any earlier lives, this loss of memory is more or less the same thing as death. The term he uses for this earlier period is *anteactam aetatem*, a phrase which can mean something like "previous time," but since he refers specifically to previous lives, it can also be "a previous lifetime." Since this lifetime is, here, a vague time-unit not related to any specific person's life, the verbiage suggests that Lucretius is thinking of a discrete time-unit equal to one lifetime, and thus his analysis may adopt the periodizing mode. And in a similar refutation that palingenesis would constitute reincarnation, at 3.843–862, Lucretius imagines an *aetas* (847) that reassembles one's original atoms after death. Democritus, another atomist, had imagined infinite simultaneous copies of himself (as described by Cicero in his *Academica* 2.125), but Lucretius talks about palingenesis as a diachronic issue (future selves) instead of a synchronic issue (simultaneous selves throughout the universe),[24] which may reflect the interaction between Epicurean physics and saecularity. Understood in conjunction with saecular notions of periodization, palingenesis upends the temporal notion of a human death.

What was the Roman familiarity with the concept of palingenesis, outside of the very specific context of Epicurean hypotheticals in the physical world? Varro also seems to have discussed palingenesis in book 4 of his *De gente populi romani*, according to an apparent verbatim quotation by Augustine.[25] Varro describes a metaphysical process promoted by certain unnamed astrologers in which souls are reunited with their original bodies after 440 years. Varro gives this process the name palingenesis, although it does not quite resemble the Epicurean version of this term. Nonetheless, the reference is quite suggestive: Varro describes the periodic return, after several centuries, of an original state.[26] As I argue in chapter 5, it is possible that Varro's writings on palingenesis influenced the antiquarian research that informed the new calculation of the Ludi Saeculares in 17 BCE. We may also consider the possibility that first-century BCE elite interest in body doubles and lookalikes reflects familiarity with palingenetic theory (since identical humans demonstrate how the same form could house two different souls).[27] And the discrete, distinct lifetimes imagined by the Epicureans parallel discrete *saecula* with distinct qualities; for example, Rome in 89 BCE looked virtually identical to Rome in 87 BCE but they are somehow not the same to a true believer of such saecular distinctions. To those Romans imagining second comings or describing new golden ages, palingenesis offered a useful intellectual foundation. Thus, beyond the specifically Epicurean explorations of Lucretius, other Romans connected palingenesis with saecular temporality.

Throughout this book, I have used the technical term metakosmesis to refer to the transition from one *saeculum* to another. Saecular transitions were the object of much (at least rhetorical) apprehension and expectation by writers at the end of the first century BCE, but for our earliest sources of saecular discourse, the metakosmesis was not a particular significant event. The Varronian explanation of the Etruscan *saeculum* system in Censorinus does mention that portents were sent by the gods to declare when each age had ended (which the Etruscan soothsayer looked for and could interpret), and in 88 BCE the sound of a trumpet rang out a shrill note that many people heard. Likewise, Sulla connected his new age to a chasm that had opened up in the earth and emitted flames, but otherwise provided little else to describe his metakosmetic moment. The transition was more than a purely academic, calculable event, but it lacked any degree of profound bombast; there was no element

46 | *Saeculum*

of a catastrophic or apocalyptic nature. Conversely, by the end of the century, the Roman thinkers and writers not only use massive cataclysms to describe changes in *saecula*, but are also using saecular discourse to discuss cataclysms; the nature of the experience has grown in importance, and the event itself is worthy of description and has assumed a larger part of the vocabulary of saecular discourse. Romans after Sulla drew from several sources in Greek philosophy in order to expand the rhetorical range of metakosmesis, with the primary one being the Stoic notion of the periodic conflagration of the universe.[28]

In the Stoic cosmological model, the universe and everything in it return periodically to a state of pure fire, a moment called "ekpyrosis" (the Stoic "conflagration"), as explained by this statement from the late fourth-century CE writer Nemesius:

> The Stoics say that when the planets return to the same celestial sign, in length and breadth, where each was originally when the world was first formed, at set periods of time they cause conflagration and destruction of existing things.[29]

Unfortunately, no direct explanation of this Stoic cosmology by an original source has survived, but regardless of what the earliest Stoic practitioners had posited, later writers uniformly understood the Stoic model of the universe to be an unending series of world-cycles begun and ended by the conflagration. This Stoic cosmology "is asserted rather than proved in our surviving evidence, but it appears to be an inevitable consequence of three basic Stoic theses," namely: the everlasting nature of God and matter (i.e., they cannot be destroyed); a deterministic physics (i.e., every event is caused by conditions that could only cause that particular event and no other); and the related idea that from the same causes come the same effects.[30] The Stoics divided the timeline of the universe, at a cosmic scale, into discrete units, each separated by a conflagration.[31]

The periodic nature of the concept of the conflagration is obvious. The ekpyrosis is the process whereby everything in the universe burns, or is turned into pure fire, marking the end of one world-cycle and the beginning of a new one:

> At certain fated times the entire world is subject to conflagration, and then is reconstituted afresh. But the primary fire is

as it were a sperm which possesses the principles of all things and the causes of past, present, and future events. The nexus and succession of these is fate, knowledge, truth, and an inevitable and inescapable law of what exists. In this way everything in the world is excellently organized as in a perfectly ordered system.[32]

The earliest Stoics, Zeno and Cleanthes, imagined that the conflagration would be started by the sun or would at least involve the sun in some way, while later Stoics such as Chrysippus said that the universe would simply devolve into light.[33] Regardless of the exact method, the Stoic conflagration marks, in a dramatic way, the change from one world-cycle to another.[34]

Since the universe was created by God and was thus perfect, some Stoics had difficulty explaining why God would then destroy the universe through the conflagration.[35] Indeed, other later Stoics gave up the idea of periodic conflagration and maintained that the universe was eternal and inviolable (aligning them with Academic and Peripatetic claims), while others asserted that God actually did not cause the conflagration.[36] No surviving Stoic text considers the conflagration to be a divine punishment for the gradual moral debasement of the world, so this would seem to be a uniquely Roman addition to the physical model when we encounter it.[37] A common solution, though, was to claim that the universe was not "destroyed" so much as simply "changed" (since no matter is ever created or destroyed).[38]

But the concept of the conflagration would return among the Roman intelligentsia in the first century BCE. Among Stoic philosophers with influence on Roman thought, special mention should be given to Posidonius, who came to Rome in the 80s BCE as an envoy from Rhodes, and ingratiated himself with the Marcelli and Junii Brutii.[39] Posidonius made some kind of impact in Roman society: he maintained a correspondence with Cicero,[40] who refers to him extensively, and was sought out directly for conversation by no less a personage than Pompey.[41] Unfortunately, his philosophical writings survive only in meager fragments, making it difficult to ascertain just how central a role he played in shaping saecular discourse at Rome during his lifetime (which lasted until the middle of the first century BCE). Although technically a Stoic, Posidonius stood noticeably far from mainstream Stoic thought.[42] However, Posidonius was an orthodox Stoic in one important regard: he

48 | *Saeculum*

returned to the Stoic belief of the periodic destruction of the earth through the conflagration, which had gone out of fashion in the Stoic school after Chrysippus.[43] This intellectual move must have had an impact on the Roman reception of Stoic doctrine and created renewed interest in the cosmology of world-cycles and their divisions by cataclysmic conflagrations.

The writings of Posidonius were voluminous and wide-ranging. Posidonius seems to have given consideration both to the cosmic-level cycles of Stoic cosmology and to cycles within the scale of human history, having written extensively about natural phenomena and even about the possibility that such catastrophes could dramatically affect the earth, such as in the disappearance of Atlantis.[44] Like the Peripatetic philosopher Dicaearchus, his writings depicted a primitivist history of the human race, beginning with a sort of Golden Age.[45] Moreover, and with particular relevance to saecularity, Posidonius was an ethnographer and seems to have had familiarity with Etruscan customs.[46] It has been suggested that his writing held some degree of influence on Augustan thinkers,[47] and given his philosophical background and his connections in the Roman intellectual world, Posidonius likely helped Roman thinkers develop the concept of the metakosmesis from a somewhat mundane calculation to a massive cataclysm.[48]

Despite the Stoic influence on the metakosmesis, it must be admitted that Stoic cosmology lacks one element that was crucial to the Roman use of saecular discourse: the Stoics never, as noted by Downing, "even raise the question whether the end of the current cycle might be in that writer's own lifetime or soon after."[49] Nor, for that matter, was apprehension toward looming metakosmesis a feature of the Etruscan *saeculum* system, or of Sulla's application of it (his saecular transition was always backward-looking, never one in expectation). Imminent cataclysm was, essentially, nothing to be afraid of. Predicting the looming end of a *saeculum*, however, became a common Roman way to use saecularity while describing generally human or specifically Roman affairs. And anxiety about natural disasters could be directly influenced by the Stoic cataclysmic temporality when wedded to saecular notions of periodized time.

As an example of this attitude (although it occurred much later than the other events I examine in this book), it would benefit us to examine the account of the public pandemonium at saecular portents in Pliny the Younger's recollection of his own experience of the eruption of Vesuvius (*Ep.* 6.20). Downing notes that among the mass of terrified refugees (whose cacophonous wailing is noted by Pliny, at *Ep.* 6.20.14), some prayed to the gods while more people instead "concluded that there were no more gods and that that extraordinary night was permanent for the whole world" (*iam deos ullos aeternamque illam et novissimam noctem mundo interpretabantur, Ep.* 6.20.15).[50] Even young Pliny himself says that he took comfort in the fact that his death would be joined by the death of the entire universe (*me cum omnibus, omnia mecum perire, misero magno tamen mortalitatis solacio credidissem, Ep.* 6.20.17). While Downing believes that his reaction suggests an Epicurean expectation regarding the mortality of the earth,[51] he (along with Sherwin-White) posits that the Stoic doctrine of periodic conflagration lies behind Pliny's account of these terror-stricken people.[52] Although the eruption of Vesuvius did not actually herald the end of the world, or even the end of a *saeculum*, the public reaction to the event as depicted by Pliny gives us an indication of the fear of saecular portents that the Stoic ekpyrosis concept may have given Romans during the first century BCE.

A more influential metakosmetic episode in Roman history, and one that contained a fiery portent no less, occurred in 44 BCE: the *sidus Iulium*.[53] Augustus writes in his memoirs that during his funeral games for Julius Caesar, a comet was visible everywhere, which the people interpreted as a sign of Caesar's apotheosis (Augustus F1 Cornell).[54] However, a *haruspex* named Vulcanius publicly declared that the comet was an omen signifying the end of the ninth *saeculum* and the beginning of the tenth (Augustus F2 Cornell). Pliny the Elder (the source of F1) tells us that, privately, Augustus interpreted the appearance of the comet as related to himself (*HN* 2.94).[55] The comet, for which there are many references throughout the literature of the period,[56] was also featured in coinage[57] and statuary. As fragment F2 shows, this portent would have heralded for the Romans a new *saeculum*,[58] and the fact that another comet appeared in 17 BCE, the year of the Ludi Saeculares, would have only enhanced this understanding.[59]

Popular belief that the assassination of Caesar heralded a new era could have been strengthened by meteorological phenomena beyond the *sidus Iulium*. Among many other ancient sources, Plutarch (*Caes.* 69.5) claims that for an entire year, the light of the sun was dimmed and cold and, as a result, the vegetation grew poorly and withered that year. In fact, ecologists have noted that there seems to have been both an eruption of Etna in 44 BCE and a major Alaskan

50 | *Saeculum*

volcanic eruption in 43 BCE that caused lasting global ecological effects visible today in, for example, the rings of bristlecone pine trees (and concurrent records from Han dynasty China report similar effects).[60] It is not unreasonable to imagine that the negative environmental consequences of these eruptions were interpreted by Romans as the sign of their entrance into a new age of Roman history. Given the various disruptions to regular life that occurred in Rome during the middle of the first century BCE, the appearance of more serious and profound changes may have caused Romans to fear the absolute worst.[61] Horace, in the first twenty lines of *Ode* 1.2, noted the public terror at the end of the late Republic surrounding the political chaos (and its attendant portents; cf. *nova monstra*, *Odes* 1.2.6). The experience of this metakosmetic moment for the Romans, despite claims that it signaled a joyous new era, may instead have increased their sense of terror, as Horace notes widespread fears of the coming "*saeculum* of Pyrrha." The influence of the Stoic ekpyrosis likely accounts for the shift between Sulla's declaration of a new age in 88 BCE (for which only a mysterious trumpet blare gave the sign) and the civic terror in response to the *sidus Iulium* of 44 BCE.

Horace's evocation of a "*saeculum* of Pyrrha" is just one of many examples of how mythology was deployed by the Romans as allegories for other sociopolitical events, and during the period after Sulla two particular myths became widespread in relation to saecular discourse: the great flood survived by Deucalion and Pyrrha,[62] and the disastrous ride of Phaethon (and the subsequent burning of the world).[63] In the coming pages, I will argue that the first-century BCE Latin authors reframe these myths as metakosmetic episodes, giving the stories a new saecular resonance that had previously gone unacknowledged. The Phaethon story, with its massive worldwide fire, has a clear link to the fiery metakosmetic portents we have seen (and their relation to the Stoic conflagration at the ends of cosmic cycles),[64] but the Romans of this period also make the same use of Deucalion's flood, a less obvious example. As a result, one product of the period of adaptation and experimentation with saecular discourse after Sulla is that by the end of the reign of Tiberius, these two otherwise unrelated myths[65] are grouped together cognitively by Romans.[66] Just as the Romans reevaluated the metakosmesis in the light of Stoic conflagrations, so they also reinterpreted these two myths using the expanded connotations of the lexicon of saecular discourse.

At the start of *Ode* 1.2, Horace describes recent terrifying weather phenomena at Rome, for which the impieties of its citizens may be responsible. Horace refers to a *saeculum Pyrrhae*, but the term here seems to be a case of transferred "epithet" as it were: Pyrrha, like Deucalion and unlike every other human at that time, lived during two *saecula* (one before the flood, one after), and the flood did not last for a *saeculum* but in fact separated two *saecula*. Thus the phrase must refer to the metakosmesis of Pyrrha, and it asserts that the cataclysmic flood ended one *saeculum* and began another, which in this poem is an actual event from human history.[67]

More importantly, Horace has described Pyrrha's flood using the temporal language of saecular discourse; the flood is not just a meteorological phenomenon, but a chronological marker. This poem has been read among earlier generations of classical scholars as an allegory for the political chaos of the late Republic, with an Archilochean metaphor of bad weather.[68] But Horace is not simply describing chaos; he is using the language of total transformative change, having refocused the myth to refer to profound historical transition.[69] A general fear of impending disaster, or at least of massive sociopolitical change, would not be out of place in the late Republic, but Horace may have a more specific reference in mind: the scholiast Porphyrion, and others after him, saw the first twenty lines of the poem as a reference to the portents following Julius Caesar's assassination.[70] In light of the comet's having been interpreted by the Etruscan seer Vulcanius as the herald of a new *saeculum* in 44 BCE, Horace's use of Pyrrha here suggests both that he reads the myth as a shorthand for a change in qualitatively defined periods and that he envisions the social unrest in the wake of the assassination as a metakosmetic moment for Roman history.

Similarly, Ovid at *Metamorphoses* 1.200–205 directly compares Rome in the wake of Caesar's assassination to the period after Lycaon's crime but before the Flood of Deucalion, given in full at 1.253–415. Ovid's version of this story has more or less become the canonical version in modern reception, but we must remind ourselves that Ovid wrote near the very end of the post-Sullan century I am investigating, and thus represents just one version of a longer process of artistic, and intellectual, experimentation (or even the culmination of it). One example of this tinkering is in the possibility of other survivors of the flood. In Ovid's version, some people do not immediately drown: a few men seek hilltops or sit in boats (including

52 | *Saeculum*

Deucalion and Pyrrha, 319), eating the fish off of treetops (293–296), but eventually they and all other creatures die of starvation (311–312). Ovid explicitly says that Jupiter saw only one man and woman left alive (325–326). But several books later, Ovid mentions a third person who actually did survive the flood: Cerambus, a man whom nymphs carried above the waters (7.353–356); unfortunately, we never hear from him again.[71] This figure may be an Ovidian invention, or perhaps an obscure reference from earlier, lost versions of the myth.[72]

Jupiter plans to punish the wickedness of the human race (or rather, the wickedness of the current *saeculum* of human history: *infamia temporis*, 1.211)[73] by destroying it, but his original plan was to use lightning; he changes his mind when he recalls that it is fated that a *tempus* (256) would come when earth, sea, sky, and the universe itself (*mundi moles*, 258)[74] would burn up, and he wants to avoid causing this cataclysm with his lightning bolts (253–261). Ovid clearly alludes here to Stoic cosmology, with Jupiter mindful of the periodic conflagrations of the universe in orthodox Stoic physics.[75] Ovid also goes out of his way, in a poetically intricate line, to remind his readers that both Deucalion and Pyrrha are related to Prometheus, a figure with saecular connotations (*inde Promethides placidis Epimethida dictis*, 390).[76] And by throwing stones over their shoulders, Deucalion and Pyrrha create not just new human beings but a new "race" (*genus*, 414), like a Hesiodic version of the Metallic Ages myth.[77] Through these details, Ovid frames the Deucalion myth within the mode of saecular discourse, giving the myth an extra connotation of qualitative historical transition.

Ovid's keen sense of detail in this passage is helpful for seeing how the Roman perception of experiencing a metakosmesis now stood: Deucalion cries heavily at the sight of the desolation of the earth (349–350), noticing even the aquatic slime left on the trees (347). In another important detail, Jupiter ends the flood by ordering Triton to blow into his conch shell (333–334), thus recalling the waters back into their usual boundaries. This divine musical signal closely resembles the loud trumpet blast[78] that was heard out of the sky in 88 BCE, which Etruscan seers interpreted as an omen indicating the end of one *saeculum* and the beginning of another.[79] Deucalion and Pyrrha, like the purported Romans of 88 BCE, must have heard that terrifying peal as well.

While I believe that the saecular connotations of the Deucalion myth came about during and after the period of experimentation with saecular discourse, Sulla may be a contributor to even this aspect of saeculaity. As Plutarch tells us (*Sull.* 14), Sulla's conquest of Athens in 87 BCE coincided with the celebration of the Chytroi festival, which honored the receding of the waters of Deucalion's flood. When the tyrant Aristion, holding out on the Acropolis, finally surrendered and came down, the god sent rain, which filled the Acropolis with water. Luke argues that Sulla would have used this incident as part of his propaganda campaign to depict himself as the bringer of a new *saeculum* to Roman history, and may even (despite the lack of a direct citation by Plutarch) have written about the episode in his memoirs.[80] Since Sulla was celebrated as a second founder of Athens on his return to the city years later,[81] it is possible that he initiated the use of the Deucalion myth in saecular discourse.

While the myth of Deucalion's flood gained increased interest within first century BCE literature, surviving contemporary visual depictions are scant.[82] However, visual representations of the myth of Phaethon at this time are more common.[83] Phaethon appears on a late first-century BCE (or early first-century CE) marble relief at Bolsena (a city said by Pliny the Elder at *HN* 2.53 to have once been destroyed by lightning, like Phaethon himself); a sardonyx cameo from the Augustan period; a late first-century BCE stucco relief; a terracotta mold from the late first century BCE; and a chalcedony intaglio from fourth- or third-century BCE Etruria. Depictions of the myth do not appear in any Greek ceramics and only one example from before Roman times survives (the aforementioned Etruscan intaglio); it has been suggested that during the end of the first century BCE an interest in artistic depictions of the Phaethon myth occurs in some connection with, in particular, the elaborate literary depiction it received by Ovid in the *Metamorphoses*.[84]

Admittedly, Ovid's long depiction of the Phaethon myth (*Met.* 1.747–2.400) lacks the same degree of metakosmetic references and saecular allusions that his Deucalion story shows.[85] One specific detail Ovid makes especially clear about Phaethon's disastrous ride is that it causes the fiery destruction of the entire earth (2.210–303); Jupiter does not strike down Phaethon's chariot with a lightning bolt until just before the entire universe (*omnia interitura*, 2.305–306) is consumed by the flames caused by Phaethon.[86] At any rate, then,

54 | *Saeculum*

Ovid's version of the myth imagines a global catastrophe, not just a tragic death for Phaethon.[87]

For language articulating Phaethon's disaster as a product of another age, the *Astronomica* of Manilius provides a firmer example. At 1.718–804, Manilius gives six different theories for the origin of the Milky Way, one of which (729–734) is that in an ancient age (*per saecula prisca*, 729) the horses of the Sun followed a different path and the old tracks of the horses formed the Milky Way. He follows this brief point with a specific example (735–749) of when the horses of the Sun were in that area: Phaethon's ride. We should not complain that Phaethon burned up the entire world (744–745), writes Manilius, because it provided us with the beautiful Milky Way.[88] Manilius also brings up Deucalion and Phaethon together later in the work: in a somewhat Lucretian passage (4.821–839), Manilius describes the extreme geological changes that are part of the natural cycle of time. Deucalion's flood (829–833) and Phaethon's fiery destruction of the world (834–837) are given as two real-life examples of natural apocalypses that altered the earth itself.

As these examples demonstrate, the imagery of the Deucalion and Phaethon myths became refashioned, after Sulla, through the discourse of saecularity. Taking on temporal connotations, the myths thus became linked through their use in periodizing rhetoric.[89] The global disasters in the myths became versions of the metakosmetic moment that creates the transition from one *saeculum* to the next.[90] While they had always been presented as large-scale events by authors, Roman writers now conceived of the cataclysms specifically in terms of the saecular discourse that used major catastrophes as metakosmetic markers separating periods on the historical timeline.

Metempsychosis, palingenesis, and the Stoic ekpyrosis influenced Roman thought on the concept of the *saeculum* and took on temporal aspects as Roman thinkers developed the notion of qualitative periodization throughout the first century BCE. In addition to the concepts found in the works of these philosophical schools, we can also find references to similar phenomena in the works of Plato and Aristotle and their followers. The Academic and Peripatetic schools were also interested in temporal organizations that could create fundamentally distinct eras, but the specific episode that energizes these explorations was the notion of societal collapse. Such a collapse could occur through a variety of different methods, such as meteorological disasters, and it could happen at various scales, from the local or regional to the global or cosmic. What distinguishes these philosophical propositions from the ones we examined previously is that this interest in societal collapse provided Romans with a language to describe the civic chaos they were perceiving not only in the political sphere but in the moral sphere as well (if those two things could even be separated). In other words, Roman fears about the potential for the destruction of the state were fed by Platonic and Aristotelian writings about the temporal frameworks that could make such disasters comprehensible, and consequently the language of saecular periodization could be adopted to popularize such sentiments with a more robust temporal vocabulary. Similar models of historical transition and repetition found in the works of these earlier philosophers thus served as comparanda for Roman depictions of civic destruction.[91]

In several of the later Platonic works, we find a recurring interest in discussions about major catastrophes that all but eliminated mankind. For example, in the *Laws*, the origins of any human civilization are imagined to be the herdsmen who are left over as survivors of a massive flood:

> **Athenian:** Do you consider that there is any truth in the ancient tales?
>
> **Clinias:** What tales?
>
> **Athenian:** That the world of men has often been destroyed by floods, plagues, and many other things, in such a way that only a small portion of the human race has survived.
>
> **Clinias:** Everyone would regard such accounts as perfectly credible.
>
> **Athenian:** Come now, let us picture to ourselves one of the many catastrophes—namely, that which occurred once upon a time through the Deluge.
>
> **Clinias:** And what are we to imagine about it?
>
> **Athenian:** That the men who then escaped destruction must have been mostly herdsmen of the hills, scanty embers of the human race preserved somewhere on the mountain-tops. (*Laws* 677)[92]

In this passage, the human race has eternally been all but wiped out by catastrophes many times, only to start over again; each catastrophe (e.g., the flood) separates each epoch of human civilization. To Benardete, the natural disaster is "a ribbon of time on which [the

56 | Saeculum

Athenian stranger] can place stages of political development that look as if they follow of necessity from the point of origin."[93] By wiping the slate virtually clean, each natural disaster compels civilization to start over again in what functions essentially as a new era of time. The merest trace of continuity from one side of the catastrophe to the other is the small number of surviving herdsmen, without any retention of culture: "The virtually complete loss of memory of city, regime, and legislation that followed the flood ensures that its survivors did not come to restore them on the basis of any half-remembered models (678a3–5). Whatever happened subsequently—cities and regimes, arts and laws—developed on its own."[94] While the Academics (unlike the Stoics or Epicureans) denied the destructibility of the earth, and could never imagine a full global catastrophic event, here in this passage we find a Platonic articulation of continuous cycles of destruction and regeneration, just at a smaller, human-level scale.

Such periodic catastrophes are also discussed in the *Critias*, wherein previous eras of civilization are seen to be fundamentally separated by the natural disasters that caused society to collapse. It is said that of the original race of people, "their names are preserved, but their works have vanished owing to the repeated destruction of their successors and the length of the intervening periods. For, as was said before, the stock that survived on each occasion was a remnant of unlettered mountaineers which had heard the names only of the rulers, and but little besides their works" (*Criti.* 109d).[95] It is imagined here that these repeated acts of destruction must have occurred by means of a deluge, as many great floods had taken place in the remote past (*Criti.* 111b). In fact, one particular night of torrential rains destroyed Attica, which is considered to be the third flood which preceded the Flood of Deucalion (*Criti.* 112a).

These theories of cyclic catastrophes are also explored in the *Timaeus*, where there are references to the great deluge and to Deucalion and Pyrrha's survival (*Ti.* 22a) and a further insistence that catastrophes such as these occur and reoccur after long stretches of time (*Ti.* 22d, 23a). Chroust sums up Plato's statements in the *Timaeus*: "In the course of time there have been many such destructions, the worst having been caused by conflagrations and floods. Whenever and wherever such catastrophes did occur, Plato concludes, mankind, or to be more exact, human civilization, had to 'start all over again,' beginning 'from scratch.'"[96] Thus the Romans could find in the Platonic corpus, with all the intellectual authority implied by such an inclusion, straightforward declarations about the regularity of civilization collapses that broke up the historical timeline into discrete units.

These speculations about massive ruptures in world history through natural disasters can be found in works by Aristotle as well. Unlike the Stoics and Epicureans, who were compelled to postulate the regular annihilation of the world itself, as Lukacher explains, Aristotle "decided to refocus the question of time" away from the cosmic perspective, with its difficulty explaining time at such a broad scale, and moving instead toward "the living present of the human subject."[97] Like Plato, Aristotle believed in the indestructibility of the world, so the large regular catastrophes he describes are not global, but they have a profound effect on human history. Aristotle "attempted to explain the recurrent declines and revivals of human civilization and of philosophy in general by insisting that due to major though localized natural catastrophes such as major deluges, men again and again find themselves compelled culturally to start from 'the beginning' in a world which knows no beginning or end."[98] He thus imagines the timeline of history broken up into similar chunks and separated by major natural phenomena.

Aristotle proposes that periodic major catastrophes appear at certain places on earth, which can explain the geological changes that are visible to human records. He writes in the *Meteorologica* (352a): "We should suppose that the cause of all these changes is that, just as there is a winter among the yearly seasons, so at fixed intervals in some great period of time there is a great winter and excess of rains. This does not always happen in the same region of the earth: for instance, the so-called Flood of Deucalion took place largely in the Hellenic lands and particularly in old Hellas."[99] Note that the Flood of Deucalion is presented here as a real-life, but localized, historical phenomenon. Aristotle brings up such periodic catastrophes to refute the claim that the universe had not existed forever but was created; he says that the rupture in human history caused by such a cataclysm would make people forget that there had ever been a time, much less a civilization, before the disaster.[100] The notion of societal collapse creates a new temporal framework that can account for the lack of evidence of previous civilizations.

Parallel to this interest in periodic natural disasters, Aristotle also describes instances of total breaks in cultural progress; human civilization reaches a certain level and then has to start back over

58 | *Saeculum*

again. This speculation about human knowledge being lost, but afterward relearned, appears in a number of Aristotelian works.[101] In the *Metaphysics*, he writes that "each art and each science has often been developed as far as possible and has again perished" (1074b10ff.). Similarly, in the *Politics*, he writes, "We ought to recall that we should not disregard the experiences of the ages. . . . For almost everything has been found out (during some previous epoch)" (1264a3ff.). And a likely reference to this concept is found in *De caelo* when he writes, "The same ideas . . . occur and re-occur in the minds of men, not just once, but again and again" (270b19–21). In these three examples, though, no mention is made of a cataclysm causing human progress to be stopped.

But Chroust has drawn a direct connection between the recurrence of natural catastrophes and of certain fundamental ideas necessary for survival: "With the 'great deluge' the technological, cultural and intellectual achievements of the past are lost, thus compelling man to begin again his emancipation from a state of utter primitivism and to repeat his climb to a higher level of technological, cultural, and intellectual performance."[102] Much like with Plato, the few survivors of a massive disaster (such as a deluge) have to re-form civilization from its very roots.

Aristotle also makes a casual mention of the theory in the *Politics*, in which it is not clear whether he is actually endorsing the idea (1269a): "And in general all men really seek what is good, not what was customary with their forefathers; and it is probable that primitive mankind, whether sprung from the earth or the survivors of some destructive cataclysm, were just like ordinary foolish people, as indeed is actually said of the earth-born race, so that would be absurd for us to abide by their notions."[103] It is apparent that Aristotle, like Plato, explored the possibility of periodic natural disasters breaking up the history of the human race into discrete units of progress.

Both Plato and Aristotle also make mention of a related concept that can be found in one form or another in almost every civilization on Earth: the idea of the "Great Year." In general, the Great Year refers to the period of time in which all the celestial rotations return to their original positions together. For example, Plato speaks in the *Timaeus* of a moment at which the solar and lunar cycles, along with the rotation of the planets and stars, all complete a full cycle at once (*Ti.* 39d).[104] While many ancient writers were interested in calculating the exact amount of time that a Great Year lasted, there is nothing inherently significant about the period of a Great Year (any more than the period of a regular year). However, in the *Meteorologica* (352a28ff.), Aristotle also links the periodic floods that destroy part of human civilization with the period of the "great year."[105] This feature would imply a greater connection between the regularity of cosmic cycles and the moments of societal collapse that punctuate the beginnings and endings of human eras. Furthermore, Censorinus (*DN* 18.11) maintains that Aristotle believed that whenever the sun, moon, and five planets all lined up again, there would be not a "great year" but a "greatest year," marked by disastrous floods (although not total cosmic catastrophes).[106] This would lend greater credence to a Roman understanding of Peripatetic belief in the connection between civilization collapse and the regular celestial movements associated with the Great Year.

One Peripatetic philosopher, Aristotle's student Dicaearchus, merits special mention for offering antecedents to saecularity.[107] Dicaearchus wrote extensively, and it is possible that he covered some of the same topics as Plato and Aristotle above, as he had a particular interest in natural catastrophes (as identified by Cicero):

> There is a book, *On the Destruction of Humans*, by Dicaearchus, a great and prolific Peripatetic who collected all the other causes of destruction (floods, plagues, famines, even sudden invasions by wild animals) by whose attacks, he teaches, certain tribes of humans have been eliminated. Then he compares how many more humans have been destroyed by the attacks of other humans, that is, by war and revolutions, than by every other calamity.[108]

There is no direct evidence, however, that Dicaearchus believed that any causes of destruction caused ruptures in human history. Dicaearchus is more relevant to saecularity in the realm of historical anthropology, where he brings in the language of the Golden Age. Dicaearchus naturalizes the mythical Ages of Man to describe the evolution of social practices (or, actually, the devolution of humans, as they move from natural to pastoral to agricultural modes of survival and with each stage increase in evil).[109] Saunders finds that "this basic threefold development in terms of the source of the food-supply is surely genuinely Dicaearchan," so this speculation

60 | *Saeculum*

about the stages of early human life can be considered an original contribution by the philosopher.[110] And while Varro spins this Dicaearchan account as progress,[111] Saunders argues that in the original text no such upward trajectory of the periodized timeline may be there, and in fact it may be a downward trajectory.[112] The removal of mythological elements in the Golden Age was later adopted by Posidonius, although he adapts the structure to describe the evolution of law and philosophy in human affairs. By breaking down human development into discrete periods, each with their own characteristics, and by integrating the mythology of the Golden Age into actual human history, Dicaearchus anticipates (and perhaps even influences) later Roman thought on human history, and contributes to the larger Roman saecular discourse of the first century BCE.

The Academic and Peripatetic schools of Greek philosophy hypothesized about the possibility of recurring natural disasters and moments of civilization collapse, at both local and global scales, which could separate distinct eras of human history without aspects of human culture or ingenuity surviving from one era to the next. In the situations imagined by these philosophers, human civilization (whether globally or in a more localized situation) is wiped out except for a small fraction of inhabitants who then go on to repopulate the area, restarting the evolution of human society from its primitive beginnings. Thus, although a slight degree of continuity is preserved (since the new community traces its origins to survivors of the old one), there is largely a lack of linkage between the destroyed civilization and the newly created one. The topic was not just a theoretical idea for philosophers to ramble about; even a sober historian like Polybius imagined periodic floods, plagues, famines, and other disasters periodically destroying all but a tiny fraction of the human race and all the skills that humanity had developed.[113] This very basic version of periodized human history thus provided an intellectual foundation for further temporal innovations by Roman writers in the first century BCE.

These earlier Greek models generally lack the idea of qualitative characteristics that define each human era, which would serve the crucial purpose of saecular discourse for the Romans. Nonetheless, the combination of two products of historical thought (namely, temporality and civilization collapse) would eventually lead to much Roman rhetoric. Through these Greek antecedents, the Romans articulated fears about the imminent collapse of their civilization using the temporal aspects of saecular discourse. Lucretius, a scorner of all things supernatural, did not believe that Deucalion's flood or Phaethon's fiery destruction actually occurred, but he nonetheless admits the possibility of massive cataclysms in a long passage in book 5 arguing against the immortality of the earth (5.324–415). This passage has been read as a direct response to Plato and Aristotle, particularly because they used the myths of Deucalion and Phaethon in their arguments.[114] He points out that if the world had always existed, there should be poems about events other than Thebes and Troy; that is, there ought to be a much larger (perhaps infinite) number of significant world events that people (including poets) remember and talk about. He offers, as a counterargument, the idea of periodic global cataclysmic events wiping out all (or nearly all) of the human race, and he never really refutes it; in fact he uses it as evidence of his own argument about the mortality of the earth (someday a powerful enough cataclysm will occur that destroys the earth).

Lucretius describes these periodic cataclysms by saying that they "destroyed the generations of men" (*periisse hominum saecla*, 339), suggesting that each disaster ended a particular *saeculum* of human history. His examples of global cataclysms include scorching heat (*torrenti vapore*, 339, like a Stoic ekpyrosis), earthquakes (*magno vexamine mundi*, 340), and floods (341–342, a *kataklysmos*). Lucretius explains how these disasters could occur in his physical model: the four elements are in constant battle with one other to master the others and that if fire prevails, the sun and all heat will drink up the waters (383–384), while if water prevails, the rivers and sea will deluge the whole earth (386–387). Here Lucretius shows that "it is quite possible that some day one of the elements will acquire such a preponderance over the others that it will overwhelm the world."[115]

Lucretius then gives an example of when each phenomenon already happened on earth (394–395): the destruction of Phaethon (396–404) and an unspecified Great Flood (411–415). Lucretius distances himself from the reality of these events with sarcastic comments (*scilicet ut veteres Graium cecinere poetae*, 405;[116] *ut fama est*, 395 and 412), and in fact after dismissing the Phaethon tale as nonsense, he then gives a rationalistic account of how fire can overwhelm the earth (temporarily [409] or entirely [410], like a true Stoic ekpyrosis)[117] which is matched by his rationalistic (and noticeably Deucalion-free) account of the flood. Thus, in this passage Lucretius describes the physical mechanisms whereby nature, through a singular phenomenon, can alter

62 | *Saeculum*

human history by wiping out humanity and starting over, and when these events happen they end the *hominum saecla*.

Cicero also engages favorably with the idea of these periodic catastrophes in a roughly contemporaneous work. In the *De republica*, he mentions the pointlessness of striving for immortality since human fame is at the mercy of periodic natural disasters (*eluviones exustionesque terrarum, quas accidere tempore certo necesse est*, 6.9.23). Yet elsewhere he notes that men who do not even care if a humanity-crippling disaster (*omnium deflagratio*) occurs after their deaths are worthy of public scorn (*Fin.* 3.64). He also claims that some men can predict such natural phenomena, even the disasters so great that they destroy the earth; that is, they are capable not simply of predicting floods, but predicting Great Floods (*Div.* 1.111). Like Lucretius, Cicero is aware of, and has reflected on, the idea that human history is broken up by natural disasters that almost totally eradicate the continuity from one period to the next.

Roman discussion of the potential end of the world seems also to have spurred Varro to compose a Menippean satire, the *Kosmotoryne*, mocking this very notion.[118] While the work survives only in a few fragments, it seems that Varro discussed end-of-the-world scenarios in relation to the perception of political (or at least moral) decline at Rome. However, unlike contemporary moralists (at whom he may have been directing his barbs), Varro insists that the destruction of the world will not be linked to any particular ethical behavior by humans, but to natural processes of decay.

As we saw earlier in chapter 1, the idea of the destruction of human civilization, at least in a localized sense, was an inherent feature of Etruscan saecular doctrine. Each city or tribe was granted a finite number of *saecula* for existence, after which it would be destroyed. In a 1994 article, Edlund-Berry evaluates the destruction of several sites in Etruscan history and suggests that the Etruscans had multiple ritual practices for cities that received damage through war or natural causes, including the "un-foundation" of sites such as Murlo.[119] The saecular doctrine thus complemented other aspects of Etruscan religion and offered another mode for people to engage with the very real fact of the ruin of entire cities. Interest in the concept of civilization collapse led to an intellectual trend among Romans in the first century BCE that I call the "post-Roman world." I use the term in a very broad sense to describe intellectual engagement with the possibility of a world which, after some cataclysmic event, lacks the existence of Rome. The fundamental aspect of this post-Roman focus is its tendency toward non-anthropocentrism; it imagines a (localized or global) setting in which a Roman civilization, or all humanity, has already vanished.[120]

We have already seen one brief reference to post-civilization engagement in Latin literature: Ovid's Deucalion looks out at the world after the flood, and it is a silent, desolate wasteland (*Met.* 1.349).[121] But the *locus classicus* for ancient thinking on time after the end of a city actually occurs at the beginning of the work of Thucydides (1.10). Thucydides imagines that in the distant future, people looking on a Sparta devoid of inhabitants and homes would underestimate its former power, while those looking on the ruins of Athens would overestimate its former power. These future humans would be investigating hypothetical cities that did not survive forever and, knowing so little about Athens and Sparta (and having no connection to them), they would completely misunderstand what the two Hellenic powers had been like during the Peloponnesian War. These are, essentially, people from another *saeculum* of human history; they have so little in common with Thucydides that they may as well be another species, or another *gens*.[122] But the Roman intellectual community of the first century BCE successfully melded this notion of post-civilization perspective with the temporal features of saecular discourse, allowing for a proleptic history of Rome to be conceived.

Post-Roman imagery most famously appears in the vision of a future Philippi given by Vergil at the end of the first book of the *Georgics* (1.489–497).[123] Vergil imagines the possibility that someday a *tempus* will come (*tempus veniet*, 493) when some farmer will plow the site of the battle and come across old javelins and helmets, as well as graves containing the bones of the dead (493–497).[124] Vergil's farmer seems to have no idea what he has uncovered: he marvels (*mirabitur*, 497) at his findings, and he considers the bones to be enormous (*grandia*, 497), as if they belonged to giants. The farmer of this future *tempus* does not simply fail to remember the events of Philippi; he seems to have no connection at all to the people who participated in the battle, as though they are a completely separate civilization.[125]

The fact that the farmer marvels at the bones as *grandia* requires further comment. The first century BCE contains several examples of large bones being uncovered and attributed to people from the mythical past.[126] For example, a story circulating in the work of Republican author Tanusius Geminus, repeated by Plutarch, claimed

64 | Saeculum

that Sertorius found giant bones in a tomb in Libya alleged to have been that of the mythical Antaeus.[127] Though he himself was skeptical, he pretended to be convinced in order to increase his standing among the Mauretanians.[128] Similarly, Sallust reports in his fragmentary *Histories* that an earthquake on Crete in the 60s BCE revealed a giant skeleton believed by many to have been that of either Orion or Otus.[129] Philodemus recorded the discovery of a giant's skeleton on Crete.[130] Later, Augustus decorated his villa at Capri with bones of massive beasts,[131] which were playfully called the "bones of the giants" (*gigantum ossa*), as well as the weapons of famous heroes. Augustus also preserved the bones of two very tall men who lived during his reign,[132] making sure to record their names so that no one failed to recognize them as with these other examples. Beagon's commentary on *HN* 7 notes at this passage that this "interest in large bone relics as evidence of the past indicates a collective historical consciousness."[133] The inability to confidently identify or contextualize these relics in history leads Romans to wonder if their own world will be treated by future humans as an inscrutable relic signifying their disconnection with the period in which the bones originate. Vergil's lines express an anxiety that Augustan Rome may end up as forgotten and misunderstood as the generation of those whose bones were uncovered in Libya and Crete.

Vergil uses the language of saecularity around this passage, suggesting that he is depicting the farmer as a member of a separate *saeculum*. The time of Julius Caesar's assassination was a wicked age (*impia saecula*, 468), and Vergil asks the gods to let Augustus live long enough to help the overturned age (*everso saeclo*, 500; *everso* anticipates the simile of the out-of-control chariot at 512–514). Vergil's wordplay also suggests an inverse relationship between his own time and that of the hypothetical farmer. While contemporary Romans are beating their curved (*curvae*, 508) scythes into swords and have no respect for the plow (*non ullus aratro / dignus honos*, 506–507), the farmer of the future *tempus* is digging up Philippi's rusty swords with his curved plow (*incurvo aratro*, 494). This farmer occupies a world that is qualitatively detached from Vergil's time; the destruction that occurred at Philippi (and/or the potential greater calamities that may follow for Rome) separates the two humans into two different *saecula*.

Beyond the bones, the farmer's discovery of material relics of an earlier *saeculum* is reflected in a comment by Pythagoras in book 15 of

Ovid's *Metamorphoses*. Pythagoras (whose soul, he claimed, embodied people from multiple ages; cf. 158–164) gives a long speech describing various changes that occur throughout nature. Early in the speech, he describes the Golden Age (*vetus illa aetas cui fecimus aurea nomen*, 96) and its eventual lapse. After several tangents, he returns to the Metallic Age myth, and says that the ages (*saecula*, 261) have metamorphosed from gold to iron. He then describes, among other many things, geological changes and the rise and fall of famous cities. Due to the many metamorphoses of bodies of water, seashells have been found far from the ocean, and an anchor was once found on a mountain (264–265). This out-of-place anchor recalls the image in the first book of Ovid's *Metamorphoses* of the anchor lodged in a meadow as a result of the flood of Deucalion (a metakosmetic event), and these uncanny discoveries resemble the armor and bones found by Vergil's farmer; in both instances, the discoverer is confronted with evidence that a past *saeculum* existed to which they have no historical connection. The presence of marine items on a mountaintop also calls to mind the "Protean herd" of seals on the mountaintop (*omne cum Proteus pecus egit altos / visere montis*, 7–8) during the *saeculum Pyrrhae* in Horace's *Ode* 1.2, and indeed Ovid shows seals occupying the land once grazed by goats during Deucalion's flood (*Met.* 1.299–300). The discoveries by Vergil's farmers force him to confront a previous *saeculum* with which he has no connection.

The fact that a farmer stumbles on the bones while plowing parallels another anxiety: a post-human *saeculum* in which nature takes over the shells of destroyed cities. Descriptions of a city's utter annihilation demonstrate this saecular transition by underscoring the discontinuity between the original settlement and what happened at the site afterward. For example, in Ovid's *Heroides* 1 (47–58), Penelope imagines that Troy's wall has been leveled and only bare ground remains (48); grain is now growing on fields grown fertile from bloodshed (53–54); the curved plow (*curvis aratris*, 55) digs up old bones; and the ruined buildings are already overgrown with foliage (56). This passage's well-established intertextual relationship to Vergil's farmer in *Georgics* 1 emphasizes Troy's complete transformation to a pre-civilization existence (where vegetation rules again). Similarly, in Horace's *Ode* 3.3, Juno describes a post-human Troy, where cattle trample the burial mounds of Priam and Paris and wild beasts use them as dens (40–42). The glory of the Trojan heroes has been

66 | *Saeculum*

completely forgotten; the people who reach Troy after its destruction will have no physical markers (σῆμα being Greek for both "sign" and "funeral mound") of its former grandeur.

Troy is not the only city described with such imagery; the Romans also choose examples closer to home. Propertius, in 4.10, describes the three *spolia opima* in the Temple of Jupiter Feretrius and how they were obtained. In the second episode, the Roman Cossus slays Tolumnius, king of Veii. As a result of Rome's domination of Veii, the site of the former richly decorated city (27–28) became fields for shepherds (29), and people reap corn over the bones of its inhabitants (*in vestris ossibus arva metunt*, 30).[134] Cairns writes, "His use of the adjective *veteres* (27) is unlikely to be casual; it should distinguish 'old Veii' from Augustus's new Veii, and thus turn the couplet into an implicit eulogy of Augustus either for having refounded Veii, or at least for planning to do so."[135] And Livy describes how Scipio Africanus's army in Spain destroyed the city of Iliturgi and burned everything to the ground, so that they might destroy the very last traces of the city (*vestigia quoque urbis*) and even the memory of it from their enemies' hearts (28.20.7).

Alison Keith has argued that throughout the *Aeneid*, references to the fall of Troy and of Carthage contain "an admonitory undertone, intimating the possibility of the imperial capital's overthrow," and that the Augustan epic poets "displace the threat of Rome's fall by projecting her destruction onto a series of prototypes and antitypes of the eternal city."[136] I contend that in these examples, the Roman poets do not displace the threat so much as allude to its plausibility. These depictions show how the history of a city can be totally forgotten; a future post-human *saeculum*, qualitatively distinct from the current one, knows nothing of its former glory.

But some Romans did imagine a specifically post-Roman world. Famously, when Scipio Africanus beheld the sight of Carthage being destroyed, he wept when considering that someday Rome too would fall. His words were recorded directly by Polybius, although the text of Polybius is lost and we only have later adaptations by the first-century BCE historian Diodorus Siculus (32.24) and Appian (*Punica* 132 = Polybius 39.6). Africanus was said to have recited two lines from the *Iliad*[137] on the future downfall of Troy, thus explicitly linking Troy's past destruction with Rome's future destruction. While Africanus had already begun thinking about a post-human Rome in 146 BCE, the trend grew stronger in the period after Sulla, when

Eternal Returns | 67

saecular discourse offered a new way to contemplate it: the new temporal possibilities of saecularity encouraged these kinds of proleptic histories through the mechanism of periodization.

In *Epode* 16, Horace imagines a Rome completely destroyed by its own wickedness. An impious *aetas* of accursed blood (*impia devoti sanguinis aetas*, 9) will ruin the city, and its very soil will be taken over again by wild animals (*ferisque rursus occupabitur solum*, 10),[138] as if returning to its pre-foundation status. Worse yet, barbarians will trample the grounds of the former city under the hooves of their horses and disturb the bones of Romulus (11–14).[139] Curiously, Horace's solution for avoiding this fate is to abandon the city and move away. This process would have the effect of achieving the exact same future for the grounds of Rome:[140] they will imitate the Phocaeans, who left their temples to be inhabited by wild boars and wolves (17–20). Thus Horace suggests a certain inevitability to the appearance of a future Roman site devoid of Romans (and possibly of any humans); whether they continue to lapse further into evil, or flee the city for the Isles of the Blessed, Rome is doomed to return (cf. *rursus*, 10) to nonexistence.[141]

Horace aligns his grim prophecy with the Metallic Ages mythology, as detailed in the poem's concluding lines (63–66). Jupiter created the Isles of the Blessed as an escape for the pious when the Golden Age (*tempus aureum*, 64) became "debased with bronze" (skipping the usual Silver Age, but clearly referring to a saecular division of history) and the ages (*saecula*, 65) were hardened with bronze, then iron.[142] Horace's plan to abandon Rome, then, is predicated on this divine response to a saecular model of the historical timeline. If the *aetas* (*altera aetas*, 1; *impia aetas*, 9) bringing about Rome's ruin is some kind of Iron Age, then the post-human Rome of wild animals and forgotten burial grounds must be the *saeculum* that follows the Iron Age: an antitype of the new Golden Age of *Eclogue* 4.[143]

The connection between the Metallic Age myth and the imagery of civilization collapse also appears in book 8 of the *Aeneid*. As Evander leads Aeneas around the site of what will eventually become Rome (306–369), though in their time it is still a wooded region, they pass by two towns with ruined walls (*duo disiectis oppida muris*, 355). Evander refers to these former settlements as *reliquias veterumque monumenta virorum* (356). These ruins are the remains of the civilization that predated Evander and the Italians, a civilization he had described a little earlier (314–336): the *Saturnia regna*. When Saturn fled Olympus and reached Italy, he found an anarchic race of men sprung from

68 | *Saeculum*

trees (*gens virum truncis et duro robore nata*, 315), and he gave them laws and ruled over them. This was, as Evander says, the Golden Age (*aurea saecula*, 324–325). This Golden Age was followed by a worse period (*deterior et decolor aetas*, 326) characterized by a madness for war and a desire for gain (*belli rabies et amor habendi*, 327). As time wore on (*tum . . . tum . . .* , 328–330), the settlements ruled by Saturn and Janus (whose domain must have preceded Saturn's),[144] collapsed into ruins, which is how Evander found them when he reached the site as an exile. Thus, Evander's Italians (and Vergil's Romans) have no connection with the people (positively described as a separate race at 315) who once inhabited this area, and whose civilization now only survives in ruined walls visible to the people coming after in a different *saeculum*.

The post-human Rome envisioned by Horace, then, was already witnessed in a way by the founder Aeneas himself in Vergil's later composition; the boars and wolves of *Epode* 16 are paralleled by the woodland briars adding grimness to the decay (*olim silvestribus horrida dumis*, 348).[145] This Vergilian depiction of an Aeneas-era Rome already featuring ruins seems to be a unique invention.[146] Even while describing Rome's very beginnings, Vergil was already thinking about Rome's ultimate end: a Rome with no Romans, a Rome with no Rome.

This Vergil passage, with the site of Rome possessing the barely recognizable ruins of a decayed Golden Age, sits uncomfortably next to the praise of the Augustan Principate and its new Golden Age that we see elsewhere in the *Aeneid*.[147] But the use of saecular discourse to imagine post-Roman futures is more than just a way to express anti-Augustan subtexts. These Romans had lived through the horrors of the civil wars, a period when the collapse of Rome seemed imminent. Once Augustus should die, the potential for renewed civil war would be an omnipresent fear. Romans writing in the 20s and 10s BCE would not be so confident that a smooth transition from Augustus to some heir would take place; a power vacuum could result in another "unholy age" finally bringing Rome to destruction.

By allowing Romans to imagine future ages distinct from the present, including ages after the death of a city, saecular discourse complicates the very notion of posterity. It is not just Augustus who could end up like the unfamiliar bones at Philippi, but anyone; Roman civilization could be totally lost to history. For poets striving for literary immortality, saecular discourse suggests the impossibility of achieving immortal fame (as I will go on to explore in chapter 6). I will explore in greater detail the consequences of such thinking by the Roman intelligentsia in the rest of this volume.

I began this chapter by noting that elements of Greek philosophy brought the idea of cataclysm (whether on a human or civic scale) into the Roman discourse of saecularity. Metempsychosis, palingenesis, and Stoic ekpyrosis altered the Roman perception of the temporality of human life and engendered cultural anxiety about the change from one era to another, especially when combined with the surviving passages in Platonic and Aristotelian thought that engage with the notion of societal collapse. Academic and Peripatetic hypotheses about human history, perhaps as a consequence of their insistence on the indestructible nature of the world, imagined that human civilization is marked by recurring natural disasters that obliterate the achievements of human culture and force the few survivors to start all over again rebuilding civilization. The existence of this train of thought helped serve as a foundation for later Roman explorations in saecular discourse, specifically because of the Roman interest in the rhetoric of social collapse in the first century BCE. Saecularity gave the Romans an intellectual apparatus to describe the distant futures in which Rome, or other cities, could be populated not by Romans but by animals or by people who had no connection, or even knowledge, of the Romans of the first century BCE. The Academic and Peripatetic interest in the idea of periodic natural catastrophes creating breaks in the timeline of human history thus influenced these later Roman temporal explorations of life after cataclysmic destruction. Moving from this discussion of the earlier Greek influences on the Roman innovation of saecular discourse, I now turn to actual applications of saecular periodization in the first century BCE.

3 | Inflection Points

Progress and Decline Narratives with Periodization

In the previous chapter, I examined the Roman rhetoric of civilization collapse, and demonstrated that the temporal structure of saecular discourse provided Roman intellectuals with a more robust way of describing the theories of societal destruction (articulated by Greek philosophers) that seemed to be particularly applicable to the political and moral chaos common to Roman life in the first century BCE. One perceived trend that influenced such pessimistic attitudes about the future of Rome was the apparent decline in moral standards among the Roman people. Telling the story of Rome's moral decline was a Roman obsession, one that certainly began before the first century BCE.[1] The temporal frameworks that Roman writers adopted to articulate the narrative of their society's moral decline varied in complexity, generally following one of three patterns. The most basic statement of moral decline—an undefined sense that mainstream behavior used to be better than it is now—demonstrated an awareness of change in civic behavior but without any claims about when, or how, this change occurred. Another typical strategy, which we may call the "lapsarian" model of moral decline, was to pinpoint a single historical moment when civic virtue was forever tarnished by the introduction of some novel vice, temporally severing the virtuous past from our inferior present. During the first century BCE, however, the spread of periodization as a temporal mode of historical narrative added increasing complexity to the story of Rome's moral decline: the saecular model grouped Roman moral history into a succession of discrete phases, and thus with multiple turning points. For such a narrative, we see not only differences of quality from *saeculum* to *saeculum* but also differences of degree, and so Roman intellectuals could promote a more nuanced story of the decline they perceived and apportion blame among a wider range of influences.

The lapsarian model was a typical approach for Roman Republican historiographers, but just what caused the transition, and when, was not agreed among them. Earl posits the existence of a "senatorial tradition" of moral decline, in which the introduction of eastern luxury ruins traditional Roman moral character.[2] The precise date of this turning point varied from the suggestion by Polybius (31.25.3–8) of 168 BCE, when debauchery, cultivated in Macedonia, first came to Rome, to the claim by Piso Frugi (Pliny, *HN* 17.244 = Piso Frugi F40 Cornell) of 154 BCE, when *pudicitia* was first threatened on a wide scale.[3] Against this tradition, centered as it is on cultural foundations of ethical conduct, Sallust's decision to peg the decline at 146 BCE, when—with Rome as the sole superpower in the Mediterranean—a fear of the enemy (*metus hostilis*) was eliminated, suggests a greater focus on the geopolitical realities causing the apparent transition than on the alleged moral devolution itself.[4] A further issue with any discussion of the concept of moral decline is that there are different "kinds" of morals, or rather different aspects of morality: sumptuary,[5] familial, sexual,[6] religious, political,[7] and so on. These aspects can be separated, combined, or given as cascading causes for one another, and thus any moral-decline narrative can take a different perspective on what constitutes "morality."

What these variations demonstrate is that any attempt to narrativize Roman moral decline, whether periodized or not, requires the creation of a highly condensed version of Roman history.[8] The lapsarian model requires a major streamlining (or, really, oversimplification) of Roman behavior before and after the chosen turning point. The entire history of a culture hinged on a single metakosmetic event, often related to a foreign war. Periodization was a useful tool for describing more nuanced versions of a decline narrative than the two-stage lapsarian versions outlined here.

Perhaps because of this long-standing habit of lapsarian rhetoric by Republican historiographers, saecular moral-decline narratives are far less prominent in prose Latin works than in poetry, and in fact we rarely find fully formed saecular narratives of decline in historiographic works before the end of the Augustan Age. Caesar's *commentarii*, for example, never adopt any kind of periodizing language. Like Sallust,[9] Livy composed his history after Sulla's promulgation of saecular discourse, yet he too adopts a lapsarian model

72 | Saeculum

of moral decline, choosing for his turning point (39.6.7) the year 187 BCE, when Manlius Vulso's army returned from Asia, laden with plunder and practicing luxurious habits. Although in his highly programmatic preface, Livy speaks of evils "which our age has been seeing for so many years" (*quae nostra tot per annos vidit aetas*, 5), from which the composition of his history (particularly of the earliest books) lets him avert his gaze, nevertheless this vague phrasing does not lend itself to characterizing a specific time-unit with specific ills, and Livy often uses the phrase *nostra aetas* to refer to the present in only a general sense.[10] In other places throughout his work, Livy makes occasional asides criticizing the current *saeculum*, but without any coherent sense of a temporal mode constructed from saecular discourse; the lapsarian model of Roman morality dominates.[11] Thus it appears that three of the major surviving historiographers writing after Sulla's propagation of the saecular temporal mode (Sallust, Caesar, Livy) were unwilling to structure their histories using the periodizing discourse already popular among their peers writing poetry and other prose genres.[12] This difference in rhetoric may reflect the greater willingness of Roman philosophical writers and poets to adopt the temporal structures implied by saecular periodization (given the cognitive foundation offered by concepts rooted in Greek philosophy, as seen in chapter 2); it was only later that Roman historiographers warmed to the idea of saecularity.

While the surviving historians of the first century BCE show no interest in a saecular narrative of moral decline, Cicero provides some more intriguing examples. Although the text of book 3 of *De republica* is poorly preserved, in one fragment (3.29) for which context is somewhat lacking (beyond a vague sense that it refers to Roman magistrates violating treaties), the character Laelius declares:

> If this habit of lawlessness [*consuetudo ac licentia*] begins to spread and changes our rule from one of justice to one of force, so that those who up to the present have obeyed us willingly are held faithful by fear alone, then, though our own generation has perhaps been vigilant enough to be safe [*etsi nobis, qui id aetatis sumus, evigilatum fere est*], yet I am anxious for our descendants [*de posteris nostris*], and for the permanent stability of our commonwealth, which might live on for ever if the principles and customs of our ancestors were maintained.[13]

A system of three *saecula* seems to emerge from this account. In the previous age, Rome's just rule kept its subordinates obeying them willingly; in the current age, Rome has introduced the habit of ruling by force, and its subordinates obey only because of fear, but the Romans have been vigilant enough to be safe; in the next age, the Romans may lack the vigilance of the present age and thus could be ruined. Notably, Cicero presents two competing narratives for the future of Rome: had the custom of ruling by justice been maintained, that earlier age could have lasted indefinitely, but because of the periodizing transition caused by the new habit of rule by force, a pattern of saecular decline inevitably follows.

A different example from the Ciceronian corpus raises a further issue about saecularity in narratives of moral decline. In the *Paradoxa Stoicorum* (49–50), Cicero initially brags about being a thrifty spender, only to admit that, given the general profligacy characteristic of the age (*morum ac temporum vitio*), he may in fact be somewhat guilty of the fault of the present generation (*in huius saeculi errore*): compared to figures from the past (and even just in the *patrum nostrorum memoria*), his expenditures might seem large. Although at first claiming to be an exception to the rule of his *saeculum*, Cicero realizes that this exceptionalism does not immediately put him at the level of frugality of Romans of an earlier age. His realization that frugality is a relative term (initially suggested at 42–47) then implies a saecular decline in Roman thrift, based on degree: Cicero gestures at an intermediate stage between parsimonious early Romans and modern profligates. Furthermore, Cicero's awareness in this early work that one's behavior can stand out within the characteristic morals of an age as an outlier, presenting a complicating factor in a saecular narrative, anticipates greater interest in the possibility of such conduct (or the depiction of such conduct) in the elegiac poetry that was yet to come at Rome.

Saecula are qualitatively defined periods of time, but a nuanced depiction of life during any such period will reveal behavior or practices that do not necessarily conform to the dominant characteristics of the *saeculum*. What happens to a person who is a saecular outlier, one who fails to fit in with the spirit of the age? Propertius and Tibullus, two elegiac poets of Augustan Rome, explored the possibilities of such a mismatch, and they use the concept of the saecular outlier in their own multifaceted self-depictions. While the presence of periodized moral histories (with their intermediate stages of decline)

74 | Saeculum

in elegiac poetry already contests the senatorial lapsarian narrative of Roman morality, the possibility of outliers in the moral *saecula* of any historical narrative (including the lapsarian model) further problematizes the simplistic streamlining of collective guilt during an allegedly corrupt age.

Propertius 1.16 is a *paraclausithyron* poem written from the point of view of the locked door of the poet's beloved.[14] This door, evidently a stern moralist, criticizes its mistress for her loose sexual morality, saying that she lives more shamefully than even the license of the age (*turpior et saecli vivere luxuria*, 12).[15] The current *saeculum* has a characteristic degree of bad morals (*luxuria*), which the woman exceeds. This *saeculum*'s morals, typified by the behavior of drunken youths in love (5–8), are themselves much worse than the *patriciae pudicitiae* (2) of earlier times, which for the door were connected to participation in foreign wars (3–4).[16] The moralizing door's narrative of the decline in morals occurs here in discrete stages, with the current moral *saeculum* being less honorable than an earlier one, but the door's mistress is out of place in her own time, as if she behaved like a Roman from a future *saeculum* (a possible anticipation of further cultural decline).

Alternatively, one can be out of place for behaving too well. In poem 2.25, Propertius says (35–38) that if this were the age (*saecla*, 35) pleasing to girls of old (which it is not), he would be like the man who could happily boast about his steady relationship. Instead, he is conquered by the current age (*tempore vincor*, 36), presumably because its girls do not behave the way they used to and (as he warned in the previous lines) will betray a man who is too confident in his relationship. But this current *saeculum* will not change Propertius's own *mores*, so he refuses to participate in the qualities with which he marks his own time.[17] Propertius situates himself outside the current moral *saeculum*, a throwback to the past.

In poem 2.31/32,[18] Propertius seeks, without hope, a girl who is similarly out of place. Propertius says that Rome is incredibly fortunate if even one girl behaves contrary to the contemporary morality of the current *tempus* (*nostro tempore*, 43).[19] While *tempus* can refer to "time" in the most general sense, attributing this usage of *tempus* to saecularity is suggested by the immediate complement (lines 49–62) of stock saecular images: the golden age (*Saturno regna*, 52), marked by its custom (*mos*) that girls prefer not to misbehave, and the epoch-closing moment of Deucalion's flood (53–54), after which improprieties emerged on earth.[20]

The saecular discourse shared by 2.25 and 2.31/32 is further emphasized by another intertextual link: Catullus.[21] After lamenting the current moral *tempus* of Rome in 2.31/32, Propertius then compares Cynthia to Catullus's Lesbia, who by committing her indiscretions with impunity set an example for Cynthia to follow or exceed (45–46). In 2.25, Propertius cites Catullus (4) as one of the elegiac predecessors who will be eclipsed by his own poetic adoration of Cynthia. Propertius nowhere else references Catullus and Lesbia by name,[22] so their appearance invites comparison of the two poems. These mutual references to successors who will surpass the deeds of their predecessors suggest that Propertius imagines the possibility of a future *saeculum* to come in which morality has reached a new degree of impropriety, a *saeculum* for which Cynthia's outrageous behavior may be the new norm.

From the comparison of the statements about moral decline in these poems, a saecular narrative of Roman moral history emerges. The "reign of Saturn" was characterized by impeccable morality, ending in Propertius's poem with the flood of Deucalion (which, as we saw in chapter 2, became a common image of metakosmesis in the first century BCE). Although the following *saeculum* saw the introduction of vice, nevertheless it was a morally sound time, typified by the examples of Tatius and the Sabines (2.31/32.47–48) as exemplars of old-time Roman virtue.[23] The *saeculum* that followed, *nostrum tempus*, has reached a new degree of immorality. Given the tendency of narratives of saecularity to separate particular *saecula* with cosmically significant events (such as the flood of Deucalion), ideally we would also find from Propertius a particular moment that demonstrates (or causes) the change from the *saeculum* of old Roman morality to modern decadence.

We find it at 2.6.27–36, where Propertius brings up erotic wall art with mythological scenes. Propertius says that the artist who first (*prima*, 27) painted erotic pictures in people's homes changed the standards of female morality at Rome, since these images taught many otherwise innocent girls about the ways of love. The *olim . . . nunc* dichotomy in 33–35 makes it clear that this act is the dividing line between a period of stern Roman morality and the current period when immorality thrives (exemplified by the fact that temples and statues of divinities have been neglected).[24] Given the earlier periodized divisions of human history with regard to morality, here Propertius is imagining the innovation of erotic wall paintings as

76 | *Saeculum*

the metakosmetic moment (spurred on by a negative culture hero) that began the current moral *saeculum* in Rome.

Ultimately, the narrative of Roman moral history in Propertius is a four-*saeculum* process: a golden age, a post-flood silver age extending through early Rome, a post-erotic art age, and a potentially worse period to follow. I would refrain from uncritically asserting, however, that Propertius is composing a sort of ethnography or anthropology of the Roman people within his elegiac corpus; this is not an intellectually serious claim about human moral history by Propertius. Rather, Propertius adopts the discourse of saecularity here to engage playfully[25] in the elegiac *topos* of moral decline in poems that are actually doing other things. By creating a timeline of human history in which the innovation (or "invention") of erotic wall art had cosmic significance, Propertius comically deflates the import of regular secular discourse, demonstrating that by his time saecularity was familiar and ripe for satire.[26]

Like Propertius, Tibullus adopts the language of saecular discourse in his discussions of Roman moral decline, such as when his *praeceptor amoris* Priapus decries the contemporary age (*haec saecula*, 1.4.57) because it "poorly manages its wretched skills" (*male . . . artes miseras . . . tractant*, 57) in the game of love. Notably, Tibullus breaks with Propertius in the latter's interest in saecular outliers, and specifically in his desire to uphold the morals of a bygone *saeculum*. In 2.3, Tibullus distinguishes the contemporary "Iron Age" (*ferrea saecula*, 35), in which men are interested in aggressively pursuing wealth instead of loving their women, from other times, such as the *priscus mos* (68) of the Golden Age (signaled by its customary acorn diet, 68–70). But while Propertius was willing to double down and stick to his own way of life in the face of a *saeculum* that had passed him by (2.25.37–38), Tibullus makes a sarcastic about-face and declares that since in this age women love rich men and fancy gifts, he will pursue wealth himself to win over Nemesis (49–52).[27]

This turn complicates the usual critique implied by narratives of moral decline, but more importantly, it directly opposes the refusal by Propertius to adapt his personal moral code to his contemporary climate; Tibullus thus depicts himself as an anti-Propertius figure. Lyne argues that Propertius and Tibullus had several literary exchanges of this kind, in which poems by one elegist respond to earlier publications by the other, often describing diametrically opposed attitudes toward some subject (such as funerals or old age) tangentially related to love.[28] This engagement through saecularity is another such example, with Tibullus's Nemesis (unlike Propertius's Cynthia) being a romantic object worth the abandonment of one's moral code.

The presence of outliers in the moral *saecula* of both Propertius and Tibullus speaks to the growing tension in the late first century BCE directed toward the traditional narrative of Roman moral history. Against the oversimplified depictions of ethical decline, these poets challenge their historian predecessors with the possibility of individual human agency within a *saeculum* characterized by a particular practice (just as the saecular model of moral decline argues for multiple turning points rather than a single powerful event). The lapsarian model, with its collective guilt during an age of moral turpitude, is undermined by this acknowledgment that every Roman can choose their own behavior.

Horace uses saecular discourse for his own sociopolitical commentary, and several of the *Odes* describe the moral decline of Rome (and the possibility, or actuality, of Augustus's reversing this decline).[29] Horace laments the wickedness of the current age in *Ode* 1.35, characterized as harsh because of its civil wars (33–34) and disrespect for the gods (35–38); Horace asks rhetorically, *quid nos dura refugimus aetas?* (34–35).[30] The final image (38–40), reforging a blunted sword, suggests that by fighting foreign enemies, the Romans can start a new age (on a "new anvil," *nova incude*, 38–39), or rather return to the moral uprightness of the *saeculum* before the contemporary one.

Horace hopes for a future *saeculum* superior in morality to the current age, but in *Ode* 3.5, Regulus instead fears that the future may be worse. In Horace's account of the exemplary behavior of Regulus (who during the First Punic War refused to let the Romans accept a humiliating truce with the Carthaginians, at the cost of his own life), he says that the foresighted mind of Regulus (*mens provida Reguli*, 13) acted specifically so that he would not create a precedent (indeed, an *exemplum*, 15) that would bring disaster on the coming age (*veniens aevum*, 16).[31] The concern by Regulus for the *veniens aevum* that will follow his own reflects the poem's critique of the soldiers of Crassus, and of the Roman people as a whole, in lines 1–12, whose *mores* have become *inversi* from the character of Regulus's time.

This decline creates some tension in the poem, because Regulus has apparently failed in his task of staving off the advance of a period with worse moral character (undercutting the power of his own

78 | *Saeculum*

exemplum); does Horace express doubt that the moral leadership of any particular Roman can prevent the degeneration of the state? Instead, I contend that it serves to elevate further the person (e.g., Augustus, or the unnamed *quisquis* of 3.24.25) who is someday capable of restraining civic license by placing him above Regulus (and any other previous *exemplum*). The stakes here are real, since Horace's narrative of moral history in *Ode* 4.15 relies on the potential for individual Romans to bring about moral progress. Horace uses saecular discourse to describe these anxieties about the Roman moral climate and its unclear future, expressing a hope for a saecular outlier to emerge who can restore Roman moral standards.

Ovid's reception of, and responses to, the temporality of these earlier authors in some sense deconstructs these moral decline narratives, challenging the stability of saecular discourse in historical narratives of Roman morality. Exemplarity can be achieved, per Ovid, through deviation, even though exemplarity is meant to define the very characteristics of an age. And the narrative of decline can be destroyed by recasting the terms of the argument into a narrative of transition; words changed in meaning are thus sapped of moralizing power.

Like Horace's Regulus ode, Ovid's use of saecular discourse shapes issues of moral exemplarity. For Ovid, *exempla* do not lose their power of efficacy even after moral *saecula* have shifted to new characteristics. The loyal relationships of Orestes and Pylades as well as Theseus and Pirithous are held up as exemplary in *Epistula ex Ponto* 2.6, such that theater audiences always cheer them (25–28).[32] The previous age (*prior aetas*, 27) admired them, and the following age (*sequens aetas*) will admire them, too. While the expression could refer simply to "before" and "after," a comparable passage in *Tristia* 5.9 encourages a reading of these *aetas* usages as saecular terminology: Ovid tells an addressee that if he had allowed Ovid to use the man's real name, both the present age (*praesens aetas*, 7) and a later age (*serior aetas*) would have known about it, terms which suggest divisions into discrete time-units. Thus, the two mythological pairs in *Epistula ex Ponto* 2.6 will retain their influence on Romans even in ages of moral degradation; to Ovid, no *saeculum* could be characterized as so wicked that the exemplary behavior of these pairs would fail to have an effect on their audience.

Livia is a special example for Ovid of exemplary moral behavior in a periodized narrative. In *Epistula ex Ponto* 3.1, Livia's virtue ensures that our age (*saecula nostra*, 116) will not be surpassed by the older Romans in terms of praise of chastity. Unlike Horace's Regulus, whose exemplary behavior nevertheless was unable to prevent the moral lapse of Crassus's soldiers (and, with them, the Roman people), Ovid's Livia has a *saeculum*-altering moral force: just by her own behavior alone, Livia elevates her own *saeculum* to the level of the early Romans and thus thwarts a narrative of periodized moral decline at Rome.[33] And unlike Propertius, Livia's chastity does not simply make her a social maverick, but effects similar behavior in the Roman people, the ultimate accomplishment of a Roman *exemplum*.

The typical (i.e., Propertian) saecular narrative of Roman moral decline appears elsewhere in Ovid's poetry, but with this decline changed into a value-neutral transition. In the introduction to the *Medicamina faciei*, Ovid contrasts men in the current *saeculum* (*saecula nostra*, 24), who love elegance (on women and on themselves), with Roman life under King Tatius, when the paradigmatically stolid ancient Sabine women shunned all profligate adornments (11–16), but this difference in the ages of women's fashion is nevertheless devoid of judgment (*nec tamen indignum*, 23). In a major section of *Ars amatoria* (3.101–128),[34] Ovid reuses the time of Tatius (118) as a period of sterner morals in contrast with the present age,[35] but without the critique of modern character. Ovid compares the different requirements for female adornment in early Rome and Augustan Rome with the changes in architecture. The current Capitol seems to belong to "another Jupiter" (*alterius Iovis*, 116);[36] the modern Curia is now far worthier of hosting the Senate than in the time of Tatius; the greatness of the Palatine Hill, now home to Apollo and Rome's leaders (the Temple of Apollo Palatinus and the house of Augustus)[37] looks nothing like its earlier pasturage. Unlike many Roman moralists, and in contrast with Propertius 2.25, Ovid declares that while old times can delight others, he himself was born at the right time; this age is suitable for his *mores* (*haec aetas moribus apta meis*, 3.122). Ovid is not an outlier in a *saeculum* that has passed him by, but instead is a man whose moral code aligns perfectly with the characteristics of his *saeculum*. But is he simply a material man in a material world?

What separates Ovid's contemporary age from that of early Rome is not its taste for riches and fancy adornment (123–126), although it is possible that Ovid is also pointing this out as another characteristic feature of the age, but the presence of *cultus* (127).[38] This *cultus* stands in opposition to the *simplicitas* (113) and especially the *rusticitas*

80 | *Saeculum*

(128) of before, which survived until our grandfathers (*priscis avis*, 128; possibly just "ancient ancestors") but no longer.[39] Parallel to this vague denotation of when *rusticitas* was replaced by *cultus* is the claim (113–114) that *simplicitas* disappeared when Rome became "golden" by possessing the great wealth of the conquered world (*domiti orbis*). The metakosmesis of Ovid's Age of *Simplicitas/Rusticitas* to the Age of *Cultus* thus is explicitly associated with Rome's imperialist adventures abroad and its acquisition of the riches of conquered territory in the east.[40] The claim that Roman morality first began to suffer when eastern wealth came into the city is in fact a standard claim by the conservative moralists of the first century BCE and earlier, as we have seen above, but Ovid has transformed this typical narrative through his open support of the new civic morality. Ovid has reframed the narrative of decline into a value-neutral shift, reflected by the word choice: Rome has not gone from righteous to wicked, as it were, but from rustic to refined.

While a decline narrative became a standard theme for Romans using saecularity in the first century BCE, progress narratives are just as feasible, and a passage from Cicero's *De republica* of the late 50s BCE will give us an example of saecularity as applied in such a historical narrative. Cicero (in the voice of Scipio Africanus the Younger) begins book 2 by describing the history of Rome from its beginnings with Romulus to show that it is the kind of ideal state that Socrates had in mind in Plato's *Republic*. At one point, discussing the career and subsequent apotheosis of Romulus, Cicero creates a timeline of Roman history in which intellectual power progressively increases from *saeculum* to *saeculum*.

Cicero writes that the *aetas* of Romulus (*haec aetas*, 2.19) was already cultured enough to reject tales that could not have actually happened. And despite the willingness of this *aetas* to mock unbelievable stories, and despite the fact that people had long ceased to believe in miracles like the apotheosis of their peers, the Romans nevertheless believed the tale told by Proculus about his apotheosis, mainly because Romulus had been such a special and successful individual. Cicero tells us that this belief in the divinity of Romulus is all the more remarkable because all other men who are said to have become gods lived in a ruder age (*minus eruditis hominum saeculis*, 2.18)[41] when people were more inclined to invent, and believe in, wild stories. On the other hand, the life of Romulus occurred in that age (*id saeculum*, 2.18) when Greece was already full of poets and poetic activity, and the only fantastical stories people could be induced to believe were about the ancient past. It was an age characterized by enough intellectual power (*temporibus ipsis eruditis*, 2.19) to be skeptical of a story like that of Romulus's apotheosis. The fact that people did believe that Romulus became a god instead of just being murdered covertly is not only exceptional but in fact a testament to the extraordinary success and virtue of Romulus himself.

But what about the contemporary time (either Cicero's or Scipio's, as no real distinction is made here)? Earlier, in describing the divine parentage of Romulus, Cicero clearly gives no credence to any mythological aspect of the life of Romulus and ascribes it to the folktales of the commoners (*famae hominum*, 2.4); indeed, a Euhemerist strand runs throughout this entire passage.[42] Thus in the period of the speaker, the learned men reject out of hand all the mythical facets of the life of Romulus that people of his own *saeculum*, though themselves as wise as the poets and scholars of nearby Greece, still believed. While they note with approval the continuing life of these fables, as they reflect well on the Roman state as a whole, they do not actually accept them as facts.

We can see in this passage that Cicero is deploying periodization to suggest a narrative of intellectual progress. Human history is divided into time-units characterized by the degree to which people are willing to believe fantastical stories about divine figures on earth (or rather, the degree to which they reject and mock such stories— how *eruditi* they are). Cicero creates three ages of increasing skepticism, which he treats positively as a form of intellectual aptitude. The earliest, and least shrewd, *saeculum* was willing to believe that superior individuals could become (or already were) divine figures. The next *saeculum* was marked by an increased unwillingness to accept such stories; this period also includes the emergence of many famous poets of ancient Greece (2.18.2), which seems to serve for Cicero as an explanation (or result) of such increased skepticism. (Crucially for Scipio in *De republica*, the earliest years of Rome's history were already at the same intellectual level as Greece was long after its civilization began, thus offering evidence of Roman greatness.)

Cicero's emphasis on poetry must be related to the fact that the marker of the beginning of this *saeculum* (a discrete unit separate from earlier human history) is the *floruit* of Homer. At *De republica* 2.18–19, Cicero calculates how long the career of Romulus had occurred after that of Homer, which is taken for granted as a benchmark of skeptical

82 | *Saeculum*

erudition about divine matters: since Romulus lived "many years" (*permultis annis*) after Homer, learned men *already* existed (*iam doctis hominibus*). Cicero also connects the existence of "writing and education" (*litteris atque doctrinis*), which also had already existed for years before Romulus lived, to the elimination of "every misconception in antiquity resulting from an uncivilized life of men" (*omni illo antiquo ex inculta hominum vita errore*). Thus, Cicero's second *saeculum*, more learned than the previous one, has benefited from (and is exemplified by) the wisdom of poetry.

Finally, the *saeculum* of greatest progress in rationality is that of the speaker himself, who does not even accept the stories about Romulus that were believed in the previous *saeculum*. In that second *saeculum*, people were willing to believe supernatural stories about people and events of the distant past but not about their contemporary time.[43] Cicero/Scipio and his peers in the third *saeculum*, on the other hand, will not even believe the legendary tales connected to Romulus, who lived hundreds of years prior to his own lifetime. Cicero gives no indication of what began this third *saeculum*, and speculation would provide little, but nevertheless he clearly distinguishes the sophistication and skepticism of his own era from that of the previous age. Thus, through this string of gradually improving ages (of a duration seemingly greater than a human generation but not profoundly longer), Cicero has created a saecular model of history with an optimistic take on religious credulity at Rome.

The notion of "progress" or "decline" as a mode of historical narrative long precedes the Roman practice of periodization; indeed, Roman moral decline narratives were already firmly an intellectual tradition well before Sulla declared himself the avatar of a new age. But the innovation of saecular periodization allowed Roman intellectuals to articulate more sophisticated temporalities in these histories and to position themselves in more nuanced ways with the larger historical framework they were claiming. The popularization of the rhetoric of periodization thus can explain the wide range of Roman writers adapting such progress and decline language to their works and can better illuminate the interest in Roman temporality that expands over the course of the first century BCE. Further developments, such as the saecular rhetoric of the political actors (see chapter 5) or the interests of historiographers during the reign of Tiberius (see the conclusion), can be better understood by grasping the intellectual power of the language of periodization.

4 | Beyond the Metallic Ages
Technical Histories and Culture Heroes

Progress and decline narratives were just two of a wide range of applications of saecular discourse demonstrated by the Roman intelligentsia of the first century BCE. Indeed, the very notion of straightforward progress or decline could be complicated by the use of periodization. Nowhere is this clearer than in the many appearances throughout the Roman literature of this period by references to what I call the "Metallic Age mythology."[1] This mythological rhetoric divides the historical timeline of the world into eras named after precious metals. Traditionally, the precious metals decline in value from era to era, thus depicting a more general decline in human life or moral standards on earth, but in the hands of Romans familiar with saecular periodization, many different historical narratives could be created. These narratives often rely on the mechanism of the "culture hero" in order to advance from one stage to the next; the culture hero is a figure whose individual innovation, action, or gift alters human history by advancing the world into a new era of civilization.

This chapter will begin with a brief overview of the range of applications of Metallic Age mythology in Roman culture in the first century BCE, a section that will conclude with a close reading of Vergil's *Eclogue* 4, focusing in particular on the temporal complexity suggested by its application of saecular discourse in the Metallic Age context. But one consequence I hope to demonstrate here is that the Romans grew less interested in the specific context of this mythological narrative and branched out into more sophisticated applications of saecular discourse in their development of Roman temporality. Thus, the Metallic Age mythology served not so much

84 | Saeculum

as a foundation for Roman explorations in cyclical history but rather as an entry point for some writers to engage in qualitative periodization, a discourse which quickly became disentangled from Hesiodic reception or utopian nostalgia and instead promoted innovative ideas for temporal frameworks. Owing to the cognitive power of saecular periodization and the increasing popularization of rhetoric developed from the Metallic Age mythology and the metakosmetic potency of culture heroes, the Romans develop a new temporal mode I call "technical history"—the saecular narrative explaining the evolution of a skill, practice, or cultural phenomenon.

The use of the Metallic Age mythology by Roman writers draws from a classical tradition that stretches back centuries in classical literature, to Hesiod's *Works and Days* 106–201, an alternative *logos* to the Prometheus/Pandora tale that it follows.[2] Hesiod describes the creation of sentient life on the planet, which began with a "golden" period of utopian ease and happiness. This was followed by an inferior "silver" period and an even worse "bronze" period, before (in an improvement) the births of the famous martial heroes familiar in Greek mythology, such as those who fought at Troy. Finally Hesiod sees himself among an "iron" period of mankind, worst of all the times that have ever existed (with fears that its behavior could further erode).

Several aspects of this passage complicate the notion that it represents a straightforward temporal narrative of social decline. Hesiod refers not to "ages" but "races" (γένεα), yet these are not simply "generations" of beings, since he refers to multiple generations of parents and children within the races themselves, and the context clearly emphasizes the chronology of the races' development over any other concern. Moreover, Hesiod's narrative arc of these metallic races is not a uniform slide into degeneracy: the decline of the golden race into silver and bronze is halted by the introduction of a fourth race, that of heroic men. This race represents an improvement over the third race, and is followed by the worst race of all, the race of iron, of which Hesiod and his readers/listeners are members. This inclusion of the heroic race problematizes one common interpretation of the Metallic Age mythology, that of the gradual decline of the human experience from an early state of pleasure; structurally, the Hesiodic narrative does not present a simple downward arc of history.

A further complication may also be implicit in Hesiod's telling of the story. The sequence of metallic races seemingly stops at the iron race, but at line 175, Hesiod imagines the possibility of having been born *after* the iron race. Does this phrase in fact hint at a superior sixth race of men, improved from the fifth race? Some scholars have interpreted the comment in this way,[3] while others have argued that it is merely a rhetorical expression and not an actual statement about the sequence of races.[4] An expectation of a sixth race superior to the fifth would complicate Hesiod's appeals to justice, since there would be no incentive for his contemporaries to avoid wickedness.[5] Lacking any other context clues, we cannot know for sure; certainly, the idea of "life after iron" is not picked up again until *Eclogue* 4 (in a manner, of course, that fundamentally alters the Hesiodic paradigm).

As I emphasized at the beginning of this chapter, Hesiod's Metallic Ages represent just one way that saecular discourse permeated Roman culture in the first century BCE, and Vergil's adaptation of Hesiod was as much a product of the intellectual movement of saecular discourse as it was an influence for further explorations by other Augustan poets.[6] Moreover, it has been argued that until Vergil, Hesiod himself was unimportant to Roman poets;[7] the poetry of Aratus had replaced Hesiod as the primary access point of Metallic Age mythology,[8] a factor which explains both the great interest in the *Phaenomena* during the first century BCE[9] and the choice of an Aratean (and not Hesiodic) conclusion to Catullus 64, which predates *Eclogue* 4. Indeed, Hesiod's Metallic Age mythology was not particularly influential even in Greek literature: while "life under Cronus" turned into a cliché of Attic comedy,[10] and some philosophers used the notion of a primitive utopia as a means to make anthropological assertions, the Metallic Age mythology only reappears in a robust way in the *Phaenomena* of Aratus.[11] It is not until the first century BCE that the explosion of references to the Metallic Ages first occurs, and this is a product of the emergence of saecular discourse at Rome.

The rhetoric of periodization in Vergil's *Eclogue* 4 draws from Hesiod, but elements of the poem also show an influence from Catullus, who himself drew from Aratus in the conclusion of his poem 64 (lines 382–408).[12] Catullus describes how the gods used to mingle freely with humans during an unspecified past time (no later than the *optato saeclorum tempore* of line 22),[13] but ever since humans have committed wickedness the gods have refused to interact so casually with mortals. This passage reflects the narrative (lines 96–136) from Aratus's *Phaenomena* in which Justice often interacts with humans in

86 | *Saeculum*

the golden race, but appears only at night to critique the more wicked silver race and permanently flees from the still more wicked bronze race. This Aratean version of the Metallic Ages creates dramatic tension for those familiar with Hesiod by stopping with the bronze race, leaving the race of heroes and the iron race ahead of the perspective of the poem and thus creating a simple decline narrative of three *saecula*.

The attitude of Justice toward the behavior of men encapsulated the qualitative characterizations of each metallic race, but the specific details of each successive age were malleable in the hands of various artists. Moreover, the structure itself of ages was not fixed by the Hesiodic original. Aratus characterized the bronze age with the invention of the sword and of consumption of meat; Cicero, in his pre-Catullan (70s BC) translation/adaptation of Aratus' *Phaenomena*, says (fr. 20E) that those attributes belong to the race of iron (*ferrea proles*), so he likely skipped the race of bronze and thus also the race of heroes.[14] By doing so, Cicero makes a radical rejection of Hesiod: Aratus created his decline narrative merely by stopping before he reached the race of heroes, but Cicero actually eliminates the race of heroes altogether (asserting a straightforward erosion of moral values in human history). Germanicus,[15] whose own later translation of the *Phaenomena* survives for us,[16] refers not to a golden race but a golden age (*aurea saecula*, 103), followed by a worse age of silver (*argenti deformior aetas*, 120) and a bronze race (*aerea proles*, 133); the altered vocabulary reflects developments in saecularity in the preceding decades, but his choice of bronze over iron (*contra* Cicero) shows his return to the Aratean source material alongside his adoption of the saecular temporal vocabulary.

It is also worthwhile to note that, for some Roman authors, a slightly different form of metakosmesis occurs at the very beginning of the mythological Golden Age. Although Hesiod's golden race was created by Zeus, by the first century BCE some Romans depicted the Golden Age as a more localized event taking place in Italy, when Saturn fled to Latium to escape the power of Jupiter. Thus, the arrival of Saturn in Latium becomes a metakosmetic moment, signaling the beginning of the Golden Age. Ovid depicts this arrival at *Fasti* 1.231, though all his Saturn seems to have found was virgin forest and some cattle (243–244) when he sailed into the area.[17] But the event of Saturn's arrival was striking enough that even in Ovid's time Janus remembers it well (*memini*, 235), and it was deemed worthy of numismatic commemoration for centuries at Rome. In fact, what starts this story from Janus in the narrative is Ovid's question about the imagery of Janus with a ship on Roman coins (the very coin Sulla used in his self-promotion campaign in the 80s BCE).

Ovid's use of the lexicon of saecularity in his conversation with Janus, during which this metakosmetic depiction appears, suggests that he is organizing Roman history into *saecula*, though not exactly the standard Metallic Age mythology we might have expected. Janus says that Ovid's age (*tua saecula*, 191) escapes his understanding if he thinks the gods don't value gifts of gold, and even in the reign of Saturn people valued wealth (193–194). However, Janus does distinguish the present from the "years of the ancient *tempus*" (*prisci temporis annis*, 197) in terms of the degree to which wealth is deemed important by Romans. And the current age (*haec aetas*, 246) calls that hill the Janiculum where Janus once had his citadel (during, presumably, an earlier *aetas*). Thus the arrival of Saturn is a feature of this saecular organization and becomes a metakosmetic moment.

One particular area of interest in classical scholarship on the Golden Age has been the inventory of the slightly different attributes that make up every author's Golden Age or the events that caused the Golden Age to end. Other scholars have pointed out the differences in the number and kind of metallic ages in each ancient writer's timeline; Murgatroyd, for example, writes that it was common to eliminate Hesiod's Heroic Age and present a simple decline narrative of four metallic ages,[18] as Aratus first did, but we do in fact see several references to the Heroic Age.[19] While I am not interested in contributing to that discussion here, it should be noted that the very fact that each Roman writer gives slightly different characteristics for the Golden Age (and slightly different criteria for when the Golden Age ended), as well as different saecular schematics for the Metallic Age mythology, demonstrates not just the flexibility of ancient mythology but also the primacy of saecularity as a discursive practice.[20]

One clear demonstration that Metallic Age mythology was more of an entry point to saecular discourse, rather than its foundation, is the variety of oppositional reactions to (and parodies of) the mythology. For example, Ovid sarcastically states that we truly live in the Golden Age now (*aurea nunc saecula*, *Ars am.* 2.277) because beloveds prefer gifts of gold to gifts of laudatory poetry and because *honos* can be purchased with gold as well.[21] Antipater of Thessalonica, an

88 | *Saeculum*

Augustan writer of Greek epigrams, wrote that the contemporary venality of love eroded distinctions between men of the Metallic Ages, because each had a precious metal to offer (*Anth. Pal.* 5.31). Humorous tweaks on the myth even emerged from the Roman populace: during the early reign of Tiberius, a couplet was produced that said he had changed the Golden Age back to Iron for as long as he lived (*aurea mutasti Saturni saecula, Caesar / incolumi nam te ferrea semper erunt*).[22] By the middle of the first century CE, the Golden Age appears on a list of hackneyed poetic themes;[23] even during the Augustan period, poets complained about the popularity of astrological poems that, if Aratus is any indication, likely featured digressions on the Metallic Age mythology.[24]

The ultimate condemnation of the Metallic Age mythology, though, appears in Horace's *Ode* 4.2. At lines 37–40, Horace refers to Augustus as the greatest thing that the fates and gods have ever given to the world, and declares that nothing will ever surpass him "even if the ages return to the ancient Golden one" (*quamvis redeant in aurum / tempora priscum*, 39–40). As Zanker has argued,[25] Horace makes this claim as a final repudiation of the Metallic Age mythology that he had mostly avoided in his poetic corpus, since the utopian unrealities of the poets' various Golden Ages were less useful to a serious discussion of contemporary Rome than Horace's own "Augustan Age," a preferable saecular narrative. As we will see in chapter 5, Horace's Augustan *saeculum* in *Ode* 4.15 lacks the supernaturalism of the Metallic Age mythology, instead presenting a realistic depiction of the benefits of Augustus's reign. Nonetheless, the rise of Augustus is depicted in several of the *Odes* as an act of divine will, so there is still an element of divine intervention in the arc of the saecular narrative Horace describes. Horace's rejection in 4.2 of the poetic Golden Age in favor of the real-life Augustan Age then represents the rejection of one saecular narrative for another, with Augustus as the divinely approved agent of metakosmesis—a culture hero in his own right.

I want to close this section with an analysis of the saecular discourse at work in a familiar example: Vergil's *Eclogue* 4. The scholarship on the poem is immense, with DuQuesnay's seminal 1977 study being the first to pay close attention to the importance of Vergil's engagement with the sequence of *saecula*.[26] My focus here, however, is strictly the periodizing temporality of the poem, so I will try to avoid a reading steeped in prior scholarship to instead focus on

Vergil's line-by-line verbiage and come to some conclusions about his application of saecular discourse. A common approach to the temporality of the poem has been to debate whether its influences are "Western" (i.e., the classical tradition, going back to Hesiod) or "Eastern" (Jewish messianic prophecies and eastern mysticism that were found in the Sibylline Oracles).[27] But as should be clear from the analyses throughout this volume, such influences and others had already contributed to the development of saecular discourse in Rome well before the composition of the *Eclogues*, and thus *Eclogue* 4 can be read less as a poetic innovation than as a product of the intellectual world of Vergil's time and place. Interpretation of this famously complex poem benefits from attention to the saecular mode that runs throughout it; indeed, *Eclogue* 4 was likely a specific influence on the approach to saeculariy of the poets and their poems (and of others in the Augustan world) that would follow. I offer here an analysis of the temporal framework of the poem with particular sensitivity to its engagement with periodizing discourse, to show how it transforms the Metallic Age mythology of its predecessors into something both familiar and innovative.

Eclogue 4 declares that now (*iam*) has come the "final age" (*ultima aetas*, 4) of the Cumaean song; evidently the ages of history are connected with Sibylline prophecy, as in the *Carmen Saeculare*. "*Ultima*" is a vague word; it can refer to the end of a line (i.e., a terminal point), but it can also refer to the end of a sequence, including a repeating sequence (or, logically, a pendular sequence).[28] Thus, at line 4 it is not yet clear either what age we have entered or what the larger shape of the metallic age sequence will be.[29]

But in the next line, we learn that the great series of ages (*magnus saeclorum ordo*, 5) is arising from the beginning. Obviously it makes little sense for the last age *and* the first age to be occurring at the same time; it is perhaps possible to have a six-unit sequence such as "Gold–Silver–Bronze–Heroic–Iron–Gold," but as we shall see, such a sequence is not at work in this poem. In the following line, we learn that now (*iam*) the Golden Age is coming back (referred to, as it commonly was, as the reign of Saturn, the *Saturnia regna*) and now a new race (*progenies*) is coming. If we read these present-tense verbs as a present continuous construction, then the actions described do not have to be occurring at this very moment, but can be in the process of occurring. If so, the new Golden Age can actually begin years from now even though its return can be vouchsafed (through Sibylline

90 | *Saeculum*

prophecy) at this moment. Such a reading fits with line 52, where this *saeculum* is about to come (*venturum*) in the unspecified future. This combination of expressing both the immediate time of the speaker and the future also resembles the similar move Hesiod makes when describing his final iron race in his version of the Metallic Ages.

Indeed, in line 8 the clarification is made that the new Golden Age is not here just yet. In the lifetime of an unspecified child (or perhaps at his birth; the *quo* of line 8 is vague), the Iron Age (*ferrea*, 8) will switch over to a new Golden Age (or, more accurately, the *aurea gens*, or a [*nova*] *aurea progenies*—in any case, a new *saeculum*). So, as we stand at line 10, the Iron Age (that *ultima aetas* from line 4) is soon to cease and be replaced by a new Golden Age, though this will occur at an unspecified future moment. Finally, in line 11, we learn that "this glory of the age" (*decus hoc aevi*)[30] "will begin" (*inibit*, 11, and thus has not quite happened yet) with Pollio as consul (*te consule*, 11): that is, in 40 BCE. Whether this means that the Golden Age will return in 40 BCE, or that the birth of the child whose lifetime will see that Golden Age must occur in 40 BCE, is left ambiguous, though the latter reading seems more likely. Somehow, Vergil envisions a chronology that will lead to the return of the Golden Age, but just exactly what this will look like is difficult to ascertain until we pay attention to the saecular discourse at work in the poem.

Before this new Golden Age can occur, the child (*puer*, 18) will read about the glories of heroes (*heroum laudes*, 26) and will have seen heroes mingling with gods (*divis . . . permixtos heroas*, 15–16). Theoxeny is a primary characteristic of the race of the heroes in Hesiod's version of the Metallic Age mythology as well as the focus of the vaguely Hesiodic denouement of Catullus 64, and so Vergil must conceive of a Heroic Age in his *ordo saeclorum*.[31] Additionally, the Golden Age will not arrive until first there is a repeat of events from Hesiod's race of the heroes (34–36), including the assembly of chosen heroes (*delectos heroas*, 35) for the new Argo. In the version of the Metallic Age mythology described by Vergil's saecular discourse in *Eclogue* 4, we first have to go back through another (*alter . . . altera . . . altera*, 34–35) Heroic Age before we subsequently (*hinc*, 37) get to the new Golden Age.

There are more obstacles to this new Golden Age, however, than simply the new Heroic Age. Vergil says traces of the old misdeeds (*priscae vestigia fraudis*, 31) will remain, and their effect will be to spur men to attempt sailing, warfare, and farming. Such activities would be depicted as evidence of "misdeeds" in only one context: the saecular discourse of the ages (usually silver, also bronze) after the Golden Age. And for these misdeeds to be *priscae*, they would need to have occurred a long time ago, which is when (relative to the speaker) they did in fact occur. Looking ahead to the future, the end of these activities (such as is described in lines 38–39) is the last step before the ultimate arrival of the Golden Age (which is clear from the imagery in 39–45); indeed, it is hard not to read the *firmata aetas* of 37 as a saecular term (or pun) rather than simply a reference to strengthened maturity making the boy a man. Thus, we can treat the *vestigia* as covert references to the future ages of bronze and silver, which precede, along with the Heroic Age, the completion of the transition from our current Iron Age to the new Golden Age.[32]

Vergil has then sent us backwards through the Hesiodic sequence of Metallic Ages. The *magnus saeclorum ordo* of *Eclogue* 4, then, is not like a clock reaching midnight and starting over, but instead like a pendulum swinging backward.[33] The Iron Age is not followed immediately by the new Golden Age but is merely the *ultima aetas*, and the sequence must run in reverse to get back to gold.[34] The utterance of the Fates, "Run on, O such ages" (*talia saecla . . . currite*, 46), is then an exhortation to the multiple *saecula*[35] that divide the Iron from Golden Age to be completed as quickly as possible. As has been long noted, this line is an allusion to the *currite* refrain of the song of the Fates in Catullus 64; while their song's bleak subtext and the subsequent absence of the presence of divinities on earth (64.382–408) give the Catullan line a negative connotation, Vergil's allusion here inverts this pessimism and instead presents a world progressing back toward the Golden Age.[36] All things rejoice in the age that is about to come (*venturo saeclo*, 52), a Golden Age not yet present on earth but nevertheless vouchsafed for us (cf. *stabili fatorum numine*, 47); thus the route by which it returns is not a simple switch from Iron to Gold but an elaborate saecular sequence.

Vergil's use of saecularity in *Eclogue* 4, although it inevitably allows him to narrativize the past,[37] is deployed primarily to describe what the future of Rome will hold; it is a forward-looking composition. By depicting a sequence of intermediate *saecula* between the current Iron Age and the impending Golden Age, Vergil creates a narrative for future Roman history in which the Golden Age is largely a sought-for goal rather than a hastily received gift. Reaching this Golden Age will not be easy or occur by magic, but will require

92 | *Saeculum*

enduring some unpleasant periods in Roman affairs; the slow but steady improvement in the *saecula* to come forms a process. Vergil's complicated (and, at times, seemingly contradictory) descriptions of *when* the Golden Age comes frustrate any attempt to fix a particular time (or a particular leader, for that matter) that will usher in that new *saeculum*; no moment or agent of metakosmesis is specified.[38] But even though the complex saecular structure between the poem's present and the future Golden Age tempers any extreme optimism for contemporary Rome, nevertheless Vergil does profess a certainty in better times to come, and the decline in human behavior that led to the current Iron Age will ultimately be redeemed by the return of the Golden Age. Could this pendulum swing from Gold to Iron and back again be a perpetual motion, with every new Golden Age destined to fail? The possibility cannot be totally eliminated, but unlike in Horace's *Ode* 4.15 there does not seem to be any indication in the text itself for such a structure. As the preceding interpretation of *Eclogue* 4 demonstrates, however, our awareness of the saecular mode of the poem's language affects how we understand Vergil's interaction with the political world of triumviral Rome and what, exactly, his prophetic song sees as Rome's future.

To summarize: Vergil's saecular history as depicted in *Eclogues* 4 is a pendulum model, in which mythological Metallic Ages devolved from an original Golden to an ultimate Iron Age, then progressed backwards to a Golden Age again. The *magnus saeclorum ordo*, having reached the *ultima aetas* of the Iron Age, would swing back in reverse to return to gold. This structure envisioned by Vergil breaks with the received tradition of not only the Hesiodic Metallic Age mythology but even the more general idea of a primitivist Golden Age to which there can be no real return. It also fails to resemble the Etruscan or Sullan versions of the *saeculum* system, which depict linear movement through the ages. Vergil has adapted the saecular discursive mode to convey a complex notion of Roman temporality in this poem.

A possible influence on this Vergilian temporal innovation is the cosmic cycle of Empedocles. The Empedoclean physical model of the universe is marked by a never-ending cosmic cycle of four stages.[39] Throughout the cycle, the four elements (earth, fire, air, water) are acted upon by two forces, Love (attraction) and Strife (repulsion). In the first stage, Love completely dominates, and the universe consists of a homogeneous sphere of all the elements. In the second stage,

Strife grows in power as the sphere separates out into the individual elements. In the third stage, Strife completely dominates, and the universe is a four-layered sphere with each element bound only to itself. The fourth stage resembles the second, only now Love grows in power instead of Strife. The first and third stages each last four thousand years, while the second and fourth stages, dynamic periods when the appearance and evolution of life occurs (zoogony), each last six thousand years.

The process of zoogony is enabled by the power of Love (as manifested in such phenomena as the desire to reproduce), and thus is particularly suited to the fourth stage (when Love's power is constantly increasing), but even in the second stage it is assumed that zoogony still occurs despite the increasing power of Strife. Because this cosmic cycle never ends, there will be an infinite amount of zoogonies, but there is no evidence that Empedocles imagined each zoogonical stage (or the zoogony of each period of increasing Love, for example) being identical.[40] This organization of time, and in particular of human history, into discrete periods with qualitative characteristics resembles a sort of prototype for later saecular discourse.[41] In fact, certain extant fragments of Empedocles have been read as references to a "Golden Age," or at least a primitivist strain, in the early phases of the increasing-Strife zoogony.[42]

While modern scholars have determined the specific lengths of the stages of the cosmic cycle, Empedocles only obliquely describes them, using ambiguous calculations. Some of the calculations for these long stages are given with the term χρόνος, and the vagueness of this term has led to scholarly debate. Rashed posits that a χρόνος was already, by Empedocles's time, a known technical term, namely a specific time-unit for a "hundred-year period," like the modern-day "century" (or like one aspect of the Latin *saeculum*).[43] However, Primavesi instead argues that it was a general placeholder term for the Greeks without any specific length, although Empedocles himself does use it to signify a hundred-year period.[44] Thus we observe Empedocles himself adapting time terminology in order to help organize his version of the periods of universal history, as the later Romans would do.

Vergil's saecular model in *Eclogue* 4 has evolved beyond the Etruscan model by adapting the structure of the Empedoclean cosmic cycle, specifically its multistage movements from harmony to discord. Vergil's pendular *ordo saeclorum* swings back and forth between a

94 | *Saeculum*

Golden Age and Iron Age that are roughly analogous to the stages dominated by Love and Strife, respectively. The intermediate stages in the Empedoclean model are represented by the ages of Silver, Bronze, and Heroes, adding more discrete divisions of cosmic improvement or decay. Thus Vergil was able to use the saecular mode while presenting human history as moving in not just one but two directions, an innovation indebted to Empedocles.

Why might Empedocles have made such an impact on Vergil's approach to the Metallic Age mythology? Of all the many Presocratic philosophers, he was perhaps the best known to first-century BCE Romans (and not simply for his supposed death by jumping into a volcano),[45] as Cicero, Varro, Lucretius, Horace, and Vitruvius all mention him by name.[46] He was more than just a famous name, though; Lucretius, although his debt to Empedocles *qua* poetry has been noted,[47] attacks elements of his philosophical works head-on at 1.716–829. Vergil was well acquainted with the works of the philosopher, and Empedoclean physics seems to have been particularly influential in both the *Eclogues* and the *Georgics*.[48] Romans seeking to use the mode of saecular discourse to describe cyclical patterns of progress and decline, without a simple linear format, could have looked to Empedocles as an intellectual authority and precedent for this kind of periodic structure. Empedoclean cosmic cyclicality added another level of complexity to saecularity in the decades after Sulla.

While Catullus borrows the theoxeny-focused decline narrative from Aratus and downplays the saecular schematization,[49] Vergil's vision of human history and Rome's future requires greater sophistication than the simple decline narrative of Catullus, so he fully adopts the discourse of saecularity for the poem and so reaches back to more complex Hesiodic imagery. Bucolic poetry is a genre known for learned and subtle allusions to predecessors, and Vergil is able in *Eclogue* 4 to allude to all his other post-Hesiodic Metallic Age mythographers: Aratus (*Virgo*, 6), Cicero (*ferrea*, 8), and Catullus (*talia saecla . . . currite*, 46). But for the intellectual heft of his saecular mode, he inverts the pessimism of the Catullan narrative and ignores the simplified readings of Hesiod in Aratus and Cicero. Vergil draws from the original complex saecular narrative in Hesiod, but with the added twist of turning the Hesiodic sequence back around and creating a pendulum shape for his timeline. Among the many examples of Metallic Age mythology in the Roman literature of the first century BCE, Vergil's deployment of saecularity in *Eclogue* 4 represents a highly elaborate narrative for history, as his sophisticated message required.

Vergil connected the inauguration of a new era with the birth of a boy, and like Sulla had declared decades prior, the appearance of a new *saeculum* was concomitant with a particular "man of the *saeculum*" who would bring about the new characteristics of the qualitatively defined era. Saecularity often emphasizes the link between the actions of one man and the cosmic trajectory of history, not just from the moral perspective but in all aspects of human civilization. Saecular narratives of history can be propelled forward by the actions of special individuals whose agency brings about the process of metakosmesis, and while this is particularly true in examples of the Metallic Age mythology that was prevalent in Roman poetry of the first century BCE, it appears in various temporal models. Saecular discourse provides a new way to describe the actions of significant figures in Roman history by crediting them with the introduction of a new era of human history.

A closely related term from the realm of anthropology which I will use frequently in this chapter is "culture hero."[50] The culture hero is a legendary or mythological individual who "enables or facilitates human civilization by such actions as overcoming monsters that obstruct the establishment of cultural order, acquiring elements such as fire or water that are necessary for civilization, or imparting important cultural information."[51] The culture hero, essentially, changes human history through his or her discovery, innovation, or invention; regular human activity is permanently altered by the addition of this new tool or activity.[52] Culture heroes are usually named figures and often divine or semi-divine personages. A similar concept of ancient thought is the motif of the "first discoverer," the *protos heuretes* or *primus inventor*.[53] The first discoverer motif, a broader version of the culture hero, imagines that any particular aspect of culture must have had a single person (often an anonymous figure whose name is lost to history) who innovated that aspect from scratch, as opposed to a gradual development over time by many hands, and who can be invoked in poetry as an object of praise or scorn.[54]

The historical narrative that a culture hero or first discoverer concept engenders is more or less identical to the lapsarian model of moral decline: a single event causes the transition from one period to another. The characteristics of the two periods are based solely on the absence or presence of the innovation introduced by the

96 | *Saeculum*

culture hero: for example, one period is characterized by a lack of farming, the other by a human knowledge of farming techniques. This change can be either a positive one (e.g., the progress of civilization through the acquisition of some beneficial practice) or a negative one (the introduction of a new vice or misdeed).[55] The culture hero or first discoverer is then, in some sense, a metakosmetic figure who causes the transition from one historical *saeculum* to another.

Saecular discourse narrativizes history by creating an arc of multiple *saecula*, so a simple change from the absence of some tool or practice to its presence in civilization is not a saecular narrative; in other words, the story of any given culture hero is not an example of saecularity. But as a metakosmetic figure, the culture hero can fit into a larger saecular narrative as the agent of transition for a particular *saeculum*. For example, we saw that for Propertius (2.6), the era of early Roman moral uprightness (one era among several) ended through the innovation, by some unknown first discoverer, of erotic wall art in private homes.[56] As argued in chapter 2, the increasing prevalence of saecularity as a mode of thought in the first century BCE led to the strengthened cognitive linkage between Deucalion and Phaethon (in their capacity as participants in metakosmetic catastrophes). It is this same dominance of the saecular mode, I argue, that explains the increased Roman interest during this time in culture heroes and first discoverers, given their potential to be the agents of metakosmesis for human history, and in the application of saecular terminology to their description.

At the outset, it is important to emphasize a few basic points. Foremost, the idea of a single person introducing a major human innovation is not new to the first century BCE. Aristotle and Theophrastus, among others, wrote entire works dedicated to the topic of first discoverers.[57] Euhemerus may have been the first to develop the comprehensive approach to mythology known now as "euhemerism" (in which myths about gods are rationalized into stories of humans highly talented in a specific realm for which they would later be misremembered as possessing divine powers), but similar views are found in earlier writers, and already at Rome euhemerism had famously been treated by Ennius in his translation/adaptation of Euhemerus's work. In Terence's *Eunuchus*, Gnatho claims that parasites used to earn a living by enduring jokes and physical abuse, but he himself invented the practice of being a yes-man or flatterer. He even says pleonastically that the old method of parasite behavior occurred "once upon a time, long ago, in a previous generation" (*olim isti f<ui>t generi quondam quaestus apud saeclum prius*, 246), but his conclusion (that just as philosophical schools take their names from their founders, the new parasites will be called Gnathonists, 263–264) demonstrates that rather than conceptualize this shift in terms of temporal units, he instead subjects the parasites of the world to a synchronic taxonomy.[58] The notion of innovation was not yet connected to periodized temporality.

Similarly, the widespread classical motif of "cursing the inventor"[59] appears even in the earliest Roman literature: in the lost comedy *Boeotia* (attributed in antiquity to Plautus), the inventor of the hours of the day and the erector of the first sundial are attacked for affecting human eating habits.[60] These metrological innovations are described as completely changing human behavior, such that the very practice of eating was totally altered from its earlier "natural" method. The speaker describes this change happening within his own lifetime but, crucially, without any of the terminology of saecularity. Thus, the development of saecular discourse certainly did not bring about the concept of the culture hero at Rome, but the assimilation of the culture hero concept to the saecular narrative is part of the evolution of periodization in the first century BCE.

Because the concept of the culture hero predates saecularity, not every reference to a first discoverer in Roman literature refers to the introduction of a new age of human history. Catullus and Ovid use the "cursing the inventor" motif without reference to any coherent narrative of changed human behavior,[61] and the common trope of the world's first ship often lacks any historicizing force.[62] (On the other hand, human innovations can emerge without the actions of culture heroes: Lucretius and Vitruvius, among others, describe innovations through gradual collective development.[63]) Various culture heroes appear almost repetitively throughout the literature of this period, from familiar mythological figures like Prometheus, Ceres, and Pan to others such as Osiris,[64] Epicurus,[65] and Icarius.[66] The vogue for culture heroes and first discoverers,[67] combined with the antiquarian interests of the first-century BCE Roman intellectual world, led to the creation by authors in the early first century CE of entire encyclopedic lists of culture heroes and their innovations.[68] Blundell suggests that the compilation of these lists is a product of a long preceding period of imagining the progress of civilization as a

98 | *Saeculum*

purely human achievement, and "with some of these lists we may be witnessing attempts to rationalize mythological culture-heroes, by suggesting that they were in reality exceptionally gifted humans who had been accorded divine or semi-divine status because of the benefits conferred by their inventions."[69]

Blundell reads the inclusion of divine figures on lists of human first discoverers as a tacit broad-scale euhemerization. Alternatively, however, we can understand these lists as encouraging the reader to consider culture heroes not in isolation but as parts of larger systems of development: a more complex narrative of periodic human progress rather than a simple absence-then-presence of a skill or tool. In other words, such lists suggest a growing preference for saecular historicization over more simplified forms. Moreover, the casual mingling of divine and human figures can also suggest, instead of a euhemerist approach, that the human innovations have a cosmic import to them (being on the same level as acts of gods), reinforcing that they too represent divine approval of new ways of life. In that sense, these lists reflect a process in the first century BCE in which culture heroes and first discoverers increasingly become seen as metakosmetic agents, understood through saecular discourse. We can observe several examples from this period where such figures are added to a saecular narrative of history.

The culture hero *par excellence* in antiquity was Prometheus, and as he himself lists in *Prometheus Bound* (442–506), Prometheus was credited with the invention of many aspects of civilization, not just the discovery of fire.[70] Although Prometheus was long associated in Greek literature with innovations for human benefit, one aspect of his myth largely ignored by authors until the end of the first century BCE is his status as the molder of the human race.[71] While certain Augustan poets mention this part of the myth,[72] it is Ovid who connects the molding of men with the beginning of the Golden Age: Prometheus becomes the inaugurator of a new *saeculum*.[73] The creation of the species and the subsequent invocation of the new *saeculum* are so strongly linked that they can even be elided, such as when Phaedrus calls Prometheus "the molder of a new age" (*saeculi figulus novi*, A5.1).[74] Of course, the son of Prometheus, Deucalion, is also a creator of men and another metakosmetic figure; the father made humans out of clay while the son "made" them magically out of rocks thrown over his shoulder. Ovid's Deucalion even intratextually wishes, immediately after the flood, that he possessed his father's

Beyond the Metallic Ages | 99

power of fashioning men (*Met.* 1.363–364).[75] During the post-Sullan period of broad engagement with saecular discourse, the Prometheus myth gains an increased emphasis on his status as the creator of the human race, since this aspect most easily casts Prometheus as a metakosmetic figure.

We find another saecular narrative using metakosmetic culture heroes in the poetry of Tibullus. Throughout the Tibullan corpus, references to Metallic Age mythology can be combined with culture-hero rhetoric to articulate a coherent saecular model of human history. As stated earlier, "cursing the inventor" was a widespread motif in classical literature, and Tibullus deploys a version of it at the beginning of 1.10 toward the inventor of the sword (*horrendos primus qui protulit enses,* 1). While the originator of war is cursed elsewhere,[76] Tibullus goes further, presenting him as one possible cause of the violence and warfare (3–4) that ended the Golden Age.[77] Although the lexicon of saecularity is not employed here, some of the standard attributes of the Golden Age (beyond the absence of war) are mentioned (7–10) to identify the mythical period. But the Tibullan version of the Metallic Ages lacks the fantastical emphasis used by other poets, instead incorporating mythological elements into a more naturalistic version of human development.[78] In 2.1, Tibullus distinguishes the acorn-eating humans of the Golden Age (37–38) from the original practitioners of agriculture in the time to follow, but this transition is not presented negatively: rural gods (37) teach farming techniques and animal husbandry to the human race, and the innovations of poetry (51–54), fertility ritual (55–58), rural cult (59–60), and love (67–78) soon follow.[79] Thus, a negative culture hero (the first discoverer of weapons of war) is joined by positive culture heroes (the unnamed rural gods) at the beginning of the age that followed the Golden Age, tempering the introduction of a new evil (war) with the complementary addition of new skills and benefits. In 1.10, then, Tibullus can depict *Pax* as the entity that first taught humans to lead oxen under the yoke (45–46) while the soldier's weapons lie neglected in the shadows (49–50); although the new age possesses warfare, it also features beneficial agriculture during periods when warfare ceases.

Even this period, however, has passed; for Tibullus, we now live in an Iron Age (*ferrea saecula,* 2.3.35). The idyllic period described in 2.1, although it did have warfare, is still preferable to the extreme (and dangerous) material avarice of modern times (2.3.36–48). The

100 | *Saeculum*

power of love, which previously only affected animals in the fields (2.1.67–71), now compels young men to lose all their money and old men to embarrass themselves in tawdry love affairs (2.1.70–78). But Tibullus has no desire to return to the previous period: he wishes to return all the way back to the Golden Age, where he would neither experience warfare (1.10.11–12) nor be separated from his beloved by the toils of farm cultivation (2.3.67–70). Thus, through saecular discourse Tibullus has divided the narrative of human history into three *saecula*: a Golden Age free of war and agriculture, an intermediate age[80] brought about through the introduction of each of those elements, and an Iron Age of mercantilism gone amok and venality among beloveds (whose attitudes Tibullus is ultimately willing to abide, as we saw in the previous chapter).

Although the Golden Age is often depicted as the first *saeculum* of human history, it should not be forgotten that an alternative version also existed in the Roman intellectual world in which an initial period of helpless anarchy led, with Saturn arriving in Italy as a fugitive, to a second but nonetheless Golden Age under his rule (as we saw above in Vergil's *Aen.* 8 and Ovid's *Fast.* 1). In this version, Saturn taught the rudiments of agriculture, or provided the fruits of the earth, and gave laws and order to humans. With these actions, Saturn serves as the metakosmetic culture hero who brought about the transition to the Golden Age. Saturn was special among divine culture-hero figures in the first century BCE because he received extra attention from euhemerist antiquarians; several writers at Rome are described as arguing that Saturn was a human being.[81] While theoretically anyone (even unnamed first discoverers) could bring about a new *saeculum*, Saturn received credit for bringing about the Golden Age, and Roman intellectuals trying to emphasize human involvement in the progress of history (as Blundell posited) thus have a special interest in arguing that the Golden Age was inaugurated by human, not divine, agency. In their many depictions and descriptions of culture heroes and first discoverers, the Romans return again and again to a narrative of human history in which one special individual brings everyone into a new era (be it metallic or otherwise).

Saecular discourse is deployed by writers in the first century BCE to craft tightly focused narratives of Roman history from a single angle. To give qualitative characteristics of an entire epoch often requires a writer to streamline (or, arguably, to oversimplify) the historical facts of that period. Understandably, then, authors use saecularity to trace the development of a single craft, art, or practice in Roman (or human) history. I refer to these narratives as "technical histories," and they are prevalent in this era of increased intellectual specialization (owing to the widespread professionalization of knowledge bodies that were formerly held by small groups of Roman elites).[82] Technical histories, more so than general histories (even those interested in moral decline), have such a narrowly focused perspective that it is far easier, and more plausible, to "flatten out" the activity of any given period to embody one specific practice.

The rise of the technical history is inextricably related to the Roman "cultural revolution" of the first century BCE, in which various intellectual fields of knowledge (such as the calendar) left the control of the Roman elite and shifted to the hands of specialists who held actual technical skill.[83] Before this shift, these fields of knowledge (including applied knowledge) were based on tradition, and thus an emphasis was placed on the static nature of the information, whereas by the end of the first century BCE, intellectual endeavors had actual scholars who were acutely aware of their place in the history of their field. These scholars then historicized the evolution of their fields, since they could historicize their own place in that evolution (and thus, unsurprisingly, many technical histories become progress narratives whose highest level of progress is simultaneous with the career of the author). Given a sufficiently broad definition of a "technical skill," we could even include something like Varro's division of all of human history into three distinct periods: the unknowable, the mythological, and the historical.[84] But what we can find when we use a narrower focus is a consciousness among actual specialists of the historicity of their given area of expertise, an expertise now validated through its absorption of the intellectual authority previously granted only to aristocratic elites. The emerging genre of the technical history, then, is a product of the sociocultural forces in the Roman intellectual community of the first century BCE.

As an example of this genre of writing, the *De medicina* of the Roman medical writer Celsus, composed during the early first century CE, applies saecular discourse to narrativize the development of medical practice. Celsus describes the practice of clystering the bowel for beneficial purging, which had undergone a threefold saecular development: originally common, the practice was reduced

102 | *Saeculum*

during the period when Asclepiades performed medicine at Rome (the late second century BCE) and generally abandoned in his own age (*saeculo nostro*, *Med.* 2.12.2). Celsus himself favors a return to the moderate application of clysters as during the Asclepiadean age of bowel therapy, leaving him at odds with the characteristics of his own age.[85] A broader, more general saecular history of medicine is also suggested in the lengthy proemium of the work. In a brief history of medical writing, Celsus writes that the Greeks developed medicine more than other peoples, but that they began this development *paucis ante nos saeculis* (1.proem.2). This would normally refer to "a few centuries before us," but Celsus then begins his history of medicine with Asclepius as the oldest authority (*vetustissimus auctor*), followed by his sons, who fought in the Trojan War. Given the Roman use of "Trojan War" as metonymous with the Hesiodic "Heroic Age" (as we saw above), Celsus instead here likely refers to fundamentally distinct epochs of medical history.

Philosophy also provides examples of this temporal awareness. Cicero's description of the history of the Academic school of philosophy in *De natura deorum* includes the report that its customary rhetorical strategy of "negative dialectic" began with Socrates, achieved a revival (*repetita*) during the tenure of Arcesilaus as its scholarch, gained a further reinforcement under Carneades, and eventually reached his own age (*usque ad nostram aetatem*, 1.11). A stock phrase like *ad nostram aetatem* virtually always means "up to now," without any saecular connotation, but the special nature of the ancient philosophical school (which had its own epochs depending on the titular head of the school, like regnal periods) lends itself to saeculated: Cicero's choice of the word *aetas* suggests that he has divided the history of the Academy into *saecula* depending on the approach of its scholarch, be it the Socratic dialectic or some other heterodoxy. Notably, he only cites by name those Academic leaders who have followed the negative dialectic that Cicero approves and uses (placing himself among them),[86] suggesting a carefully tailored narrative of events; it is as though the opponents have been whitewashed from his saecular history of the Academy.

It is not just prose specialists who adopt this discursive mode; the poets also use such language. The Ovidian corpus provides a saecular history of abortions at Rome. In the *Nux*,[87] a poem told from the point of view of a walnut tree, the narrator draws a connection

Beyond the Metallic Ages | 103

between the modern vogue for shade-producing trees over fruit-producing trees and the current popularity of abortions among Roman women. Abortions are so common now, says the walnut tree, that it is rare in this age (*in hoc aevo*, 24) for a woman to be a parent; in that *tempus* (*illo tempore*, 16) when times were better (*tum cum meliora fuerunt tempora*, 7–8), being a mother was more common. Thus the tree is imagining multiple ages, each characterized by its relation to (or affinity for) abortions,[88] with one metakosmetic moment being the time when the first woman[89] performed one. This woman appears in *Amores* 2.14 (*quae prima instituit teneros convellere fetus*, 5), the follow-up to the poem (2.13) in which Corinna attempts an abortion and falls ill. Ovid says in 2.14 that had the popularity of abortions been the same (*mos idem*, 9) for ancient Roman mothers, then the human race would have died out and another Deucalion and Pyrrha would have needed to be found to throw the stones in the empty world[90] and restart it (11–12). This reference to the single most famous metakosmetic myth during the first century BCE signals Ovid's adoption of saecular discourse.

Other Ovidian examples can be found. Ovid gives an abstract history of the Roman city at *Metamorphoses* 15.446, where Pythagoras tells Numa that Helenus told Aeneas that men other than Aeneas will make Rome powerful through the long ages (*per saecula longa*). This phrase *per saecula longa* is a common stock periphrasis for "forever," but since the Etruscan definition of the term involved the lifetimes of cities, here there seems to be some atypical relevance to saecular discourse. Furthermore, this passage sits near the long speech of Pythagoras that describes the change that the earth undergoes, and which begins with Pythagoras saying that the ages (*saecula*, 261) have metamorphosed from gold to iron. He then describes, among other things, geological changes and the rise and fall of famous cities.[91] The *saecula* that Pythagoras refers to here, then, may in fact be the divisions of history by which cities are given their terminal points in the Etruscan divinatory realm. Ovid also seems to gesture at a history of exiles in *Epistulae ex Ponto* 1.3. After a list (from recent, less-recent, and mythological history) of famous exiles, Ovid declares that no one in all ages (*omnibus aevis*, 83) was exiled to a more forbidding place far from home than he. I interpret his use of *aevum* here to refer to an organization of history into time-units, perhaps the division of history into the three Varronian *saecula* of unknowable, mythological,

104 | *Saeculum*

and historical time mentioned earlier; such a division would best account for the temporal unity that must be implied by that range of historical and mythological examples.

The later Augustan period, from which some of these Ovid poems date, seems to have been a fertile ground for technical histories. The Augustan didactic poet Grattius, in his *Cynegetica*, prefaces a list of superstitious treatments against rabies by calling them "the old tricks and contrivances of an unsophisticated age" (*priscas artes inventaque simplicis aevi*, 399–400), having earlier given more solid advice on how to identify and treat the malady; this language is suggestive of a saecular history of dog-rearing.[92] Similarly, in book 1 of his *Astronomica*, Manilius says that in times of great upheaval the occasional age (*rara saecula*, 816) has seen comets and shooting stars. This is perhaps a reference to the Vergilian "iron age" of Julius Caesar (cf. Vergil, *G.* 1.468, below), or perhaps also a reference to a meteorological history of the earth, in which each *saeculum* features telltale comets, shooting stars, and other celestial phenomena that distinguish it from others.

We also see in Manilius a gesture at geological saecularity. After noting the rise and fall of empires on earth in book 1, Manilius says that it would be tedious to chronicle the *saecula* (513) and tell how often the sun has returned to its initial starting position; Manilius seems to draw a parallel between the cycles of empires and the cycle of the sun. Using saecularity as a segue, he proceeds to declare that everything created by mortals is subject to change, and that the earth (as opposed to the night sky), having been worn out by the turning years (*vertentibus annis exutas*, 516–517), bears an appearance that varies through the ages (*per saecula*, 517).

Given Manilius's well-known familiarity with the poetry of Lucretius, it is likely that he drew the language for this idea from a passage in the *De rerum natura* that in fact denies this very saecular geological narrative. Lucretius describes, at the very end of book 2, the gradual decay of the fertility of the earth (1150–1174).[93] The laws of Epicurean physics prohibit the possibility of sudden drastic change (especially cosmically preordained or divinely instigated change), so only a gradual (d)evolution of nature is possible, and this is made explicitly clear: *omnia paulatim tabescere* (1173). While the earth naturally will be less fruitful over time, Lucretius situates himself at a moment in geological history when the realities are particularly bleak; indeed, his *aetas* is "broken" (*iamque adeo fracta est aetas*, 1150).[94] As a result of

Beyond the Metallic Ages | 105

this, the old farmers and vine-dressers of his time compare the present with the past (*tempora temporibus praesentia confert / praeteritis*, 1166–1167) and subsequently praise the fortunes of their parents (*fortunas parentis*, 1167).

But because of their misunderstanding of the laws of nature, with no grasp of Epicureanism to rely on, these old farmers and vine-dressers foolishly create a saecular narrative for geological history to explain the change.[95] They attack the current *saeculum* (*saeclumque fatigat*, 1169)[96] and grumble that the ancient stock of Romans could easily endure their epoch, despite narrow holdings, because it was full of a sense of duty (*antiquum genus ut pietate repletum / perfacile angustis tolerarit finibus aevom*, 1170–1171). Thus, they attribute the failure of the soil to produce a bountiful harvest not to the natural decay of the earth but to the moral failings of contemporary Roman life, and they create a saecular narrative of geological decline parallel to (and presumably caused by) moral decline.

For Lucretius, this geological saecularity is an error caused by a failure to understand Epicurean physics; he describes this technical history only to refute it. This last example, then, demonstrates an awareness even in ancient Rome that the ease with which saecularity can narrativize the history of a narrowly focused topic can lead to a gross oversimplification or outright distortion of historical truth.[97] As we saw earlier in the chapter, Roman poets expressed concerns that challenged narratives of moral saecularity or lapsarian models of Roman moral decline. The moral history is, in some sense, a kind of specialized history similar to the technical history (although it is less interested in historicizing a discipline than in finding a target for censure), so those poets perform an operation not unlike what Lucretius does here.

What distinguishes the Lucretian reaction to geological saecularity, however, is his simultaneous presentation of a counternarrative: the Epicurean-influenced gradual devolution of the fecundity of the earth is a total rejection of the saecular model of geological decline (being, as it is, bound up with moral issues). The other Roman poets argue less from an alternative position on the forces of the universe than from an interest in raising issues with the simplicity of the saecular moral narrative. Lucretius's own intellectual foundation explains his dismissal of a saecular technical history: technical histories emerge because of the rise of disciplinarity and specialist knowledge in the first century BCE, whereas Lucretius is not a

106 | *Saeculum*

scholar of geology but a proponent of the thoughts of a philosopher who lived centuries before his own time. In that sense, Lucretius rests his intellectual authority on the kind of source material that saecular technical histories were meant to refute in the first place.

Similar issues arise in some of the works of Cicero. As we have seen, Cicero occasionally makes use of saecularity in his historical narratives, but it is far from his usual approach. One impediment to any argument for or against Cicero's potential use of saecular narratives is the lack of clarity of his relevant time terminology. For example, in *De republica* (2.2), Cicero records the idea (apparently a favorite of Cato the Elder) that Rome was superior to other famous nations because its republic was not founded by one man, but required a process lasting longer than the lifetime of a man (*una hominis vita*): Rome's republic was founded in *aliquot saeculis et aetatibus*. This brief expression can be interpreted several ways. It could be a case of *variatio*, and thus Cicero uses two different words to describe the exact same concept, or it could be a case of rhetorical expansion, and thus the terms are distinct ("so many centuries and, indeed, epochs"), or Cicero could be referring back to the prior mention of the lifetime of one man ("so many centuries and lifetimes"). Given the familiar connection between a lifetime and a *saeculum*,[98] and given Cicero's (and other Roman authors') frequent use of the word *aetas* to refer to a human lifetime, it is easy to see why the two words would be joined together. Since, in two speeches, Cicero joins *saeculum* with another time word,[99] the temptation is to treat the word to mean "century" in all cases.

But in *De natura deorum* (1.21), Cicero complicates this possibility. Velleius, the representative of the Epicurean school, attacks the Stoic theology of Balbus and asks why God waited so long, lying dormant for innumerable *saecula* (*innumerabilia saecula*), to create the universe, insisting that even though the universe did not exist yet, *saecula* still did. He then distinguishes the *saecula* that are periods of a certain number of days and years, which cannot exist without the universe, from *saecula* "not measured by specific units of time" (*nulla circumscriptio temporum metiebatur*), which can describe the indefinable eternity marked only by the presence of God. The extreme opacity of this passage (owing somewhat to the fact that a figure hostile to Stoic theology is describing it) makes it difficult to understand what Cicero is saying, but it does demonstrate that for Ciceronian literature, the term *saeculum* meant different things in different contexts.

Earlier in this chapter, we saw how Cicero describes an increasing skepticism in human (and especially Roman) history toward supernatural events, with multiple saecular stages of skepticism. A similar narrative is described by Balbus, the Stoic representative in book 2 of Cicero's *De natura deorum*. Balbus suggests that the persistence with which belief in God has lasted is a sort of proof of its veracity, and even though belief in all other supernatural matters (such as the Chimaera or Hippocentaur) has faded away with time, belief in God seems to have grown stronger with "the ages and epochs of men" (*saeclis aetatibusque hominum*, 2.5). Balbus alludes to a multistep process rather than a single transition, and in the light of that previous passage, the impression we get is a reference here to a saecular narrative of increasing skepticism (in the face of which a belief in God has held steady or even strengthened).[100]

This chapter has demonstrated three interrelated contours in the rise of the discursive mode of periodization and saecularity in the first century BCE. The growing popularity of a particularly temporal-minded version of the Metallic Age mythology encouraged Romans to see the world around them in terms of qualitatively distinct periods. To help explain such historical narratives, Romans frequently adapted the "primus inventor" trope and credited culture heroes with providing the innovations that created the metakosmetic moments transitioning history from one period to the next. And this periodized approach to the timeline gave rise to the rhetoric of technical histories, as the newly energized specialist class of Roman intellectuals took stock of the evolution of their chosen fields and articulated historicized accounts of their specialty to further obtain intellectual authority. From prose authors and politicians such as Varro, Cicero, and Celsus, to poets like Lucretius, Ovid, and Manilius, saecular discourse emerged throughout the Roman intellectual community in order to propagate sophisticated new narratives about Roman history and the achievements of the Roman people.

5 | Acting Your Age

Periodization in Roman Politics after Sulla

I have argued that Sulla was the key promulgator of the language of periodization in first-century BCE Roman culture: his deployment of saecular discourse to depict himself as the inaugurator of a new "era" of Roman history spurred the broad development of the rhetoric throughout the intellectual community. However, in the immediate aftermath of Sulla's retirement and death, there does not seem to be any evidence of subsequent Roman politicians adopting this language for themselves. Possibly this is the result of Sulla's negative posthumous reputation; it is likely that his career of atrocities and persecutions had left saecular discourse too tainted for anyone to use in the following years.

Eckert has demonstrated that Sulla's infamy began as soon as he died and not (as some scholars have claimed) in the wake of Caesar's assassination decades later; if Sulla had liked to declare his own importance through the innovative discourse of periodization, then others may have wished to avoid such associations.[1] Furthermore, Rosenblitt has shown that navigating the political landscape at Rome in the aftermath of Sulla's reign was dangerously tricky, and evocations of temporal transitions may simply have been too risky.[2] Alternatively, it may be possible that articulations of new eras and Roman rebirths existed not in the public sphere but in the private world of aristocratic traditions. Sallust (*Cat.* 47) speaks of a prophecy, often mentioned by Lentulus Sura, that a Sibylline oracle proclaimed that three members of the Cornelius family would at some point rule over Rome; with Cinna and Sulla having been the first two, Lentulus believed himself to be the third and so felt emboldened to join Catiline's conspiracy. Such aristocratic family oracles were likely the

Acting Your Age | 109

intended target of the great 12 BCE editing project of the Sibylline books by Augustus, in which prophetic writings in circulation were collected and burned en masse while a new authoritative edition of the Sibylline Books was composed and stored in the Temple of Apollo Palatinus.[3] The loss of Sallust's *Histories* perhaps also deprives us of some examples from the revolt of Lepidus (although, given the literary parallels between Sallust's Catiline and his Lepidus of the surviving fragments, we might suspect that these would be inauthentic retrojections by the historiographer).

Where did periodization go in Roman political discourse? Or rather, what might it have looked and sounded like before declarations of an "Age of Augustus" became mainstream? Luke has argued that in the 60s and 50s BCE, Cicero made attempts to elevate first Pompey and then himself using this periodizing language.[4] We might expect Pompey to have been willing to adopt saecular discourse in the political sphere, given his undeniable connections to Sulla and his ambitious career. The exceptional resume of Pompey may have suggested to many Romans that he was a unique figure in Roman history and could best be understood through periodizing discourse. When in 66 BCE Cicero gave his support to the proposal that Pompey take sole command of the war against Mithridates, he described Pompey in the *Pro lege Manilia* as a seemingly divinely authorized figure (*de caelo delapsum*, 41) with godlike virtue (*divina virtus*, 33; 36) and possessing a divinely authorized luck (47–48), superior to every other commander in Roman history (27), and sent via some plan of the gods to eliminate war (42). For Luke, this indicates that Pompey was "a Sullan-style savior who would inaugurate a new *saeculum*."[5] But Cicero's praise for Pompey in this speech, although lavish, nevertheless lacks any kind of discursive gesture toward temporality that would situate Pompey at a particular moment in history; he is a special person, but there is nothing special about his time.[6]

Luke further suggests that during and after his own consulship, Cicero tried to depict himself as a "man of the *saeculum*" whose activities saved the Republic and brought about a new era of Roman history. Per Luke, Cicero exploited an omen in 65 BCE portending (as interpreted by Etruscan seers) the possible collapse of Rome (*Cat.* 3.19–21) by claiming that disaster was averted by the actions of his own consulship in 63 BCE. Thus, the much-mocked hexameter line from his poem *De consulatu suo*, "O blessed Rome, born with me as consul" (*O fortunatam natam me consule Romam*), was meant to suggest that

110 | *Saeculum*

Cicero himself had brought about a "rebirth" for Rome, and that a new age had begun through his drastic intervention during the Catilinarian conspiracy.[7] Cicero's unpublished epic, the suggestively titled *De temporibus suis*, may also have articulated some kind of large-scale periodized version of Roman history, given its divine apparatus and "council of the gods" scene.[8]

It is true that later Romans drew a connection between Cicero and a *saeculum* of his own: the Augustan orator Arellius Fuscus wrote that Cicero, although proscribed in one age, would himself proscribe Antony to all ages through the survival of the *Philippics*.[9] But in fact, despite the examples of saecular discourse examined in our previous chapter, it seems that Cicero largely denied that Roman history (in the sociopolitical sense) should be understood with any kind of periodization. Cicero expresses a familiarity with the Polybian anacyclosis,[10] against which he argues for his version of the ideal republic.[11] For Cicero, the inevitable dissolution of each of the three Polybian forms of government into their uglier twin proves that all three forms are inferior to the mixed form of government that forms the ideal (and noticeably Roman) state; his ideal state will never change or be overthrown, but will remain the same forever. Indeed, he explicitly claims (*Rep.* 3.34) that states should not naturally die, like people do, but rather the death of a perfect form of government would be like the death of the universe.[12] Furthermore, Cicero forgoes the application of saecularity, or even any periodizing terminology, in his letter to Lucceius (*Fam.* 5.12) on the proper composition of a history. It seems safer to conclude that while Cicero had a greatly inflated sense of his own importance to Roman history (and was keen to impart this attitude to others), he did not try to depict his actions in Roman politics as the inauguration of a qualitatively distinct age of history.

Curiously, Julius Caesar seems not to have adopted any significant degree of saecular language in his public displays of his career and role at Rome (nor, as noted in chapter 3, in his historiographic works). If we are to believe the alleged timelines of Republican-era Ludi Saeculares (on which see below), Romans would have expected a celebration of the festival during the early 40s BCE, yet no source says anything about any plans by Caesar to undertake one. Instead, more enticing possibilities emerge only after the assassination of Julius Caesar; the tumultuous nature of the political realm at this time, combined with the increased distance from the atrocities of

Sulla's career, perhaps made saecular discourse more palatable to Roman politicians, most notably Octavian (soon to be Augustus). I will consider two less obvious personages, Messalla Corvinus and Agrippa, before analyzing the broad adoption of saecular discourse under the *princeps*.

Messalla Corvinus, a politician and patron whose allegiances shifted throughout the civil wars, was the object of praise in several poems of the first century BCE (as one might expect of a man connected with a circle of poets including the elegist Tibullus). Two of these poems, the epyllion *Ciris* and the encomiastic *Catalepton* 9, are not very well known and are sometimes dated to the Imperial period by scholars who believe they were forgeries or exercises written to resemble older poetry. However, recent scholarship by Kayachev has convincingly argued that these are authentic works from around the Triumviral period, with the *Ciris* likely composed between 45 and 30 BCE and *Catalepton* 9 at a similar date.[13]

In the prologue of the *Ciris*, the poet gives a somewhat formal blessing to his patron Messalla and describes him as "the incredible glory of the age" (*mirificum decus saecli*, 12–13).[14] What makes this otherwise commonplace sentiment stand out is its context within the proem of the epyllion, a proem which is particularly focused on cyclical repetitions of time: much attention is paid to the image of Athena's robe and its use in the ritual practices at Athens (20–35), specifying its five-year cycle (*confecto redeunt quinquennial lustro*, 24) and declaring, "that day is called happy, and that year is called happy; happy are they who are able to see such a year and such a day" (*felix illa dies, felix et dicitur annus / felices qui talem annum videre diemque*, 27–28). The poet goes on to express a hope that this praise of Messalla will survive (along with the poem itself) "unto elder eras" (*senibus saeclis*, 41). Not only does this verbiage resemble "Neoteric" attitudes toward aesthetic periodization (see chapter 6) but it also appears in *Catalepton* 9, a poem purporting to be the foreword to a collection of Messalla's Greek bucolic poetry; the poem, which refers to Messalla as "the glory of a great triumph" (*magni decus triumphi*, 3), promises that Messalla's literary works will be received by future ages (*saeclis accepta futuris*, 15) and will outlive the proverbially aged Priam and Nestor. In these expressions of praise toward Messalla's military, political, and artistic achievements, which the poet considers scarcely human (*vix hominum*, 56) in their impressiveness, the temporal context of the qualitative and personality-defined era is a consideration, albeit a small one.

112 | *Saeculum*

What role might saecular discourse play, in the wake of the civil wars, for a Roman politician without a coterie of poetasters but with just as much ambition and influence? For a detailed case study, I would like to examine Marcus Vipsanius Agrippa's tenure as Rome's curule aedile in 33 BCE, and specifically one particular action during that tenure: his cleaning of Rome's oldest and greatest sewer system, the Cloaca Maxima, and the public demonstration he made by sailing a boat through it.[15] It is not entirely clear whether Agrippa's maintenance of the Cloaca consisted merely of an inspection and cleaning or of renovations and additions, but I am primarily interested in the publicity regarding the operation (especially the boat) rather than the details of it, because of its potential as political imagery. The public presentation of the cleaning and the boat ride was meant, I argue, to appropriate mythological associations to Hercules that had been originally sought by Sulla. Agrippa makes use of the "culture hero" connotations of Herculean mythology (and his labor of cleaning the stables of Augeas) in order to visually articulate a new periodized history of Roman infrastructure, in which he himself plays a role as a "man of the *saeculum*" to lead Rome into a new age of peace and prosperity.

Previous scholarship analyzing Agrippa's exceptional aedileship has focused on the practical benefits of Agrippa's renovations and construction projects.[16] Agrippa's maintenance of the Cloaca Maxima can also be understood using comparable episodes of political performance in the career of Sulla, who used public works projects as a demonstration of his epochal nature as a leader in Roman history.[17] In particular, Sulla's cultivation of Herculean associations was meant to portray the man as a Roman culture hero, who like the mythological Hercules brought order and stability to the world. Hercules, like any mythological culture hero, was regarded as a benefactor of mankind through his labors. Sulla's attempts to connect himself to Hercules are well documented, as was demonstrated in chapter 1.[18] Sulla began to cultivate associations with Hercules in 88 BCE, a year marked by an Etruscan omen about the introduction of a new *saeculum*,[19] and it is this omen that Sulla exploited to depict himself as a leader inaugurating a new age of Roman history.

Among the canonical labors of Hercules, the cleaning of the stables of Augeas tends not to command the same sort of renown that the other labors do, and in fact explicit extant literary references to the deed date back only to the first century BCE.[20] The few earlier narratives are more ambiguous: Pindar mentions an unspecified service by Hercules to Augeas for which the latter would not pay,[21] and Pseudo-Theocritus's *Idyll* 25 also has some kind of telling of the story of Hercules and Augeas that does not actually narrate Hercules' cleaning of the stables.[22] It seems that the Augean stables tale was a local Elian myth, but since its depiction appeared among the metopes decorating the Temple of Zeus at Olympia, it achieved a higher level of Mediterranean familiarity.[23] Hercules' Twelve Labors themselves only were effectively codified by the end of the Roman Republican era, just as explicit literary references to the Augean stables labor (and the detail of the diversion of water to clean them) appear.

Thus, the period of the late Republic was evidently the time when the tale of Hercules clearing the Augean stables with a river began to flourish in the Mediterranean consciousness. The Roman polymath Varro uses the myth in a fragment of his *Bimarcus*, a lost Menippean satire now typically understood to be an internal debate between two sides of Varro's brain: one a stern moralist lamenting contemporary Rome's changed social mores, the other an optimist happy to be alive in the greatest period of Roman success.[24] In the fragment, moralist Varro complains that Rome is so full of moral filth that even Hercules, who cleaned out the Augean stables, could not handle it.[25] Here Varro treats Hercules as emblematic of a culture hero solving problems, though in this instance the social problem is Rome's shifting morality. Since Roman morality was, at this time, often subjected to the discourse of epochal periodization as well, the Augean stables tale thus seems to have achieved such a growing popularity in first-century BCE Rome that it was adapted into this moral history of Rome.

Agrippa's cleaning of the Cloaca Maxima in 33 BCE thus meets an audience now better familiar with the Augean tale, and naturally the cleaning resembles this labor of Hercules in many ways, most obviously his purgation of waste from a structure and the manipulation of waterways.[26] The Cloaca was used not only to conduct the water from seven different streams but also to withstand the backwash pressure of Tiber floods (whose potential damage to the city was immense, particularly for the urban poor). Given the many documented floods of the Tiber in Rome in the first century BCE,[27] Agrippa's service in solving this serious civic problem puts him in the role of a

114 | *Saeculum*

Herculean culture hero.[28] The much-attested rowing through the Cloaca by Agrippa allowed him to highlight himself publicly as the contributor, as well as depicting him as the Hercules figure.[29]

Agrippa's resemblance to Hercules, or at least to a Sullan Hercules, goes beyond the Cloaca to other areas of political performance. Like Sulla, Agrippa wrote an extensive autobiography (now lost but mentioned by Pliny the Elder and Servius), and we know from a reference in Pliny that he recollected the details of his aedileship in that autobiography (to say nothing of the official commentary on his actions as the magistrate, which Frontinus makes mention of throughout his *De aquis urbis Romae*).[30] No doubt the work mentioned and praised, if not emphasized, Agrippa's unique Cloaca treatment. Like Sulla, Agrippa made connections to Hercules numismatically: bronze coins were minted in Spain (though probably only after 27 BCE) with Hercules on the obverse and Agrippa's name on the reverse.[31]

Attempted associations with Hercules seem to have been effective in the later remembrance of Agrippa's career. Diodorus Siculus apparently connected Agrippa's aquatic building activities to those of Hercules: Sulimani has argued that in his *Bibliotheke*, Hercules is described by Diodorus constructing works around Lake Avernus (4.22.2), which Sulimani reads as a likely reference to the deeds of Agrippa (building harbors and canals) in the 30s during the time Diodorus wrote his history; as Diodorus often conflates activities by mythic heroes with actual human actions, his readers would cognitively link Agrippa and Hercules via such waterworks.[32] For another such link, we can recall Seneca the Younger's line from his *Apocolocyntosis*: Claudius, addressing Hercules, speaks not of the stables of Augeas but of the cloacas—the sewers of Augeas.[33] I read this verbal slip as further evidence that Agrippa's activity in the Cloaca Maxima was viewed later by Romans in light of the Augean stables myth; the similarity has further linked Agrippa to Hercules.

Parallels aside, one may quibble that Hercules diverted a river to clean the stables of Augeas, while Agrippa merely saw to it that the Cloaca was thoroughly cleaned. But later writers would attribute an act of river diversion to Agrippa as well. What survives of Porphyrio's commentary on Horace's *Ars poetica* includes a scholion in which Agrippa is said by the commentator to have diverted the stream of the Tiber, like Julius Caesar had allegedly wanted to do (and of course as Hercules had done in the Augeas tale).[34] This (apparently inaccurate) recollection is the product, I argue, of Agrippa's Sullan attempts to appear like a Herculean culture hero.

It is reasonable to ask: is sailing in a sewer a sensible way to glorify oneself politically? We are told by Seneca the Elder that Agrippa was self-conscious about his rustic name and background, and Pliny mentions his reputation for lacking refinement.[35] Perhaps sailing a boat through the Cloaca did not improve that reputation—or perhaps, paradoxically, it demonstrated that Agrippa was a serious politician: in the 30s BCE, while Antony was rumored to be gallivanting around with Cleopatra in Egypt, the Augustan government's public message was that they were taking care of business: providing services, cleaning up the city, and restoring order (if not quite restoring the Republic itself). The temporal associations of a public works undertaking like this, centered on a piece of monumental civic architecture connected to the oldest days of the city, contributes to the sense of "re-foundation" that many Roman leaders (Augustus among them) hoped to cultivate in the first century BCE. Although Agrippa ultimately was not seen as ushering in a new era of Roman history through his aedileship, it is reasonable within its historical context that he may have aspired to make himself look like a Cloacan culture hero through this highly publicized episode.

Roman saecular discourse underwent a period of experimentation and evolution during the decades after Sulla's dictatorship, but many of the best-preserved examples of its application in not only literature but also other areas of culture appear during the reign of Augustus.[36] Saecularity allowed Romans to describe the Principate (and the actions of the *princeps*) as something both revolutionary for Roman history and traditional; the saecular model of historical narrative insists that the new age be qualitatively different from the previous one, but also allows it to resemble an earlier period. As we will see in this chapter, Horace's *Ode* 4.15 depicts the Augustan Age as a return to the moral standards of an earlier, bygone era, but nonetheless sharply different from its immediate predecessor. And as we saw earlier, Vergil in his fourth eclogue sees the radically new Golden Age to come as part of an unending cycle, thus promising that the changes in Roman history are part of a divine order (and have already occurred before in the past). The expansive presence of saecularity as a means of discussing or describing the sociocultural world in Augustan Rome, perhaps best represented by the modern scholarly shorthand of the "Augustan Age," has already been mentioned; in

116 | *Saeculum*

this section I would like to concentrate more closely on a few aspects of the Augustan world and examine how saecular discourse was deployed in a variety of media. Rather than full overviews of the major topics, the emphasis here will be a very tight focus on, and thus a brief look at, some significant features of Augustan art, architecture, literature, and society.

Literary works played a significant role in the development of the ancient Roman concept of the Augustan Age, and of the numerous examples of saecular discourse pertaining to Augustus in Roman literature, a few passages stand out as important markers of an Augustan *saeculum*. The importance of the *saeculum* in the Vergilian poetic corpus, and chiefly in the *Aeneid*, has long been well understood, and familiar passages in books 1, 6, and 8 describing prophetic views of the future unsurprisingly feature saecular terminology.[37] In the *Georgics*, an impious age (*impia saecula*, 1.468) feared that they had slipped into an eternal night (*aeternam noctem*)[38] when an eclipse occurred after Caesar was murdered. With Augustus having not yet taken over the moral leadership of Rome, Vergil asks the gods not to prevent this young man from helping an overturned age (*everso saeclo*, 500). The fact that the age is overturned, like an out-of-control chariot (cf. 1.512–514), reminds one of the course of the ages (*magnus saeclorum ordo*, *Ecl.* 4.5), as though the substantial impiety of the previous *saeculum* somehow stalled the course of history: the guidance of Augustus must reset the world so that the natural return to the Golden Age can occur. But Vergil was not the only Roman using such terminology to explain the new temporality that the reign of Augustus seemed to inaugurate. To these more familiar examples of the notion of an Augustan *saeculum*, I would like to add some others so that the breadth of possibilities articulated by Roman authors can be better understood (and so that Vergil can be treated less as a center of gravity for saecular discourse in the Augustan milieu in classical scholarship).

All Roman writers knew that Augustus was destined to leave this world someday, but there was ambiguity about what was to happen next: would the benefits to Roman culture provided by the *princeps* continue even after his death (a perpetual "Augustan Age"), or would a new (and potentially worse) age follow? The language used to address this question was not uniform. For example, in his prophecy about Augustus at the end of Ovid's *Metamorphoses*, Jupiter says that he, "looking forward to an age of future time and of coming generations" (*inque futuri / temporis aetatem venturorumque nepotum / prospiciens*,

15.834–836), will order Tiberius to bear Augustus's name and the burden of his cares. This wording suggests that the Augustan Age will last forever, and that subsequent generations (including Tiberius himself) will constitute the "future time" of the unending age. On the other hand, as we will see below, Horace's *Ode* 4.15 implies that the length of the Augustan Age is contingent on the presence of Augustus as the guardian of the state of affairs, and in his ultimate absence something new will take its place. The temporal possibilities produced by the discourse of an Augustan Age were multiform.

Augustus was not simply written *about* as an inaugurator of a new *saeculum*; he also wrote of his own *saeculum* in his *Res Gestae* and his (lost) memoirs.[39] Augustus describes his revival of exemplary ancestral practices which he claims had already deteriorated by his *saeculum* (*ex nostro [saecul]o, Res Gestae Divi Augusti [RGDA]* 8.5). Thus, this Augustan revival was directed toward a Roman audience of posterity for them to imitate (*imitanda posteris*). Augustus was also the only man in his age (*meae aetatis, RGDA* 16.1) to settle soldiers using his own funds.[40] And (as analyzed in chapter 2) in the second book of his *commentarii* memoirs,[41] Augustus describes the Etruscan seer Vulcanius (or Vulcatius), who declared that the comet that appeared after the death of Julius Caesar signaled the metakosmesis of the Etruscan *saecula*. The *princeps* was thus familiar with the language of periodization and actively participated in the saecular discourse that for modern scholars is so closely linked to his own career.

As a point of comparison with these other evocations of an Augustan *saeculum*, I want to examine Horace's *Ode* 4.15,[42] from his collection usually dated to 13 BCE.[43] Generally speaking, the poem is a lyric encomium of the reign of Augustus, framed by allusive considerations of the poet's own genre and predecessors as well as depictions of the appropriate ways for Romans to celebrate the new world Augustus has given them.

> Phoebus volentem proelia me loqui
> victas et urbis increpuit lyra,
> ne parva Tyrrhenum per aequor
> vela darem. tua, Caesar, aetas
>
> fruges et agris rettulit uberes,   5
> et signa nostro restituit Iovi

118 | *Saeculum*

derepta Parthorum superbis
postibus et vacuum duellis

Ianum Quirini clausit et ordinem
rectum evaganti frena licentiae   10
iniecit emovitque culpas
et veteres revocavit artis,

per quas Latinum nomen et Italae
crevere vires, famaque et imperi
porrecta maiestas ad ortus   15
solis ab Hesperio cubili.

custode rerum Caesare non furor
civilis aut vis exiget otium,
non ira, quae procudit ensis
et miseras inimicat urbis.   20

non qui profundum Danuvium bibunt
edicta rumpent Iulia, non Getae,
non Seres infidive Persae,
non Tanain prope flumen orti.

nosque et profestis lucibus et sacris   25
inter iocosi munera Liberi
cum prole matronisque nostris,
rite deos prius apprecati,

virtute functos more partum duces
Lydis remixto carmine tibiis   30
Troiamque et Anchisen et almae
progeniem Veneris canemus.

Phoebus struck me with the lyre when I was wishing to speak
of battles and conquered cities, so that I might not spread my
small sails upon the Tyrrhenian Sea. Your era, Caesar, brought
back abundant harvests to the fields, and restored to our Jupiter the standards ripped down from the proud doorposts of the
Parthians, and it closed the Temple of Janus Quirinus, devoid
of battles, and it placed a restraint upon audacity, wandering

beyond the proper limit, and it removed sins, and it called back the ancient skills through which grew the Latin name and Italian strength and the reputation and grandeur of the empire stretched from the western bed of the sun to its rising. With Caesar as guardian of our affairs, civic frenzy or force will not drive out peace, nor will anger, which forges swords and makes enemies of wretched cities. Those who drink of the deep Danube will not break the Julian edicts, nor will the Getae, nor will the Seres or the treacherous Persians, nor the people born near the river Tanais. And we, on regular days and holidays, among the gifts of happy Liber, with our wives and children, having duly invoked the gods first, will sing in the custom of our fathers of leaders having acted in virtue, in a song accompanied by Lydian pipes, and of Troy and of Anchises and of the offspring of dear Venus.

In the bulk of the poem, Horace describes how the Augustan age (*tua, Caesar, aetas, 4.*) changed the world through a variety of improvements to domestic and foreign affairs. This second-person construction lies in opposition to the customary first-person "our generation" (*nostra aetas* vel sim.) that Horace and other Romans commonly use;[44] while the first-person construction clearly operates as a formulaic, value-neutral periphrasis for "the present time," this *tua aetas* instead marks the age with some sort of "Augustan" quality. The phrase gestures toward Augustus's influence on Roman politics and (especially) culture, implying a palpable mark left by Augustus himself on the characteristics of the era. Additionally, the grammar of the poem suggests that the *aetas* itself had some effect on the world at large; note that it is *aetas* that is the subject of the verbs *rettulit, clausit, emovit*, etc. The qualitative aspect of saecular temporality lends itself to such a rhetorical shift in a way that a mere chronological function (such as "Augustus's present" or "Augustus's life") would not.

The discourse of saecularity divides history into discrete units, but in this poem we are given no explicit indication of when this *aetas* began (or when it will end). Since Augustus essentially is the primary agent behind the accomplishments that his age has brought us, then its duration must line up with his assumption of power. It cannot begin with his birth (to take *aetas* here to mean "lifetime"), since the lifetime of Augustus saw many negative aspects of Roman history: civil war, bloodshed, and the murder of Roman leaders. Much as with the curious (and unsuccessful) proposition by the senator in

120 | *Saeculum*

the Suetonius passage earlier, honoring the entire lifetime of Augustus lends itself to uneasy references which seem out of place in this poem. Crucially, there are no claims to permanence for any of the aspects of his age (5–24), and in fact the ablative absolute phrase "with Caesar as guardian of our affairs" (*custode rerum Caesare*, 17) suggests a temporal boundary: once Caesar is no longer in charge of affairs, new occurrences will happen.[45] Even if the word *aetas* inevitably contains a connotation of "lifetime" then we can still acknowledge that, in Horace's mind, Augustus would likely stop being the *princeps* only at death, thus ending his lifetime and his reign (and thus also his "age"). This, of course, assumes that Augustus would not pursue a retirement like Sulla, which no contemporary source ever seems to suggest.

If we analyze *Ode* 4.15 in consideration of his use of periodization, we will find Horace imagining several *saecula* in this poem. The clearest is the present *saeculum*, the *tua aetas* of line 4. This age is marked by fertility (5), peace (6–9, 17–24), morality (9–11), and the general prestige of Rome (12–16). While this description is perhaps an exaggerated depiction of the situation at Rome in 13 BCE, the flattery does not go so far as to mythologize the present condition; Horace has not applied Metallic Age mythology here but has instead created a *sui generis* "Augustan" age.[46] Necessarily, however, the *aetas* of Augustus that is so characterized must have been preceded by an *aetas* that lacked such qualities (in opposition to this *tua aetas*), and so Horace simultaneously creates a previous age with crop failures, wars, and *licentia* and *culpae*. And, since Augustus is bringing back (*rettulit, restituit, revocavit*) positive characteristics that had been lost (*veteres artis*, 12), we can also read into the poem a still earlier age strongly resembling that world which the *aetas* of Augustus has restored. The close of Augustus's *aetas* will occur, per our earlier reading of the poem, when he stops being the *custos rerum* and a successor takes over. In 13 BCE, life after Augustus was not exactly easy to predict: Marcellus was dead, Gaius and Lucius were still children, and Agrippa was rarely in Rome itself. To Horace, it would not be out of the question to imagine a future Rome wracked by another civil war (through a succession crisis) and renewed chaos upon the death of the *princeps*. This subsequent inferior *aetas* lingers at the edge of *Ode* 4.15, with Augustus (through his work as the *princeps* more so than through distant prophecies) being the sole guarantor of the benefits of his own age.

As we can see, *Ode* 4.15 engages in saecular discourse to create a complex narrative for Roman history, and a reader (Roman or otherwise) sensitive to saecularity will grasp these implicit messages. Horace's organization of Roman history into qualitatively defined time-units gives Augustus high esteem as the initiator of a positive new *saeculum*, redeeming the ugly preceding age and resembling a still earlier one. With the unstated but perceptible potential for new decay after Augustus, Horace constructs a pendulum model of Roman history that swings back and forth between ages of virtue and peace and ages of sin and war. What helps Rome emerge from bad *saecula* into good ones is the work of men like Augustus, "leaders having acted in virtue" (*virtute functos duces*, 29). This perspective on Roman temporality, dominated by the actions of a unique "man of the *saeculum*," reflects positively on the *princeps* and justly ranks him with the *progeniem Veneris* (32).

Readers of this final collection of odes in 13 BCE are meant here to be reminded of the dark saecular prediction at the end of *Ode* 3.6 which, through the guidance of Augustus, 4.15 has shown to be in error. *Ode* 3.6, often dated to 23 BCE as part of the simultaneous publication of the first three books of Horace's *Odes*, features the same meter as 4.15 (Alcaic stanzas), begins its final line with same words as 4.15 (*progeniem*), and makes significant use of saecular discourse, all of which invites comparison between the two poems. At the beginning of 3.6, the current generation of Romans will keep paying for the sins of the previous generation (*delicta maiorum*, 1) until the temples are repaired and the piety toward the gods reestablished, even though the current Romans are themselves guiltless (*immeritus*, 1). But this attitude has changed by the end of the poem (45–48), where we learn that the *aetas* of our parents begot the present generation, who are more evil than they were (and they were worse than *their* parents), and we will beget an even worse generation (*progeniem*, 48); this passage seems to depict the current Romans as not actually *immeritus*. Here Horace likely alludes to the speech of the Maiden in the *Phaenomena* of Aratus, who correctly predicts that an inferior race of bronze will follow the race of silver, but he strips away any trace of the Metallic Age mythology.[47] What Augustus has done, in *Ode* 4.15, is render this cycle null and void; his *aetas* has reversed the devolution predicted by these lines (composed a decade prior) and restored the virtues of the exemplary Middle Republican period (perhaps through, among other things, the reparation of those temples).

122 | *Saeculum*

A similar saecular resonance with 4.15 occurs earlier in the poem. At 3.6.17–32, Horace claims that multiple *saecula*, each productive of crime (*fecunda culpae saecula*, 17), first destroyed marriage, the family, and the home, and that from this source all the current problems of Rome have sprung. Horace usually refers to a single time-unit as a *saeculum*[48] (although other writers commonly use the poetic plural to refer to the singular), so Horace is probably referring here to multiple time-units: the first generation to ruin family values (our fathers'), and then the current one (and thus, our fathers' generation is worse than our grandfathers', and we are worse than our fathers'), both of which were the first Roman generations to do so (*primum*, 18). Although he predicts that what follows the current generation will be even more sinful (*vitiosiorem*, 48), the *aetas* of Augustus has instead removed crime (*emovit culpas*, 4.15.11) and thus nullified that prediction in *Ode* 4.15.

Horace's *Ode* 4.15, per my reading above, saw the leadership of Augustus (*custode rerum Caesare*, 17) as the temporal and causal marker of the Augustan Age, with Augustus himself as the sole guarantor of the benefits of his own age; his presence as a Roman leader was a requirement for the characteristics of his age to exist. One other previous composition by Horace affects our reading of saecular discourse in *Ode* 4.15: the *Carmen Saeculare* from 17 BCE. Perhaps for reasons of *variatio*, Horace never uses the word *saeculum* in the *Carmen*, but saecular discourse nonetheless looms large, as would be expected.[49] Horace connects the new *saeculum* (*certus undenos decies per annos / orbis*, 21–22) to the Sibylline Books (*Sibyllini versus*, 5) and says that with its arrival, virtues (Faith, Peace, Honor, Modesty, Virtue) that had been neglected will now (*iam*, 55) dare to return. Thus the new *saeculum* is marked by a morality that once existed at Rome but, at least in the previous *saeculum*, was no longer present (cf. 45, where Horace hopes that the gods will instill good *mores* in the youth). This sentiment lines up nicely with the similar idea in 4.15 that the Augustan *aetas* ended the ills of the previous age by revisiting the boons of the age before that.

The sentiment is expressed again at 67–68, when Rome will get another *lustrum*[50] and another better age (*aevum*, 68). Yet by insisting on the specifics of the ritual and its regularity (e.g., it will happen every 110 years (21)), and by noting that Phoebus's looking with favor upon Rome is a condition for success and not guaranteed (65), Horace cannot help but demonstrate that there will be other *saecula* and thus other opportunities for Apollo *not* to smile on Rome. In other words, Horace imagines the possibility of multiple futures, since future *saecula* may turn out well for Rome or turn out poorly (or actually improve, if the cycle is truly *melius semper*). Again, as in 4.15, Horace's guarded attitude toward the future suggests that the blessings bestowed on the Augustan *aetas* are not permanent.

Discussions of Horace's *Carmen Saeculare* naturally invite questions about the nature and contemporary reception of the Augustan celebration of the Ludi Saeculares, the ritual festival purportedly celebrated by the Romans at the transitional moment of two *saecula*.[51] The watershed celebration of the Ludi Saeculares took place in 17 BCE, and its primacy in our understanding of the ritual is no doubt the result of its well-preserved details (in both the *Carmen Saeculare* of Horace and in the epigraphic texts of the *Acta*). The Augustan celebration seems to have been notably influential in the succeeding iterations of the Ludi Saeculares in the Imperial period, but the history of the Ludi Saeculares in the centuries before Augustus is far less certain, due to a lack of evidence, conflicting (or absent) accounts, and biased theories by ancient writers.[52]

One major stumbling block for any analysis of Republican era celebrations of the Ludi Saeculares is that it is not clear when any of the alleged celebrations took place, owing to the existence of two competing timelines in ancient scholarship. Censorinus records two systems (17.3–5): one established by Augustus's *XVviri* in 17 BCE and counting backward by 110 years (and thus arriving at dates of 456 BCE, 346 BCE, 236 BCE, and 126 BCE), and another laid out by Valerius Antias (and sometimes followed by Livy or Varro), which began in 509 BCE under P. Valerius Publicola, restarted in 348 BCE, and then followed with hundred-year periods (thus leading to celebrations in 249 BCE and 149 BCE).[53] Of course, it is also possible that neither of these systems of reckoning accurately captures the dates of the Republican celebrations. The process of figuring out which dates are authentic, miscalculated, or outright fabricated has activated modern scholarship for years: "The proper chronological order for the [Ludi Saeculares]," writes Hall, "has been contested no less vividly in modern times than in antiquity."[54] There is much reason to be skeptical that a formal celebration of the Ludi Saeculares that actually resembles what Augustus put on in 17 BCE ever happened, and to instead conclude that earlier iterations are better understood either as other festivals or as total fabrications.[55]

124 | *Saeculum*

It may be that the interest of antiquarians and historiographers in determining this Republican history of the Ludi Saeculares was the result of broader interest in saecularity in the Roman intellectual world after Sulla. Valerius Antias, a historian from the middle of the first century BCE, has long been accused (even since Livy) of distorting or fabricating Roman history in ways that promote the Valerii clan, and his description of the history of the Ludi Saeculares was possibly a consequence of Sulla's promulgation of the concept. Two Roman sources from the first century BCE contend that the first celebration of what they could possibly consider the Ludi Saeculares occurred in 249 BCE, when the *XVviri* consulted the Sibylline Books after negative portents during the First Punic War.[56] Pseudo-Acron, a scholiast at line 8 of Horace's *Carmen Saeculare*, writes that the Augustan antiquarian Verrius Flaccus claimed the Ludi Saeculares began in 249 BCE. After lightning struck part of the city wall and collapsed it, Verrius says, the Sibylline Books instructed that the festival be celebrated every 110 years in honor of Dis and Proserpina, with children singing hymns to the divinities on the Capitol on three days and nights. If this instruction was carried out (at least in the first iteration), the Romans would win the war against Carthage, as it was understood by the Romans. Thus, as Verrius Flaccus describes it, the ceremony was invented completely at this time, with no precedent; the Ludi Saeculares came about entirely because of this pronouncement.

The other ancient source, Varro (preserved in Censorinus 17.8), has a different story. Varro says that as a result of lightning striking part of the city wall, the *XVviri* consulted the Sibylline Books, but their report was that the Ludi Tarentini, a preexisting ceremony for Dis and Proserpina at the Campus Martius, should become a three-day event performed every one hundred years. Varro states this last detail, that the ceremony should be repeated every one hundred years, "as if that had not previously been the case."[57] Varro, writing decades before the Augustan Ludi Saeculares, records a 100-year cycle, unlike the 110-year cycle of Verrius Flaccus, a discrepancy which must reflect the changes effected by the *XVviri* in 17 BCE. Varro also connects the Ludi Saeculares to an otherwise unknown Ludi Tarentini, giving the Ludi Saeculares some sort of continuity with rituals from before 249 BCE.

Hall argues that the ritual of 348 BCE already resembled later Ludi Saeculares.[58] He bases this on the surviving text of the

"Saecular Prayer," a prayer to Apollo preserved in the Severan Acta and believed to be at least roughly similar to the text of the Augustan Ludi Saeculares. The prayer mentions "keeping the Latins obedient," which Taylor argued must be a reference to the fourth century BCE before the Latin League dissolved in 338 BCE.[59] Hall believes that Ateius Capito, a well-respected scholar of Roman history who had a major supervisory role in 17 BCE, accurately preserved the text of the original Ludi Saeculares ritual, having been tasked by Augustus to do so by stripping away elements added in later rituals.[60] An alternative explanation, though, is that the text of the prayer is a pseudo-archaic forgery meant to create the illusion of greater continuity with a more remote past.[61]

Ultimately, however, I find it best to accept the conclusions drawn by Dunning in her work on the history of the Ludi Saeculares, a summary of which I give here.[62] Dunning writes that a ritual performed at the Tarentum in the Campus Martius had been overseen by the Valerii clan for centuries, but was brought under state control in 249 BCE (or possibly 348 BCE) during a moment of civic crisis (and by the authority of the Sibylline Books). Valerius Antias was perhaps the first to claim that the duration between regular celebrations of the festival was one hundred years, but the festival did not have a saecular character (in the sense of a transition from one qualitatively defined era to another) during the Republic. The celebration by Augustus was the first to possess this aspect, and through the antiquarian research publications of Ateius Capito, a new chronology of the Ludi Saeculares was created that extended backward in time and (falsely) asserted the metakosmetic nature of the previous iterations.

The celebration by Augustus of the Ludi Saeculares in 17 BCE was a major episode in the evolution, and public promulgation, of the concept of saecularity. In light of the saecular discourse used in Augustan literature to describe the place of the *princeps* within Roman society, the saecular resonances of the ritual would have been obvious to the Roman intelligentsia, as they are to modern scholars. But a more critical question to answer is the extent to which the Ludi Saeculares attempted to convey a sense of cosmic transition, a metakosmetic moment from one epoch to another, to the general Roman populace.

From the start, it appears that this epochal nature of the celebration was stressed to the Roman people; Zosimus (2.5) records that

126 | *Saeculum*

well before the ceremony, officials went around the city hyping the event to everyone,[63] stressing that it would be a spectacle they had never seen before and never would again (presumably since the next celebration was supposed to occur 110 years later). This aspect of the ceremony evidently made such an impression on the people that for the premature Claudian performance of the Ludi Saeculares in 47 CE, when the proclamation was again made that the ceremony would be a spectacle no one had ever seen before, there was public mockery; there was an understanding that Claudius had violated the idea of saecularity with his own performance.[64] This emphasis on the once-per-*saeculum* aspect of the Ludi Saeculares also appears in Ovid's *Tristia*, when he describes Horace's hymn being performed "at that time when Caesar celebrated the Ludi that each age sees just once" (*quo tempore ludos / fecit quos aetas aspicit una semel*, 2.25–26). Regardless of further mysticism, what seems to have resonated very well with the Romans is the idea that each *saeculum* should be marked by just a single celebration of the Ludi Saeculares.

While officials promoted the performance in the time leading up to the ceremony, it is also possible that the Roman people had been expecting such a momentous civic celebration for several years. Several scholars have argued that Augustus originally planned to celebrate the Ludi Saeculares in 23 or 22 BCE (perhaps in relation to the reforms passed in the Second Settlement).[65] The flexibility of calculations for the occurrence of the Ludi Saeculares was explained above, but further evidence of Augustus's adjustment of the date is the fact that the official oracular pronouncement for the appropriate time to celebrate the Ludi Saeculares (discovered, or "discovered," in 19 BCE) points to a celebrate date of 16 BCE, not 17 BCE.[66] The scholarly consensus holds that this 16 BCE calculation is accurate, and no real explanation for the discrepancy has ever been given, so Luke may be right to suggest that Augustus moved up the date to coincide with Lucius Caesar's birth (and thus connect the new *saeculum* to the birth of a special child, a la *Eclogue* 4).[67]

One last point about the Augustan recalculation of the saecular duration, to 110 years, should be noted. Varro, in his *De gente populi romani*, had written of a particular strand of the concept of palingenesis, whereby after a period of 440 years a man would be "reborn" (*renascendis*) through the perfect reassembly of his constituent atoms.[68] By recalibrating the system of the Ludi Saeculares to 110-year periods, Augustus could perform his celebration exactly 440 years after the legendary first Ludi Saeculares had been celebrated. To those Romans familiar with Varro's work, Augustus could thus represent himself performing a civic palingenesis.[69]

While the preparations for the Ludi Saeculares stressed their once-in-a-*saeculum* nature, the actual performance of the ceremony itself included aspects that stressed its periodizing resonance. Admittedly, it is extremely difficult, or perhaps impossible, to recreate what any Roman's experience of the Ludi Saeculares would have been like. Rüpke aptly describes the challenge for modern scholars: "The exegetic pressure to which each individual element of the ritual was exposed by the particular context of the genre treating it, together with the narrow available repertoire of explanatory strategies (etymology, mythic archetype/portrayal [typology], genetic explanation), created meanings that were distorted and greatly inflated in comparison with the spontaneous, contemporaneous interpretations of participants."[70] We cannot know what the Ludi Saeculares "meant" to the average Roman participant; our knowledge of what is written about its function and mythology is not enough to make those sorts of claims. Horace (*Odes* 4.6.41–44) writes that those Roman boys and girls who participated in the chorus of the Carmen Saeculare would someday boast of having sung that hymn "when the *saeculum* brought round the festal days" (*saeculo festas referente luces*, 42). And the spectacle made enough of an impression on Livy that he used it as a benchmark for all Roman games, noting that the splendor and variety of the Taurian Games of 186 BCE were "almost as much as the games of this *saeculum*" (*prope huius saeculi copia ac varietate*, 39.22.2).[71]

Nonetheless, we can assert confidently that a major component of the experience of the Ludi Saeculares was its lustral nature: the ceremony was like an amplified version of the purification that concluded a lustral period.[72] Given the frequency of the *lustrum* (occurring every five years), the general Roman populace would have understood the nature of that ceremony well, and thus the comparison of the Ludi Saeculares to a familiar Roman cultural experience would have guided the popular perception of the performance of 17 BCE.[73] But a purificatory act described in saecular discourse becomes exponentially more powerful: if the act leads to a new *saeculum*, then one is left with not a purified version of what existed before, but a fundamentally new and different version. The *saeculum*, like the *lustrum*, divided Roman history, but the simple quantitative aspect of the *lustrum* was exceeded by the qualitative, cosmic change of the

128 | *Saeculum*

saeculum.[74] This parallel between the *saeculum* and the *lustrum* perhaps explains how, at this time in Rome, both Vergil and Horace appear to use the word *lustrum* in their works to refer to a qualitatively defined period, that is, the *saeculum*.[75]

The importance of the celebration, and the suffusion of its imagery throughout wider Roman culture, is reflected in the numismatic record. While it is true that numismatic images do not offer a clear explanation of sophisticated concepts, nonetheless we can look to Roman coinage for general guidance regarding the interests of the contemporary community. A gold piece issued in 16 BCE commemorating the Ludi Saeculares features a wreathed Augustus on the obverse side and, on the reverse, a depiction of the *suffimenta*, in which Augustus (among other priestly officials) distributed purificatory incense cakes to Roman citizens in the days before the ceremony.[76] It is notable that the *suffimenta*, an interaction of the *princeps* with individual citizens, is the aspect of the ceremony chosen for commemoration; the participation of the people is stressed over any elite-flavored symbolism.[77] Through the burning of their own incense cakes, the Roman populace took part in the ritual cleansing of the city and so helped bring about a new *saeculum* of Roman history. The saecular nature of the Games was not an aspect presented solely to the antiquarian interests of the Roman intelligentsia, but was promulgated to a wide (and presumably comprehending) audience of the Roman people.

As we can see, the idea of the "Augustan *saeculum*" was a contemporary one, and the senatorial proposal to enter the term as such in the Roman Fasti, as we saw earlier, would only give a technical imprimatur to what was already an understood concept. The senator from the Suetonius anecdote proposed changing the Roman calendar to reflect that a new era of human life began on the day that Augustus was born. The wider Roman Empire saw another version of this concept: requiring a recalibration of all calendrical counting in certain provinces to begin with the date of Augustus's birth.[78] This additional Augustan epoch further integrated the *princeps* into his subjects' perception of the universe's divine order through saecular discourse, while simultaneously activating the skills of calendar specialists to deliberate on the facts about the date of this origin.

The proconsul Paullus in the province of Asia, in 9 BCE, proposed (unsuccessfully, it seems) that the Greek cities use the birthday of Augustus as the starting date for a new epoch.[79] A similar document,[80] in its explanation for why this unwieldy calendar change would be appropriate, notes that "the time for life begins from his birth."[81] It was in 9 BCE that Augustus first reformed the Julian calendar to account for a miscalculation of the intercalation of leap days,[82] so calendrical reform was already a major sociopolitical topic at this time; the proconsul's proposal did not come out of nowhere. But the qualitative characteristics associated with this temporal shift are highly suggestive of saecular discourse; the dating system reflected the fact that Augustus's birth heralded a new period of time distinct in some way from what came before it. To Friesen, "The proconsul's proposal to realign the calendar characterized the pre-Augustan period as a time of descent into chaos, the end of a degenerative process in which a disintegrating world was ready to fling itself headlong toward destruction. The birth of Augustus, however, represented the origin of a new age, the (re)creation of this world. Corporate existence and personal life were so profoundly affected that the birth of Augustus could be reckoned as the beginning of time."[83] Unlike the reform of the Julian calendar, which was a response to actual technical problems with the calculation of intercalary days, this proposed Augustan dating epoch, similar to actions of eastern kings of the Hellenistic era, was purely honorary in nature: "the realignment of Asia's calendars was not presented as a pragmatic proposal because pragmatism was not the paramount issue. . . . Augustus would make sense of time."[84] The new Augustan *saeculum* needed to be reflected in the way that people recorded time itself.

The province of Asia was not the only place in the empire to imagine an Augustan *saeculum*. The Ara Numinis Augusti, set up at Narbo in 12 or 13 CE, celebrated the birthday of Augustus and commemorated the day when the "good fortune of the age" brought about a new leader for the entire world: *qua die eum saeculi felicitas orbi terrarum rectorem edidit*.[85] And Bickerman records that in certain eastern calendars, a new era of calculation began on the date of Augustus's victory at Actium;[86] choosing this moment as the metakosmetic transition into a new era, as opposed to the otherwise unremarkable day of Augustus's birth in 63 BCE, requires a less cosmic approach to a saecular narrative of the Augustan world.

The importance of the date of Augustus's birth in these calendar proposals may reflect a similar contemporary interest in the horoscope, and astrological sign, of Augustus.[87] The fact that Augustus was born before the Julian reform of the Roman calendar greatly

130 | *Saeculum*

increased the difficulty of selecting the date of Augustus's birth and, more importantly, under which sign the *princeps* was born (Capricorn or Libra).[88] There seems to have been no Roman consensus about this fact: Vergil (*G.* 1.32–35) and Manilius (4.546–551, 4.773–777) suggest that it was Libra, but elsewhere Manilius (2.507–509) as well as Germanicus (558–560) point to Capricorn.[89] Suetonius (*Aug.* 94.12) records an anecdote that Augustus had his full horoscope taken by a seer named Theogenes, who immediately recognized Augustus as a cosmically authorized figure. This so pleased Augustus that he struck a silver coin with the sign of Capricorn on it, and even published the results of the horoscope (Cassius Dio 56.25.5). Crucially, this gave Augustus the same horoscope as Rome's founder, Romulus, as Varro had earlier recorded.[90] Through this horoscope, Augustus then appears as a palingenetic or metempsychotic rebirth of the legendary founder; the new Augustan *saeculum* is a second Romulan *saeculum*.

The very idea of the Augustan epoch (especially as a benchmark for calendrical dating), beginning on the date of his birth, has an obvious connection to the actions of several Hellenistic kings, as has been long understood.[91] But it is crucial also to understand these developments in the context of the emergence of periodization as a dominant mode of intellectual thought in the first century BCE. Saecularity, through its connection to Etruscan divination, gives Augustus a divine imprimatur (via the cosmic control of a city's saecular timeline) and connects him and his age with the rest of Roman history, rather than isolating his reign as a *sui generis* period. Furthermore, the debate over the specifics of his birth reflects the specialized skill of technical scholars (who flourished in the decades preceding Augustus's rise) and their desire to understand with precision every aspect of their new version of history. The presence of Augustus on the calendar reifies the concept of the Augustan *saeculum* as a foundational attribute of world chronology from which further calculations must derive. It resembles the Suetonius anecdote's proposal as an honorific statement of his importance to a narrative of Roman history, but by merging saecular discourse with the technical discourse of ancient calendars, it necessarily expands the breadth of periodization's influence on the temporal perception of human history.

The rise of periodization and the prominence of saecular discourse among Roman intellectuals in the first century BCE made it easier for the Romans (including Augustus himself) to portray the Principate and its deeds as both revolutionary and reactionary; saecularity negotiates the tension between rupture and continuity by accounting for both as expressions of divine cosmic order. Nowhere is this negotiation more evident in the Augustan world than in the "Palatine Complex," a site that offers multiple examples of the power of saecular discourse to express the new reality of Rome under the Principate. Here the geographical location interacted with its markers of temporality to produce periodizing associations.

The Palatine Hill was the site of a variety of architectural projects during the first century BCE, in particular the personal home of Augustus himself, as well as the Temple of Apollo Palatinus and its adjacent Bibliotheca.[92] These buildings also played a part in the saecular discourse of Augustan triumphalism as evocations of the new Augustan *saeculum*. The Palatine, for Romans of the Augustan period, had a rich pedigree: it was the site of the grotto where the legendary she-wolf suckled Romulus and Remus, the site where Romulus had his own hut, and the site where Evander founded the first settlement at Rome. When Aeneas arrives in Italy in *Aeneid* 8, Vergil's Evander shows him (as we saw in chapter 2) the ruins of Saturn's Golden Age settlement around the Palatine. (If Augustus wanted to bring about the return of the Golden Age, it was perhaps no surprise that he would do so much of his work on the Palatine.) The Romulus connection of the Palatine, in particular, lends itself to the trend of Augustus depicting himself as the Romulus of the new *saeculum*;[93] in fact, he allegedly almost took the title "Romulus" instead of "Augustus" when these titular options were first debated.[94] Although the edifices in Augustus's Palatine Complex were new additions for a new Augustan Age, they nevertheless interacted with these fabled sites from Rome's legendary past, binding the complex to more familiar elements of Rome's history and suggesting temporal reoccurrences.

One such interaction involved Augustus's decision, when he became the *pontifex maximus*, not to move to the traditional residence near the Temple of Vesta in the Roman Forum, but to dedicate part of his house on the Palatine to the worship of Vesta as a *domus publica*.[95] The sacred fire of Vesta, maintained in the temple, was a symbol for the health and security of Rome as a city (and a people). By associating Vesta with his own home on the Palatine, Augustus encouraged the perception that by his personal oversight, the fortunes of Rome

132 | *Saeculum*

would be guarded anew (such as in *Ode* 4.15.17, *custode Caesare*); the Augustan Age was secure under the close supervision of the *princeps*.

A far greater application of periodizing connotations can be found in various elements of the Temple of Apollo Palatinus, dedicated in 28 BCE.[96] The choice of a temple to Apollo, as opposed to any of the other gods of the Roman pantheon, has invited comment, with one explanation being Apollo's relatively few prior associations in Roman architecture at that time.[97] But there may have been a saecular component to this as well: Nigidius Figulus, in his *De diis*, had described an Orphic sequence of *saecula* for human history ending with a permanent "Age of Apollo," as mentioned earlier.[98] Nigidius was also well known in Rome for allegedly predicting Augustus's eventual world domination on the day of Augustus's birth, during the deliberation of the Senate on the Catilinarian conspiracy.[99] Luke suggests that, partially because of this prediction in 63 BCE, Augustus may have appealed to the theological expertise of Nigidius and chosen to build a temple to the god whose *saeculum* was thought to usher in a permanent era of peace and happiness.[100]

Whether or not Augustus was thinking of such esoteric Orphic eschatology when he conceived of the details of the temple, certain Roman poets nevertheless connected it later with saecular discourse, as shown in earlier chapters. Propertius, in his visually engaged celebration of the opening of the temple in 2.31/32,[101] ultimately concludes the poem by giving a saecular narrative of Roman moral history, complete with the Saturnian Golden Age ending with a metakosmetic Flood of Deucalion. Ovid uses the entire Palatine complex (comparing, e.g., its current golden roof to its earlier thatched one) as a symbol of the age of *cultus* that had superseded the age of *rusticitas*.[102] And Ovid's Phaethon episode (*Met.* 1.747–2.400), examined in chapter 2 as a paradigmatic metakosmetic moment, has also been read in connection with the temple.[103] For the poets of the Augustan world, the temple inspired ideas about saecular transitions; these would have been further enhanced by the strong presence of the Palatine complex in the performance of the Ludi Saeculares (the site of the *suffimenta*, the sacrifice to Apollo and Diana, and the singing of the *Carmen Saeculare*).

Indeed, one effect of the prominence of the Palatine Hill, both in Roman life in general and in the Ludi Saeculares in particular, is that the Capitoline Hill, with its venerable (though recently rebuilt)

Temple of Jupiter Optimus Maximus, began to become less important in Roman cultural life. Feeney points out that Apollo (and Diana) are far more crucial than Juno and Jupiter in Horace's *Carmen Saeculare*: "The eclipse of the old Capitoline deities by the Palatine gods of the *princeps* is most remarkable, and it has been exposed more nakedly in ten minutes of singing than it had been in three days of ritual action."[104] Horace himself had described the hymn as a prayer to Apollo and Diana, not mentioning other deities (*Ode* 4.6.37–38). Huskey has shown, in a perceptive article, that Ovid's wandering *libellus* in *Tristia* 3.1 completely ignores the Capitoline Hill, as though it does not even exist anymore; its focus is mainly on the Palatine complex.[105] The Capitoline Hill mattered for the previous *saeculum*, but in the Augustan *saeculum* it is the Palatine that is the sociocultural *omphalos* of the city.

A diachronic perspective on the Temple of Apollo Palatinus reveals two primary phenomena about Roman sociopolitical interactions with the temple.[106] The first is the eventual association of the Temple of Apollo Palatinus not with the lightning prodigy that resulted in its construction,[107] nor with the Battle of Naulochus, after which the temple was announced, but with the Battle of Actium,[108] which preceded the dedication of the temple. Thus the poems of Horace and Propertius from the late 20s BCE focus on those aspects of Apollo associated with music and poetry (pastimes of peace),[109] while later works by Vergil and Propertius imply or flatly declare the temple's connection with Actium.[110] The other phenomenon apparent from this study is the slow transfer of social importance from the Temple of Jupiter Optimus Maximus to the Temple of Apollo. A visual and topographical competitor with the Temple of Jupiter since its dedication, the Temple of Apollo increasingly takes on the associations of its Capitoline rival (such as in triumphs and the storage of the Sibylline Books)[111] to the point that Ovid could viably ignore the Capitoline completely. These processes were gradual, and interactions with Apollo Palatinus were not static but dynamic and shifting throughout the Augustan Age; the addition of saecular resonances no doubt played a part in both these shifts. Indeed, saecularity helps explain the transition as both revolutionary and traditional: the Palatine takes on several of the aspects formerly connected to the Capitoline, but still preserves them as recognizable elements of Roman culture. Another example will clarify this process: the Sibylline Books.

134 | *Saeculum*

Perhaps the most significant connection to saecularity in the Temple of Apollo Palatinus, and another example of cultural importance shifting from the Capitoline to the Palatine, is its housing of the Sibylline Books transferred from the Temple of Jupiter Optimus Maximus by Augustus, where they were managed by the *XVviri*.[112] In 12 BCE, upon becoming *pontifex maximus*,[113] Augustus placed the Sibylline Books in gold cases beneath the cult statue of Apollo inside the temple,[114] having removed spurious verses from the rolls. While the contents of the Sibylline Books were meant to be state secrets, consulted only when necessary, the general understanding was that they contained prophetic writings of the Cumaean Sibyl and instructions for expiating malign omens. It was through the *XVviri*'s consultation of the Sibylline Books that Augustus justified his recalibration of the saecular counting system. The citation by Vergil of "Cumaean song" containing a cycle of *saecula* (*Ecl.* 4.4–5) further contributes to this perception that the Sibylline Books held the authority to describe a saecular narrative for Roman history.

This perception explains the otherwise unaccountable presence[115] in Tibullus 2.5 of a brief reference to the transition of the Saturnian Golden Age to the Silver Age ruled over by Jupiter (9–10):[116] the poem begins by describing the installation in 21 BCE of Messallinus (son of Tibullus's patron Messalla) as a new member of the *XVviri*, handling the Sibylline Books in the Temple of Apollo Palatinus. As a member of this priestly college, Messallinus has access to the saecular lore of the Sibylline Books and can learn about any impending (or recent) metakosmesis while within the walls of the temple. Thus the Temple of Apollo Palatinus, through its housing of the Sibylline Books, was a site understood to house the very instruments of saecular discourse. The Sibylline Books demonstrate how Augustus could explain his actions as a rupture in Roman history (through the new edifices on the Palatine) while also maintaining continuity with the past (since the Palatine, like the Capitoline before it, was the site of the consultation of the Sibylline Books after major omens, and the books were, like the Ludi Saeculares, primarily lustral in purpose). Saecular discourse allows Augustus to alter the urban landscape dramatically without suggesting that a total break in the narrative of Roman history has occurred.

6 | Pyramids and Fish Wrappers
Roman Literary Periodization

In chapter 4 I examined the phenomenon of the "technical history," which appeared prominently during the first century BCE and made much use of the language of periodization. While I demonstrated examples of histories in a variety of fields, such as law and medicine, I neglected to discuss the history of one particular field: literature. Literary histories can be considered special examples of Roman technical histories because they can be interpreted by readers, or created by writers, in two ways. One method is the narrative description of literary development in a direct way, just like any other technical history; Cicero and Horace, and later Quintilian and Tacitus, give us examples of such histories. Alternatively, through one's own discursive practices in one's own works of literature, an author can articulate a literary history without an explicit declaration of intent. Hinds has written that, through allusive practices, Roman authors produce strategic literary histories into which they can situate their own works even as they write them.[1] Thus, whether as an "objective" outsider analyzing literary history from a level of remove, or as a participant in that literary history itself, Roman writers were actively involved in narrativizing the history of Roman literature.

In the most general sense, Roman writers were able to discuss literary history in a number of structural possibilities. For example, they could create a canon, and by so doing select which authors "mattered" in a timeless sense or were otherwise worthy of rereading throughout posterity. Ovid, to name just one author, articulates literary canons in several of his works: *Amores* 1.15 gives a long list of Greek and Roman authors who have achieved particularly noteworthy fame, and even more pointedly, in his *Ars amatoria* (3.329–348)

136 | *Saeculum*

Ovid supplies a list of canonical Roman authors that a well-educated woman ought to know. A similar method of creating a simplistic history of literature is through the use of a chronology, or a list of names of dates: Cornelius Nepos, in his *Chronica*, provides the years during which various writers were alive and active, without any larger structure or explicit aim. The canon and the chronology offer no analysis of the arc of literary history, but simply give a static list of major authors possibly arranged in chronological order.

There are certainly other methods of demonstrating one's literary predecessors in a basic way. But when Romans wanted to narrativize literary history, particularly the history of Roman literature, they needed a more complex model, one in which the changes in literature over time seem to have occurred in a coherent way. One such model, as should be clear, was saecular discourse: periodization inherently narrativizes history by creating a broader arc for the *saecula* to follow (and we saw several examples of such arcs in chapter 4's account of technical histories). In this chapter, I will examine the influence of periodization on the Roman cognitive organization of literature and analyze examples of saecular approaches to literary history. But I will begin first by discussing the two alternative models with which periodization competed: I term these alternatives the "evolutionary model" and the "genealogical model."[2]

Cicero's *Brutus*, in his account of the history of oratory in Rome, provides the most robust example of the evolutionary model of literary history.[3] In this model, Roman literary development (primarily in oratory for Cicero, but ultimately in all fields of art, including poetry and sculpture) improves incrementally from major author to major author, with the underlying assumption that all authors are in some way derivative of an immediate predecessor; eventually, literature achieves a state of perfection, beyond which there can be no further positive development. Indeed, the *Brutus* gives a narrative that is not only evolutionary but also teleological,[4] aiming toward a level of mastery that is (implicitly) the oratory of Cicero himself. This process is a deterministic one: Cicero "explains Roman oratory by presenting its history within a general scheme of literary progress that applies Aristotelian concepts of inherent nature (*physis*) and goal (*telos*) to literary phenomena."[5]

Cicero aptly summarizes the thrust of the evolutionary model at *Brutus* 70–71, where he describes the step-by-step progress to perfection that occurred in the visual arts; no art is invented and perfected at the same time (*nihil est enim simul et inventum et perfectum*), he explains. The danger to literary culture offered by the evolutionary model is that earlier authors can fade into obscurity as they are supplanted by better works, in a cruel "survival of the fittest." Cicero points out that the most well-known speech of the orator Curio, which was hailed as a masterpiece even in Cicero's boyhood, had by the time of writing become almost totally forgotten in light of newer and "superior" works (122). Hinds makes clear that one major goal of the *Brutus* is to reaffirm the importance of Cato the Elder to modern Roman oratory, lest he be forgotten; for Cicero, the evolutionary model compels anyone praising the perfect artists to acknowledge the importance of those predecessors through which the process of development has achieved such perfection.[6]

Cicero is not the only Roman author to describe literary history with the evolutionary model: Vitruvius, in the preface to book 7 of his *De architectura*, suggests a similar explanation for the technical arts.[7] Vitruvius describes the process of technical writing as a gradual accretion of knowledge, in which works grow from generation to generation (*singulis aetatibus crescentia*, 7.pr.1) as authors take the *commentarii* and *praecepta* of their predecessors and add their own knowledge (as Vitruvius himself did with architectural knowledge). Writers should not claim to have brought entirely new and original technical works into the world, Vitruvius suggests, as illustrated by two anecdotal examples from literary scholars at Alexandria (7.pr.4–9). Just as Cicero sought to reaffirm for his contemporaries the importance of Cato the Elder to Roman literary history, Vitruvius insists that writers should not suppress their sources, and he himself writes that he does not hide his authorities from other ages but openly credits them (7.pr.10).

Thus, one way to tell the "story" of Roman literary development was to posit a slow, gradual development in the quality and range of Roman literature from its origins to a possible climax, with each writer building off of the work of previous others. Another option for narrativizing the history of Roman literature was the genealogical model: authors situate themselves and/or their works within a sort of "family tree" of influence and adaptation, distinguishing them from other contemporaries and other participants in the history of the field. Genealogies were always an important aspect of elite Roman culture, and in the first century BCE in particular there was a trend of aristocratic genealogies tracing an elite family's lineage back to a

138 | *Saeculum*

divinity or some participant of the Trojan War.[8] It is perhaps no surprise, then, that Roman writers felt compelled to concoct literary family trees to enhance their own prestige or justify their aesthetic choices. The scope of the genealogical model can vary; for example, it can be used to trace the history of all of Roman literature or a particular genre (such as elegy or satire). By doing so, an author achieves literary authority through situating himself in a lineal succession with other well-known literary figures. The impression created by such a narrative, though, is that the genre (or whatever the focus is) has no meaningful differences from writer to writer within the tree; the narrative aspect of the model can only explain how one differed from one's peers.

Propertius provides us with a paradigmatic example of the genealogical model. At the end of Propertius 2.34, the last ten lines of the poem create a family tree of Roman elegists, with their five names placed as the last words of each hexameter line: Varro (of Atax), Catullus, Calvus, Gallus, Propertius. Each man is connected to the name of his single beloved, further making it clear that Propertius is depicting these men as elegiac poets. Thus, Propertius narrativizes the history of Roman elegy, with himself as the latest in a long line of elegists (and thus in some sense already a peer of the other four).[9] Later, Ovid will go one step further and make his genealogical model fairly explicit at *Tristia* 4.10. The poem acts as a quasi-autobiography for Ovid, and at lines 41–56 he describes looking up to the older famous poets when he was first writing. In just one couplet, Ovid tells the compressed history of Roman elegy. Tibullus was the *successor* (53) to Gallus, and Propertius to Tibullus, and Ovid to Propertius; Ovid declares himself fourth in the series (54). As Cairns points out, "each [poet] is trying to present himself in the most acceptable light of the moment, and in both cases special pleading is manifest."[10] Both poets present artificial literary genealogies, with major names tendentiously included or excluded, in order to create a narrative of Roman literary history.

It is not elegy alone that is the focus of such historicizing. Horace often depicts himself as the only son of Lucilius within Roman satire (thus writing Ennius, who also wrote satires, out of the family tree), but in *Satires* 1.4 Horace depicts Lucilius himself as a follower (*secutus*, 6) of Eupolis, Cratinus, Aristophanes, and other playwrights of Old Comedy (1–2). In their willingness to pick on public figures deserving of reproach, the men of Old Comedy had something in

Pyramids and Fish Wrappers | 139

common with Lucilius, and so in Horace's narrative of ancient literature, Lucilius acts as an heir to their legacy.[11] Horace even narrativizes the early history of drama at Athens (*Ars P.* 275–284), in which Thespis founds the line, Aeschylus follows him, and the Old Comedy playwrights succeed (*successit*, 281) him before drama decays into ribaldry.

The genealogical model can thus focus on the history of one particular genre. Alternatively, an author can use the genealogical model to demonstrate the literary history of his own source material. We see this approach in the prologues of Roman comedy (thus suggesting that the genealogical model is older than the evolutionary). At its simplest, the playwright indicates the Greek source of his comedy, such as is typical in Plautine prologues.[12] Terence tends to use the model in a more complex way, demonstrating the full range of source material he has used in his play. For example, in the prologue to the *Andria*, Terence not only argues for his play being the product of two Menander originals, but also declares Naevius, Plautus, and Ennius (with their similar "contaminations") to be his methodological models (*auctores*, 19).

The comic playwrights trace genealogies back to Greek originals while avoiding connections to earlier Latin comedies. In the prologue to his *Adelphoe*, Terence stresses that although his play contains a word-for-word adaptation of a scene from an earlier Diphilus comedy, it has nothing in common with the Plautus play that drew more heavily from Diphilus (6–14). Consequently, the genealogical model can, in the hands of an enemy, be a criticism instead of a source of authority. In the prologue to his *Eunuchus*, Terence describes how his enemy Luscius argued that the *Eunuchus* did not trace its lineage directly to the Menander original but was fourth in a line that also included plays by Naevius and Plautus. Terence is forced to deny that he adapted these earlier Latin plays, and he insists that any resemblance to them comes from his adaptations of an entirely different Menander play with a similar structure (27–34).

Thus, the comic playwrights narrativize Roman literary history to obtain a measure of poetic authority from their family tree; in their case, status is improved by declaring succession from a Greek original and worsened by the possibility of having succeeded an earlier Latin author. But furthermore, they also use their genealogies to demonstrate how their works are adaptations, and thus are different not only from their predecessors but also, more importantly,

140 | *Saeculum*

from their competitors (who may also draw a lineal succession from the same origins). Essentially, these playwrights draw a connection to an earlier model in order to demonstrate something special about their works, almost as if promoting a sense of literary development within their family tree.

The narrativization of the history of the genre through the genealogical model can take a variety of forms, depending on what sort of "story" one wants to tell. Ovid's family tree of elegy is tantalizingly different from Propertius's, though unfortunately Ovid does not clarify why he excludes Varro, Catullus, and Calvus, nor does Propertius do so for his exclusion of Tibullus; various explanations have been given.[13] As we have seen, the genealogical model can be used to create historical narratives of literary stasis, joining writers who are not obviously similar in order to exploit key linkages; alternatively, the narrative created by such a literary genealogy could occlude certain influences or emphasize developments that distinguish branches of the tree. Obviously, there are some points of overlap between the evolutionary and genealogical models; one could perhaps make the argument that Cicero's *Brutus* is a sort of genealogical narrative of Roman oratory not dissimilar to Ovid's narrative of elegy, and Horace's genealogy of drama is very nearly a (d)evolutionary description.

I have devoted considerable space to describing the various methods of historical narrativization among literary figures because I wanted to demonstrate that there was nothing inevitable about the popularity of periodization in the first century BCE; satisfactory methods of historiography already existed. Choosing a model of literary narrativization was a strategic decision, since in essence each model holds a potentially competing view of Roman literary history. Cicero gives himself honors by showing how different (i.e., better) he is from the people at the beginning of his oratorical lineage, whereas Ovid acquires prestige by stressing how very similar he is to Gallus at the head of his line. Furthermore, the genealogical model serves writers who are at a status disadvantage (literary and otherwise), while the evolutionary model benefits more established figures: the youthful works of Ovid gain an enhanced position when presented in the company of already respected works by Gallus, Propertius, and Tibullus, while Cicero (writing the *Brutus* long after his reputation as an orator had been made) seeks to claim for himself special status above earlier famed orators, having no need merely to align himself with them. Both the evolutionary and genealogical models give historical narratives that stress continuity, but as we will now see, the saecular model is a story of abrupt historical ruptures. Periodization was a dominant mode of discourse throughout the first century BCE, and it found popularity in the realm of Roman literary history as well.

The "Neoteric" Poets and the Saecular Model

While the evolutionary and genealogical models described above continued to be used throughout the first century BCE and beyond, a periodizing model emerged during the middle of the first century BCE that instead organized Roman literary history into *saecula*. The emergence of this model is most associated with those Latin poets who have tended to be labeled "neoteric" by scholars, after a comment by Cicero (*Att.* 7.2).[14] Much scholarly debate has centered on the specifics, or even the existence, of just such a poetic "school" in Rome at this time. The evidence to suggest that there was a homogeneous community of poets with identical aesthetic criteria is so slender that some scholars have suggested that we simply stop using the word "neoteric" to describe them.[15] Although I fully concede that the neoteric poets' (hypothesized) claims of Parthenius-inspired revolution hide their real debt to earlier Latin poets,[16] nonetheless I will continue to use the term "neoteric" throughout this project. I use it not to define a coherent aesthetic movement but simply to refer to Hellenistic- or Callimachean-minded poets in the decades before Vergil.[17] These neoteric poets, whatever their interest in Callimachean poetics may be, nonetheless share a more genuinely innovative view of temporality with regard to Roman literary history, as my readings will show. I argue here that, in response to the evolutionary model, these neoteric poets use the word *saeculum* as a signifier for a particular narrative about Roman literary history, which for them is a history divided into *saecula*.

The forces shaping this periodized schematic are twofold: Roman literary history is organized into qualitative *saecula* defined both by popular appeal and by aesthetic evaluation. It is a reformulation of the idea of poetic immortality; renown is a function of temporary sociocultural forces, but the best poetry survives the changing tastes both of the general public audience and of the more selective art

142 | *Saeculum*

world (two communities whose participants do not always overlap). The neoteric poets use periodization to demonstrate the fickleness of popularity while hoping for a fame that lasts for all *saecula*, not just one. Their awareness of the desultory tastes of the Roman literary audience compel their organization of Roman literary history into *saecula*, and they hope to produce a work of literary greatness that subverts this very saecularity and thus achieve literary immortality (i.e., by writing a work that will be celebrated in every *saeculum*). Not every reference to poetic immortality, of course, must be read as part of a saecular model of Roman literary history, but such references do occur frequently in a poetic context of qualitative aesthetic *saecula*. Both the saecular model and the evolutionary model suggest changing tastes, but there is a crucial ideological difference: for Cicero (whose focus is largely elite and culturally conservative), these changes are gradual and explicable, whereas for first-century BCE poets with a cynical perspective toward the opinions of both tastemakers and the masses, shifting trends occur suddenly, sharply, and largely at random.

It will be useful to start by examining the best-preserved of these neoteric poets, Catullus, who evokes saecular literary histories in three poems (1, 14, and 95). In the first poem, Catullus expresses the hope that his poetic *libellus* will last (*maneat*, 10) more than one *saeculum* and possibly endure forever (*perenne*, 10). The line is well known to allude to Callimachus's *Aetia* 1 (fr. 7.13–14 Pfeiffer), but whereas Callimachus uses the word ἔτος ("year," or perhaps "time"), Catullus chooses the far more culturally loaded term *saeculum*. The wish for a fame that will last more than one *saeculum* is directed toward the "patron goddess" (*patrona virgo*, 9) of Catullus, implying that control over the extension of literary fame to more than one *saeculum* is held at a cosmic level.[18]

Catullus offers this *libellus* to Cornelius Nepos, a noted Roman historian who had written the *Chronica*, a three-volume work (*tribus chartis*, 6) on the history of the world, or perhaps on "each and every age" (*omne aevum*). The phrase *omne aevum* is a peculiar one in this context; virtually every other first-century BCE usage of *omne aevum* (e.g., *Aen.* 9.609, Pollio's *Historiae* fr. 7; even slightly later works such as Manilius's *Astronomica* 1.46) refers to the entirety of one person's life, but here the sense is clearly something larger in scope. Skinner would like to read *omne aevum* as a phrase that refers to all of recorded time, such as the *memoria aevi* of Livy 26.22.2 and Tacitus, *Annales* 4.35, but "the employment of the generalized abstraction *omne aevum* as a substitute for the actual technical term *memoria* (in the sense of 'tradition, history', *OLD* s.v., 7) does not occur elsewhere in classical Latin (see *TLL* 1.1167.50–62)."[19] Indeed, I contend that with this phrase Catullus does not speak in general terms of "history" or "time" but specifically emphasizes multiple *saecula* of history: all of history can be divided into multiple ages, and Nepos has written about each one.[20]

Based on the scant fragments of the works of Nepos that have survived, we can hypothesize why Nepos was chosen by Catullus to be the object of the formulaic dedication for his *libellus*. In certain surviving fragments Nepos discusses the poets Homer and Hesiod, as well as Archilochus (F1 and F4 Cornell); at the very least, he discusses their relative dating. Starr suggests that Catullus dedicates the *libellus* to Nepos because the latter's inclusion of certain poets in his chronographic work confers the kind of eternal significance (within a chronologically minded setting) that Catullus is expressly seeking.[21] Catullus hopes to last more than one *saeculum* because that would mean his poetry's fame was not the fleeting, crowd-pleasing fame that his poetic rivals earned (such as he will mention in poems 14 and 95); Nepos, as a discerning historian, included in his work only those poets who achieved such a lasting fame, and thus Catullus chose him as the dedicatee of the *libellus* in this programmatic intro.[22]

Catullus 14 also discusses literature in terms of literary saecularity, but its focus is on the other side of the equation: poorly written poems. Catullus receives a book of lousy verse as a holiday gag gift from his friend and fellow neoteric poet Calvus, and he threatens to return the favor. These bad poets are described as the detriments, or burdens, of the current age (*saecli incommoda*, 23), but for whom are they burdens? If they are popular enough to take up space on the shelves of the booksellers (*librariorum scrinia*, 17–18), then they must not be universally loathed. Either they are burdens on the new era of neoteric aesthetics (by providing overwrought competition), or they are burdens for Catullus and his friends of similar taste during this particular era of poetry, and the gifted book of terrible poetry certainly seems to be a burden on Catullus. The gag gift, when understood as such (aided by the Saturnalian context evoked at line 15),[23] can express Catullus's and Calvus's aesthetic tastes just as much as sincere gifts can.[24]

144 | *Saeculum*

As we can see, poems 1 and 14 in the surviving Catullan corpus have a clear structural and linguistic similarity, and the poems present "positive and negative paradigms of his poetic doctrine."[25] Not only do both refer to *libelli* presented as gifts and address distinguished literary figures, but as Hubbard points out, both poems give special emphasis to the term *saeculum*: "Catullus prays to the Muse that his book last more than one *saeclo* (1.10, the last word of the last line), while the poets of Calvus' book are a pain to the present *saecli* (14.23, the first word of the last line)."[26] Bad poetry is not instantly forgotten, and in fact the works of these bad poets in 14 are successfully being sold (and in this case, purchased by Sulla, the client of Calvus). But unlike the Catullan *libellus*, these bad poets have no future to hope for; they will be a burden on the current *saeculum*, but no future ones.

The fate of bad poetry is described in Catullus 95, a poem contrasting the erudite *Zmyrna* of the neoteric poet Cinna with the bloated *Annales* of the poet Volusius of Hatra and the similarly swollen Antimachus.[27] The pages of Volusius will soon end up not in an elegantly appointed scroll but as a fish wrapper, and in the same Paduan backwater they were born, they will die (*morientur*, 7).[28] This death is a crucial point: bad poetry has no hopes for the sort of literary immortality that Catullus and the neoteric poets seek.[29] While the Catullan *libellus* will outlive one *saeculum*, and the *Zmyrna* of Cinna will be read by so many *saecula* of readers that the *saecula* themselves will turn gray (*cana saecula*, 6, the poem evidently outliving time itself), the *Annales* of Volusius will not survive; regardless of how well Volusius sells in the booksellers' market or how much the *populus* (10) praises Antimachus in the current era, bad poetry will not reach another *saeculum*. The implication must be that fame granted by a *populus*, instead of by a *patrona virgo* or a scholar like Nepos, is doomed to single-*saeculum* length.[30] The bad poetry attacked in Catullus 14 will soon be garbage as well, and in preparation for dying in its birthplace, Catullus punningly orders it to "go back thither whence you brought your wicked feet" (*abite illuc unde malum pedem attulistis*, 14.21–22). Space complements time here, as bad poetry dies in its birthplace while Cinna's *Zmyrna* travels the world (95.5).

Thus, in poems 1, 14, and 95, Catullus repeats certain important details: discussions of poetics, considerations of literary posterity, and the use of the word *saeculum*.[31] Given the significance of these poems as programmatic statements of Catullus's approach to aesthetics,[32] we should consider *saeculum* (a word found so prominently placed in 1 and 14) as a term with special connotations for Catullus's sense of literary history.[33] We can also discern in the fragments of other neoteric poets some further examples of the language of saecularity.[34] Cinna (fr. 14 Hollis) expresses with familiar language a hope similar to that of Catullus 1.10 when he writes, "May our Valerius Cato's *Dictynna* last for *saecula*" (*saecula permaneat nostri Dictynna Catonis*).[35] Batstone, noting the affinity between Cinna fr. 14 Hollis and Catullus 1.10, posits that "these are poets who know each other's poetry and who share a common language and common aesthetic values."[36] Here the shared attitude is toward the ability of learned verse, as opposed to popular drivel, to survive the vicissitudes of audience taste.

Not every use of the term *saeculum* in neoteric poetry must be a reference to a saecular model of literary history. Elsewhere,[37] Cinna mentions "huge heaps of gifts piled up from everywhere over innumerable centuries" (*innumerabilibus saeclis*, fr. 6.2 Hollis). In context, it is fairly certain that Cinna refers here with *saeclis* merely to hundred-year periods (and not ideologically marked periods), since he is describing historical time; the fragment refers to a great religious shrine to which offerings have been made from every source going back to such mythical figures as Cecrops, Cadmus, Danaus, and Aegyptus. But Q. Mucius Scaevola, another poet of this time, allusively spins the phrase into saecular discourse (fr. 91 Hollis) in his praise of the *Marius* of Cicero: "It will grow old during innumerable *saecula*" (*canescet saeclis innumerabilibus*). Hollis contends that the twist by Scaevola of Cinna's phrase into a loaded aesthetic valuation reflects the widely divergent composition methods of Cinna and Cicero (the former took nine years to finish his *Zmyrna*, while the latter could write five hundred lines in one night).[38] It may be surprising to see the poetry of Cicero described with terminology more normally associated with the neoterics he so detested, but as Knox points out, the youthful Cicero embraced the Hellenistic tradition (though not the Callimacheanism of Catullus and his friends).[39] Although Cicero's conception of Roman literary history in the *Brutus* was the evolutionary model and not the saecular model, one must keep in mind that it is Scaevola, not Cicero, who invokes saecularity here in his description of poetic posterity.

Catullus's friend Furius Bibaculus may provide a further example of the neoteric attitude toward literary periodization. A fragment of his poetry (preserved at, and perhaps misunderstood by, Suetonius's

146 | *Saeculum*

Gram. et rhet. 9.6) asks, "Where on earth is Orbilius, literature's forgotten man?" (*Orbilius ubinam est, litterarum oblivio,* fr. 83 Hollis). Hollis has suggested, following the argument of Nisbet, that this line refers to a writer who was formerly famous but who has been replaced by changing aesthetic preferences—in other words, disfavored in a new literary *saeculum*.[40] Furius Bibaculus also seems to have discussed the poet and scholar Valerius Cato in three other fragments (fr. 84–86 Hollis), where he seems to have treated Cato as a canon-forming tastemaker "who alone chooses and makes poets" (*qui solus legit ac facit poetas,* fr. 86 Hollis).[41] Although these fragments are too meager to allow us to draw any large inferences, one cannot help but wonder if Furius Bibaculus participated in the same sort of rhetoric of periodized aesthetics that his neoteric peers seem to have followed.

The pattern that emerges from these various examples of neoteric use of saecular terminology is the creation of a forward-looking Roman literary history through periodization.[42] The neoterics imagine discrete *saecula* based on popular appeal, which is not fixed and thus cannot confer the literary immortality they seek. In order to maintain renown from *saeculum* to *saeculum*, the poetry must possess a transcendent genius that will be identifiable in any *saeculum* of aesthetic taste (instead of just the trends of the moment). Moreover, the saecular model of literary history can serve as a weapon to use against one's rivals: even if a poetic enemy is currently successful and popular, the saecular model provides a way for one to explain how that enemy will nevertheless fall eventually into obscurity. Such a weapon is inherently unstable, however, since such discourse must necessarily also apply to one's own works. Hence, Roman poets embracing a saecular literary history are particularly interested in declaring their own immortality, or more specifically, in declaring that their works will survive not just one *saeculum* but all of them. Of course, one could also interpret the use of the saecular model as a latent attack on the readership aptitude of the Roman people in general (since their tastes are almost randomly fickle), which provides a further attack: anyone who appeals to the general populace is already tainted. The only true way to transcend saecular tastes, in this interpretation, is to ignore the crowd altogether and to focus solely on the appreciation of a small circle of friends and *literati*; this inward-looking approach to literature and aesthetics is another common feature of the work of the neoteric poets.

Horace on the Saecular Model

Cicero's *Brutus*, the earliest surviving Latin work that explicitly tackles Roman literary history, narrativized Roman literature with an evolutionary model. The next surviving example of direct historical analysis, Horace's *Epistula* 2.1, lacks as obvious and rigid a structure as Cicero's approach but nonetheless clearly demonstrates an interest in the saecular model of literary history, perhaps reflecting the influence of the periodizing mode propagated by Catullus and the neoteric poets. While the neoteric poets conceived of saecular literary history as a way to dismiss the popularity of upstart rival poets, Horace, receiving periodization as an established approach to understanding Roman literature, adapts the model to explain how the Roman people can reject all new poets (rival and friend alike) in favor of older works. Although the exact target of Horace's criticisms in this work cannot be known (and it may not be in reference to specific Romans), he clearly discusses the saecular model of literary development as a valid, well-known concept in the Roman intellectual world. Saecular discourse would appear to have permeated wider Roman audiences by the time Horace discusses periodization within Roman literary history.[43]

Horace's main complaint in *Epistula* 2.1 is that the saecular model can too easily be perverted by uncritical Roman readers whose artificial systems of literary organization are hopelessly, perhaps dangerously, inaccurate (but nonetheless influential). Primarily, Horace targets divisions into "old" and "new" Roman literature, in which any work of old literature is given blanket preference over new works. Horace's mockery of contemporary aesthetes whose zeal is directed solely at antiquities includes a *sorites* argument to demonstrate the absurdity of separating literature into "old" and "new" periods (34–49). But his point is not so much that periodization itself is fatally flawed; rather, his critique is that literature cannot be judged by its date of composition and instead must be judged by its literary merit, a valuation that permits both old classics and new successes (such as Horace's own poetry production) to be considered worthy of praise.

Horace stages an argument (36–39) between himself and a hypothetical critic (perhaps a stand-in for the general reading public) to decide how far in the past "old" literature must be. They declare that a writer who has been dead over one hundred years can

148 | *Saeculum*

be considered "old" (and thus superior), and that anyone else is to be considered "contemporary" (and thus inferior). Horace chooses a specific time limit solely to demonstrate the absurdity (through his *sorites* argument) of making aesthetic valuations based only on chronology, but his chosen duration here is more pointed. The word *saeculum*, as a term for a time period, had two primary definitions, the more general of which was simply "a period of one hundred years" (such as the modern "century"). This hundred-year *saeculum* was in contrast to the more variable Etruscan *saeculum* or, more to the point, the qualitative *saeculum* of saecular discourse. Horace's number is thus not randomly chosen: he demonstrates that a quantitatively defined chronological marker (particularly one defined by this rolling turning point between old and new) is an insufficient criterion for a saecular model of literary history, which requires a new structure based on aesthetic criteria.[44]

The sloppy periodization of Rome's current batch of readers leads to an extreme "flattening out" of the distinctions between the Roman poets of Horace's ancient past. For the popular audience in Horace's Rome, Roman literature in the period (*aevum*, 62) of Livius Andronicus that precedes Horace's own period (*ad nostrum tempus*, 62) is totally undifferentiated. As a result, the *populus* (18) knows no better than to treat even the rough prose of the Twelve Tables and early treaties as literary works inspired by the Muses (23–27), since all they consider is that these writings are old works. Ennius may have seen himself at the time as superior to Naevius, even a second Homer (*alter Homerus*, 50), but now the two are placed on the same vague level of quality (50–54).[45] When one misapplies the saecular model, Horace points out, every old poem is equally venerable, regardless of actual merit (*adeo sanctum est vetus omne poema*, 54).[46]

Despite these criticisms, Horace seems to be aware of, and in favor of, periodization. He supports the idea that Lucilius and he himself occupy different aesthetic ages in *Satires* 1.10.67–71, where he declares that if Lucilius were alive in the current *saeculum* (*nostrum aevum*, 68) he would follow its particular aesthetic guidelines.[47] Although Lucilius himself was more polished (*limatior*, 65) than the group of older poets preceding him (*poetarum seniorum turba*, 67), he would need to pare down his poetry to fit the aesthetics of Horace's time (69–71). This language of "smoothing" or "paring down" his poems signals the Callimachean aesthetics that are closely associated with Catullus and his contemporaries, the introducers of saecular

Pyramids and Fish Wrappers | 149

literary history to the Roman intellectual world.[48] Thus Horace is ready to imagine a set of aesthetic criteria characteristic of his own literary *saeculum* to which Lucilius would be obligated to adhere (and different sets for previous *saecula*).[49]

Were this neo-Lucilius transplanted to Horace's literary world unwilling to alter his poetry, it would presumably end up sent out of Rome to the provinces, its pages eaten by moths, a fate he elsewhere suggests may come to his own book of letters (*Epist.* 1.20.11–13). This image is a Horatian twist on the neoteric fear of poetic mortality in a provincial backwater, such as is expressed in Catullus 95 (7–8) and appears again at the end of *Epistula* 2.1 (*quidquid chartis amicitur ineptis*, 270). The intertextual link to Catullus's other *saeculum* poems is clear in this later Horatian example: *chartis* recalls 1.6, and the context of an unwanted gift (*munere*, 267) of bad poetry resembles poem 14, where Calvus's gift (*munere*, 14.2) of bad poems is a blight on the *saeculum*.[50] In the case of *Epistula* 1.20, Horace imagines that the book will receive this fate only after "the *aetas* abandons you" (*te deserat aetas*, 10). The suggestion here is that after a shift in the aesthetic preferences of the contemporary literary *saeculum*, a work that once seemed beloved will be scorned and forgotten.[51] While Catullus and his contemporaries (and the Augustan poets that followed them) hoped for a fame that transcended the shifting tastes of literary *saecula*, here Horace more modestly predicts that the popularity of this first book of epistles cannot avoid future oblivion. In Horace's periodized literary history, being considered passé is the mark of a work aligned with the wrong era, and aesthetics out of step with the trends of the age will doom any piece of literature.[52]

Thus Horace gives two possibilities of saecular literary histories at Rome. In *Epistula* 1.20, works praised by the people in the current *saeculum* will be validly ignored in the next (as this is the natural progression of tastes).[53] But as a more disillusioned Horace describes in *Epistula* 2.1, works are unjustly ignored by the people in the current *saeculum*, and will be unjustly praised in the next, because the tastemakers have selected the wrong criterion (namely, composition date) for their aesthetic valuations.[54] His insistence on qualitative judgments (cf. *Epist.* 2.1.63–75) over strictly quantitative groupings reinforces the necessity of a historical narrative focused on aesthetics, and his awareness of the shifting aesthetic sensibilities of various periods of Roman literary history (and the ways in which changing tastes can negatively affect the appreciation of a work of literature)

150 | *Saeculum*

aligns with the anxieties of the earlier neoteric poets who sought a fame that would last forever in spite of the shifts of public opinion. The fact that the epistle is (at least nominally) addressed to Augustus himself further suggests that Horace was not thinking simply about his own literary reputation, moreover, but that he had in mind a much greater scope: the entire Roman literary culture, whose health and well-being he naturally cared for and which he deemed threatened by the misuse of critical judgment. While there remained several ways for Romans to talk about the history of their own body of literature, Horace's analysis of its development shows that the saecular model of Roman literary history had become a familiar option.

Augustan Anxieties

Because so much of the neoteric poetry of the mid-first century BCE is lost, it is difficult to gain a clear picture of exactly how, or how much, Catullus and his contemporaries used this saecular model of literary history, but in the better-preserved Augustan poetry that followed this period, we can find more obviously stated interactions with this model. I will begin with Horace's *Odes*; in 3.30, the final poem in his first composition of lyric poetry, we find a reflection on the poet's status as an immortalized artist. We can see in this programmatic conclusion to the entire *Odes* publication that Horace seeks a kind of poetic immortality similar to what the neoteric poets sought: a protection against the shifting tastes of the popular audience. This similarity is strengthened by several intertextual markers connecting him to earlier neoteric *saeculum* poems: *innumerabilis* (4; cf. the fragments of Cinna and Scaevola); *monumentum* (1; cf. Catullus 95.9, where Cinna's *Zmyrna* verses are *parva monumenta*); and *perennius* (1; cf. *perenne* at Catullus 1.10). While the term *saeculum* never appears in the poem, Horace may periphrastically approach the term with *innumerabilis annorum series* (4–5) and *temporum* (5).

One particular aspect of Catullus's reflections on poetic immortality that Horace transforms in *Odes* 3.30, however, is the fear of being relegated to a rural backwater upon a change into a new literary *saeculum*. Catullus threatens that the *Annales* of Volusius will die out by the river Padua (95.7)—but Horace, a proud product of Venusia, actually aspires to reach audiences at the Aufidus and Daunus Rivers in southern Italy (10–12). Thus Horace hopes his literary renown will

Pyramids and Fish Wrappers | 151

achieve geographical breadth as well as temporal length, an attitude distinguishing him from the neoterics.[55] Catullus and his friends only wanted to appeal to a certain kind of readership, namely a small, familiar, urban audience of his peers (or, to put it another way, the neoteric poets only cared about that kind of readership, to the exclusion of others); this inward-looking attitude is characteristic of Catullus and probably also the other neoteric poets. It is true that the Horatian attitude in the *Odes* is different from the one we get in *Epistula* 1.20 (where being sent to the provinces is a sign of aesthetic devaluation by the Roman populace), but achieving a breadth of popularity is presented positively in *Ars poetica* 345–346. This latter passage also mentions the Sosii, who appeared at *Epistulae* 1.20.2—perhaps this later work is responding to the earlier work with a changed attitude.[56]

Horace and the neoteric poets are closer in temperament, though, in their desire for a stable fame and for the achievement of a poetic mastery that would transcend the shifting tastes of each literary *saeculum*. Horace's claim of staying fresh with the praise of posterity (*usque ego postera crescam laude recens*, 3.30.7–8) suggests that in each *saeculum* to come, he will receive popular acclaim, preventing any loss of renown. Thus the structure of his immortality is periodized: no aesthetic *aetas* ever deserts him, but to every *aetas* he always seems *recens*, and by standing this saecular test of time (which physical objects like bronze and the pyramids ultimately cannot do), his renown will grow with each *saeculum* that he survives. The underlying fear, then, is that Horace might in some future *saeculum* achieve the *senectus* that doomed his book in *Epistula* 1.20; only by staying *recens* at each *aetas* can one avoid literary mortality.

With the saecular model, the possibility of poetic immortality is complicated by the awareness of the ever-changing status of public taste. For the neoteric poets, this discourse was a weapon against their enemies more than it was a problem for their own legacies. But the Augustan poets had actual concern for their popularity and success with readers, and periodization provided a solution for defending poor success in one's own lifetime. Ovid expresses his anxiety about the possibility of future *saecula* of readers and poets changing their opinion about his immortal fame, with comments appearing in three programmatic conclusions to his works: *Amores* 1.15, *Tristia* 4.10, and the *sphragis* of *Metamorphoses* 15 (871–879). Multiple intertextual markers show the relationship between these three poems, so it

152 | *Saeculum*

is clear that Ovid is contemplating the same questions about literary immortality in all three: for example, we find references to envy (*livor*) which physically gnaws (*edax*) on artists and their art; an immortal fraction (*pars*) of the author which will survive (*superstes*) after death and even live forever (*vivam*); claims being conditional on the ability of prophets to see the future accurately.[57] *Amores* 1.15 sits at the end of the first book of Ovid's erotic elegies and situates the poet within the larger history of classical literature, while the *sphragis* of the *Metamorphoses* similarly looks back on the accomplishment of the epic and predicts that it will allow Ovid to achieve lasting fame; *Tristia* 4.10, more pessimistically, sees Ovid sitting in exile at Tomis hoping that though his physical presence in Rome is no longer possible, his literary reputation will ensure that he is not forgotten. A close reading of these poems reveals Ovid's attempts to come to grips with his literary posterity in the face of saecularity's inherent instability.

Ovid's poetic mission statement is first given voice in *Amores* 1.15. Ovid seeks a *fama perennis* (7), which can only be granted by poetry; for this reason he skips not only military service (4), a trope of elegy, but also a career as a jurist or lawyer (5–6). Jurists were known to write works of legal scholarship (Ateius Capito being the most famous of the Augustan period) and lawyers' oratory was a genre of prose composition, so Ovid has begun this poem with claims about literary immortality: prose writers cannot achieve it, only poets. While not every declaration of immortality by Ovid must signal saecular discourse, Ovid's use of *perennis* to describe everlasting fame situates these claims, and this poem as a whole, within the tradition of saecular literary models invoked by Catullus (*perenne*, 1.10) and Horace (*perennius*, *Odes* 3.30.1).[58]

Ovid continues to formulate his claims of immortality with the language of periodization in the next section (9–30), now adding hints of the potential for failure. In this section, Ovid lists a variety of Greek and Latin poets who have achieved everlasting fame through the strength of their compositions. The Greek authors seem secure, but complications arise during the section of Roman authors. Ovid asks, "What *aetas* will not know of Varro and the first ship and the golden fleece sought for the Aesonian leader?" (21–22). At first glance, this rhetorical question is just an elaborate variation on the same kind of praise Ovid has been giving poets throughout this poem. But reading the language he uses in a literal sense, one sees that Ovid actually suggests the possibility of future ages that will not

Pyramids and Fish Wrappers | 153

know Varro of Atax and his *Argonautae*. Unlike Ennius and Accius, each of whom possess a name that will cease at no *tempus* (*nullo tempore*, 20, wording that gestures at literary saecularity), Varro has a fame that is less certain; Rome may enter an *aetas*, a *saeculum* of literary history, in which readers and poets have forgotten about Varro, and his renown will disappear (as when the *aetas* deserts a work, as Horace imagines at *Epist.* 1.20.10). This literary saecularity is implied all the more by the metakosmetic reference to the Argo as the world's first ship (*primam ratem*, 21) and the visual pun created by the verbal juxtaposition of *aetas* and *aurea* (21–22, though *aurea* modifies the neuter plural noun *terga*); the Golden Age, and with it the saecular discourse of historical periodization, is hinted at for the reader who associates this myth with metakosmesis.[59]

Elsewhere in *Amores* 1.15, Ovid claims that certain poets will maintain their fame only as long as certain *dum*-conditions apply, conditions which are thematically related to the poets' works (e.g., Hesiod will be known as long as grapes and grain are grown [11–12]). But for Lucretius, Ovid actually provides a set date for the mortality of the *De rerum natura*: Ovid asserts that Lucretius's *carmina* will die on the day when the earth is destroyed (23–24, an allusion to *De rerum natura* 5.95). One can read this either as a tautology (obviously everything will perish on the day the earth is destroyed) or as a facetious impossibility (such as Ovid provides for several other authors, for example, Hesiod), but given the use of saecular discourse to discuss cataclysmic world events (including the destruction of the earth, such as examined in chapter 2), we should perhaps read into these lines a gesture at the subordination of literary immortality to saecular instability. Moreover, the statement curiously contradicts Ovid's later claim that *carmina* "lack a death" (*carmina morte carent*, 32).

More dubiously, Vergil will be read (*legentur*, 25) only as long as Rome is the capital of the conquered world, which as we saw in chapter 2 was considered by some Romans to be a finite period (and the origin of saecularity, of course, was in predicting the end of a *civitas* through divination).[60] Ovid has left possible a future period of Roman history in which these authors (and, by extension, all authors) will lose their seemingly permanent renown. The poet has demonstrated that even ostensibly "immortal" poets are nonetheless susceptible to changes wrought by saecular metakosmesis, and thus he has envisioned, metaphorically, a narrative of literature being subjected to the power of saecular change. With this language, *Amores*

154 | Saeculum

1.15 subtly expresses anxieties about the potential for "immortal" poets to achieve only a temporary immortality.[61]

This anxiety lies behind the particular wording of Ovid's prayer for poetic glory in the *sphragis* at the end of *Metamorphoses* 15. In this passage (whose affinities with Horace's *Ode* 3.30 are well known), Ovid expresses a desire to live on in fame *per omnia saecula* (15.878). Similar phrases appear throughout Latin works of the first century BCE as a periphrasis or poetic variant for "forever."[62] In light of the anxiety expressed in *Amores* 1.15, however, here the best interpretation is that Ovid hopes to counter the changing interests of Roman poetic audiences by surviving through *all* literary *saecula*. The obvious similarity to the desires of Catullus and his contemporaries is found also in the spatial wish to be famous in all of Rome's territorial holdings (877; cf. Catullus 95.5) along with the temporal immortality that will, just as in Catullus 1, make him *perennis* (875). But unlike Catullus, who contrasted the appeal of Cinna's *Zmyrna* with the praise given by the *populus* to the bloated verse of Antimachus (95.10), Ovid revels in the fact that he will be famous forever among the *populus* (878), since Ovid has no reason to fear the shifting tastes of the *populus* if he is simultaneously granted fame throughout all literary *saecula*.

To achieve a lasting fame would perhaps require the achievement of poetic merit, whereas temporary fame could be granted simply by popular support. Although Ovid had earlier proposed that one's posthumous fame is equal to what one deserves (*Am.* 1.15.40), here he is less certain. Indeed, Ovid suggests at the end of *Tristia* 4.10 that his *fama* may be the result not of the merit deserved by his works but by the favor granted to him by his *lectores* (131–132). This would explain why, in his own literary *saeculum* (*saecula nostra*, 125), Ovid does not consider himself to be the best poet but is nonetheless considered so by others (127–128).[63] Underlying this claim seems to be an assumption that poetic renown in any given *saeculum* is more a function of popular approbation than some "objective" standard of literary merit. Thus, while Ovid is considered the top poet in this *saeculum*, the tastes of Rome's poetry readers may shift in a future *saeculum* to come. Only by securing a form of literary immortality *per omnia saecula* can Ovid hope to avoid the pitfalls to which Varro of Atax and the other "temporarily immortal" classical poets are subjected.

Luckily, Ovid has at least achieved worldwide fame in his own lifetime, a rarity (*Tr.* 4.10.121–122). As Horace noted in *Epistula* 2.1 (see above), the contemporary zeal for antiquities often leaves living

Pyramids and Fish Wrappers | 155

poets in the shadows of their elders until they have been dead long enough to be considered "classics." A similar phenomenon is identified by Phaedrus, the Augustan fabulist. In the ten-line prologue to book 5, Phaedrus notes that in the current *saeculum* (*nostro saeculo*, 4), artists and sculptors often falsely attribute their new works to famous predecessors (Praxiteles, Zeuxis, etc.) in order to sell them for higher prices. Phaedrus explains that "biting envy" (*invidia mordax*, 9; cf. *livor edax*, above) gives preference to antiquity, even if falsely ascribed, over the talented works of the current age. (For Cicero's evolutionary model of literary history in the *Brutus*, the predecessors would have to be a step backwards in quality; with a saecular model, authors can depict a wider variety of historical narratives.) Surprisingly, Phaedrus has no qualms about engaging in the practice, and so warns the reader that although he has sufficiently credited Aesop as a source for his writings, he may invoke his name again later in book 5 solely for the prestige (*auctoritatis gratia*, 3). Phaedrus was certainly attuned to the cultural forces, literary and otherwise, of his contemporary milieu,[64] so we can read this passage, as with Horace in *Epistula* 2.1, as a comment on the public preference for material from a previous age, perhaps hoping that in a *saeculum* to come, fabulists would falsely cite his name to add to their own prestige.

The neoteric poets, as we saw, deployed saecular discourse as a weapon against their foes as a way to emphasize the mortality of their popularity and works. By so doing, they inevitably suggested the possibility of failure for their own immortality, and thus had to insist on a renown that survived multiple *saecula*. For the Augustan poets that followed, saecular narratives of Roman literary history were almost solely a source of anxiety; although anyone was able to use saecularity to explain away his current unpopularity (and Phaedrus and Horace, in *Epist.* 2.1, similarly predict an increase in popular praise only once they have become "old" authors), nonetheless the knowledge of fickle literary tastes changing from *saeculum* to *saeculum* in the future complicated the hope for immortality. From a strategic standpoint, then, the use of the saecular model is more inherently unstable than either the evolutionary model or the genealogical model of narrativizing literary history. Unlike those two narratives, the saecular model precludes the ability to assert a fixed status within the literary realm, unless an author is able to achieve a certain exceptional kind of literary immortality that transcends the saecular historical timeline itself (essentially, becoming ahistorical[65])—and it

156 | *Saeculum*

is not altogether clear that anyone was sure that that could be possible. The growing deployment of saecular discourse within the intellectual world of the Romans thus introduced a powerful complicating factor in the ongoing game of praise, condemnation, and self-awareness within the Roman literary community.

The Bibliotheca at the Temple of Apollo on the Palatine

This discussion of literary saecularity has so far focused largely on the abstract components in the world of literature, but I shift now to a very tangible object for Roman writers of the late first century BCE: the Palatine library (hereafter referred to as "the Bibliotheca"), which joined the Temple of Apollo Palatinus in the Augustan Palatine complex and stored a wealth of both Greek and Latin texts.[66] The Bibliotheca was dedicated in 28 BCE along with the Temple of Apollo (Dio Cassius 53.1.3).[67]

While large private libraries had existed during the Republic for many years, the concept of the "public" library was more recent: Asinius Pollio had opened a library in the Temple of Libertas before the Bibliotheca (Pliny, *HN* 35.10), which came in the wake of aborted plans by the late Julius Caesar to construct a massive public library in Rome run by Varro (Suetonius, *Iul.* 44.2; cf. Cicero, *Fam.* 9.4.1). This absorption by Pollio of a public benefaction set to be granted by Augustus's own kin may explain one impetus to construct the Bibliotheca.[68] A library in the Porticus Octaviae would soon follow, but there was nothing else comparable in Rome.[69] Augustus was actually involved in the process of establishing the Bibliotheca: it was he who selected Pompeius Macer to be in charge of organizing the interior and acquiring the book rolls, sending him direct written instructions (Suetonius, *Iul.* 56.7); later, the mythographer Hyginus, a freedman of Augustus, was put in charge of running it (Suetonius, *Gram. et rhet.* 20).[70]

The Bibliotheca was not simply an element of a prominent temple complex in Augustan Rome, but was also an important addition to the environment of the Roman *literati*.[71] It was in some sense a participant in that literary community, not as a writer but in its capacity as a facilitator of a literary history narrative, not unlike the *critici* of *Epistula* 2.1. By having a site that housed all of ancient literature with some kind of organizing principle, as it must have, the Bibliotheca shaped how Romans understood their own literary history. Its existence, whether or not this effect was intentional and planned, compelled the perception of Roman literary history in a certain way. Its effect was both backward-looking, as its collection constituted an organized database of previous literature, and forward-looking, since it was regarded as a spur to literary activity. This historicizing mode effected by the institution of the Bibliotheca created a saecular model of literary history, which provides this ability to narrate past and future simultaneously so easily.

The Bibliotheca's creation was itself an act of literary historicization, in part by providing in one single public area the corpus of earlier Greek works that Roman writers sought to imitate. Roman claims to be the first to perform some literary feat (such as to compose Latin poetry in Archilochan meter), or to be the Roman version of a particular Greek poet, could in a way be evaluated in the Bibliotheca itself: one look at the shelves would test the claim.[72] Even if the specific claims made by surviving Roman poets are not so simple as to make this possible (there was probably not a specific shelf dedicated to Archilochan verse), nonetheless we can perceive such statements through the perspective of the Bibliotheca's organizational scheme, which inevitably invited comparison of Greek and Roman contributions to the various genres. Thus, Roman authors talk about joining the canon of classical poets (e.g., Horace, *Odes* 1.1.35–36) not simply in an abstract sense but also in the tangible sense of the canons that were classified by librarians.[73] The Bibliotheca thus presents a challenge to Roman writers to match the contributions of the earlier Greek world.[74]

I use the phrase "earlier Greek world," but of course the Bibliotheca must not have housed Greek works only from centuries prior; it is unlikely that it would have failed to include more recent works of history, epigram, and philosophy.[75] Moreover, Romans were still consuming contemporary Greek literature at this time. But Roman writers (poets in particular) who discuss Greek literature invariably ignore these contemporary works, even if their own writing suggests familiarity with them; for them, "Greek literature" generally ends with Callimachus.[76] For example, Ovid's list of immortal poets in *Amores* 1.15 goes no further than the third century BCE, at which point he begins with Ennius and the early Roman poets. Similarly, Horace in *Epistula* 2.1 describes how many Roman authors inevitably get compared to Greeks, but always to Greeks many centuries prior

158 | *Saeculum*

(e.g., 50–58; 156–167). Thus, it appears that when Augustan Romans speak of "Greek literature," they are thinking not geographically (i.e., things written by people east of us) but temporally (things written by people before us).

Undoubtedly, this cognitive phenomenon began earlier than 28 BCE. But the Bibliotheca, with its Greek and Latin holdings available for all to see, both responds to and participates in that temporal perception of Greek literature.[77] In the narrative of literary history that the Bibliotheca cultivates, Greek literature occupies an earlier *saeculum* that ends, regardless of subsequent publications, with the arrival of Latin literature. The effect of its collection and organization of previous literary works was the perception of a saecular history of ancient literature. The construction of the Bibliotheca responded to the "new age" of Roman literature: Rome was now finally ready to compete with the old Greek masters in all genres.

This temporal model affects the self-fashioning of Roman writers. Horace describes a scene (*Epist.* 2.2.91–101) in which he and an elegist friend (often assumed to be Propertius) walk around the Bibliotheca admiring its holdings, and begin to compare themselves to Alcaeus and Callimachus.[78] This scene models the intellectual approach to literary history encouraged by the structure of the Bibliotheca itself: a *saeculum* of Greek literature and a *saeculum* of uncultivated Latin literature (one which never even attempted lyric or learned elegy) have both passed away, and contemporary poets can now participate in a new *saeculum* of Roman literature in which they can match the famous Greek poets of centuries past.[79] The existence of a newly thriving Latin portion of the Bibliotheca in competition with the already immortalized Greek portion contributes to the narrativization of Roman literary history, and the mechanism of this narrativization lies in the relationship between the Roman literary world and the *princeps*.

The Bibliotheca was staffed by librarians with direct connections to the emperor, and literary evidence demonstrates that emperors made recommendations about what should (or should not) be in it; "both personnel and policy could therefore be and sometimes though not always actually were in imperial hands."[80] While the *princeps* had some degree of influence in the literary sphere, this is not to say that Augustus was personally encouraging the composition of specific works by specific authors; rather, he provided (not least through the creation of the Bibliotheca itself) a more general spur to the Roman

Pyramids and Fish Wrappers | 159

creative class to give Rome works with which it could compete with Greece (and stock the Bibliotheca with Latin contributions to match the Greek ones, a tangible goal to embody the abstract one).[81] The Bibliotheca provided a physical space to house and support, essentially, sociocultural forces that were already emerging at Rome: "in most cases the imperial inclusion of a library in a larger monumental program was a response to cultural expectations nurtured by the progressive Hellenization of Rome and Italy."[82] In other words, the Bibliotheca served to reify the contemporary Roman literary competition with ancient Greece (as perceived by its own Roman participants) by showing the tangible results of that competition on the shelves of its literary holdings.

This phenomenon was made possible by the literary historicization that the Bibliotheca enacted; a Greek *saeculum* and an early Roman *saeculum* had already come and gone, and a new *saeculum* of Roman literature had been founded anew by Augustus (one finally talented enough to match Greece when displayed together). And the Palatine complex was already a site with saecular associations (as shown in chapter 5); chief among these was its housing of oracular texts in the Temple of Apollo (such as the Sibylline Books and Etruscan documents). The religious/legal scholarship performed by Ateius Capito, through which he authorized the recalculation of the Roman *saeculum* to 110 years, likely took place in the Bibliotheca itself.[83] It was on the Palatine that the *Carmen Saeculare* was sung during the Ludi Saeculares, announcing the new *saeculum* to all the Roman people. Of all the possible sites to construct a library in Rome, Augustus chose the hill on which he was exerting the most energy in declaring a new *saeculum* for Roman history. The Bibliotheca, in its own way, announced a new *saeculum* in Roman literary history as well, one in which Rome could finally match Greek literature roll for roll, as the shelves themselves would soon visibly attest.[84]

Given the level of control that the *princeps* held over the "personnel and policy" of the Bibliotheca, management of the site was a way for him to engage with the popular perception of the Roman literary world. The Bibliotheca was a *princeps*-controlled depiction of literary history for an audience of all Romans: "The whole sanctuary became a place of *memoria*, a historically pregnant archive of books, documents, portraits and works of art. And yet, the library right in the center of the palace was accessible to private citizens, open for any reader to inspect. . . . It was in easy reach of anyone who lived

160 | *Saeculum*

on the Palatine or had any business being there."[85] Even the interior decoration of the Bibliotheca was a means of exerting some influence on the public perception of Roman literary history: Petrain notes how the senatorial authorization of portraits for Germanicus and Drusus demonstrates that the Bibliotheca's decorative program was "a sophisticated tool allowing the emperor to harness and manipulate the prestige of the literary tradition, and as such its details were publicized throughout the empire."[86]

Presence on the shelves of the Bibliotheca conferred a literary legitimacy that was otherwise unavailable, which is why Ovid's walking, talking *liber* tries so hard to gain access into the Bibliotheca (*Tr.* 3.1.59–68). As Neudecker writes, "Ovid did not only think of his future literary fame, but also about the rehabilitation of his status, when he begged Tiberius to let his works have entry into the *Palatina*. He insists on the fundamental difference between '*statio publica*' and '*privatus locus*' of all books."[87] We saw earlier (in chapter 5) how *Tristia* 3.1 demonstrates the ultimate domination of the Palatine over the Capitoline as the hill with the most cultural cache at Rome, adding to its saecular associations.[88] The Bibliotheca performs a similar operation for the periodized history of Roman literature, inviting Roman writers and readers to think of themselves as inhabiting a new *saeculum* of Roman literary history. The competition with earlier Greek models, encouraged by the very structure of the Bibliotheca, contributed to an intellectual model of Roman literary history in which Augustan poets were quasi-palingenetic reappearances of figures from the older Greek *saeculum* of classical literature. Failure to secure a spot within the Bibliotheca is a tangible variant of the "abandonment by the *aetas*" that filled Augustan writers with anxiety; to lack a place in the "canon" that the Bibliotheca's shelves constituted was to miss out on the immortality the poets so explicitly sought.

There has been considerable scholarly debate regarding the possible division of the Bibliotheca into two halves. Suetonius (*Aug.* 29) describes the building as *bibliotheca Latina Graecaque*, which has led some to conclude that Greek works were physically separated from Latin works, as if in separate halls or wings. However, recent archaeological work "has in any case made it clear that this Augustan library was a single apsed hall. . . . Traces of contemporary tufa walls exclude the presence of a second adjacent library room in the Augustan phase."[89] Tucci further notes, "The Augustan building was referred to both in the singular and the plural by ancient authors, but the literary evidence is not sufficient to argue that its original phase had separate Latin and Greek halls."[90] But Corbier posits, based on a papyrus describing an embassy received in the "Roman bibliotheca," that the Greek and Latin collections were nevertheless housed in two separate areas of the Bibliotheca.[91] This separation is further suggested by epigraphic evidence from the later Julio-Claudian period of slave workers in the Bibliotheca, which shows that some slaves worked exclusively in the Greek collection, others only in the Latin.[92] Wiseman makes the crucial point that "the use of the Bibliotheca for Senate meetings implies an unusually large reading-room space," implying that there would not have been a need for separate buildings for Greek and Latin literature.[93] While there were probably not separate Greek and Latin wings of the Bibliotheca, there still likely was a clear division of Greek and Latin works within the literary holdings.

In a 1993 article, Horsfall makes the case that the opening of the first bilingual libraries (Pollio's, then the Bibliotheca) contributed to the self-perceived inferiority of Roman literary culture in comparison with the Greek by making visually clear the "literature gap" between Greece and Rome: one could simply look at the shelves holding the Latin works in the Bibliotheca and find them noticeably barer than those shelves holding Greek works.[94] His speculative reconstruction (perhaps relying on an overly literal reading of *vacuam Romanis vatibus aedem* at *Epist.* 2.2.94) imagines a fully stocked Greek section in the Bibliotheca sitting alongside a Roman section largely empty, visually inviting contributions from Augustan writers to fill its bare shelves with works matching earlier Greek models. But the construction of the Bibliotheca was not solely a challenge to Rome's literary class, but also a validation: only now, in this new age of Roman literature, could the city's authors credibly be displayed next to the canonized works of ancient Greece. As Wiseman points out, in 12 or 13 CE an embassy from Alexandria was received by Augustus in the Latin portion of the library, "no doubt to remind them that there was now a literature beyond what their own library held."[95] The building offered a new historical consciousness for Roman authors, an awareness of their new elevated status within literary history. Horsfall's imagined layout would convey even more strongly the saecular historicization of Roman literature that the Bibliotheca's existence encouraged.

Saecular discourse provided a language for Roman authors to depict a literary history, like any other technical history, that can be

162 | *Saeculum*

periodized with qualitative *saecula*. These *saecula* are defined by the aesthetic tastes of the Roman audience and their attitudes toward poetry both contemporary and older. This approach complemented the evolutionary model, used by Cicero and Vitruvius among others, which narrativized Roman literary history through a gradual process of refinement culminating in a final stage of literary perfection, as well as the genealogical model, in which "family trees" of authors within a certain genre or sharing a certain trait were created for various strategic purposes.

The saecular model, associated especially with the neoteric poets of the middle of the first century BCE, provided the means for a more sophisticated analysis of literary development. Horace, expanding on the claims of the neoterics, demonstrated how popular appeal drove the changes from *saecula* to *saecula* and shaped the dominant aesthetic criteria in each. The stakes were high for Roman poets, because cultural rejection could lead to the mortality of one's works (and thus of the poet himself), and the ever-changing standards created by readers and poets created anxiety for anyone hoping to achieve literary immortality. No poets were safe; even those who were revered as loftier than the pyramids in their own time, or afterward, could someday become reviled as a fish wrapper in the eyes of a different *saeculum* of readers. If at all possible (and this was not certain), poets hoped that their works could achieve such a level of distinction and inherent quality that they could be praised in every *saeculum*, avoiding the pitfalls of the fickle mob's changing tastes in poetry. The creation of the Bibliotheca contributed to the saecular narrativization of Roman literary history by suggesting that the contemporary Roman poets would now match old Greek masters in all genres of literature. Among technical histories of such topics as legal scholarship and medicine, the saecular literary history emerged in the first century BCE as a new way to narrativize the history of Roman literature.

Conclusion
Spaces after Periods

Within the scope of the present volume, I have examined texts, personages, and other cultural objects in the Roman intellectual world from the rise of Sulla until the end of the reign of Augustus. Future scholarship could pick up on the activities of the Romans during this time and pursue the aftereffects of these events in the time outside this range. We can see the consequences of this long intellectual trend in temporal rhetoric by noting key differences in the ways that later Roman authors talk about the history of Rome, and about the timeline of a particular cultural trend, or in the vocabulary that they deploy when describing the past (and possible future). For example, it is generally understood that while Tacitus was clearly influenced by Cicero's *Brutus* in composing his own literary history on Roman oratory, the *Dialogus*, he was nevertheless more interested in historicizing the trends of Roman oratory with an awareness of the political events that had produced distinct eras of quality and demeanor among Roman orators; Tacitus has taken for granted that the way to understand the evolution of Roman oratory is to think not genealogically like Cicero but in terms of qualitatively defined eras of oratory. Likewise, among the Neronian writers such as Seneca the Younger, evocations of a new Golden Age under the young emperor are less indebted to Hesiodic (or even Vergilian) notions of cosmic cyclicality and more influenced by a general appreciation of Roman history as an unending timeline of discrete periods dominated by significant individuals.[1]

I have said very little about Jewish and Christian use of periodization and the possibility that the Romans drew an influence from the east. Jewish Messianic texts had been appearing since the

164 | *Saeculum*

Hellenistic era, and the prophecies predicting the coming of an exceptional figure who would inaugurate a new time period are certainly suggestive of the "man of the *saeculum*" pronouncements we see in the Roman world. The biblical Book of Daniel offers an apocalyptic worldview that would not be out of place among the Greek-inflected cataclysms I examined in chapter 2.[2] Moreover, the Book of Daniel features Nebuchadnezzar's dream of a man with various metallic body parts (head of gold, breast of silver, belly of bronze, legs of iron, and feet of clay) that is interpreted by Daniel as representing the successive world empires that will all be outlasted by the sovereignty of God.[3] The parallels to the Metallic Age mythology of the Romans are immediately apparent.

One possible source for Jewish influence on the Roman development of qualitative periodization is the body of texts known as the Sibylline Oracles, or *Oracula Sibyllina*.[4] These writings come down to us in fourteen books, composed in Greek dactylic hexameter, purporting to be revelations uttered by ancient Italian Sibyls. Because of the anonymous nature of the compositions, as well as the haphazard system of later accretions on earlier texts, dating the works is extremely difficult. Most of the corpus seems to have been composed during the imperial period (and largely by Christian authors), but book 3 of the collection is generally believed to have been the work of Hellenistic Jewish contributors and thus was potentially available to Roman intellectuals during the first century BCE. Scholars since at least Tarn[5] have explored the similarities between the prophecies articulated in book 3 of the *Oracula Sibyllina* and the language of Vergil's *Eclogue* 4, and various explanations have been given for how Vergil might have come into contact with this esoteric Jewish tradition. Others have been more skeptical of this Roman–Jewish interaction and instead have asserted (like I did in chapter 4) that the Hesiodic tradition of Metallic Age mythology is sufficient to explain the entirety of Vergil's complex temporal scheme in the poem.[6] In a recent volume, Machinist examines the use of periodization from three case studies in the Old Testament and concludes that "while the biblical authors were mindful of describing the past in periodic units, they did not do so with fully articulated and explicit schemes; the latter began to appear only later, in the Second Temple period of Hellenistic and Roman Judaism."[7] Quantitative periodization, *translatio imperii* motifs, and temporal markers associated with dating and eras (such as in the Seleucid world) did appear in Jewish writings

Conclusion | 165

before (and perhaps were accessible to) the authors of my study, but it seems that the kind of qualitative periodization I am describing with saecular discourse did not appear in the Jewish intellectual world until after the first century BCE.

The Christian reception of Roman saecular discourse, on the other hand, is so profoundly extensive as to be worthy of its own book. The prayer formula *in saecula saeculorum*, the widespread popularity of "second coming" millennialism, and the epochal dating system of Dionysius Exiguus (and the creation of the "Era Vulgaris") all have associations with the saecular discursive mode of the first-century BCE Romans. One aspect with particular relevance to saecularity is the realm of eschatology: while the Romans often contemplated the possibility of massive cataclysms that could destroy the city or the entirety of human civilization, Christian (and Jewish) eschatology essentially postulated an endpoint to the sequence of ages, a true *"ultima aetas"* culminating in the end of history with the arrival of the Kingdom of God. Apocalyptic scenarios like the depiction in the Book of Revelations and various temporal schemes involving tribulation and "end times" situations all have potential antecedents in the Roman authors I have examined in this book.[8]

As I explained in the introduction, my primary chronological range of interest has been roughly 88 BCE to 17 CE. In planning this volume, I decided that saecularity in Jewish and early Christian thought was a topic beyond the scope of this book, and that it would be best to leave the questions they raise to other scholars. I am reluctant to contribute further to the culture of "intellectual silos" that separate classicists from biblical studies scholars, but my focus in this volume ultimately stayed within the Greco-Roman(-Etruscan!) world. I hope that further scholars of ancient temporality will be able to draw the connections between Roman and Judeo-Christian thought on the notion of saecular periodization.[9]

But I wish to conclude this volume by briefly examining a more immediate successor to the first century BCE and the cultural actors from the Augustan reign. A generation of writers one might call the "Tiberian Age" of Roman literature provides us with several tantalizing examples of what we could consider to be the product of decades of fully absorbed saecular historical consciousness within Roman intellectual culture.[10] For example, the Roman historian Fenestella (whose work survives only in brief fragments) seems to have composed a full history of Rome with a particular interest in changing

166 | *Saeculum*

social trends and revolutionary cultural innovations.[11] Fenestella's obsession with the *primus inventor* theme may even have earned him the mockery of later writers.[12] It also seems that Fenestella used Sulla's memoirs as a source for his history; perhaps Sulla's saecular historicity had become so ingrained in Roman culture by the Tiberian age that Fenestella felt comfortable rejecting the set pieces and annalistic announcements of earlier Republican historians and devoted more space to technical histories and moral *saecula*. A telling phrase appears at fragment Fenestella F25 Cornell: Fenestella writes that small, low-price pearls became trendy "around the Sullan period" (*circa Sullana tempora*), which Pliny the Elder identifies as a clear mistake in the chronology of events.[13] This phrase is perhaps evidence that already by the Augustan Age, Sulla's political periodization of Roman history was working. Nicolaus of Damascus, who composed a universal history roughly around this time period, also seems to have placed emphasis on the sociocultural sphere and on innovations that led to changes in behavior on a broad scale.[14] This focus may have interpreted such events as metakosmetic moments in a saecular history of the human race.

We also find, in the Tiberian historian Velleius Paterculus, an articulation of a saecular literary history spanning both Greece and Rome in all genres, and he uses all four of the primary Latin terms for a time-unit: *aetas*, *aevum*, *tempus*, and *saeculum*. At the conclusion of book 1 of his history, Velleius goes on an unexpected tangent (1.16–18) about the artistic phenomenon he perceives in which the greatest practitioners of a particular literary genre or artistic talent all tend to appear within the same time period: tragedy, Old and New Comedy, philosophy, and oratory all follow this pattern, in the eyes of Velleius. Nor is this phenomenon true only of the Greeks, but also of the Romans (although in their case, Velleius can think of some slight exceptions). Velleius speculates on the reason for this temporal pattern, ultimately concluding that emulation inspires genius and that this fact will naturally cause such sharp peaks in the quality of any artistic pursuit. Here again, we see the temporal framework of qualitatively defined periods as the unstated cognitive foundation for the divisions Velleius makes on the literary timelines of Greece and Rome. The "national conversation" on Roman literary history in which, as we saw in chapter 6, a variety of Roman writers participated, has brought forth the sort of historical consciousness Velleius takes for granted in this passage.

Conclusion | 167

The final Tiberian age example I would like to analyze here comes to us from a fragment[15] of the *Histories* of Seneca the Elder, although its debt to Cicero is somewhat emphatic.[16] Cicero, at *De republica* 2.3, had prepared to describe the Roman republic at its birth, its growth, its maturity, and its final strong and healthy state (*et nascentem et crescentem et adultam et iam firmam atque robustam*).[17] Something ostensibly similar, and yet fundamentally different, occurs in this Tiberian work. Lactantius (7.15.14) tells us that Seneca the Elder, in his historiographical writing,[18] divided the history of Rome into *aetates* (*Romanae urbis tempora distribuit in aetates*). Born and reared under Romulus, Rome's monarchy period was like its childhood (*pueritia*); the expulsion of the Tarquins began its adolescence (*adulescentia*); its maturity began (*coepisse iuvenescere*) with the end of "the Punic War";[19] and with the rise of civil wars and the return to a sole ruler, the city entered old age (*senectus*) or rather a second childhood (*altera infantia*).

Seneca here divides Roman history into four periods, each with its own characteristics related to its relationship with political power (at home and abroad).[20] Using human maturation as an allegory for the development of the Roman state is not an original idea of Seneca the Elder, but he is possibly the first writer to conceive of a saecular history of Rome divided into such stages of life.[21] Crucially, Seneca gives actual moments for transitions of ages: the expulsion of the Tarquins in 509 BCE, the end of the Third Punic War in 146 BCE, and "rule by a single authority" (*regimen singularis imperii*; surely described within the work itself, and probably referring to the beginning of the Augustan Principate). These *aetates* are discrete units (not vague ideas, like these stages of human maturation themselves are),[22] and unlike the "lapsarian" moral decline narratives that have only a single turning point,[23] here in his full history of Rome Seneca provides three. Unfortunately we do not seem to have a direct quotation, and it is Lactantius who refers to these periods as *aetates*, so our understanding of Seneca's specific terminology is lost, but it seems fairly clear that Seneca the Elder's history was a saecular narrative of Rome.

By using the metaphor of the life of a human to describe the life of a state, Seneca enters on dangerous ground, because the metaphor creates a finite narrative and thus implies that Rome will someday fall. As we saw earlier, Cicero explicitly rejected that comparison at *De republica* 3.34, saying that states should not naturally die, like people do. Adopting the metaphor would seem to suggest that even

168 | *Saeculum*

states have a natural life cycle, which includes the destruction of the state. But Seneca neatly avoids the issue by describing the principate both as the *senectus* of Rome and alternatively as a second childhood. With this alternative, Seneca opens the door for a neverending cycle in which Rome will revert to childhood (with periodic embrace of one-man rule) rather than reaching old age and then dying.[24] Thus Seneca, like Vergil in *Eclogue 4*, adapts a finite saecular model for the historical narrative of Rome to allow for infinite cycles through the same phases. Perhaps Seneca the Elder, along with Fenestella, Nicolaus of Damascus, and Velleius Paterculus, can point us in the direction of a "Tiberian period" type of historical consciousness influenced by the preceding century of saecular discourse in the Roman intellectual community.

The Romans of the Republic were not natural periodizers: the organization of their civic life into consular years and censors' *lustra* never suggested to them the possibility that these periods could have distinct qualitative characteristics. Although celebrations of Ludi Saeculares may possibly have taken place in the second and even third centuries BCE, this form of historical organization did not develop into any sort of sophisticated language of periodization until the rise of Sulla. Sulla deftly wedded the cosmic Etruscan divinatory connotations of the term *saeculum* to the rhythms of Roman political history, announcing himself as the "man of the *saeculum*" who was inaugurating a new age of Roman life. Subsequent additional connotations came from the influence of Greek philosophy: cyclical successions of periods, metempsychosis and palingenesis, and new models for periodic destruction and rejuvenation. The result of such intellectual experimentation was a new discursive mode, one which allowed Romans to narrativize history through qualitatively defined periods in the past, present, and future. The century after Sulla could practically be described as its own cognitive *saeculum*, an Age of Saecularity.

The effects of this new discursive mode were manifold. Some were highly specific. The mythological figures of Deucalion and Pyrrha would now be permanently linked with the figure of Phaethon, not simply for their catastrophic tales but as signifiers of epochal rupture and transition. Romans already knew how to imagine the demise of Rome in an abstract sense, but now they had a robust language for describing the discontinuity of a future world after Rome had been obliterated.

The traditional narrative of Roman moral decline became more complex: rather than try to pinpoint the lapsarian moment when Roman decadence began, Romans could organize their history into various moral stages (each with culture heroes to introduce new phenomena) and explain how the arc of Roman morality did not have to be one-directional. Experts in a single *ars* could historicize their innovations within a longer technical history of development. Roman poets could explain away their current obscurity with expectations of future fame, while holding this model of unstable popular appeal as a weapon against more celebrated rivals. Saecularity offered a new lens through which to perceive history, one with new facets for refracting the facts of the past into narratives for the present.

Between the language of the renewed Golden Age and such contemporary statements as the motion to declare his lifetime the *saeculum Augustum*, it is all too easy to see Augustus at the epicenter of Roman saecular discourse. What this survey of the Roman intellectual world of the first century BCE has attempted to show, however, is that Augustus (or Vergil, for that matter) was not the foundation on which all other uses of the *saeculum* were built. Saecularity had a long history of adoption and adaptation, an earlier tradition of qualitative periodization, in the decades that preceded the career of Augustus. The "Augustan Age" appeared alongside many other unrelated "ages," competing with (rather than dominating) these alternative saecular histories. The prominence of saecularity in European thought in the two millennia that followed stands as a testament to the power that the Romans gave to the intellectual authority of this discursive mode in the first century BCE.

Notes

Introduction

1. White 1980, 27.

2. Generally, periodization applies only to past events; as we will see, however, the Roman version of periodization this volume focuses on includes categorization of future events as well.

3. Zerubavel 2003, 84.

4. Zerubavel 2003, 85.

5. Zerubavel 2003, 96.

6. Zerubavel (2003, 96), in discussing the use of centuries or decades as periods, contends that the idea of the century as a distinct historical unit only began in the seventeenth century, and the qualitative identification of individual decades is a product of twentieth-century thought.

7. Livy (2.1.2) encourages the reader to imagine each Roman king as a new founder of the city, or at least a founder of the new part each king added to the city, but this falls short of actual regnal periodization. On the difficulties of seeing periodization at work in the Imperial Roman understanding of its Republican past, see Roller 2015.

8. Purcell 2003, esp. 26–34.

9. Within classical scholarship, other sources merit mention: Hannah 2005 and 2009 are wide-ranging works on the Roman conceptions of time, although periodization receives less attention than other forms of chronographical organization (such as calendars). Rawson 1985 remains a useful (although rather general) resource on the Roman intellectual community's forms of historical organization. Blundell (1986, 103–134) thoroughly covers the general idea of cyclical history in Greek and Roman thought. Jaeger (1997, 5 n. 13) provides a helpful summary of research on the temporal shape of Roman historiography. More recently, Short (2016) investigates the cognitive

172 | Notes to Pages 5–9

organization of Roman time discourse, although he does not discuss time at the epochal level. Outside the field of classics, Eliade (1954, 112–129) provides an overview of cosmic cycles in nearly all world cultures, and Lukacher (1998, 1–49) focuses on eternal recurrence in ancient Mediterranean thought (primarily, though, in the works of Ovid). Kermode (1967) touches on many issues of narratology within historiography that are later expanded on by White. Whitrow (1988) covers various cultures' views on time and periodization throughout human history.

10. From a technical standpoint, geologists use the words "age," "epoch," "period," "era," and "eon" as distinct terms, but I will use them interchangeably throughout this book.

11. The *saeculum* is probably most familiar to modern nonspecialists (aside from its appearance on the reverse of the Great Seal of the United States in the phrase "Novus Ordo Seclorum," which is printed on the one-dollar bill) through the political theory writings of William Strauss and Neil Howe, whose 1997 book *The Fourth Turning: What the Cycles of History Tell Us about America's Next Rendezvous with Destiny* predicted various social upheavals in twenty-first century America (and was apparently deeply influential for Steve Bannon, former chief strategist for President Trump). But Strauss and Howe's theories of cyclical shifts in culture have largely been criticized by serious scholars.

12. Suetonius, *Aug.* 100.2–3.

13. Although the suggestion was perhaps not entirely revolutionary—many poets had spoken of an Augustan Age, as we will see.

14. On the Etruscan origins of the term and its lexical range, see chapter 1.

15. Censorinus, *DN* 17.7–11.

16. The senatorial habit of proposing outlandish honors for the *princeps*, in life and at death, suggests that the senators may not have considered the repercussions of their proposals with such calculation, though arguably these sorts of proposals were in fact the very moves senators used to jockey for position in an increasingly competitive Roman elite world and thus would receive greater attention.

17. Although in Hesiod they are races (γένεα) and not ages, as is discussed further below.

18. Censorinus, *DN* 17.6; see the extensive discussion below in chapter 1.

19. See for example Cathryn Carson's 2010 volume *Heisenberg in the Atomic Age: Science and the Public Sphere.* (The nomenclature even appears in classical scholarship, with a slight variation, in the title of Richard Ned Lebow and Barry S. Strauss's 1991 book *Hegemonic Rivalry: From Thucydides to the Nuclear Age.*)

20. See esp. Flower 2010, 3–17.

21. Very rarely, and only by Vergil and Horace in the period I am studying in this project.

Notes to Pages 9–18 | 173

22. For obvious reasons, certain words that refer to offspring or a generation (*proles, progenies, nepos*, etc.) can be used for saecularity, but only in special contexts (e.g., when such terms clearly have a chronological function).

23. Van Noorden (2015, 24–27) rightly notes that for the Metallic Age mythology, rigid scholarly distinctions between the "anthropological" terminology (largely Greek) and "historical" terminology (especially in Roman translations) are unhelpful and largely inaccurate. While she posits the influence of Vergil or Ovid for the use of *aetas* and *saeculum* as Roman translations of the original γένος in Hesiod, I intend to explain it as a result of an already-present trend of saecularity in Roman thought.

24. See also West 1978, 165–166 on hypotheses about pre-Hesiodic connections between Deucalion and Prometheus, another figure important to saecular discourse.

25. In Ovid's account of Phaethon's story in *Met.* 1–2, he also includes an anthropomorphic embodiment of the Saeculum (2.26) but leaves it otherwise undescribed; given the context (he is joined by other anthropomorphized time-units), this Saeculum may in fact refer to a century. See Bömer 1969.

26. Cf., among other places: Horace, *Ode* 1.3; Cicero, in prose (*Tusc.* 5.7) and poetry (the fragment of his translation of Aeschylus' *Prometheus Unbound* in *Tusc.* 2.23); Phaedrus, *Fabulae Aesopiae* App. 5.1 (*saeculi figulus novi*). Van Noorden (2015, 12) reads the list of metals at line 502 of [Aeschylus]'s *PV* as a possible allusion to Hesiod's Metallic Age mythology.

27. See, e.g., Martin 1991, where Thucydides 1.22.4 is offered as a characteristic statement.

28. The Etruscan divinatory model, in fact, assigned a finite sequence of *saecula* for each individual *civitas*, such that one *civitas* could be in its final *saeculum* while a nearby *civitas* has several more remaining. For much more on this topic, see chapter 1.

29. Even modern classical scholars can be found using such terminology: Keith (2006) writes, "Matthew Santirocco, in his 1979 article 'Sulpicia Reconsidered,' inaugurated a new saeculum in Sulpician studies by eschewing biographical speculation for careful examination of the 'technique and traditional features' of Sulpicia's poetry" (3).

30. Columella 8.16. On the Roman historical consciousness of fishponds, see esp. the study by Bannon (2014).

Chapter 1: Omen History

1. As Lewis (1991, 509 n. 1) rightly notes, "memoirs" is not an entirely accurate description of the work, which Plutarch (*Sulla* 37.1) calls "*hypomnemata*" and Cicero (*Div.* 1.71) calls "*historia*," but for lack of a better English word (and

174 | Notes to Pages 18–22

because of a general scholarly convention) I will refer to it as such throughout this project.

2. The major sources of modern scholarship on this work are Calabi 1950; Frier 1971; Valgiglio 1975; Keaveney 1982 (revised 2005); Bates 1983; Lewis 1991; Smith 2009; Thein 2009; Wiseman 2009. See also the collection of fragments and testimonia in Cornell 2013.

3. Frier (1971, 585) imagines that in the 80s Sulla must have employed "an extensive propaganda campaign: agents and counter-agents, a barrage of pamphlets."

4. The issue of when this omen took place, and where "Laverna" was, has seen some scholarly debate; see Cornell 2013, 3.294.

5. So posited by Luke (2014, 43).

6. Trans. Perrin (1916, 341).

7. Ramage 1991, 97.

8. Luke 2014, 42–44; Lewis 1991, 515–516. In Plutarch's biography, the story immediately follows a fragment cited by Plutarch specifically as coming from the dedication, and the two fragments can conceivably be read continuously; Luke suggests that all of *Sull.* 6.5–7 may be a compressed version of the preface.

9. Trans. Perrin (1916, 337).

10. Bates 1983, 235.

11. Plutarch helps us gain a better sense of the tone of the entire work when he notes at 6.7 that Sulla too often exaggerates in the memoirs how much aid came to him from the gods, as opposed to by chance or through normal human decision-making.

12. Trans. Perrin (1916, 347).

13. Plutarch also writes (7.6) that the soothsayers predicted, based on a sparrow flying into the temple with a grasshopper in its mouth, that the omens suggested a quarrel between wealthy landowners and the populace, but the Greek text is corrupt and this story may be a later interpolation.

14. Luke 2014, 44–45; cf. Turfa 2006, 82: the *saecula* system was "published (or outright manipulated) by Sulla as announcing a regime change for the better." Keaveney (1982, 194) likewise asserts an understood connection between the *saeculum* prodigy and Sulla, writing that with the interpretation of the omen by the soothsayers, "Sulla's position in the divine scheme of things was made manifest."

15. Lewis (1991) demonstrates that there was ample space for Sulla in the memoirs; Keaveney (1982) posits that the period from 88 BCE to 86/5 BCE took up eight books.

16. Lewis 1991, 517.

17. Kendall 2013, 39: "Based on what Plutarch chooses to cite from these memoirs it is reasonably certain that what Sulla recounts of himself is heavily shaded by self-promotion and the desire to blacken his opponents."

Notes to Pages 22–24 | 175

18. For Plutarch's frequent use of Sulla as a source not only in the *Sulla* but also the *Lucullus*, the *Marius*, and the *Moralia*, see Schettino 2014; for his antiquarian interests, see Paven 2014.

19. Balsdon 1951, 2.

20. Bates 1983, 235; see also Cornell 2013, 1.285–286.

21. Luke 2014, 45: "the connection between the Lavernan prodigy and the declaration of a new *saeculum* in 88 was likely even clearer in Sulla's memoir than it is in Plutarch's account." Flower (2016, 214) confidently asserts that in the memoirs, "Sulla appears as a man chosen by the gods for a predestined role at an epochal time in the history of Rome and its empire. The Etruscan haruspices noted the prodigies that marked the change of the age and that predicted civil war."

22. Weinstock 1971, 197. On the use of new era calculations by Hellenistic kings, see esp. Kosmin 2018.

23. Flower 2010, 134.

24. Crawford 1974, 731.

25. Crawford 1974, 368.

26. Cf. Ovid, *Fast.* 1.229–240.

27. Ramage 1991, 104; also, 104 n. 59: "Janus was best known as the god of beginnings . . . and so Sulla is perhaps also using this idea to announce a new era for Rome under his leadership." But see Athenaeus 15.692e on how several Mediterranean cities minted coins with Janus on one side and a ship on the other.

28. Crawford 1974, 732, though he also notes that "it is difficult not to see in all this traces of a new, individualistic attitude toward the *res publica*, an attitude which is incompatible with the collective ideology of oligarchic rule and which eventually finds expression in autocracy."

29. On the details of Sulla's building works, I draw especially from Ramage 1991, 111–115. While I am focusing solely on Sulla's activities in Italy, it is worth mentioning that Sulla's destruction of cities in the east possibly contributed to the later discourse of saecular civilization collapse.

30. Purcell 1995, 326: "there is the closest relationship between the spaces of Rome's topography and the working of its social and political institutions: naturally, the effect will have been at its most intense in the Forum Romanum (and on the Capitol)."

31. Flower 2010, 131.

32. On Sulla's activity in the Forum, see Coarelli 1985; on Sulla's civic building policy in general, see esp. Davies 2017, 205–208.

33. Appian, *B Civ.* 1.97.

34. Velleius Paterculus 2.61.3.

35. Ramage 1991, 111, reading Cicero, *Phil.* 9.13.

36. Crawford 1974, 381.

37. Ramage 1991, 111.

176 | Notes to Pages 24–27

38. Ramage 1991, 120.

39. Purcell 1995, 333.

40. For a detailed assessment of the slaughters in the Forum during the proscriptions, see Keaveney 1982, 150–155.

41. On the possible Roman reaction to this "whitewash," see Davies 2017, 208.

42. Luke 2014, 54.

43. Pliny, *HN* 36.45.

44. Keaveney 1982, 178.

45. Flower 2010, 127: "his interest in the state religion can be seen in a number of measures."

46. Flower 2010, 132.

47. Tucci 2005, 28.

48. Tucci 2005, 28.

49. Purcell 1995, 331.

50. See Keaveney 1982, 193 for details; Gellius (13.14.3–4) explicitly says Sulla sought the distinction of doing it (*proferendi pomerii titulum quaesivit*). Ramage 1991, 115: "the fact that this was the first time since the reign of Servius Tullius that the pomerium had been enlarged must surely have put Sulla in a unique position in the minds of the Romans . . . here was further evidence that he was bringing a new era."

51. Sallust, *Hist.* fr. 1.49 (Ramsey).

52. Flower 2010, 133–134; Sulla also gave out a new law code in Dicaearchia shortly before his death (Plutarch, *Sull.* 36). See also Santangelo 2007, 214–224 for Sulla as a "new founder of Rome." On saecular culture heroes, see chapter 4.

53. Flower 2010, 131.

54. On Sulla's associations with Hercules, see also Santangelo 2007, 220; Flower 2010, 127; Davies 2017, 185–187. See also Thein 2002, 130–132 for how Sulla's associations with Bellona may have contributed to his evocation of a new age.

55. Ramage 1991, 114.

56. Ramage 1991, 115.

57. Plutarch, *Sull.* 35.1; Keaveney 1982, 191.

58. Statius, *Silv.* 4.6.85–88.

59. Fears 1981b, 880.

60. Fears 1981b, 880. See also Ramage 1991, 118–119 on how Sulla sought identification with Hercules as a bringer of civilization and peace, like a culture hero.

61. Keaveney 1982, 191.

62. Flower 2010, 120.

63. Fears 1981a, 790.

Notes to Pages 27–32 | 177

64. Ramage 1991, 121.

65. Ramage 1991, 100: "Sulla was the first to recognize the fact that, if his efforts at self-promotion were to be effective, he had to take his message to all parts of the world and that to do this he had to adapt his propaganda to two quite different social and political situations. This was a policy that his successors followed."

66. Fears 1981b, 877–878.

67. Trans. Perrin (1916, 347–349).

68. For these dates, see *Sull.* 21.4 and 37.1.

69. Dating explicit at Censorinus 21.6.

70. I follow Parker's text and translation here, although other scholars have read "100 years" instead of 105.

71. Trans. Parker (2007).

72. Hall 1986, 2567–2568.

73. See Turfa 2012, 31 for thoughts on the origins (real and alleged) of the Etruscans' saecular system.

74. Turfa 2012, 106: "Cultures were determining factors in the doctrine," at least in the minds of those who believed Rome would last for twelve *saecula* (see chapter 5 for the story of the seer Vulcatius in the memoirs of Augustus).

75. Cornell 1976, 422.

76. For the fullest recent analysis of the work of Censorinus, see Freidin 2020. Modern scholars disagree on his aptitude as an antiquarian. Grafton and Swerdlow (1985, 461): "his treatment is neither scientific nor historical despite his efforts to separate the credible from the fabulous . . . grossly inconsistent in quality . . . and supinely credulous about Etruscan predictions and the like," but (454) the work is "all couched in language so jejune as to suggest that he added little or nothing to what he read"; Parker (2007, xi–xii): Censorinus was "a compiler, not a scholar" but is "admirably clear in explaining even the complexities of astrology and mathematics"; Santangelo (2013, 117): his composition is a "learned work."

77. Weinstock (1971, 192): Censorinus "depends on a good antiquarian, no doubt Varro."

78. Including the etymology of the word *saeculum*, at Varro, *Ling.* 6.11; Hall 1986, 2567, citing Diehl 1934, 255.

79. Cornell 1976, *passim*.

80. Cornell 1976, 431–432.

81. Cornell 1976, 437.

82. Note that Plutarch uses the Greek word γένεα, like Hesiod, instead of the technical term *saeculum* (for which there was no Greek loan word or transliteration, as shown in the Greek version of the *Res Gestae*).

178 | Notes to Pages 33–37

83. The total of eight ages would also conflict with other sources, such as Servius, *ad Ecl.* 9.46 (see chapter 5), where the *haruspex* announces the beginning of the tenth age in 44 BCE. At *Dem.* 2.2, Plutarch admits that he is not a strong reader of Latin, which perhaps may account for some of these issues.

84. The Varronian material need not be seven hundred years old to be authentic: Smith (2014, 89–90) points out that the Etruscan "sense of their own ultimate demise" put forward in their saecular doctrine "may be a prophecy after the event—after the Roman conquest when it was clear that there was a limit to Etruscan autonomy."

85. Van der Meer 2011, 116–117.

86. Van der Meer 2011, 117.

87. For evidence of *saeculum*-level longevity among Etruscans, we have the epitaph of a certain Felsnas Laris, who died at 106 years old; see Turfa 2012, 30 on Felsnas and the (suspicious?) longevity of many members of the Etruscan aristocracy.

88. See Schultz 2006, 222–223; Luke 2014, 44–45. Adams (2003, 182) argues, based on linguistic analysis, that the text is actually an imperial forgery, but Luke points out that such a dating "does not exclude the possibility that the imperial version was based on an earlier Republican-era tradition."

89. Source of text: Lachmann 1848, 350–351; trans. De Grummond and Simon (2006).

90. Luke 2014, 45.

91. Briquel (2014, 118–121) collects many stories of mockery directed toward soothsayers by Cato the Elder, Plautus, and Pomponius and skeptical attacks by Lucretius and Cicero, as well as hostile Roman stories of Etruscan seers deceptively exploiting Roman ignorance (though without denying the validity of the *Etrusca disciplina* itself).

92. Rosenblitt 2019, esp. 115–140.

93. Rosenblitt 2019, 99.

94. On the "atypical" qualities of Sulla contributing to his claims that "a new age had begun," see also Davies 2017, 213–214.

95. Balsdon 1951, 1. Other examples: Sulla was the first to exhibit untethered lions in the Circus (Seneca, *De brevitate vitae* 13.6); Sulla was the first member of the Cornelii to be cremated (Pliny, *HN* 7.187); Sulla's stepson Scaurus was the first Roman to own a gemstone collection (*dactyliotheca*; *HN* 37.11); small, low-price pearls (Fenestella F25 Cornell) and floor mosaics (*HN* 36.189) first came into vogue under Sulla; Sulla was the first Roman to bother to plunder a library (Strabo 13.1.54; Plutarch, *Sull.* 26). Sulla's cultural iconoclasm may have contributed to the later perception of him (best exemplified by Sallust, *B. Cat.* 11) that many Roman vices were first introduced to their culture by Sulla. On Sulla's eclecticism more broadly, see Vollenweider 1958/1959, 27–28.

Notes to Pages 37–38 | 179

96. Gagé (1955, 431) notes that the first attested occasion of the Etruscan system of *saecula* in Rome is the Sullan portent of 88 BCE.

97. Sulla himself would even become a new Latin verb: Cicero (*Att.* 9.10.6.8) uses *sullaturit*, "it has been Sulla-minded," to describe Pompey's attitude; Quintilian later made note of this coinage (*Inst.* 8.3.32, 8.6.32). (This verb elegantly captured Cicero's sentiment, expressed previously to Atticus at 8.11.2.8 and 9.7.3.11, that Pompey was desirous of the leadership method of the *Sullani regni*.) Cicero frequently made mention of a Sullan Age (*Verr.* 2.1.43; *Paradoxa Stoicorum* 6.46; *Har. resp.* 18; *Mur.* 49; *Dom.* 43 [where it was characterized by *acerbitas*] and 79; *Fam.* 13.4.1 [where it was also characterized by *acerbitas*] and 13.5.2), as did Pliny the Elder (*HN* 13.88, discussing the destruction of the Sibylline Books and in relation to the burning of the Capitoline) and Suetonius (*Gram. et rhet.* 11 and 13), as well as Servius, *ad Aen.* 6.73 when discussing the *XVviri*. The first instance, however, of a Roman using *saeculum* with such a descriptor is Seneca the Younger, *De ira* 1.20.4, *sullano saeculo*.

98. See Rawson 1985, 303–315 on divination in Rome during the first century BCE. For broader Roman interest in Etruscan culture, see Hall 1996, 149–286; De Grummond 2013, 543–544.

99. Nigidius Figulus, in book 4 of his *De diis*, notes that certain authorities (including apparently Orphic rituals) connect gods with *saecula*, and he mentions a connection between *saecula* and conflagrations (F67 Swoboda = Servius, *ad Bucol.* 4.10): *quidam deos et eorum genera temporibus et aetatibus <distinguunt>, inter quos et Orpheus: primum regnum Saturni, deinde Iovis, tum Neptunium, inde Plutonis; nonnulli etiam, ut magi, aiunt Apollinis fore regnum, in quo videndum est, ne ardorem, sive illa ecpyrosis adpellanda est, dicant.* The phrase *eorum genera* seems to imply the kind of qualitative periodization I am arguing for here. Servius goes on to say that the reference to Apollo and Lucina at *Ecl.* 4.10 were understood by some to be references to Augustus and Octavia, with the reign of Augustus being the final Apolline *saeculum* articulated by Nigidius.

100. See Rawson 1985, 303–315 on divination in the Roman intellectual world during the first century BCE. For broader Roman interest in Etruscan culture, see Hall 1996, 149–286; De Grummond 2013, 543–544. Livy and Diodorus Siculus recorded the various omens associated with the outbreak of the civil war in 88 BCE, according to Suda 1337, and Cicero (*Har. resp.* 9.18) seems also to be recalling the Etruscan soothsayers explaining the portents of 88 BCE. Assuming they did not get this information directly from Sulla's memoirs, it must have been circulating in other ways (including official senatorial records). See Rawson 1979 for the argument that Sisenna's (lost) history "certainly recorded portents at the start of the Social War, with the haruspices' interpretation of them" (341) and probably featured Sulla in an emphatic, and romanticized, role.

180 | Notes to Pages 40–42

Chapter 2: Eternal Returns

1. Among many sources for the history of Greek philosophy at Rome, I will single out Zetzel 2016 for the various venues of Roman engagement with philosophy, as well as the Barnes and Griffin 1997 volume, relevant especially for this chapter.

2. Star 2021 appeared too recently for me to be able to incorporate its research into my study. Its first three chapters (13–126) cover many of the same intellectual topics from the Greek philosophical tradition and their influence on later Roman poetry as I do throughout this chapter.

3. Among other examples, see Horace, *Epod.* 15.21 (*Pythagorae arcana renati*), and especially in a mocking sense, such as *Fast.* 3.153 and the claims at Horace, *Sat.* 2.6.63 that Pythagoras had beans for relatives (*Pythagorae cognata*).

4. On the distinction see Riedweg 2005, 62–63; for an alternative understanding of Pythagorean metempsychosis, see Luchte 2009. For what "Pythagoreanism" meant in the ancient world, see Kahn 2001.

5. See, e.g., Ovid, *Met.* 15.158–175.

6. Rawson 1985, 292.

7. This bold claim, though, made Ennius a target for abuse in the first century BCE by poets such as Lucretius (1.124) and Horace (*Epist.* 2.1.52). Hardie (1986, 17–22 and 79–83) posits that Ennius took this idea directly from Empedocles, making the Pythagorean connection indirect.

8. For fullest recent treatment of the history of Pythagoreanism at Rome and its renewed flourishing in the first century BCE, see Volk 2016.

9. Swoboda 1964, 83 (F67); see note 99 at the end of chapter 1 and the discussion in chapter 5 below for more on this passage.

10. Rawson 1985, 291–294; Riedweg 2005, 123–124. The fact that Cicero brings up Nigidius Figulus in his translation of the *Timaeus* is perhaps related to that work's own discussion of periodic catastrophes; see more below.

11. Farrell 2013, 83: "The idea that Cicero bequeathed to Vergil a Pythagorean conception of Plato is borne out by the fact that in almost every passage where Servius detects Platonic influence it is influence of a sort that is compatible with Pythagorean teachings."

12. Galinsky 1975, 48.

13. E.g., *vetus illa aetas cui fecimus aurea nomen*, *Met.* 15.96; *sic ad ferrum venistis ab auro, / saecula*, 15.260-1; perhaps also a reference to Etruscan city foundations and saecular doctrine at 15.446.

14. Gruen (1990, 159) writes that the connection in Roman minds between Pythagoras and Numa is so strong that Cicero and Livy take great pains to refute it (although Ovid will later treat it like a fact again).

15. However, some scholars have argued for a later dating. For a particularly thorough analysis of the work related to these issues, see Peirano 2012, 117–172.

Notes to Pages 42–46 | 181

16. Crucially, the poet also declares his willingness, if Messalla should need it, to jump into the flames of Mount Aetna (*vivum Aetnaeae corpus committere flammae*, 196), a direct reference to the supposed death of Empedocles in an attempt to prove or justify his own profession of Pythagorean metempsychosis.

17. Note that Censorinus gives one definition of the word as "the longest period of human life" (17.2).

18. κατὰ περιόδους τινάς τά γενόμενα ποτε πάλιν γίνεται, Dicaearchus fr. 40 Mirhady = Porphyry, *Vita Pythagorae* 19. See also Riedweg 2005, 62–63.

19. It is actually mathematically possible for time to extend infinitely without having every possible configuration of atoms happen or repeat, but no ancient writers seem to demonstrate an awareness of this.

20. *Sent. Vat.* 14.

21. There was no hard Epicurean orthodoxy, although preference is usually given to Epicurus's own writings. On this issue, see Longo Auricchio and Tepedino Guerra 1981; Annas 1989, 164; Erler 1992, 178ff. Per Annas, whatever Epicurus himself did not make completely clear was argued over by later Epicureans.

22. Rawson 1985, 284: Epicurean treatises other than that by Lucretius existed in the Latin literature of the first century BCE; we know of works by Amafinius, Rabirius, Catius, and Philodemus. Philodemus seems not to have been interested in physics, but Catius evidently was (Quintilian, *Inst.* 10.1.124). Costa 1984, 74: Lucretius (5.335–337) claims that he is the first to describe Epicureanism in Latin, which seems to be untrue, so maybe he means that he is the first to discuss Epicurean physics.

23. For discussion on Lucretius and his treatments of this palingenesis issue, see Warren 2000, 2001, and 2004, as well as Schiesaro 1994.

24. Warren 2004, 358.

25. *Genethliaci quidam scripserunt . . . esse in renascendis hominibus quam appellant paliggenesian Graeci; hac scripserunt confici in annis numero quadringentis quadraginta, ut idem corpus et eadem anima, quae fuerint coniuncta in homine aliquando, eadem rursus redeant in coniunctionem* (*Civ. Dei* 22.28).

26. On this Varro fragment and its relation to Lucretius, see Schiesaro 1994 and 2021.

27. Pliny the Elder, likely working with an earlier source (perhaps Varro?), gives a list of examples at *HN* 7.52–56, the most famous being the plebeian lookalikes of Pompey (cf. Valerius Maximus 9.14).

28. On the topic of Stoic cyclical conflagration, see also the summary in Long 2006.

29. Nemesius 309.5–311.2 = SVF 2.625 = Long and Sedley 1987, 52C1; trans. Long and Sedley (1987).

30. Long and Sedley 1987, 311.

182 | Notes to Pages 46–48

31. Alternatively, a Stoic may imagine a circular timeline, like a clock face, with the conflagration at midnight, at which point the same period starts over again.

32. Aristocles (Eusebius, *Praep. evang.* 15.14.12) = SVF 1.98 = Long and Sedley 1987, 46G; trans. Long and Sedley (1987).

33. Zeno: *Alexander Lycopolis* 19.2–4 = Long and Sedley 1987, 46I; Cleanthes: Plutarch, *Comm. not.* 1075D = SVF 1.510 = Long and Sedley 1987, 46L.

34. Long and Sedley 1987, 278: "On this conception . . . the universe is a cyclical process which alternates forever between an ordered system, of which we ourselves are parts, and a state of pure fire, or 'light' in Chrysippus' interesting formulation."

35. Here the Stoics were directly responding to Plato, who had argued in favor of the eternity of the world in *Timaeus* 41a–b by objecting to the possibility that a perfect God would destroy his own creation.

36. Salles 2005, 74.

37. Although Heraclitus had argued for an explanation like this in his own works, as the later Stoics understood him. Finkelberg 1998, 219–220: "[This] portrayal of conflagration, this time not as the final outcome of fire's gradual transformations but as an impetuous descent of avenging justice upon the world, driving it to an instantaneous destruction, reveals the eschatological purport of Heraclitus' cosmogonical doctrine."

38. Long and Sedley 1987, 279: "The end of the present world will not be a 'destruction' in any qualified sense; it introduces no discontinuity in the life of the world at its most extended, but only a 'natural change.'" Cf. Ju 2009, 116: "The conflagration . . . is understood by the Stoics as the devastation of the world's arrangement as such, so that 'all,' namely the whole of the world, is resolved into, and unified with, a single element, 'fire.' This process also represents a sort of rarefaction, but, unlike the normal referent of the term 'rarefaction,' the conflagration is unidirectional and does not at once accompany condensation, rather determining the world's periodic destruction into fire at very long intervals of everlasting recurrence. In Stoic physics the conflagration is in this light a particular form of resolution, applying above all to the destruction of the elements, the world, the gods other than Zeus, and the souls of sages."

39. Rawson 1985, 8.

40. E.g., *Att.* 2.1.2.

41. An anecdote told by many, e.g., Pliny the Elder, *HN* 7.112.

42. Posidonius often "lies outside the Stoic consensus" (MacGregor 2005, 65); "It is typical of Posidonius that he read previous philosophers and especially Plato constructively for his own purposes, rarely venturing purely disinterested comments" (Ju 2009, 123).

43. Ju 2009, 116–117.

Notes to Pages 48–49 | 183

44. Fr. 49EK (EK = Edelstein and Kiss 1989). Humphreys (1997, 214–216) argues that Posidonius may have integrated his Stoic perspective with the Polybian *anacyclosis* model of human political states shifting in cycles, a tantalizing possibility of major influence on Roman saecular discourse.

45. Fr. 284EK. See below for Dicaearchus and his demythologized primitivist account of the Golden Age, which survives in Seneca the Younger's piece-by-piece refutation (*Ep.* 90).

46. Fr. 53EK.

47. Galinsky (1996, 96) notes that the Posidonian claim that "good *mores* make *leges* superfluous" appears in Horace, *Ode* 3.24.

48. Even if few Romans totally accepted Stoic doctrines on the physical model of the universe or based their temporal notions of human history on them, Stoicism nevertheless provided a set of terms and images that could be usefully adapted to describe metakosmesis; for Roman discourse on time, the words and images used are "just as likely to be regarded as true concepts as they are poetic figures" (Lukacher 1998, 5).

49. Downing 1995, 101.

50. Downing 1995, 104.

51. On this expectation, see the Lucretius passage in chapter 4.

52. Sherwin-White 1998, 380.

53. The most important recent work on this episode in Roman history is Pandey 2013. I essentially agree with the argument made throughout it, but at 412 n. 21 Pandey argues that Octavian was insufficiently aware of the possibilities of saecular discourse and Etruscan divinatory terminology to have included the second half of this story (about the seer Vulcanius or Vulcatius) in his memoirs, and that this must be an interpolation from a later source. As this book demonstrates, it is actually very likely that Octavian understood the significance of Vulcanius's declaration immediately.

54. On the funeral games and the comet, see Weinstock 1971, 88–91, 370–386. Cornell (2013, 3.538) claims a crucial difference between comets (which tended to be seen as negative) and stars; Augustus had to toy with the nomenclature throughout his career. The slippage between the status of this astronomical entity as a "comet" or as a "star" has been noted by many scholars; see Koortbojian 2013, 26–28 for a review of scholarship.

55. See Smith and Powell 2009 for further analysis of this passage.

56. A sampling: Vergil, *Ecl.* 9.47, *Aen.* 8.681; Horace, *Odes* 1.12.46–47; Propertius 3.18.33–34, 4.6.59; Ovid, *Met.* 15.845–850.

57. See the examples in Zanker 1990.

58. Cornell 2013, 3.538: "the new *saeculum*, and its portent, were presented by the Caesarians as a promising new beginning."

59. Weinstock 1971, 379: "It can only mean a revised version of the prophecy of Vulcanius: in 44 as well as in 17 the comet announced the beginning of a new *saeculum*."

184 | Notes to Page 66

60. On the possible effects of this event in Rome, see McConnell et al. 2020 (as well as the response letter by Strunz and Braeckel 2020).

61. Jal (1963, 238–251) describes how, beginning with the fighting between Marius and Sulla, Romans came to expect oracular signs to accompany civil war and were prepared to explain their meanings in terms of changing eras.

62. Beyond the material analyzed below, a few other passages are worth noting. It is possible that "from Deucalion" had long been a colloquial Roman expression meaning "very old"; see Lucilius F284 Warmington (old cots dating from Deucalion, *a Deucalione grabati*). Juvenal 15.30 uses *a Pyrrha* in the same way, and Ammianus Marcellinus 30.4.12 makes a similar joke about an entity dying ages (*saeculis*) prior alongside Evander's mother. In a more substantially saecular reference, Vergil says in the *Georgics* that Nature provided laws and characteristic benefits for certain places as far back as the *tempus* of Deucalion's propagation of the human race (1.61–62). Vergil also writes, in *Ecl.* 6, that Silenus sings about Pyrrha (*lapides Pyrrhae iactos*, 41) in the same two lines that he mentions the Golden Age (*Saturnia regna*, 41) and Prometheus as a culture-hero (*furtum Promethei*, 42), suggesting more clearly a link in Vergil's works between the Deucalion myth and saecularity. Later, Columella mentions the "Deucalionian rocks" (*Deucalioneae cautes*, 67) from which humans were created in his Vergilian poem at the beginning of book 10 of his *De agri cultura*.

63. Phaethon is often referenced obliquely, sometimes only as a negative exemplum of hubris or in connection with his sisters' creation of amber, but I am only interested in references to Phaethon for his role in a world disaster. Nonetheless there are several brief references to Phaethon's flames specifically, which allude to the disaster: Catullus 64.291 (*flammati Phaethontis*); a fragment of Varro of Atax's *Argonautae* (*tum te flagranti deiectum fulmine Phaethon*; see fr.11 Courtney); *Culex* 128; Horace, *Odes* 4.11.25 on Phaethon's smoking corpse (about which see Reckford 1972, 429); Ovid, *Tr.* 4.3.65.

64. Galinsky 1975, 105 on the Phaethon story and its connection to Pythagoras; see above for Pythagorean influence on the development of saecularity. More recently, Closs (2020) has drawn connections between first-century BCE fears about destruction and Phaethon imagery; at 13–16, Closs explicitly connects Phaethon to both the Stoic ekpyrosis and the notion of the *saeculum*.

65. In one version of these myths, found in the *Fabulae* of the Augustan mythographer Hyginus, though it seems to be a much later interpolation, the flood of Deucalion is caused in order to put out the global fire caused by Phaethon's disaster; see Diggle 1970, 15–22. Much later, Nonnus attributes the flood to an attempt to put out a worldwide fire caused by lightning bolts aimed at the Titans (*Dion.* 6).

66. See, e.g., Ovid's *Fast.* 4 passage and Manilius's *Astronomica* 4 passage below; also Lucan 1.651–657, Martial 5.53, Servius on *Ecl.* 6.41, *Phoenix* 11–14.

An epigrammist of the Neronian period, Lucillius, has a humorous poem in the *Greek Anthology* (11.214) about an artist who has painted a Deucalion and a Phaethon, and another Lucillian poem (11.131) links the two as famous killers of men; the former poem may reflect the growing popularity of the imagery of these two myths in the visual arts in the years preceding the Neronian era. And note that this pairing was not an inevitable mental link for the Romans: for a contemporary example of a mythological combination of fire and water that does not mention Deucalion and Phaethon, see Tibullus, 1.9.49–50.

67. Nisbet and Hubbard 1970, 23: "In our poem Horace describes his flood not as a quaint impossibility but as something that has actually happened."

68. Commager 1962, 179; Dyer 1965, 79; Nisbet and Hubbard 1970, 23.

69. Cf. Taylor 1962, 37, who reads here "an echo of the cyclical view of human history, in the national and political context," recalling both Stoic physics and a cosmic cycle "in which the dominant trend was always downward." Nisbet and Hubbard (1970, 22) see this as a reference to the Great Year doctrine, for which every cosmic cycle ends with fire or flood, but this does not seem to be a likely application.

70. Fraenkel (1957, 243) sees the *iam satis* as an allusion to the similarly contextualized prayer at the end of Vergil's *G.* 1 (*satis iam,* 501), about which see more below, but he points out (246) that unlike the supernatural omens of Vergil's depiction of the post-assassination period (469–488), Horace's imagery in 1.2 is natural.

71. Grant (1950, 185) notes that Theophilus of Antioch (115–181 CE) draws from some mythographical source the information that "a certain Klymenos was in a deluge after Deucalion (3.18); this may possibly refer to Klymenos the father of Phaethon (Hyginus, *Fab.* 154), and regard Phaethon as the first king after the original deluge (Plutarch, *Pyrrh.* 1). Or it may be a mistake for Cerambus (Ovid, *Met.* 7.353–356). It is obviously very erudite."

72. Bömer (1969, *loc. cit.*) says that a story recorded in the third-century CE *Metamorphoses* of Antoninus Liberalis expands on the account in Ovid (Cerambus offends the nymphs and is turned into a beetle), and he speculates that it probably came from the lost *Metamorphoses* of the second-century BCE poet Nicander. Bömer also (*loc. cit.*) points out that the term *inobrutus* (356) is a *hapax legomenon,* which is all the more appropriate since Cerambus is a singular figure in his own right.

73. *Contra* Bömer 1969, *loc. cit.*, on the force of *tempus:* "Singuläre Junktur." Cf. *Met.* 8.97, where Minos addresses Scylla as *O nostri infamia saecli.*

74. Cf. Lucretius 5.96, *moles et machina mundi,* in a passage also describing the inevitable destruction of the world; Ovid alludes to this very line of Lucretius in his prophecy of Lucretius's fame in *Am.* 1.15.23–4, so he must be aware of the metakosmetic connotation of his allusion.

186 | Notes to Pages 52–53

75. Lee 1984, 100–101.

76. For more about Prometheus and his saecular aspects, as well as those of all culture-heroes, see chapter 4. Ovid also refers to Pyrrha as the niece of Prometheus at *Ib.* 544.

77. A *durum genus*, alluding to Vergil's Deucalion passage at *G.* 1.63. The native Italians self-describe as a *durum genus* at *Aen.* 9.605, perhaps suggesting a temporal connection to the age of Deucalion and Pyrrha.

78. Triton's signal is also associated with destruction: at *Aen.* 6.162ff., Misenus is famed for his ability to blast loud trumpet calls, but by blaring out on a conch shell he stirs the wrath of Triton and is drowned by that very divinity. But Propertius describes a fountain in a statue of Triton that made a pleasing sound at 2.31/32.15–16.

79. See also the portent of an Etruscan trumpet blast in the sky at *Aen.* 8.526. The conch shell's metakosmetic connotations are expanded by Germanicus in his *Aratea* (554–562), in lines greatly embellishing the original material in Aratus. He describes the discoverer of the conch (*cochlidis inventor,* 554), with a blast of which the happier age (*laetior aetas,* 555) of the gods went into battle with the Titans. The next zodiacal sign given by Germanicus is Deucalion (562), even though technically it ought to be Aquarius; Hyginus 2.29.1.5 tells us that Hegesianax equated Deucalion with Aquarius, so here Germanicus chooses to use the name with a metakosmetic resonance for his Roman audience.

80. Luke 2014, 49–52. On Plutarch's citation practices, see chapter 1.

81. Santangelo 2007, 215–216.

82. In the *LIMC,* the only secure surviving depiction from antiquity is a sarcophagus relief from Ostia from around 180–190 CE, in which the pair are throwing the stones over their shoulders which turn into newly born humans (the inscription reads *homines nati*); cf. the brief entry on Deucalion in the *EAA.*

83. See *LIMC* for details on these objects.

84. *LIMC s.v.* Phaethon, 353: "C'est à la fin du Ier av. J.-C. que le mythe semble s'etre imposé dans les arts figurés, au moment où Ovide lui donnait, dans la littérature, sa forme la plus élaborée." Note also Diggle 1970, 7: "There is little of Phaethon in Roman literature before Ovid."

85. One potential link between stories: seals appear both in the flood of Deucalion (1.299–300, in an area where goats had previously grazed) and in the fiery destruction caused by Phaethon (2.267–268, floating dead on the water because of the scorching heat of the air). Also, the personified Saeculum appears standing next to the throne of Phoebus (2.26), but since Day, Month, and Year are joining Saeculum, this figure most likely represents a Century, although Ovid may invite us to read it in multiple ways.

86. Bömer 1969, 318: "Das Fatum dieser Stelle hat eine enge Parallele in der Deucalion-Geschichte."

Notes to Pages 54–59 | 187

87. Van der Sluijs (2006, 71) suggests that Ovid's depiction of the death of Phaethon (*Met.* 2.319–322) sees him metamorphose, with his hair and long trail, into a meteor or comet. This depiction calls to mind Caesar's comet in 44 BCE, interpreted by the Etruscan seer in Augustus's memoirs as the herald of a new age. Cf. Gale 2013, 287–288, arguing that Vergil's reference at *G.* 1.466–468 to the eclipse after Caesar's assassination (during which the *impia saecula* was in a state of fear) alludes to the Phaethon myth, for which (in Ovid's depiction) the Sun refuses to give light to the world after Phaethon's death.

88. On the story that Phaethon created the Milky Way, cf. Aristotle's *Mete.* 345a, Diodorus Siculus 5.23.2; Diodorus, a first-century BCE writer, also attests the wide popularity of the myth, saying many poets and historians (πολλοὶ τῶν τε ποιητῶν καὶ τῶν συγγραφέων) have mentioned it. Aristotle describes the Phaethon explanation for the origin of the Milky Way as a Pythagorean view.

89. The *Bibliotheca* of [Apollodorus], dated to the first or second century CE, associates Deucalion with the end of the bronze age (1.7.2); this designation may reflect the development of apocalyptic Deucalion imagery in saecular thought in the first century BCE.

90. In particular, Phaethon's connection to epoch-making global catastrophes was developed throughout the century after Sulla such that the emperor Tiberius occasionally said that in his patronage of Caligula, he was rearing a viper for the Roman people and a Phaethon for the whole world (*se natricem populo Romano, Phaethontem orbi terrarum educare*; Suetonius, *Calig.* 11.1).

91. Blundell (1986, 103–134) draws several connections between Roman approaches to cyclical history and their Greek antecedents in the Platonic and Aristotelian works.

92. Trans. Bury (1926).

93. Benardete 2000, 92.

94. Benardete 2000, 95.

95. Trans. Bury (1929).

96. Chroust 1973, 113.

97. Lukacher 1998, 4.

98. Chroust 1973, 120.

99. Trans. Lee (1952).

100. McDiarmid 1940, 245.

101. All translations that follow are from Chroust 1973, 116.

102. Chroust 1973, 117.

103. Trans. Rackham (1932).

104. This concept was known to the Romans; e.g., Cicero writes about it at *Nat. D.* 2.51.

105. Solmsen (1951, 8) claims on the other hand that, to Aristotle, major floods on earth do not reflect the developments of the heavenly region.

188 | Notes to Pages 59–64

106. Chroust 1973, 115–116. Aristotle mentions or alludes to "cosmic catastrophes" also in *Mete.* 339b19ff., *Cael.* 270b16ff., *Metaph.* 1074a38ff. and 1074b10, and *Pol.* 1264a3ff., 1269a5ff., and 1329b24ff.

107. It is notable that Dicaearchus was very familiar with the life and work of Pythagoras (see fr. 40–42FS), in particular the Pythagorean ideas about metempsychosis.

108. *Off.* 2.16–17 = fr. 78FS; trans. Fortenbaugh and Schütrumpf (2001).

109. Fr. 53–56bFS.

110. Saunders 2001, 242.

111. Fr. 54–55FS.

112. Saunders 2001, 243.

113. Polybius 6.5.5–6; he cites an unspecified λόγος (perhaps a tradition?) that this has happened multiple times before already. Cf. Cicero, *Div.* 1.112, for a city destroyed by an earthquake; Pliny the Elder, *HN* 2.53, on the destruction of the city Bolsena by lightning.

114. Costa 1984, 74.

115. Costa 1984, 76.

116. At 405, "the sarcastic comment dismisses the childish fairy-tale" (Costa 1984, 77).

117. Costa 1984, 76: while Lucretius does not believe in the myth of Phaethon, "he seems to think of it as a sort of allegory of the phenomenon he is envisaging."

118. On this satire, see the commentary by Cèbe (1983), as well as the more recent work by Schiesaro (2019).

119. Edlund-Berry 1994.

120. Gardner (2019, 116–134) comments on Roman perceptions of civilization collapse via the temporal construct of ages.

121. Ovid also proleptically describes a post-civilization earth earlier (1.246–249), when the council of the gods fears what the world will look like after the flood; he uses language that recalls the post-Roman wastelands of Horace and Propertius (see below).

122. Rood 2016, 359: for Thucydides, "future ruins reflect an idea of historical rupture."

123. On this passage and the post-Roman connotations, see also Betensky 1979, 110–111; Farrell 1991, 167–168.

124. *Contra* Erren (1985, *loc. cit.*), whose claim that the use of *scilicet* means Vergil is being "sarkastischer" is an overinterpretation.

125. Cf. Jenkyns 1993, 119: "it may be implied . . . that the farmer who digs up the remains of the dead of Philippi will not know their significance, so great is the expanse of time between."

126. Mayor, perhaps the authoritative source on this topic, has collected and analyzed these and other examples from all of antiquity (2000).

127. Plutarch, *Sert.* 9.6–7; cf. Tanusius Geminus F1 Cornell.

128. Thus Konrad (1994, 60) suggests.

129. Pliny the Elder, *HN* 7.16; cf. Sallust, *Hist.* fr. 3.49 Ramsey.

130. *On Signs* fr. 4 De Lacy.

131. Suetonius, *Aug.* 72.3.

132. Pliny the Elder, *HN* 7.16.

133. Beagon 2005, 255.

134. Heyworth 2007, 497: the "primary point" is "that Veii is now forgotten"; he contrasts this with Ovid's Troy, "where it is only ten years since the sack of Troy and agriculture has not fully covered its bones."

135. Cairns 2009, 292. This passage "fulfills that other proper function of elegy, to mourn for the dead" (Cairns 2009, 357).

136. Keith 2016, 171–172.

137. 6.448–449: "A day will come when holy Ilium will die, and Priam and his people" (ἔσσεται ἦμαρ ὅταν ποτ᾽ ὀλώλῃ Ἴλιος ἱρὴ / καὶ Πρίαμος καὶ λαός).

138. Harrison (1993, 145–146) notes the motif of animals playing among the ruins of a great city. See also Rissanen 2015, 123–139 on the Roman attitude to wolves; he notes that wolves prevent the repopulation of the grounds of Carthage during Gaius Gracchus's failed colonization attempt (Plutarch, *C. Gracch.* 11.1).

139. Mankin (1995, 250) suggests that these lines are intended to recall the Gallic sack of Rome in 390 BC, and that Horace's suggestion to abandon Rome matches those Romans' plan, which Camillus famously rejected (Livy 5.49–55).

140. This paradox is noted by Miles (1980, *loc. cit.*).

141. Mankin (1995, 250) notes the lack of "Golden Age" optimism that usually accompanies depictions of pre-Romulan Rome in Latin literature. Sertorius is said to have dreamed of sailing to the Isles of the Blessed (Sallust *Hist.* fr. 1.87–90 Ramsey; Plutarch, *Sert.* 8.1–9.2).

142. Mankin (1995, 271–272), like many scholars, notes the Roman preference for the "'temporal' rather than 'racial'" depiction of the myth, suggesting that perhaps the myth appealed to the Romans as "history" rather than as "anthropology" (as it would to the Greeks).

143. Several scholars, but most fully Zanker (2010), argue that Horace composed *Epod.* 16 as a direct response to (and as a corrective for) the overly intangible Golden Age of *Ecl.* 4.

144. Cf. *Fast.* 1.231ff., described above.

145. Santangelo (2013, 124) notes that since *olim* can refer to the future as well as the past, the thickets on the Capitol may return; cf. Feeney 2007, 165. This reading complements my reading of *Ecl.* 4 in chapter 4 that Vergil's *ordo saeclorum* is a neverending pendulum.

146. White (1993, 186) points out that Vergil's Aeneas sees a Capitoline that was "a numinous spot where relics of a long-extinct settlement were

190 | Notes to Pages 68–72

visible," while Tibullus says that it was inhabited by shepherds in the time of Aeneas (2.5.26–30). Propertius, too, ignores this earlier settlement and imagines Aeneas coming upon virgin woodland at 4.1.1–2. See also Propertius 3.9.49; Ovid, *Ars am.* 3.119–120.

147. On this passage, see esp. the analysis of Feeney (2007, 163–166).

Chapter 3: Inflection Points

1. On this ancient Roman tendency, see esp. Earl 1961, 41–59.

2. Earl 1961, 41–59.

3. Although Piso F38 Cornell mentions the beginning of a new (civic) *saeculum* in 158 BCE, see Cornell 2013, 3. 213: "There is no direct indication in the other fragments of Piso that he divided Roman history into *saecula*."

4. In *Cat.* 6–13, Rome's fall occurs after 146 BCE but only as the result of bad fortune; in *Iug.* 41 Sallust clarifies that the removal of *metus Punicus* caused internal strife; in *Hist.* fr. 9, a more general *metus hostilis* is credited for keeping Rome together, which after 146 BCE had disappeared. See McGushin 1992, 78.

5. See Cicero, *Paradoxa Stoicorum* 49–50, discussed below; cf. Cato (speaking in Cicero, *Sen.* 55), who admires the frugality of Manius Curius and the instruction of the age (*temporum disciplinam*) in which he lived, instruction presumably related to that very frugality.

6. Cf. Cicero's discussion at *Cael.* 48 on whether young men's indulgence in *meretrices* is typical of the *saeculum* (*ab huius saeculi licentia*) or was actually a custom of earlier Romans (*maiorum consuetudine*) as well.

7. Cf. Cicero, *Off.* 2.75, when Pontius the Samnite wishes he had been born in that age (*ad illa tempora*) when Romans began to accept bribes; this practice, says Cicero, began *multa saecula* later.

8. For emphasis on the artificiality of any Roman decline narrative, see Galinsky 1992, 53–73, and especially his appendix of no less than 210 explanations for Rome's decline.

9. Sallust, for what it is worth, never deploys saecular discourse in any of his extant works, preferring instead these two-stage accounts; given his hostility to Sulla, perhaps he was unwilling to adopt the temporal rhetoric popularized by the deceased dictator.

10. Cf. 1.19.3, 2.14.1, 7.14.6, 28.12.12, 34.51.5. For Livy, *aetas* tends to refer to a "generation" because he pairs it so frequently with genitives such as "of our fathers," "of our elders," etc.

11. At 3.20.5, Livy notes that the Romans of 460 BCE did not possess the "disregard for the gods which now holds the *saeculum*" (*quae nunc tenet saeculum neglegentia deum*), but while this brief digression marks his own *saeculum* with a

Notes to Pages 72–76 | 191

characteristic impiety, there is no larger saecular narrative of impiety. Similarly, at 26.22.15 Livy writes that the "worthless and flimsy authority even of parents against their children in this *saeculum*" (*parentium quoque hoc saeculo vilis levisque apud liberos auctoritas*) makes his account of young men asking their elders which consul to vote for in 211 BCE seem like a hardly credible story, but beyond the idea that the past was better than the present, there is little here in the way of saecularity.

12. Earl (1961, 43) argues that Livy consciously chose to align himself with the "senatorial tradition," perhaps rendering it impossible for him to use saecularity in his narrative. But see Miles 1995, 75–109 for a larger conception of moral cyclicality in Livy, requiring periodic refoundations of the city by exceptional *conditor* figures.

13. Trans. Keyes (1928).

14. For the text of Propertius, I follow Goold 2006.

15. Heyworth (2007, 72) deletes lines 11–12, owing to the difficulty he perceives in comparing the mistress to *luxuria* itself and to the hexameter's "strange expectation that the woman's bad reputation (n.b. *infames*, 9) might enable her to save her good reputation," but I find Goold's text and interpretation here adequate.

16. Livy 10.23 describes a cult of Pudicitia Patricia.

17. See Shackleton Bailey 1956, 115 for *saecla* as equivalent to *mores*, for which Lucan 10.110 (*nondum translatos Romana in saecula luxus*) is given as a comparandum.

18. Luck (1979, 85–88) makes the case for continuity between the two poems.

19. Heyworth (2007, 254) reads this hexameter as an echo of Cicero's *O fortunatam natam me consule Romam* (fr. 8 Courtney); this is relevant, in the light of arguments that Cicero depicted himself as a second founder of Rome through statements such as that line of verse (see chapter 5).

20. Heyworth (2007, 257) points out the oddity of Propertius seemingly suggesting that infidelity began *during* the flood (*cum*, 53); he also notes that here Propertius uses the flood of Deucalion to end the Golden Age, when typically it ended the Bronze Age (or, in Ovid, *Met.* 1.125–347, the Iron Age).

21. The talking door in Propertius 1.16 also recalls a similar device in Catullus 67.

22. One exception: the book-closing 2.34, where Propertius explicitly lists all of his elegiac forerunners at the finale of the poem.

23. Cf. Ovid, *Ars am.* 3.118, *Medic.* 11 (see below) for Tatius and the Sabines as typical references to old Roman morality.

24. See Leach 1988, 412–413.

25. Heyworth 2007, 137: "The tone of the whole passage [on the inventor of erotic wall art as a negative culture hero] is not easy to judge," but he finds it "jocular, perhaps a jibe at the *princeps*, whose programme of moral

192 | Notes to Pages 76–79

reform is comically at odds with the morality of the art he displays in his homes (cf. Ov. *Tr.* 2.521–8)."

26. Cf. Newman 1997, 438: Propertius "does not 'reflect' art in his poems. He distorts it there to serve quite independently conceived, satiric/sexual purposes." For a (perhaps) more serious attempt by Propertius to narrativize Roman moral decline, see 3.13, where increasing love for wealth combined with neglect of the gods causes a general decline.

27. Murgatroyd (1994, 107–108) instead reads a "helplessness" and "hopelessness" in these lines, declaring the presence of humor only "for the uninvolved reader."

28. Lyne 1998.

29. Particularly 3.6.45–48, where each generation begets another marked by increasing wickedness, and 4.15, where Augustus has initiated a *saeculum* of moral improvement after an earlier decline; these poems are discussed in chapter 5. See also chapter 2 for similar sentiments in *Epode* 16.

30. With a first-person plural verb and *aetas* in the nominative case, Horace refers here to "our harsh age," using the same construction as in line 9 of *Epode* 16: *impia perdemus devoti sanguinis aetas.*

31. This *aevum* would be distinct from that of Regulus himself, of course; a good deed can become an *exemplum* instantly, but a gap of time helps (see Roller 2018). Here *aevum* does not mean "time" in general, although Horace sometimes (not always) uses the word that way; typically Horace uses the phrase *in omne aevum* or *in longum aevum* to mean "forever" or to refer to all of posterity (cf. *Epist.* 1.2.43, 1.3.8, 2.1.159), so Horace refers here to a specific discrete time-unit with this *aevum.*

32. In Cicero's *Amic.* 15, three or four unnamed pairs of famous friends (usually considered to refer to Orestes/Pylades, Theseus/Pirithous, and Achilles/Patroclus) are cited as the only examples "from all the ages" (*ex omnibus saeculis*); at *Amic.* 24, Orestes and Pylades are explicitly named. Manilius, at *Astronomica* 2.583–593, cites Orestes and Pylades as an exemplary pair of friends, the only pair "through the ages" (*per saecula*) who each tried to die for the other, whereas wickedness is common through all ages (*per saecula cuncta*).

33. Similarly, in the pseudo-Ovidian *Consolatio ad Liviam*, Livia "holds her *animus* against her age" (*sua saecula*, 45), maintaining strict morals despite the evils of her contemporary world. Having one's "own *saeculum*" in that phrase's grammatical sense is surprisingly unique; no one until Martial (5.10.8) modifies *saeculum* with the reflexive possessive adjective—except Lucretius (*ad sua saecla*, 2.1113), who clearly does not use *saecla* to refer to time-units, but to different species (such as in his stock phrase, *saecla ferarum*).

34. On this important passage, see Myerowitz 1985, 105–109; Steudel 1992, 105–116; Gibson 2003, 128–148.

35. Given that book 3 of the *Ars amatoria* is addressed to Roman women, and that this passage in particular is about cosmetics, it is not all that

Notes to Pages 79–85 | 193

remarkable that we see some similarity to, or expansion of, the *Medicamina faciei* passage, with Ovid taking on a didactic persona in each.

36. One can detect a trace of Epicurean palingenesis in Ovid's joke; see chapter 2.

37. See chapter 5 for more on the saecular resonance of the Palatine complex.

38. See Gibson 2003, 128 for a definition of this *cultus*.

39. *Rusticitas* is an uncommon word and appears in the Ovidian corpus securely in only two other places: at *Ars am.* 1.672 a man who kisses his beloved without transitioning to sex has failed to meet the expectations of the times, and this failure demonstrates *rusticitas*, not modesty; the old *anus* of *Am.* 1.8 (whose position as a *praeceptrix amoris* closely resembles Ovid's in *Ars am.* 3) associates *rusticitas* (44) with the naivete of a young wife who refuses to cheat on her husband, and again this *rusticitas* is compared with the stern morality of Romans in the time of Tatius and the Sabine women (39–40, with clear verbal echoes to *Medic.* 11–12).

40. Cf. the claim by Janus in *Fast.* 1 (see chapter 4) that Romans have always loved money but have only in Ovid's time (*tua saecula*) been able to acquire much of it.

41. The plural *saeculis*, as with *temporibus* at *Rep.* 2.19, is commonly used as a rhetorical plural for the singular term.

42. Zetzel 1995, 175.

43. *Rep.* 2.18.2; Zetzel 1995, 176.

Chapter 4: Beyond the Metallic Ages

1. Of the many contributions to this body of scholarship, some of the authoritative surveys of previous generations are Baldry 1952, Gatz 1967, DuQuesnay 1977, Wallace-Hadrill 1982. More recent work on the ancient reception of the Metallic Ages (such as Versnel 1994, Brown 1998, and Evans 2008) has brought it closer to the topics I examine in this chapter. Golden Age scholarship is extensive, but most scholars focus on the deployment of rhetorical tropes of Golden Age life (e.g., Zanker 2017, 204–210) or treat a certain kind of utopian primitivism from an anthropological perspective; I am more concerned in this book with the temporal aspects that Metallic Age mythology, among other schemes, can possess.

2. Van Noorden (2015) and others refer to this story as the "myth of the races," given the verbiage Hesiod uses; since the Romans contribute significantly to the shift from "races" to "ages" and their activity is my focus in this book, I refer to this mythology throughout with the more general phrase "Metallic Ages."

3. Vernant 1960; Hunt 1981, 37; also a scholiast on lines 160–161, as in Pertusi 1955, 25.

194 | Notes to Pages 85–87

4. Rosenmeyer 1957, 275–276; Verdenius 1985.

5. Clay 2003, 84; Van Noorden 2015, 84.

6. For a thorough analysis of the Romans' reception of Hesiod, particularly in regard to his Metallic Age mythology, see Rosati 2009, 365–369.

7. Farrell 1991, 315.

8. Van Noorden 2015, 41.

9. Van Noorden 2015, 170. For a deep analysis of the Roman reception of the *Phaenomena* and explanations for its popularity, see Volk 2015.

10. Baldry 1953.

11. Hesiod, Aratus, and the epigrammist Antipater of Thessalonica provide the only surviving examples of the Metallic Age mythology in Greek literature before the first century BCE. See Gatz 1967.

12. For a reading of Catullus 64 particularly attuned to questions of saecular discourse, see esp. Feeney 2007, 123–127.

13. Feeney 2007, 125: the awkward conjunction of the synonymous *tempus* and *saeculum* in that phrase "is there to highlight the theme of successive epochs that have been lost."

14. Text in Ewbank 1933. Unfortunately, we lack most of the text from the poem's Metallic Ages passage.

15. The authorship of this poem is disputed, with some claiming that Tiberius actually composed the poem; see Gain 1976, 16–20. For the purposes of my argument, I rely simply on an early imperial authorship.

16. Many others do not; Martin (1956) discusses the flourishing of this literary trend.

17. Vergil tells the same story in *Aen.* 8.314ff., but Saturn comes from the sky, not a boat; Green (2004, 113–114) notes that Ovid is the first surviving Latin author to depict Saturn arriving by boat, which serves as an explanation for the imagery on the familiar Roman coin. Aside from the cattle, some kind of people (not exactly human, but born from oak trees [*Aen.* 8.315]) are already there, while it is less explicit in Ovid's version that there were people present: the *gens* takes the name "Saturnian" from that moment (*Fast.* 1.237), but it not clear if there is a *gens* already at that time. (There seems to have been a *volgus* present already [245], and Janus counts people as subjects [247ff.] by some point.)

18. Murgatroyd 1980, 101.

19. Other than Catullus 64 and Vergil, *Ecl.* 4: Cicero mentions a Heroic Age three times: *Tusc.* 5.7, *Nat. D.* 3.54, and most famously *Div.* 1.1. Propertius 1.4.7 talks about an age of beauty (*formosi temporis aetas*) that seems to be related to the legendary figures of the Trojan War. [Tibullus] also imagines a time-unit with a characteristic degree of beauty occurring in the past: at 3.4.25–26 he writes that no age (*aetas*) of our forefathers or house of heroes produced a man more lovely (*formosius*) than the Apollo who appeared in his dream.

Notes to Pages 87–91 | 195

20. In noting the "great variation in ancient descriptions of the golden age," Zanker (2017, 194) writes that "one is tempted to speak not of essential properties but rather of a loose set of family resemblances whose variety stems from the different motivations and aims of the individual authors."

21. Cf. Ovid's similar punning sentiment at *Fast.* 1.191.

22. Suetonius, *Tib.* 59. On this anecdote, see Baldwin 1978 and Slater 2014.

23. In the pseudo-Vergilian epyllion *Aetna* (usually dated after Manilius), lines 9–16.

24. See above for translations/adaptations of Aratus's *Phaen.*, to which the *Astronomica* of Manilius is also greatly indebted. *Recusationes* of astronomical poetry appear at Propertius 2.34.51–54, Tibullus 2.4.17–18, [Tibullus] 3.7.18–23. Philodemus, epigram 31 uses Aratus and astronomical poetry as the basis for an obscene joke. On the popularity of astronomical poetry during this time, see Lewis 1984; Fantham 1985 (esp. 245–246 n. 11); Lewis 1989 (esp. 104–105, where he suggests that the extended mythological digressions, such as that of Dike, contributed to the popularity of the *Phaen.*); Pasco-Pranger 2006, 7.

25. Zanker 2010.

26. Though Gatz (1967, esp. 87–103) anticipates some of the contributions of DuQuesnay (1977). For a useful modern summary of the many vectors of *Ecl.* 4 scholarship regarding *saecula*, see Perkell 2002, 12–18.

27. Summarized in Nisbet 1978. On the Sibylline Oracles, see the conclusion.

28. Clausen 1994, 131: "strictly speaking, the last age has not come yet, but the poet eagerly anticipates it."

29. Coleman (1977, 130) notes that the "golden line" pattern of 4 "suggests the cyclic symmetry of the ages."

30. On the ambiguity of this phrase, see Coleman 1977, *loc. cit.*

31. Clausen (1994, 133) notes the intertextual references to Catullus 64 in these lines.

32. Coleman (1977, 141) reads *heroum laudes* in line 26 as preparation for the "reference to this second Heroic Age."

33. Coleman (1977, 141–142) argues that the chronological structure here recalls "the pendular movement of the world to and from God" in Plato's *Plt.*, where the end point of the swing is described in Hesiodic Golden Age terms. However, Coleman reads the new Heroic Age as occurring within, not before, the new Golden Age.

34. This interpretation (a reversal of the Hesiodic sequence) has had its adherents since Rose (1942), but to my knowledge no one has focused specifically on the ability of saecular discourse to explain the chronological structure.

196 | Notes to Pages 91–95

35. While *saeculum* is often used in a poetic plural, here the context and the *hapax* phrase *talia saecla* must be referring to multiple *saecula*, which I understand as the *ordo saeclorum* from Iron through Heroic, Bronze, and Silver back to Gold.

36. Coleman 1977, 153; Clausen 1994, 140–141.

37. By dubbing the present time an Iron Age, Vergil implicitly creates some kind of decline narrative for Rome, since the ages must decline to ultimately reach the Iron Age. Thus, between the lines of this poem is a pessimistic critique of the previous decades (and beyond?) of Roman history, although Vergil does not explore it in much detail here.

38. The *puer* is unnamed and may not even represent an actual person; on the many attempts at identification, see Coleman 1977, 150–152. The consul Pollio serves only as a chronological anchor in the poem; there is no suggestion that he himself will effect any change.

39. The last hundred years of scholarship have seen a great deal of debate on the specifics of this cycle (see Barnes 1979 for a discussion of the various arguments), but recent papyrus and scholia findings seem to have secured a clearer picture. On the details of the cycle, I follow Primavesi 2008 except where noted.

40. Inwood 2001, 40; *contra* Barnes 1979, 2:8.

41. For some modifications to the zoogony doctrine (including phases within zoogonies and a distinction between the zoogonies in the Love-increasing and Strife-increasing stages), see Mansfeld and Primavesi 2011.

42. Inwood (2001, 63), reading fragments 122/128 and 123/130.

43. Rashed 2001.

44. Primavesi 2006, 27–28.

45. As mentioned by, e.g., Horace, *Ars p.* 465.

46. Direct mentions of Empedocles by name are frequent in Cicero; they also appear in *Eumenides*, a Menippean satire of Varro; Lucretius 1.716; Horace, *Epist.* 1.12.20 and *Ars p.* 465; Vitruvius, *De arch.*, preface to book 8.

47. Castner 1987; Sedley 1989; Campbell 2014, *passim.*

48. Farrell 2014, 61–90.

49. The Hesiodic *Catalogue of Women* contains suggestions that the Heroic Age was characterized solely by theoxeny, thus possibly being a non-Aratus source for this material in Catullus 64; see Van Noorden 2015, 35.

50. For a useful overview of this term (and its use in the history of anthropological studies), see Long 2005.

51. Hansen 2004, 141. For more on the culture hero as an element of ancient mythology, see Blundell 1986, 169–171; Hansen 2004, 141–143; Sulimani 2011, 13–15.

52. Long 2005, 2091: culture heroes affected a society's "attitude toward space, time, and mortality."

Notes to Pages 95–97 | 197

53. See esp. Kleinguenther 1933, although his focus is primarily the appearance of the concept in Greek literature.

54. Farrell 2005, 420: "the ancients tended to posit the existence of a *protos heuretes* even in areas where modern scholars are absolutely sure that there was none, and to exaggerate the importance of the earliest known practitioners in any given field." For a list of first discoverers in Latin poetry in the first century BCE, see Boucher 1965, 419.

55. For an example of a "negative culture hero," beyond Propertius 2.6 above, cf. Tibullus 1.4: Priapus decries the contemporary age (*haec saecula*, 57) because it "poorly manages its wretched skills" (*male . . . artes miseras . . . tractant*, 57), presumably a reference to skills in love. One tangible result of the age's characteristic problems is that beloveds are now accustomed to want gifts, and the blame for this increased materialism among beloveds is placed on the unknown man "who first taught people to sell love" (*qui venerem docuisti vendere primus*, 59).

56. Elsewhere, Propertius also mentions another "first artist" (2.12.1–4), the first man to paint Love as a boy, who first saw (correctly) that lovers behave erratically (like children). Paintings are important to the Propertian history of human culture; on the importance of visual culture in the poetry of Propertius, see Hubbard 1984.

57. Nisbet and Hubbard 1970, 50. Posidonius, in Rome during the first century BCE, also had a research interest in the topic.

58. Barsby 1999, 131: "This is a comic extension of the Greek and Roman habit of recording the 'first inventor' of things."

59. On this motif, see Murgatroyd 1980, 151.

60. Gellius 3.3.3–5 preserves the fragment (and the debate over its attribution).

61. Catullus 66.48ff. on the inventor of mining; Ovid, *Am.* 2.3.3 on the originator of the castration of eunuchs.

62. Cf. Propertius 1.17.13, Tibullus 1.7.19, Ovid, *Am.* 2.11.1 (who identifies the ship as the Argo); Horace (*Ode* 1.3) gestures at the idea of a change in human history but without any saecular terminology (although he connects technological innovation with moral decline); Catullus 64 does not link the end of the heroic age with the launching of the Argo but with the behavior that occurred after the wedding of Peleus and Thetis.

63. Lucretius gives many examples in the "anthropology" section (5.771–1457) of the *De rerum natura*; Vitruvius provides a similar history of architecture in *De arch.* 2.1. Ovid (*Fast.* 4.107) says that love (with some ambiguity as to whether he refers to the goddess Venus or to the abstract force of romance) compelled several inventions to be made, though it did not quite "give" them to humans.

64. Tibullus 1.7.29ff., crediting Osiris with teaching agriculture to the human race.

198 | Notes to Pages 97–99

65. Unsurprisingly, exponents of Epicureanism (such as Velleius in Cicero's *Nat. D.* 1.43 and Lucretius 5.8) describe Epicurus in the traditional way, as a godlike genius whose teachings ended human superstition.

66. Propertius curses his knowledge (given by Bacchus) of wine at 2.33.27–30. In the *Panegyric of Messalla*, [Tibullus] imagines the possibility that a later age (*longior aetas*, 11) might deny the theoxeny of Icarius, but claims that the constellations Erigone and Canis will testify to his good deed for all time.

67. The late Augustan didactic poet Grattius included no less than four culture-hero figures in his short (541 lines) *Cynegetica*: Diana, Hercules, and the mortal inventors Dercylos and Hagnon. Gale (2018, 86–88) notes that all of them can be partially linked with the author himself in a metapoetic sense. Moreover, the hunting knowledge discovered by Dercylos and Hagnon and the divine approval of hunting suggest "apparently wholehearted confidence in the positive benefits of cultural development in general" (85), which distinguishes Grattius from his didactic predecessors Lucretius and Vergil, with whom his poem maintains an allusive relationship.

68. E.g., Hyginus, *Fab.* 274–277; Pliny the Elder, *HN* 7.209. It is likely, although far from universally accepted, that the Hyginus to whom the *Poet. astr.* and *Fab.* are attributed is the same Hyginus who was a freedman of Augustus, master of the Palatine Library (Suetonius, *Gram. et rhet.* 20), and dedicatee of Ovid (cf. *Tr.* 3.14).

69. Blundell 1986, 170.

70. Note that Cicero's translation of the lost *Prometheus Unbound*, which survives in fragments, is the only extant work of Cicero's poetry that uses the word *saeculum* (preserved at *Tusc.* 2.23); Cicero refers to Prometheus as a real-life culture hero at *Tusc.* 5.7.

71. Although we do see this detail in Sappho (fr. 207, from a Servius scholion), Callimachus (*Ia.* 2 fr. 192.1–3; *inc.* fr. 493), and in several of Aesop's fables. Prometheus was present at the divine fashioning of the human race in Plato, *Prt.* 320c–322a, though did not contribute.

72. Horace, *Odes* 1.16.13; Propertius 3.5.

73. Ovid, *Met.* 1.78ff.; cf. Hyginus, *Poet. astr.* 2.42.1.4: "in that *tempus*, Prometheus made men" (*quo tempore Prometheus homines finxerit*).

74. Cf. also the obscene jokes about Prometheus in his role as molder of men at *Fabulae Aesopiae* 4.15–16.

75. Elsewhere in the *Met.*, Ovid says that the ancients claimed that in the first age (*aevo primo*, 7.392) men's bodies sprang up from mushrooms at Corinth. On Ovid's repetition of (seemingly contradictory) myths of human creation, see Wheeler 2000, 34–35.

76. E.g., Propertius 4.3.19.

77. Though not the only one: lines 5–7 suggest the alternative possibility that desire for gold, having subsequently led to warfare, was the real cause

of the end of the Golden Age, and that the invention of weaponry was value neutral.

78. On Tibullus and human progress see Murgatroyd 1994, 40–41; Murgatroyd 1980, 111–116; Maltby 2002, 369. In 1.3, Tibullus presents a then-versus-now narrative, with a Golden Age under Saturn (*Saturno rege*, 35) giving way to a period under Jupiter (*Iove sub domino*, 49) marked by all the negative traits that the Golden Age lacked, but there is no indication of when or how this transition occurred.

79. These subsequent innovations lack first discoverers, but seem to emerge organically as natural responses to life in the countryside; like the lists of culture heroes by Hyginus and Pliny the Elder, divine intervention and human ingenuity are both present.

80. Tibullus nowhere uses the term "Silver Age," although it is perhaps noteworthy that his only use of the word "silver" is in a description of a warfare item (a soldier's battle armor) at 1.2.69.

81. Varro, Cornelius Nepos, and the Augustan orator Cassius Severus, as well as the Greek writers Diodorus Siculus and Thallus, a chronographer and freedman of Augustus; see Nepos F2a–d Cornell.

82. Vitruvius (*De arch.* 2.pr.5) seems to mention a common trend of technical writers giving histories of their fields, though he himself provides an evolutionary account (with day-by-day progress) of the history of architecture, in the Lucretian style.

83. See, e.g., Wallace-Hadrill 2008.

84. As reported by Censorinus, *DN* 21. Varro separated the first two periods with the cataclysmic Flood of Ogyges (*cataclysmon Ogygi, Rust.* 3.1.3).

85. This is not the only time Celsus refers to his contemporary *saeculum* of medical history: he says the recently deceased Cassius was the most talented doctor of the age (*ingeniosissimus saeculi nostri medicus, Med.* 1.proem.69), and he mentions the claims of certain doctors of the age (*quidam medici saeculi nostri,* 1.proem.54) who follow the Methodic school of medicine.

86. Philo of Larissa, named by Cicero at *Nat. D.* 1.7 as a teacher of his, was also the teacher of Antiochus of Ascalon, who broke doctrinally from the Academy; Cicero may use his saecular history of the Academy strategically to position himself as the "true" heir of Philo and the Academic scholarchy, through his faithful defense of negative dialectic. On the history of such debates about the Academy, see Long and Sedley 1987, 448–449.

87. The authorship of the *Nux* is much debated, and while most scholars seem convinced that the work is an imitation, some still credit the poem to Ovid (Richmond [1981] lays out the argument in favor without committing to it). Since the possibility nonetheless remains, even if Ovid did not compose the *Nux*, that a Roman poet roughly contemporary with him did compose it, I include it in this study.

200 | Notes to Pages 103–107

88. Ovid mentions at *Tr.* 2.415–416 a certain Eubius, who had written a work about abortions and whom he describes as "the author of a foul history" (*impurae conditor historiae*). Perhaps the author of the *Nux* has in mind this lost work.

89. McKeown 1998, 296: "It suits Ovid's rhetoric to assume that it was a woman who first devised abortion. Pliny, however, makes the same claim at *NH* 10.172."

90. *in vacuo orbe*, 12; McKeown (1998, 299) reads this as an echo of Vergil's *vacuum in orbem* at his mention of the Deucalion myth in the *G.* (1.62), which intertextually connects the Ovid passage to the Deucalion myth (although neither Deucalion nor Pyrrha is explicitly named).

91. For discussion of the out-of-place seashells and anchor from 15.264–265, see chapter 2.

92. Verbal ambiguity allows some to interpret the *non* in line 400 as referring to *metus falsi* and thus read Grattius taking the talismans seriously. But Green (2018, 47 n. 76) admits that it could refer to mockery, and cites various previous scholars. Gale 2018, 83: "Like Lucretius, he warns against the vagaries of fashion, preferring tried and tested methods (*experti usus*) to *novitas* (114–116)."

93. Gardner (2019, 108–111) also discusses this passage for its saecular temporal perspective.

94. A similar sentiment is expressed at 5.821–836: the earth, like an old woman, will eventually be unable to bear life, and it is gradually reaching that point, since it can no longer produce the wide variety of living things that it used to.

95. Thus, although hostile in nature, this passage suggests the possibility that saecular discourse even occurred among non-elite Romans during the first century BCE.

96. This is a rare use of *saeclum* in the singular in Lucretius; the only two other cases refer to the "female race" (*muliebre saeclum*).

97. Hardie (2009, 44–45) argues that Vergil alludes to this passage with his future farmer, unable to recognize the bones of Pharsalian veterans, at *G.* 1.493–497.

98. E.g., Varro's etymology of *saeculum* as the longest duration a human could live; the calculation of Etruscan *saecula* with the lengths of the longest-lived men in the city.

99. At *Verr.* 2.3.21, Cicero uses *saeculum* as an expansive form of *annus* ("after so many years and even centuries"). At *Cat.* 2.11, he says that removing the Catilinarians will prolong the life of the Republic not for a brief instant but for many centuries (*non breve nescio quod tempus sed multa saecula*).

100. Cf. *Div.* 2.117, where Cicero gestures at this saecular narrative of increasing Roman skepticism in his history of the Oracle of Delphi. Cicero claims that not only in our age (*nostra aetate*), but for a long time, no one has

Notes to Pages 108–110 | 201

cared about Delphic oracular responses; apologists claim that this is because the holy power of the place gradually dissipated (*evanuisse*), but Cicero retorts that it dissipated only after men began to be less credulous.

Chapter 5: Acting Your Age

1. Eckert 2019.

2. Rosenblitt 2019, 4 on the sense of civic trauma that Roman society felt after the civil wars and massacres of the Sullan reign.

3. On aristocratic family oracles, cf. Fenestella F19 Cornell; on the editing of the *Sibylline Books*, see Suetonius, *Aug.* 31.1, Cassius Dio 54.17.

4. Luke 2014, 86–89.

5. Luke 2014, 86–87. More darkly, Cicero later wrote to Atticus in 49 BCE and said that "our Pompey has desired an imitation of Sulla's reign" (*Gnaeus noster Sullani regni similitudinem concupivit, Att.* 9.7.3).

6. Years later, in the *Balb.* of 56 BCE, Cicero considers it "a particular blemish and defect of the age" (*saeculi quaedam macula atque labes*, 15) that Pompey's success is held against him by envious competitors, since if Pompey's career had taken place five hundred years prior (*annos quingentos*; note that Cicero does not use the phrase *quinque saecula* to refer to five hundred years), no one would fault him for his extralegal actions in the light of his military success. But Cicero is not suggesting that Pompey has brought about a new *saeculum* of Roman history; this comment instead is a moral critique of the tendencies of Roman conduct in the current time.

7. Luke 2014, 88–90. Havas (2000) likewise argues that Cicero tries to present himself as a second Romulus in this poem and in parts of the *Rep.*, including through exploitation of the Roman septuacentennial that fell during his political career.

8. On the few recoverable details of this poem, see Harrison 1990.

9. Seneca the Elder, *Suas.* 7: *uno proscriptus saeculo proscribes Antonium omnibus.* While the phrase *omnia saecula* sometimes is used as a periphrastic expression for "forever," the use of the phrase *uno saeculo* here as well indicates that at least one discrete *saeculum* is imagined; note also the context, for which "century" seems less likely to be the meaning than "age" (being too prosaic and technical for such an aphoristic, lapidary line).

10. For an explanation of Polybian anacyclosis, see the introduction. See Trompf 1979, 180–181 for Cicero's nuanced appraisal of this anacyclosis.

11. Cf. *Rep.* 1.45, 1.69, 2.45.

12. Similarly, in *Rep.* 3.29, Cicero imagines that had Rome maintained its traditional strategy of ruling subordinate peoples with justice and not force, the state could have survived indefinitely. Unfortunately, this section lacks greater context, being highly fragmentary, and its exact sentiments are unclear.

202 | Notes to Pages 111–113

13. On the *Ciris*, see Kayachev 2020, 5–30. On *Catal.* 9, see Kayachev 2016.

14. See Kayachev 2020, 87–88 on the debates about restoring these textually suspect lines: "The idea of a new golden age (*mirifici . . . saecli*) may not be out of place here" (88).

15. As described at Cassius Dio 49.43.1; Pliny, *HN* 36.104.

16. Osgood (2006) has situated the importance of public works projects such as Agrippa's within larger Triumviral period propaganda, whereby Romans earned popular support not only for the building projects' immediate benefits (e.g., clean water) but also the beautification of the city (through new monumental architecture). Hopkins (2012) details the extent of the renovations to the Cloaca Maxima and analyzes its treatment as not simply efficient maintenance but, in context with Roman social life, a sort of quasi-religious veneration, though Hopkins does not connect Agrippa himself to the religious sphere through his Cloaca project. For a full-length study of Agrippa, see Powell 2015.

17. Davies (2017, 207) notes the importance of Sulla's work on the sewers, which both "suggested a purging of the city's miasma" as well as gestured toward the notion of a civic refoundation.

18. See also Ramage 1991, Keaveney 2005.

19. As noted by Keaveney (1982).

20. Diodorus Siculus 4.13.3; Hyginus, *Fab.* 30.7.1; [Apollodorus] *Bibliotheca* 2.5. For a thorough treatment of the history of the Augean stables labor and its canonicity and alternative versions, see Gantz 1996, 392–393 and Mitchell 2021, 80–94.

21. *Ol.* 10.28–30.

22. Callimachus's *Aitia* likely included the story in a (now-lost) portion. Moreover, the earlier treatments of the myth seem to depict Hercules cleaning the stables by hand, whereas the diverting of the river to clean the stables may have been a later addition, perhaps as late as Diodorus Siculus. The depiction of this Labor in the visual arts is also ambiguous until the Augustan period. Many sources tell of a famous bronze statue of Hercules sitting on a basket, which some have interpreted to be an emptied dung basket, with the seated Hercules tired out from all the cleaning. Versions of Hercules potentially connected by modern scholars to this myth include a variety of items in hand and poses, some focusing more on the diverting of the river than on the dung-related activity. As the *LIMC* notes, "The lack of any coherent imagery for this labor is striking."

23. On this accounting of the myth, see *LIMC*, *loc. cit.* The labor of the Augean stables appeared on the last of the twelve metopes, although the story would later be placed fifth in order; only during the Hellenistic period did the canonical number of labors settle at twelve, and although the temple itself probably gave the authority for this canonization, it seems to have been a long

Notes to Pages 113–116 | 203

process only ending with the mythographers of the first century BCE. On the "canon" of the Twelve Labors, see Ogden 2021, xxi–xxxi.

24. Here I agree with the claims, now better vindicated, of Mosca (1937), as well as the more recent scholarship of Gellar-Goad (2018).

25. *non Hercules potest, qui Augeae agessit* κόπρον (fr. 21 Cebe). See Cebe 1974, *loc. cit.*

26. Furthermore, Luce (2006) compiles the many examples of waterway manipulation that appear in the folktales of the Hercules mythology canon. Maticic (2022, 348) even reads the Hercules and Cacus episode from *Aen.* 8 and Propertius 4.9 in light of Agrippa's building projects, including the cleaning and sailing of the Cloaca: "one may read the Herculean drainage activities in the site of Rome as a commentary on [the Augustan regime's] hydrological activity."

27. Such as documented by Aldrete (2007, 15); there were eight in the first century BCE alone.

28. For an example of Hercules being understood as a civilizing culture hero by the time of the Augustan Age, see Grattius, line 69: *ipse deus cultorque feri Tirynthius orbis.*

29. The symbolism could hold useful moral overtones as well: in an authoritative article on the "meaning" of the Cloaca Maxima at Rome, Gowers (1995, 28) writes that Agrippa's stunt "can be seen as a symbolic gesture in the context of contemporary medicine: purging was a standard element in bodily regimen, too."

30. Pliny, *HN* 7.148.

31. Burnett, Amandry, and Ripolles 1992, 78; cf. Powell 2015, 124.

32. Sulimani 2011, 178.

33. *Tu scis, quantum illic miseriarum tulerim, cum causidicos audirem diem et noctem, in quos si incidisses, valde fortis licet tibi videaris, maluisses cloacas Augeae purgare, Apoco.* 7.5.3. Note that in this Seneca passage, like in Varro's *Bimarcus*, the comparison is drawn between moral filth and literal filth.

34. Porphyrio, *ad Horatii Artem poeticam* 67–68: *Tiberim intellegamus. Hunc enim Agrippa derivavit, qua nunc vadit; antea per <V>ela<b>rum fluebat.*

35. Seneca, *Controv.* 2.4.13; Pliny, *HN* 35.26: *vir rusticitati propior quam deliciis.*

36. Cooley 2019 is a useful diachronic overview of the sociocultural elements that contributed to eventually give rise to an ancient perception of a meaningful Augustan Age.

37. Jupiter declares that the rough age (*aspera saecula, Aen.* 1.291) will grow mild, with wars having been ceased, when Augustus rules Rome; an age will come (*veniet aetas,* 1.283) when Rome controls Greece, with *lustra* gliding past (*lustris labentibus,* 1.283). Anchises associates Augustus with the re-foundation of the Golden Age (*aurea saecula,* 6.792–793). Vulcan, while forging the Shield of Aeneas, is described as "not unknowing of the age to come" (*haud venturi*

204 | Notes to Pages 116–123

inscius aevi, 8.627) just before crafting a visual narrative of Roman history that will climax with the Battle of Actium.

38. Not unlike certain descriptions of Stoic universal destruction; see chapter 2.

39. On the *Res Gestae* (including a reconstruction of its text), see Cooley 2009; on the memoirs, see Smith and Powell 2009.

40. Luke 2014, 230: "Augustus explicitly refers to his own time as his *saeculum* (*ex nostro saeculo*) as he closes out the chapter, thereby identifying himself as the 'man of the *saeculum*' in the tradition of Sulla, Pompey, Cicero, and Caesar." Cf. Luke 2014, 254–259, where he argues that the *RGDA* are organized to demonstrate that a coherent "Augustan Age" began with the Ludi Saeculares.

41. Servius, *ad Ecl.* 9.46.

42. For another reading of this poem similarly sensitive to the periodizing rhetoric it employs, see Breed 2004.

43. There is debate over this date and several alternatives have been given (the most extreme being that of Williams [1972, 44–49], who argues for 8 BCE). I follow the general scholarly consensus (see Putnam 1986, 23 n. 6).

44. Cf. *Odes* 1.35.34–35; Cicero, *Nat. D.* 1.11; Livy 2.14.1; Ovid *Ars am.* 1.241.

45. So Putnam 1986, 264: "the name of Rome's ruler is absorbed into an ablative absolute construction that could connote causality (since) or duration (while, so long as), or even hint at conditionality (if)."

46. Cf. Zanker 2010.

47. See chapter 4 for this Aratus passage. This allusion strengthens the interpretation of Horace's "generation" terminology in *Ode* 3.6 as part of saecular discourse.

48. E.g., *Odes* 1.2.6, 4.6.42; his use of *saecula* at *Ep.* 16.65 clearly must be plural.

49. Horace does reference the performance of the *Carm. saec.* in *Odes* 4.6.29–44. He imagines one of the female chorus-singers from the performance, now older, recollecting her participation in the event, "when the *saeculum* brought around its festival days" (*saeculo festas referente luces*, 42). This line also serves as evidence that some Roman writers did in fact consider the festival to be the event that marked the change from one *saeculum* to another in Rome or marked the beginning of the "Augustan Age."

50. Here being used, perhaps for the first time, to mean something like "saecular time-unit" and not "five-year period"; see Galinsky 1996, 408 nn. 63 and 66. But an *Aen.* usage at 1.283 may precede it.

51. On the major aspects of the Ludi Saeculares from Augustus onward, see Pighi 1941; Galinsky 1996, 100–106; Beard, North, and Price 1998, 71–72 and 201–206.

52. On the Imperial versions, see especially the work of Dunning (2016).

Notes to Pages 123–127 | 205

53. Censorinus 17.10; the text here is unfortunately lacunose, but the sense has been adequately reconstructed by Forsythe (2012, 171 n. 6).

54. Hall 1986, 2575. This dating ambiguity, combined with the meager details of these earlier celebrations, had led some scholars, such as Weiss (1973), to doubt the very existence of any authentic celebrations of the Ludi Saeculares before Augustus, a claim now more convincingly argued by Dunning (2020).

55. Scholarship on the pre-Augustan history of the Ludi Saeculares, and the possibility of its nonexistence, is extensive. Important sources are Taylor 1934, Pighi 1941, Palmer 1974, Hall 1986, Coarelli 1993, Bernstein 1998, Forsythe 2012; most recently, Dunning (2020) gives a possible reconstruction of the earliest Republican celebrations of the Ludi Saeculares as a cult ritual of the Valerii clan.

56. Weinstock 1971, 193; Hall 1986, 2570; Galinsky 1996, 101; Beard, North, and Price 1998, 71.

57. Forsythe 2012, 60–61.

58. Hall 1986, 2573.

59. Taylor 1934, 107–111.

60. Hall 1986, 2586–2587.

61. Momigliano 1941, 165. See also Cooley 2006. Similarly, Beard, North, and Price (1998, 205) suggest that the Sibylline oracle (preserved in Phlegon's *De macrobiis* 5.2) dictating the ritual was "an antiquarian product of the Augustan age, incorporating or imitating earlier material . . . to give an antique flavor to the text." Seeking the obedience of the Latins appears in this oracle as well as in the Saecular Prayer.

62. Dunning 2020.

63. Rüpke (2011, 134) argues based on this detail that the Ludi Saeculares were celebrated with "the fullest possible degree of public mobilization."

64. Suetonius, *Claud.* 21.2.

65. For a summary of this scholarship, see Luke 2014, 216 n. 73. In particular, Merkelbach (1961) reads *Aen.* 6.65–70 and 6.791–794 as evidence of an original plan to celebrate a new *saeculum* in 23 BCE; Mattingly (1934, 162–163) gives an explanation for 22 BCE being a better choice.

66. Text preserved in Zosimus 2.6; see Beard, North, and Price 1998, 1:205 n. 126.

67. Luke 2014, 226.

68. Preserved in Augustine, *De civ. D.* 22.28. For more on palingenesis, see chapter 2.

69. See Luke 2014, 225: "secular doctrine found ritual expression in ceremonies aimed at renewing and perpetuating the state."

70. Rüpke 2011, 137.

71. Cooley 2019, 82: "Their staging on temporary structures raised for the purpose over several nights and days and the emphasis on the participation

206 | Notes to Pages 127–130

of all members of the citizen body in the celebrations make clear that the festival must have had enormous impact upon Rome's citizen population."

72. Poe 1984, 59: "The function of the Secular Games was lustral." Galinsky 2007, 77: "The underlying idea clearly was that of a historical marker and of an extended *lustrum* or periodic occasion for purification." Luke 2014, 224: "Like the *lustrum*, the *saeculum* marked a greater division of time, but one that was less precise than momentous and ritually significant. . . . To close out a census period with a *lustrum*—a purification of the people—was symbolically akin to closing out a *saeculum* through the celebration of the Secular Games."

73. Indeed, metakosmesis can be presented as a purificatory process, such as when the Flood of Deucalion washes away the wicked members of the human race; cf. Ovid, *Met.* 1.188ff.

74. Hence the connotations of a re-founding of the city that were absent at lustral ceremonies. Here the Cloaca episode of Agrippa provides another comparandum.

75. Vergil, *Aen.* 1.283; Horace, *Carm. saec.* 67.

76. See Cooley 2009, 205. Another coin of this time, with the face of Julius Caesar on the obverse, has been interpreted as depicting on the reverse side a herald announcing the Ludi, but this is far from clear and other valid explanations have been given. For possible numismatic representations of the Ludi Saeculares, including the 17 BCE celebration, see Scheid 1998.

77. E.g., Pedroni (1999) argues that sun and moon symbolism on Republican coinage represents a coded typology for the Ludi Saeculares, a connection that would seem to be apparent only to the most antiquarian tastes of the Roman citizenry.

78. Hannah 2005, 146–147.

79. *OGI* 458.I.4–10 (= *Die Inschriften von Priene* 105). On this inscription and the following one, see Hannah 2005, 131.

80. *OGI* 458.II.30–77.

81. Hannah 2005, 131.

82. Bickerman 1980, 43–47; Hannah 2009, 48.

83. Friesen 2001, 123–124.

84. Friesen 2001, 125.

85. Desau, *ILS* 112 (E.-J. 100); cf. E.-J. 98a (Halicarnassus). See Weinstock 1971, 196.

86. Bickerman 1980, 73.

87. On the horoscope's importance in the ancient world, especially for Augustus, see Hannah 2005, 125–130.

88. For the details of this enduring scholarly question, and for an intriguing possible solution, see Bowersock 1990, 384–387.

89. Hannah 2005, 127. On Augustus's astrological sign, and astrology more broadly, in a variety of Augustan authors (especially Manilius), see Green 2014.

Notes to Pages 130–133 | 207

90. Plutarch (*Rom.* 12) relates that Varro asked his friend Tarutius, an Etruscan seer, to calculate the date of Romulus's birth based on the major events of his life, and Tarutius then compiled a horoscope for Romulus based on this date.

91. See especially Kosmin 2018; also Bickerman 1980, 70–78.

92. For a review of the construction projects on the Palatine during the life of Augustus, see Nielsen 2013, 51–55, and Wiseman 2017. On the Palatine Bibliotheca, see chapter 6.

93. On the Romulan connections to the Palatine, see Galinsky 1996, 213–215.

94. Suetonius, *Aug.* 7.2.

95. Galinsky (1996, 301) calls this decision "a characteristic blurring of private and public domains."

96. For an overview of the details of this temple, see Kellum 1985.

97. Galinsky 1996, 215–216: "the likely reason was the latitude of possible associations and the concomitant opportunity for further development" (215).

98. F67: *quidam deos et eorum genera temporibus et aetatibus <distinguunt> inter quos et Orpheus: primum regnum Saturni, deinde Iovis, tum Neptuni<um>, inde Plutonis; nonnulli etiam, ut magi, aiunt Apollinis fore regnum, in quo videndum est, ne ardorem, sive illa ecpyrosis adpellenda est, dicant* (Swoboda 1964, 83). Cf. Vergil, *Ecl.* 4.10: *regnat Apollo.* See also chapter 1.

99. Suetonius, *Aug.* 94.5; in the middle of his indirect discourse describing this anecdote, Suetonius inserts the phrase *nota ac vulgata res est*, suggesting that it was a common story familiar to many.

100. Luke 2014, 257 n. 78.

101. For a detailed explication of this poem's description of the temple, see Lange 2009, 168–171.

102. *Ars am.* 3.101ff. On this passage, see also Hay 2020.

103. On the Temple of Apollo Palatinus and Ovid's Phaethon episode, see Barchiesi 2009, 173ff. See also Galinsky 1996, 219 for the saecular connections of Sol's quadriga on the roof of the temple.

104. Feeney 1998, 34.

105. Huskey 2006. To some extent, this is due to the presence on the Palatine of the Bibliotheca.

106. For this perspective, see especially Gurval 1995.

107. Hekster and Rich (2006, 151–152) identified a terracotta plaque from the temple (published by Carettoni [1972]) depicting a tapered pillar that they believe existed in the temple itself, marking the site where the lightning prodigy struck the ground.

108. See, e.g., Kellum 1993, 77; Quenemoen 2006.

109. On Horace, see Babcock 1967; on Propertius, see Bowditch 2009.

110. See, e.g., Bell 2009.

111. As noted by Miller (2000, 412).

208 | Notes to Pages 134–139

112. On the *XVviri*, see Smith 1979, 445.

113. Suetonius, *Aug.* 31.1. While Suetonius seems to suggest that Augustus moved the books from the Capitoline in 12 BCE, this is impossible (based on Tibullus 2.5, below), so modern commentators have interpreted Suetonius to mean that the books had been somewhere in the Temple of Apollo Palatinus since its dedication but only moved to the gold case in 12 BCE.

114. Servius *ad Aen.* 6.72 says that the *libri vegoici* were also housed there, perhaps referring to Etruscan texts such as the Prophecy of Vegoia (see chapter 1).

115. No explanation is given by the commentators (Smith 1979; Murgatroyd 1994; Maltby 2002) beyond the obvious connection of Apollo, in his otherwise unattested performance at the metakosmesis of the Golden Age to Silver Age.

116. Cf. Tibullus 1.3.49, where the Silver Age under Jupiter is negatively characterized by constant deadly peril and warfare; cf. also Vergil, *G.* 1.121ff.

Chapter 6: Pyramids and Fish Wrappers

1. Hinds 1998, esp. 123–144.

2. Despite the similarity of their terminology, I should note that this "evolutionary model" of Roman literary history differs from modern mainstream biological evolutionary theory, which uses the mechanism of natural selection and so lacks a teleological component.

3. For a recent book-length examination of the *Brutus*, see Van den Berg 2021, who says that Cicero's "major accomplishment was to compose . . . a framework for documenting the history of an artistic practice" (245).

4. Van den Berg (2021) refers to this model as not only "evolutionary" or "teleological" but also "accretive, as each speaker or generation supplements past innovations and refinements" (246).

5. Goldberg 1995, 6.

6. Hinds 1998, 64–65.

7. For in-depth analysis of this preface, see Oksanish 2019, 59–93; on the substance of *commentarii* as Vitruvius suggests here, see Riggsby 2006, 137–138.

8. See esp. Toohey 1984.

9. Cairns 2009, 315: "It is clear that Propertius, having criticized Varius and 'polemicized' against Vergil, is now establishing a literary genealogy for himself as an elegist, with all the poets listed fitting roughly into this category."

10. Cairns 2009, 315.

11. On Horace's connection of Roman satire and Old Comedy, see especially the treatment of Ferriss-Hill 2015.

12. The prologue-speakers in Plautus's *Asin.* (10–12) and *Cas.* (31–34) point out that their plays are translations of originals by Demophilus, and the

Notes to Pages 140–143 | 209

characters speaking in the prologues in the *Trin.* (Luxuria, 18–21) and the *Merc.* (Charinus, 9–10) cite Philemon as the source for their plays.

13. Cairns 2009, 315–316: "Ovid sought to appear as a major adherent of a 'modern' school of major elegists who wrote elegy exclusively, while Propertius wanted to dilute his enormous poetic dependence on his former patron, the recently disgraced Cornelius Gallus. . . . Hence Propertius promoted to the status of elegist three writers (Varro, Catullus and Calvus) who did write erotic elegy, but whose main contributions were not elegiac, in order not to have Gallus as his sole predecessor." Lyne (1998) has posited a poetic rivalry between the contemporaneous Tibullus and Propertius that perhaps would have precluded the latter from including his rival in this genealogy.

14. Alternative labels being *poetae novi* (*Orat.* 161) and *cantores Euphorionis* (*Tusc.* 3.45).

15. Perhaps most forcefully Courtney (1993, 189).

16. On this phenomenon, perpetuated by much classical scholarship, see Hinds 1998, 74–83.

17. Johnson (2007) acknowledges the strength of the skepticism of scholars such as Courtney but nonetheless wishes to refer to a "neoteric" interest in innovative versification and diction, as well as an original (almost amoral) approach to subject matter that distinguishes these poets from their predecessors and from more conservative poets such as Cicero and composers of historical epics; I take a cue from this argument.

18. See Gratwick 2002 on the textual emendation of line 9; other variations have been suggested, but none of them seriously affects my claims about *saeculum* in line 10.

19. Skinner 1987, 22.

20. Varro, not uniquely among classical historians, divided the history of the world into three essential periods: the unknowable, the mythological, and the historical (see chapter 4, note 84). It is possible that the "three volumes" noted in this poem refer not to actual written divisions of the *Chronica* but to Nepos breaking up the history of mankind into these three *saecula*, i.e., three *aeva* of ancient history. (The plural form of *aevum*—in both cases modified by *omnis*, as it were—is attested in Ovid at *Met.* 2.649 and *Pont.* 1.3.83.)

21. Starr 2010.

22. See also the work of Rauk (1997), who writes that time is the "unifying theme of the poem" through which Catullus links Nepos to himself as "two writers who are inspired by literary values that would challenge conventional notions about the hierarchy of genres." Gale (2015) further elucidates anxieties about future reception in this poem.

23. Although see Starr 2012, 119, arguing that Catullus would have expected a gift of a good book, not a bad one, at this time.

24. For a sincere gift of good poetry, see, e.g., Cinna's gift of Aratus, fr. 13 Hollis.

210 | Notes to Pages 144–146

25. Hubbard 1983, 226–227; Starr 2012.

26. Hubbard 1983, 226–227.

27. These last two lines (9–10) are not included by all editors with poem 95, though I believe they must be; see Solodow 1987 on the textual criticism of this poem.

28. In poem 36, it is Catullus himself who will help kill off the horrible *Annales* of Volusius; the intertextual phrase *pessimi poetae* (although genitive singular and not vocative plural) links Catullus 36 also with 14.23.

29. Noonan (1986) argues that "the unexpressed concept of a poem's lifetime" (304) connects all the obscure details alluded to in the poem in mockery of Volusius and Antimachus.

30. Starr 2012, 125: "Immortality, for Catullus, does not depend on the number of his readers or on bookstores: it depends on the quality of his poetry and the sophistication of his readers."

31. Catullus also uses the word *saec[u]lum* in poem 43, one of the two obscene poems addressed to an Ameana. However, Hendren (2014) has interpreted the "Ameana cycle" poems to be metaphorical criticisms of literary aesthetics, which would further strengthen my argument in this section.

32. See also Batstone 2007 for programmatic poems in Catullus.

33. In the first poem of his surviving corpus, Catullus refers to a *"libellus"* composition of his. There have been many scholarly attempts to determine the exact nature and content of the Catullan *libellus*; see Skinner 2007b for a survey of the long history of the debate over the arrangement of the Catullan corpus and claims about the various collections that make it up. Hubbard 1983 (and affirmed in Hubbard 2005) provides a convincing argument that poems 1 through 14 (but not the fragment 14b) form the *libellus*. If this reconstruction were accurate, it would point to an even greater emphasis on saecularity in Catullus's aesthetic doctrine.

34. All fragments from Hollis 2007.

35. Cf. Alfonsi 1962 on the resemblance of this fragment to a Cicero passage, although to my mind the resemblance is more trivial than Alfonsi allows.

36. Batstone 2007, 242.

37. Hollis (2007) places fr. 14 among Cinna's epigrams while making fr. 6 part of the *Propemptikon Pollionis*.

38. Hollis 2007, 147.

39. Knox 2011; see Lyne 1978 on the importance of Callimachus to the usual group of "neoteric" poets.

40. Hollis 2007, 136–137.

41. Hollis 2007, 142–143, again following Nisbet.

42. Hollis (2007, 148) identifies as I do the frequency of saecular terminology in the neoteric poems about literary posterity but merely writes,

"Varying ways of describing a poem's longevity became an ingenious neoteric game."

43. At times Horace targets the *populus* (18) and the *volgus* (63), but he also takes aim at the more limited group of *critici* (51).

44. On this passage, see also van den Berg 2014, 261–262 for its engagement with a Ciceronian analogy to the aging of wine.

45. See Hinds 1998, 69–70 and van den Berg 2014, 254–255 and 260–261.

46. Note van den Berg 2014, 291: "The signal importance of Horace's version lies not solely in the idea that modern authors update their predecessors, as Cicero had claimed, but in its use by an epigone to challenge the authority of the past."

47. Horace likely used as a model for this notion a fragment of the epigrammist Astydamas, though he crucially alters the sense: the original imagines that if the author and his predecessor swapped (vague undefined) time periods, they'd each be considered the top poet. Horace, however, imagines Lucilius needing to adopt new aesthetic criteria to survive in Horace's time. See van den Berg 2014, 291 for this allusion.

48. Cf. Catullus 1.2, where his poetic *libellus* is polished with pumice (*pumice expolitum*), as is Horace's book of epistles in *Epist.* 1.20.2.

49. He also, in *Epist.* 2.1, speaks of "the present age and the one after it" (*et praesens et postera aetas*, 42), unprompted by the hypothetical opponent in his *sorites* argument, and thus he imagines a future *saeculum* that complements those two eras, the age of "beloved antiquity" and the age of "ignored contemporary poetry."

50. Brink 1971, 265: "Thus the grotesque finale is set against a Catullan background of *ars* and *facetiae*."

51. While some commentators read *aetas* here to refer to youth (an uncommon reading of the word), Horace later describes old age (*senectus*, 18, and not a generic word for "time") seizing the book as an additional (*hoc quoque*, 17) fate that awaits it, suggesting that the abandonment by the *aetas* refers to some other phenomenon.

52. Feeney (2002, 186–187) lucidly makes this final point clear by arguing that for the Romans, the sole cultural activity borrowed from Greece that was celebrated and cultivated rather than feared and misunderstood was literature, specifically poetry; thus poetry always has a dangerous tendency to find itself "at odds with the national character" as manifested by dismissive critical tastes.

53. Gale (2015, 98) writes that just as Catullus 1 "points to an awareness that the value of the literary work is something that lies ultimately in the power of the reader rather than the writer," so Horace, *Epist.* 1.20 "is depicted as vulnerable to the whims of fashion." Gale (2015, 102–103) also detects this phenomenon in Catullus 14.

212 | Notes to Pages 149–155

54. Hardie (2005, 38) writes that in *Ars P.* 69–72, where Horace describes changing tastes, he "repeats a Lucretian insistence on the transience of fashion in the culture history of book 5 (1273–1280 and 1412–1418, both of which look back to the programmatic statement of the mutability of successive phases of the earth's history at 5.828–836)."

55. Cf. *Epist.* 1.20.4, *paucis ostendi gemis et communia laudas* ("you lament being shown to few people, and you praise public things").

56. At *Ars P.* 345–346, the *aevum* of the writer is "prorogated," which we might read as analogous to a period of holding *imperium* (and, thus, as a finite, discrete time-unit).

57. Among other parallels, we find: *Livor edax* (*Am.* 1.15.1), *edax* (*Met.* 15.872), *Livor iniquo dente* (*Tr.* 4.10.123–124); *parsque mei multa superstes erit* (*Am.* 1.15.42), *parte tamen meliore mei super alta perennis astra* (*Met.* 15.875–876); *siquid habent veri vatum praesagia* (*Met.* 15.879), *siquid habent igitur vatum praesagia veri* (*Tr.* 4.10.129); *vivam* (*Am.* 1.15.42, *Met.* 15.879). Most of these intertexts also connect Ovid to *Ode* 3.30.

58. Moreover, Ovid's claim that he will be sung *in toto orbe* (8) bespeaks the Augustan acceptance of limitless spatial fame, unlike the neoteric poets' narrower interest in their audience.

59. Catullus 64 had previously connected saecular change with the Argo as the first ship in human history (perhaps his own invention, or a borrowing from Accius, but definitely a departure from the tradition as given by Apollonius of Rhodes; on Varro's relationship with this detail in Catullus 64, see Polt 2013). The Golden Age is called *aurea aetas* by Ovid at *Met.* 1.89 and 15.96; apparently he was the first Latin poet to use the phrase.

60. And compare Horace's *Odes* 3.30.8–9, where his immortality is also contingent on the survival of the city of Rome (with a *dum*-condition); see also *Tr.* 3.7.50–52.

61. Vessey (1981) reads *Am.* 1.15 as an irony-heavy mockery of the very idea of literary immortality. In particular (610), he reads *fama perennis* in an allusive relationship with *cura perennis* at 1.3.16, where Ovid's claims of non-desultory love are almost surely ironic; the two avowals, so linked, are meant to "draw our attention to the flaws which underlie them."

62. Cf. *omnia saecula* at Livy 8.34.11, 7.36.5; *per saecula* at Vergil, *Aen.* 6.235; phrases such as *per saecula longa, vel sim.* are common. Latona, not the Ovidian narrator, uses *per omnia saecula* to mean "forever" at *Met.* 6.208.

63. On Ovid as the focus of his own literary *saeculum*: Seneca the Elder reports (*Controv.* 3.7) that Cestius referred to Ovid as "a man who filled this *saeculum*" with erotic poetry (*qui hoc saeculum . . . implevit*). But the third book of the *Controversiae* survives only in excerpts, some of which possibly were edited.

64. On Phaedrus and his engagement with the Roman reception of Callimachus in his own time, see Glauthier 2009.

65. Cf. the *Zmyrna* outliving the *cana saecula* themselves in Catullus 95.6, above.

66. For an overview of the Palatine complex, including the Bibliotheca, see Wiseman 2019, 135–138, as well as Gros 1993.

67. Although some scholars (in particular, Thompson [1981]) have argued that, in light of the failure of poets celebrating the dedication of the temple to mention the Bibliotheca, it must have opened several years after the dedication of the temple.

68. Bowie (2015, 239) writes, "The rapidity with which the creation of this prestigious library followed that of Pollio can hardly be accidental." On Varro's involvement in earlier library projects, see Hendrickson 2015.

69. While the purpose of the building was chiefly to house writings, some Senate meetings also occurred in the Bibliotheca during the reign of Augustus, particularly during his senescence (Suetonius, *Aug.* 29.3).

70. As understood by Houston (2014, 220–224).

71. Such that it is mentioned numerous times in contemporary literary works; for just one example, Horace at *Epist.* 2.2.92–94 talks about how Roman poets would look around with pride when in the Bibliotheca and ponder its cultural weightiness (*molimine*, 93).

72. Horsfall 1993, 63–64. Conversely, Horace (*Epist.* 1.3.15–20) advises a younger poet not just to borrow from all the other poems in the Bibliotheca (because the proximity of all his sources increases the risk that his borrowing will be exposed) but to create original material.

73. Horsfall 1993, 61–62.

74. Babcock (1967) reads *Ode* 1.32 as evidence that Horace was spurred to write Alcaean verse (and, in a broader sense, to write the *Odes*) directly as a result of the dedication of the Palatine complex and, perhaps, the empty shelves on the Latin side of the Bibliotheca.

75. We have seen in previous chapters the social elevation of the philosopher Posidonius in first-century BCE Rome, to name just one figure, and there are countless examples of Hellenistic epigrams that the Roman poets of the first century BCE were familiar with (to say nothing of contemporary epigrammists).

76. Cf. Horace's comment at *Epist.* 2.1.28–29 that it was generally believed that the oldest literature of the Greeks was the best. The silence (or, at best, muted credit) regarding Parthenius and his influence on lyric is perhaps the most egregious example of this phenomenon.

77. Especially given that Greek and Roman literature would have been separated: Petrain (2015, 334) notes that "literary and epigraphic testimonia make it certain that the Palatine library did house from its inception distinct Latin and Greek collections."

78. On this passage, see in particular Brink 1971, 320–325. For a broader look at Horace's textual responses to the opening of the Bibliotheca, see Blum 2017.

214 | Notes to Pages 158–163

79. We should perhaps understand claims of being a new Callimachus, for example, in light of saecular discourse regarding palingenesis, though metaphorically and not literally; see chapter 2.

80. Horsfall 1993, 60–61, citing a variety of examples of emperors adding (or sometimes subtracting) works to the Bibliotheca.

81. Horsfall 1993, 62–63. In *Epist.* 2.1.216–218, Horace suggests that these were the conscious goals of Augustus in erecting the Bibliotheca; see Brink 1971, 239.

82. Bowie 2015, 259, citing the Bibliotheca as a specific example of this concept in action.

83. A scholiast on Juvenal 7 records that the Bibliotheca held many volumes of Roman juridical texts.

84. Petrain 2015, 334: "The emphasis on comparison and competition between the two literatures is an unmistakable feature, certainly the fruit of deliberate reflection on how a public library should function in the city of Rome."

85. Neudecker 2015, 322.

86. Petrain 2015, 342; cf. the Tabula Hebana, an inscription of the senatorial decree whose text has been found as far off as Spain.

87. Neudecker 2015, 329–330.

88. As argued by Huskey (2006).

89. Tucci 2015, 286.

90. Tucci 2015, 286.

91. Corbier 1992, 899.

92. Houston 2014, 220–222. Houston also argues (247–248), based on a note from Galen (admittedly two hundred years later), that writings were classified in the Bibliotheca both by genre and author as well as by "named collection" (seemingly if the volumes in question belonged to a larger personal collection acquired by the Bibliotheca). If true, this would have broader implications on the perceived development of Roman literature in competition with earlier Greek sources.

93. Wiseman 2019, 137.

94. Horsfall 1993, 60.

95. Wiseman 2019, 137.

Conclusion

1. On the renewed Roman interest in Golden Age rhetoric under Nero, particularly by Seneca the Younger, see esp. Evans 2005. Star (2021) also examines Seneca's ideas about the end of the world and their relation to periodic cataclysms.

Notes to Pages 164–167 | 215

2. On apocalyptic temporal schemes in Jewish and Christian thought, see, e.g., Hellholm 1983, Downing 1995, de Villiers 2000, Buitenwerf 2013.

3. See Lucas 1989 for a useful analysis of this passage.

4. See Buitenwerf 2003 and Lightfoot 2007 for overviews of this body of literature and its connections with the Roman world.

5. Tarn 1932.

6. E.g., Nisbet 1978.

7. Machinist 2019, 237.

8. For a useful overview of such scenarios and their classical connections, see Star 2021, 1–6. On the combination of metallic age mythology with Christian eschatology in Lactantius, see Zanker 2017.

9. Goldhill 2022 represents a major contribution to the study of the Christian reception of classical thought on time and to the Christian intellectual developments regarding temporality during Late Antiquity. Unfortunately, it was published too late for me to integrate its conclusions more fully into this study.

10. On the characteristics of Tiberian age historiography (mainly Velleius Paterculus), see Oakley 2020.

11. See Cornell 2013, esp. 1.493, for considerations of what Fenestella's work may have been like (as well as the possibility that Pliny the Elder used Fenestella more frequently than he explicitly cites for information on epochal shifts in cultural trends).

12. Seneca the Younger may have Fenestella or Cassius Hemina in mind at *De brevitate vitae* 10.13.6; see Cornell 2013, 3.580. Seneca may also be mocking Fenestella's emphasis on antiquarian details at the expense of actual important events at *Ep.* 108.30–31, but see the defense at Cornell 2013, 3.573.

13. Fenestella F25 Cornell; Pliny, *HN* 9.123.

14. Fenestella is said by Cornell (2013, 1.493) to have down-dated some instances of moral decline when compared to other authorities, and in this regard is compared to Nicolaus, who similarly had blamed Lucullus (*FGrHist* 90 F77) for introducing some of the extravagances witnessed during the Augustan Age (1.493, n. 17).

15. See Scappaticcio 2020 for a recent conference volume analyzing this work.

16. Seneca the Elder F2 Cornell. There are scholarly debates about whether this passage comes from Seneca the Elder, Seneca the Younger, or even Florus (see Cornell 2013, 3.596–597).

17. Cicero picks up the metaphor again at 2.21, where he says that the state was not left like an infant crying in its bed but was left full-grown and nearly in manhood.

216 | Notes to Pages 167–168

18. For which there is a testimonium, and possibly one other surviving fragment at Suetonius, *Tib.* 73.2; see Cornell 2013, 2.982–985.

19. I.e., *fine Punici belli*; this must refer to the Third Punic War, because Seneca describes Rome then acting "with Carthage gone" (*sublata Carthagine*).

20. On the use of periods by Seneca and its relation to the extant work of Florus, see Renda 2020.

21. Klotz (1901) posits an Augustan archetype, while noting the similarity of the Cicero passages in *Rep.*; this possibility is noted by Griffin (1976, 195 n. 2). Alternatively, Riposati (1939, 258) and Vittinghoff (1964, 558 n. 3) suggest that Varro systematized the metaphor. See Cornell 2013, 1.508 n. 30.

22. Cf. Cicero, *Sen.* 33, where he also divides human life into four periods, each with their own characteristics, but does not give specific moments when they begin and end. Aside from the *depositio barbae* (poorly attested before the imperial period and considered by Wiedemann [1989, 116–117] to have held no formal significance) and the assumption of the *toga virilis*, there were no obvious moments of transition from one period of life to another in ancient Rome.

23. Cornell (2013, 1.505–508) suggests a possible Sallustian influence on the decision to mark 146 BCE as a (though not *the*) turning point in Roman history.

24. On the implications of this passage, see esp. den Hengst 2000, 68.

Bibliography

Adams, J. N. 2003. *Bilingualism and the Latin Language.* Cambridge: Cambridge University Press.

Aldrete, G. S. 2007. *Floods of the Tiber in Ancient Rome.* Baltimore, MD: Johns Hopkins University Press.

Alfonsi, L. 1962. "Su Cicerone e i 'poetae novi.'" *Aevum* 36: 319.

Annas, J. 1989. "Epicurean Emotions." *GRBS* 30: 145–164.

Arnott, W. G. 1970. "*Phormio parasitus*: A Study in Dramatic Methods of Characterization." *G&R* 17: 32–57.

Babcock, C. L. 1967. "Horace *Carm.* 1.32 and the Dedication of the Temple of Apollo Palatinus." *CP* 62: 189–194.

Baldry, H. C. 1952. "Who Invented the Golden Age?" *CQ* 11: 83–92.

———. 1953. "The Idler's Paradise in Attic Comedy." *G&R* 22: 49–60.

Baldwin, B. 1978. "Verses in the Historia Augusta." *BICS* 25: 50–58.

Balsdon, J. P. V. D. 1951. "Sulla Felix." *JRS* 41: 1–10.

Bannon, C. 2014. "C. Sergius Orata and the Rhetoric of Fishponds." *CQ* 64.1: 166–182.

Barchiesi, A. 2009. "Phaethon and the Monsters." In *Paradox and the Marvelous in Augustan Literature and Culture*, ed. P. Hardie, 163–188. Oxford: Oxford University Press.

Barnes, J. 1979. *The Presocratic Philosophers.* 2 vols. London: Routledge.

Barnes, J., and M. Griffin. 1997. *Philosophia Togata* II: *Plato and Aristotle at Rome.* Oxford: Clarendon Press.

Barsby, J. 1999. *Terence: Eunuchus.* Cambridge: Cambridge University Press.

———. 2001. *Terence.* 2 vols. Cambridge, MA: Harvard University Press.

Bates, R. L. 1983. "Memoirs and the Perception of History in the Roman Republic." PhD diss., University of Pennsylvania.

Batstone, W. W. 2007. "Catullus and the Programmatic Poem: The Origins, Scope, and Utility of a Concept." In *A Companion to Catullus*, ed. M. Skinner, 235–253. Malden, MA: Blackwell.

218 | Bibliography

Beagon, M. 2005. *The Elder Pliny on the Human Animal:* Natural History *Book 7.* Oxford: Clarendon Press.

Beard, M., J. North, and S. Price. 1998. *Religions of Rome.* 2 vols. Cambridge: Cambridge University Press.

Bell, R. 2009. "Revisiting the Pediment of the Palatine Metroon: A Vergilian Interpretation." *PBSR* 77: 65–99.

Benardete, S. 2000. *Plato's "Laws": The Discovery of Being.* Chicago: University of Chicago Press.

Bernstein, F. 1998. *Ludi Publici: Untersuchungen zur Entstehung und Entwicklung der öffentlichen Siele im Republikanischen Rom.* Stuttgart: F. Steiner.

Betensky, A. 1979. "The Farmer's Battles." In *Virgil's Ascraean Song: Essays on the Georgics,* ed. A. J. Boyle, 108–119. *Ramus* 8. Melbourne: Hawthorn Press.

Bickerman, E. J. 1980. *Chronology of the Ancient World.* London: Thames and Hudson.

Blum, B. 2017. "Studiorum instrumenta: Loaded Libraries in Seneca and Horace." In *Horace and Seneca: Interactions, Intertexts, Interpretations,* ed. M. Stöckinger, K. Winter, and A. T. Zanker, 211–238. Berlin: de Gruyter.

Blundell, S. 1986. *The Origins of Civilization in Greek and Roman Thought.* London: Croon Helm.

Bömer, F. 1969. *P. Ovidius Naso: Metamorphosen.* Heidelberg: C. Winter.

Boucher, J.-P. 1965. *Études sur Properce: Problèmes d'inspiration et d'art.* Paris: de Boccard.

Bowditch, L. 2009. "Palatine Apollo and the Imperial Gaze: Propertius 2.31 and 2.32." *AJP* 130: 401–438.

Bowersock, G. 1990. "The Pontificate of Augustus." In *Between Republic and Empire: Interpretations of Augustus and His Principate,* ed. K. A. Raaflaub, 380–394. Berkeley: University of California Press.

Bowie, E. 2015. "Libraries for the Caesars." In König, Oikonomopoulou, and Woolf 2015, 237–260.

Breed, B. W. 2004. "Tua, Caesar, Aetas: Horace *Ode* 4.15 and the Augustan Age." *AJP* 125: 245–253.

Brink, C. O. 1971. *Horace on Poetry. Epistles Book II: The Letters to Augustus and Florus.* Cambridge: Cambridge University Press.

Briquel, J. 2014. "*Etrusca disciplina* and Roman Religion: From Initial Hesitation to a Privileged Place." In *Religion and Competition in Antiquity,* ed. D. Engels and P. Van Nuffelen, 112–132. *Collection Latomus* 343. Brussels: Peeters.

Brown, A. S. 1998. "From the Golden Age to the Isles of the Blest." *Mnemosyne* 51: 385–410.

Büchner, K. 1974. *Das Theater des Terenz.* Heidelberg: C. Winter.

Buitenwerf, R. 2003. *Book III of the Sibylline Oracles and Its Social Setting.* Leiden: Brill.

———. 2013. "The Tiburtine Sibyl (Greek)." In *Old Testament Pseudepigrapha: More Noncanonical Scriptures,* vol. 1, ed. R. Bauckham, J. R. Davila, and A. Panayotov, 176–188. Grand Rapids, MI: Eerdmans.

Burnett, A., M. Amandry, and P. P. Ripolles. 1992. *Roman Provincial Coinage*. Vol. 1. London.

Bury, R. G. 1926. *Plato. Laws*, vol. 1: *Books 1–6*. Cambridge, MA: Harvard University Press.

———. 1929. *Plato. Timaeus. Critias. Cleitophon. Menexenus. Epistles.* Cambridge, MA: Harvard University Press.

Calabi, I. 1950. "I commentarii di Silla come fonte storica." *MAL* ser. 8.3: 245–302.

Campbell, G. 2014. "Lucretius, Empedocles, and Cleanthes." In Garani and Konstan 2014, 26–60.

Carettoni, G. 1972. "Terrecotte 'Campana' dallo scavo del tempio di Apollo Palatino." *RendPontAcc* 44: 123–139.

Carson, C. 2010. *Heisenberg in the Atomic Age: Science and the Public Sphere.* Cambridge: Cambridge University Press.

Castner, C. J. 1987. "*De Rerum Natura* 5.101–103: Lucretius' Application of Empedoclean Language to Epicurean Doctrine." *Phoenix* 41: 40–49.

Cèbe, J.-P. 1974. *Varron, Satires ménippées.* Vol. 2. Rome: École française de Rome.

———. 1983. *Varron, Satires ménippées.* Vol. 6. Rome: École française de Rome.

Chroust, A.-H. 1973. "The 'Great Deluge' in Aristotle's *On Philosophy.*" *L'Antiquité Classique* 42: 113–122.

Clackson, J. 2015. *Language and Society in the Greek and Roman Worlds.* Cambridge: Cambridge University Press.

Clausen, W. 1994. *A Commentary on Virgil: Eclogues.* Oxford: Clarendon Press.

Clay, J. S. 2003. *Hesiod's Cosmos.* Cambridge: Cambridge University Press.

Closs, V. M. 2020. *While Rome Burned: Fire, Leadership, and Urban Disaster in the Roman Cultural Imagination.* Ann Arbor: University of Michigan Press.

Coarelli, F. 1985. *Il Foro Romano: Periodo repubblicano e augusteo.* Rome: Quasar.

———. 1993. "Note sui *ludi Saeculares.*" In *Spectacles sportifs et scéniques dans le monde étrusco-italique*, 211–245. Collection de l'École française de Rome 172. Rome: École française de Rome.

Coleman, R. 1977. *Vergil: Eclogues.* Cambridge: Cambridge University Press.

Commager, S. 1962. *The Odes of Horace.* Bloomington: Indiana University Press.

Cooley, A. E. 2006. "Roman Religion in the Age of Augustus." In *Religion in Republican Italy*, ed. C. E. Schultz and P. B. Harvey, 228–252. Yale Classical Studies 33. Cambridge: Cambridge University Press.

———. 2009. *Res Gestae Divi Augusti: Text, Translation, and Commentary.* Cambridge: Cambridge University Press.

———. 2019. "From the Augustan Principate to the Invention of the Age of Augustus." *JRS* 109: 71–87.

Corbier, M. 1992. "De la maison d'Hortensius à la *curia* sur le Palatin." *MÉFRA* 104: 871–916.

Cornell, T. J. 1976. "Etruscan Historiography." *ASNP* III 6.2, 411–439.

220 | Bibliography

———, ed. 2013. *The Fragments of the Roman Historians*. 3 vols. Oxford: Oxford University Press.

Costa, C. D. N. 1984. *Lucretius:* De Rerum Natura V. Oxford: Clarendon Press.

Courtney, E. 1993. *The Fragmentary Latin Poets*. Oxford: Clarendon Press.

Crawford, M. H. 1974. *Roman Republican Coinage*. Cambridge: Cambridge University Press.

Daviault, A. 1981. *Comoedia togata: Fragments*. Paris: Budé.

Davies, P. J. E. 2017. *Architecture and Politics in Republican Rome*. Cambridge: Cambridge University Press.

De Grummond, N. T. 2013. "Haruspicy and Augury." In *The Etruscan World*, ed. J. M. Turfa, 539–556. New York: Routledge.

De Grummond, N. T., and E. Simon. 2006. *The Religion of the Etruscans*. Austin: University of Texas Press.

De Melo, W. 2011. *Plautus*. 5 vols. Cambridge, MA: Harvard University Press.

den Hengst, D. 2000. *"Senium imperii."* In *Ultima Aetas: Time, Tense and Transience in the Ancient World*, ed. C. Kroon and D. den Hengst, 61–70. Amsterdam: VU University Press.

Denzler, B. 1968. *Der Monolog bei Terenz*. Zurich: Keller.

Dettmer, H. 1997. *Love by the Numbers: Form and Meaning in the Poetry of Catullus*. New York: P. Lang.

de Villiers, P. G. R. 2000. "Pagan Oracles and Jewish Apocalypses in Graeco-Roman Times." *Acta Patristica et Byzantina* 11: 47–73.

Diehl, E. 1934. "Das Saeculum: Seine Riten und Gebete." *RhMP* 83: 255–272, 348–372.

Diggle, J. 1970. *Euripides: Phaethon*. Cambridge: Cambridge University Press.

Dittenberger, W. 1905. *Orientis Graeci Inscriptiones Selectae: Supplementum Sylloges Inscriptionum Graecarum*. Leipzig: S. Herzel.

Downing, F. G. 1995. "Cosmic Eschatology in the First Century: 'Pagan,' Jewish, and Christian." *L'Antiquité Classique* 64: 99–109.

Dunning, S. 2016. "Roman Ludi Saeculares from the Republic to the Empire." PhD diss., University of Toronto.

———. 2020. "The Republican Ludi Saeculares as a Cult of the Valerian Gens." *Historia* 69: 208–236.

DuQuesnay, I. M. 1977. "Vergil's Fourth *Eclogue*." *PLLS* 1: 25–100.

Dyer, R. R. 1965. "'Diffugere nives': Horace and the Augustan Spring." *G&R* 12: 79–84.

Earl, D. C. 1961. *The Political Thought of Sallust*. Amsterdam: Hakkert.

Eckert, A. 2019. "Reconsidering the Sulla Myth." In *Sulla: Politics and Reception*, ed. A. Eckert and A. Thein, 159–172. Berlin: de Gruyter.

Edelstein, L., and I. G. Kidd. 1989. *Posidonius: The Fragments*. Cambridge: Cambridge University Press.

Edlund-Berry, I. E. M. 1994. "Ritual Destruction of Cities and Sanctuaries: The 'Un-founding' of the Archaic Monumental Building at Poggio

Civitate (Murlo)." In *Murlo and the Etruscans: Art and Society in Ancient Etruria*, ed. R. D. De Puma and J. P. Small, 16–28. Madison: University of Wisconsin Press.

Eliade, M. 1954. *The Myth of the Eternal Return*. Trans. W. R. Trask. Princeton, NJ: Princeton University Press.

Erler, M. 1992. "Orthodoxie und Anpassung: Philodem, ein Panaitios des Kepos?" *MH* 49: 171–200.

Erren, M. 1985. *P. Vergilius Marro. Georgica*, vol. 2: *Kommentar*. Heidelberg: C. Winter.

Evans, R. 2008. *Utopia Antiqua: Readings of the Golden Age and Decline at Rome*. London: Routledge.

Ewbank, W. W. 1933. *The Poems of Cicero*. London: University of London Press.

Fantham, R. E. 1985. "Ovid, Germanicus, and the Composition of the *Fasti*." *PLLS* 5: 243–81.

——. 1998. *Ovid. Fasti: Book IV*. Cambridge: Cambridge University Press.

Farrell, J. 1991. *Vergil's Georgics and the Traditions of Ancient Epic*. Oxford: Oxford University Press.

——. 2005. "The Origins and Essence of Roman Epic." In *A Companion to Ancient Epic*, ed. J. M. Foley, 417–428. Malden, MA: Wiley-Blackwell.

——. 2012. "Calling Out the Greeks: Dynamics of the Elegiac Canon." In *A Companion to Roman Love Elegy*, ed. B. K. Gold, 11–24. Malden, MA: Wiley-Blackwell.

——. 2014. "Philosophy in Vergil." In Garani and Konstan 2014, 61–90.

Fears, J. R. 1981a. "The Theology of Victory at Rome: Approaches and Problems." *ANRW* 2.17.2, 736–826.

——. 1981b. "The Cult of Virtues and Roman Imperial Ideology." *ANRW* 2.17.2, 827–948.

Feeney, D. 1998. *Literature and Religion at Rome: Cultures, Contexts, and Beliefs*. Cambridge: Cambridge University Press.

——. 2002. "*Una cum scriptore meo*: Poetry, Principate, and the Traditions of Literary History in the *Epistle* to Augustus." In *Traditions and Contexts in the Poetry of Horace*, ed. T. Woodman and D. Feeney, 172–187. Cambridge: Cambridge University Press.

——. 2007. *Caesar's Calendar: Ancient Time and the Beginnings of History*. Berkeley: University of California Press.

Ferriss-Hill, J. L. 2015. *Roman Satire and the Old Comic Tradition*. Cambridge: Cambridge University Press.

Finkelberg, A. 1998. "On Cosmogony and Ecpyrosis in Heraclitus." *AJP* 119: 195–222.

Flinterman, J.-J. 2014. "Pythagoreans in Rome and Asia Minor around the Turn of the Common Era." In *A History of Pythagoreanism*, ed. C. A. Huffman, 341–359. Cambridge: Cambridge University Press.

Flower, H. I. 2010. *Roman Republics*. Princeton, NJ: Princeton University Press.

222 | Bibliography

———. 2016. "The Rapture and the Sorrow: Characterization in Sulla's Memoirs." In *Fame and Infamy. Essays for Christopher Pelling on Characterization in Greek and Roman Biography and Historiography*, ed. R. Ash, J. Mossman, and F. B. Titchener, 209–223. Oxford: Oxford University Press.

Forsythe, G. 2012. *Time in Roman Religion*. New York: Routledge.

Fortenbaugh, W. W., and E. Schütrumpf, eds. 2001. *Dicaearchus of Messana: Text, Translation, and Discussion*. New Brunswick, NJ: Transaction.

Fowler, W. W. 1910. "The *Carmen Saeculare* of Horace and Its Performance, June 3 BC 17." *CQ* 4: 145–155.

Fraenkel, E. 1957. *Horace*. Oxford: Clarendon Press.

Frazer, J. G. 1929. *The Fasti of Ovid*. London: Macmillan.

Freidin, A. B. 2020. "The Birthday Present: Censorinus' *De die natali*." *JRS* 110: 141–166.

Frier, B. W. 1971. "Sulla's Propaganda: The Collapse of the Cinnan Republic." *AJP* 92: 585–604.

Friesen, S. J. 2001. *Imperial Cults and the Apocalypse of John: Reading Revelation in the Ruins*. Oxford: Oxford University Press.

Gabba, E. 1981. "True History and False History in Classical Antiquity." *JRS* 71: 50–62.

Gagé, J. 1955. *Apollon romain. Essai sur le cult d'Apollon et le développement du "ritu Graecus" à Rome des origins à Auguste*. Paris: de Boccard.

Gain, D. B. 1976. *The Aratus Ascribed to Germanicus Caesar*. London: Athlone.

Gale, M. R. 2013. "Vergil's Caesar." In *Augustan Poetry and the Roman Republic*, ed. J. Farrell and D. Nelis, 278–296. Oxford: Oxford University Press.

———. 2015. "*Aliquid putare nugas*: Literary Filiation, Critical Communities and Reader-Response in Catullus." In *Latin Literature and Its Transmission*, 88–107. Cambridge: Cambridge University Press.

———. 2018. "'*Te sociam, Ratio . . .*': Hunting as Paradigm in the *Cynegetica*." In Green 2018, 77–96.

Galinsky, G. K. 1975. *Ovid's* Metamorphoses: *An Introduction to the Basic Aspects*. Oxford: Blackwell.

———. 1992. *Classical and Modern Interactions: Postmodern Architecture, Multiculturalism, Decline, and Other Issues*. Austin: University of Texas Press.

———. 1996. *Augustan Culture: An Interpretive Introduction*. Princeton, NJ: Princeton University Press.

———. 2007. "Continuity and Change: Religion in the Augustan Semi-century." In *A Companion to Roman Religion*, ed. J. Rüpke, 71–82. Malden, MA: Wiley-Blackwell.

Gantz, T. 1996. *Early Greek Myth: A Guide to Literary and Artistic Sources*. Baltimore, MD: Johns Hopkins University Press.

Garani, M., and D. Konstan, eds. 2014. *The Philosophizing Muse: The Influence of Greek Philosophy on Roman Poetry*. Cambridge: Cambridge University Press.

Gardner, H. H. 2019. *Pestilence and the Body Politic in Latin Literature.* Oxford: Oxford University Press.

Gatz, B. 1967. *Weltalter, goldene Zeit und sinnverwandte Vorstellungen. Spudasmata* 16. Hildesheim: G. Olms.

Gellar-Goad, T. H. M. 2018. "Varro's *Bimarcus* and Encounters with the Self in Plautus's *Epidicus* and *Amphitruo.*" *Arethusa* 51: 117–135.

Gibson, R. K. 2003. *Ovid: Ars Amatoria, Book 3.* Cambridge: Cambridge University Press.

Gill, C. 1980. *Plato: The Atlantis Story.* Bristol: Classical Press.

Glauthier, P. 2009. "Phaedrus, Callimachus and the *Recusatio* to Success." *CA* 28: 248–278.

Goldberg, S. M. 1986. *Understanding Terence.* Princeton, NJ: Princeton University Press.

———. 1995. *Epic in Republican Rome.* Oxford: Oxford University Press.

———. 2005. *Constructing Literature in the Roman Republic: Poetry and Its Reception.* Cambridge: Cambridge University Press.

Golden, M., and P. Toohey, eds. 1997. *Inventing Ancient Culture: Historicism, Periodization, and the Ancient World.* New York: Routledge.

Goldhill, S. 2022. *The Christian Invention of Time: Temporality and the Literature of Late Antiquity.* Cambridge: Cambridge University Press.

Gomme, A. W. 1945. *A Historical Commentary on Thucydides.* Oxford: Clarendon Press.

Goold, G. P. 2006. *Propertius: Elegies.* Cambridge, MA: Harvard University Press.

Gotoff, H. C. 1981. "Cicero's Style for Relating Memorable Sayings." *ICS* 6: 294–317.

Gowers, E. 1995. "The Anatomy of Rome, from Capitol to Cloaca." *JRS* 85: 23–32.

Grafton, A. T., and N. M. Swerdlow. 1985. "Technical Chronology and Astrological History in Varro, Censorinus and Others." *CQ* 35: 454–465.

Grant, R. M. 1950. "The Problem of Theophilus." *HTR* 43: 179–196.

Gratwick, A. S. 2002. "*Vale, patrona virgo*: The Text of Catullus 1.9." *CQ* 52: 305–320.

Green, S. J. 2004. *Ovid, Fasti I: A Commentary.* Leiden: Brill.

———. 2014. *Disclosure and Discretion in Roman Astrology.* Oxford: Oxford University Press.

———, ed. 2018. *Grattius: Hunting an Augustan Poet.* Oxford: Oxford University Press.

Griffin, M. T. 1976. *Seneca: A Philosopher in Politics.* Oxford: Clarendon Press.

Gros, P. 1993. "Apollo Palatinus." In *LTUR*, vol. 1, 54–57.

Gruen, E. 1990. "Philosophy, Rhetoric, and Roman Anxieties." In *Studies in Greek Culture and Roman Policy*, 158–192. Leiden: Brill.

Gurval, R. A. 1995. *Actium and Augustus: The Politics and Emotions of Civil War.* Ann Arbor: University of Michigan Press.

224 | Bibliography

Hall, J. F. 1986. "The *Saeculum Novum* of Augustus and Its Etruscan Antecedents." *ANRW* 2.16.3, 2564–2589.

———. 1996. *Etruscan Italy: Etruscan Influences on the Civilizations of Italy from Antiquity to the Modern Era.* Provo, UT: Brigham Young University Press.

Hannah, R. 2005. *Greek and Roman Calendars: Constructions of Time in the Classical World.* London: Duckworth.

———. 2009. *Time in Antiquity.* New York: Routledge.

Hansen, W. F. 2004. *Handbook of Classical Mythology.* Santa Barbara, CA: ABC-CLIO.

Hardie, P. 1986. *Virgil's* Aeneid: *Cosmos and Imperium.* Oxford: Oxford University Press.

———. 2005. "Time in Lucretius and the Augustan Poets: Freedom and Innovation." In *La représentation du temps dans la poésie augustéenne = Zur Poetik der Zeit in augusteischer Dichtung*, ed. J. P. Schwindt, 19–42. Heidelberg: Universitätsverlag Winter.

———. 2009. *Lucretian Receptions: History, the Sublime, Knowledge.* Cambridge: Cambridge University Press.

Harrison, S. J. 1990. "Cicero's 'De Temporibus Suis': The Evidence Reconsidered." *Hermes* 118: 455–463.

———. 1993. "The Literary Form of Horace's Odes." In *Horace: L'oeuvre et les imitations; un siècle d'interpretation*, ed. W. Ludwig, 131–162. Geneva: Fondation Hardt.

Hartog, F. 2000. "The Invention of History: The Pre-history of a Concept from Homer to Herodotus." *History and Theory* 39: 384–395.

Havas, L. 2000. "Romulus Arpinas: Ein wenig bekanntes Kapitel in der römischen Geschichte des Saeculum-Gedankens." *ACD* 36: 71–88.

Hay, P. 2019. "Saecular Discourse: Qualitative Periodization in First-Century BCE Rome." In *The Alternative Augustan Age*, ed. Kit Morrell, Josiah Osgood, and Kathryn Welch, 216–230. Oxford: Oxford University Press.

———. 2020. "The Programmatic 'Ordior' of Silius Italicus." *Syllecta Classica* 30: 49–71.

Hekster, O., and J. Rich. 2006. "Octavian and the Thunderbolt: The Temple of Apollo Palatinus and Roman Traditions of Temple Building." *CQ* 56: 149–168.

Hellholm, D., ed. 1983. *Apocalypticism in the Mediterranean World and the Near East.* Tubingen: J. C. M. Mohr.

Hendren, T. G. 2014. "Catullus's Ameana Cycle as Literary Criticism." *Mnemosyne* 67: 1–14.

Hendrickson, T. 2015. "An Emendation to a Fragment of Varro's *De bibliothecis* (Fr. 54 *GRF* Funaioli)." *CQ* 65: 395–397.

Heyworth, S. J. 2007. *Cynthia: A Companion to the Text of Propertius.* Oxford: Oxford University Press.

Bibliography | 225

Heyworth, S. J., and J. H. Morwood. 2011. *A Commentary on Propertius: Book 3*. Oxford: Oxford University Press.

Hinds, S. 1998. *Allusion and Intertext: Dynamics of Appropriation in Roman Poetry*. Cambridge: Cambridge University Press.

Hollis, A. S. 2007. *Fragments of Roman Poetry c. 60 B.C.–A.D. 20*. Oxford: Oxford University Press.

Hopkins, J. N. 2012. "The 'Sacred Sewer': Tradition and Religion in the Cloaca Maxima." In *Rome, Pollution and Propriety: Dirt, Disease and Hygiene in the Eternal City from Antiquity to Modernity*, ed. M. Bradley and K. Stow, 81–102. Cambridge: Cambridge University Press.

Horsfall, N. 1993. "Empty Shelves on the Palatine." *G&R* 40: 58–67.

Houston, G. W. 2014. *Inside Roman Libraries: Book Collections and Their Management in Antiquity*. Chapel Hill: University of North Carolina Press.

Hubbard, T. K. 1983. "The Catullan *Libellus*." *Philologus* 127: 218–237.

———. 1984. "Art and Vision in Propertius 2.31/2.32." *TAPA* 114: 281–297.

———. 2005. "The Catullan *Libelli* Revisited." *Philologus* 149: 253–277.

Humphrey, J. H. 1985. *Roman Circuses, Arenas for Chariot Racing*. Berkeley, CA: University of California Press.

Humphreys, S. C. 1997. "Fragments, Fetishes, and Philosophies: Towards a History of Greek Historiography after Thucydides." In *Collecting Fragments / Fragmente sammeln*, ed. G. Most, 207–224. Göttingen: Vandenhoeck and Ruprecht.

Hunt, R. 1981. "Satiric Elements in Hesiod's *Works and Days*." *Helios* 8: 29–40.

Huskey, S. J. 2006. "Ovid's (Mis)guided Tour of Rome: Some Purposeful Omissions in *Tr*. 3.1." *CJ* 102: 17–39.

Inwood, B. 2001. *The Poem of Empedocles*. Toronto: University of Toronto Press.

Jacobson, H. 1977. "Demo and the Sabbath." *Mnemosyne* 30: 71–72.

Jaeger, M. 1997. *Livy's Written Rome*. Ann Arbor: University of Michigan Press.

Jal, P. 1963. *La guerre civile a Rome: Étude littéraire et morale*. Paris: Presses Universitaires de France.

Jenkyns, R. 1993. "Virgil and the Euphrates." *AJP* 114: 115–121.

Johnson, S. E. 2015. "The Ages We Live By: Historical Periodization in Social and Political Thought." PhD diss., University of Chicago.

Johnson, W. R. 2007. "Neoteric Poetics." In Skinner 2007a: 175–189.

Johnston, P. A. 1980. *Vergil's Agricultural Golden Age: A Study of the Georgics*. Leiden: Brill.

Ju, A. E. 2009. "Stoic and Posidonian Thought on the Immortality of the Soul." *CQ* 59: 112–124.

Kahn, C. H. 2001. *Pythagoras and the Pythagoreans: A Brief History*. Indianapolis, IN: Hackett.

Kayachev, B. 2016. "*Catalepton* 9 and Hellenistic Poetry." *CQ* 66: 180–204.

———. 2020. *Ciris: A Poem from the Appendix Vergiliana*. Swansea: Classical Press of Wales.

226 | Bibliography

Keaveney, A. 1982. *Sulla: The Last Republican*. London: Croom Helm.

——. 2005. "Sulla and the Games of Hercules." *AC* 74: 217–223.

Keith, A. 2006. "Critical Trends in Interpreting Sulpicia." *CW* 100.1: 3–10.

——. 2016. "City Lament in Augustan Epic: Antitypes of Rome from Troy to Alba Longa." In *The Fall of Cities in the Mediterranean: Commemoration in Literature, Folk-Song, and Liturgy*, ed. M. R. Bachvarova, D. Dutsch, and A. Suter, 156–182. Cambridge: Cambridge University Press.

Kellum, B. 1985. "The Temple of Apollo on the Palatine." In *The Age of Augustus*, ed. R. Winkes, 169–176. *Archaeologia Transatlantica* 5. Louvain: Institut Supérieur d'Archéologie et d'Histoire de l'Art; Providence, RI: Brown University.

——. 1993. "Sculptural Programs and Propaganda in Augustan Rome: The Temple of Apollo on the Palatine." In *Roman Art in Context: An Anthology*, ed. Eve D'Ambra, 75–83. Englewood Cliffs, NJ: Prentice Hall.

Kendall, S. 2013. *The Struggle for Roman Citizenship: Romans, Allies, and the Wars of 91–77 BCE*. Piscataway, NJ: Gorgias Press.

Kenney, E. J. 1982. *Latin Literature*. Cambridge: Cambridge University Press.

Kermode, F. 1967. *The Sense of an Ending: Studies in the Theory of Fiction*. New York: Oxford University Press.

Kleinguenther, A. 1933. *Prōtos heuretēs: Untersuchungen zur Geschichte einer Fragestellung*. Philologus Supp. 26.1. Leipzig: Dieterich.

Klotz, A. 1901. "Das Geschichtswerk des Aelteren Seneca." *RhM* 56: 429–442.

Knox, P. E. 2011. "Cicero as a Hellenistic Poet." *CQ* 61: 192–204.

König, J., K. Oikonomopoulou, and G. Woolf, eds. 2015. *Ancient Libraries*. Cambridge: Cambridge University Press.

Konrad, C. F. 1994. *Plutarch's Sertorius: A Historical Commentary*. Chapel Hill: University of North Carolina Press.

Koortbojian, M. 2013. *The Divinization of Caesar and Augustus: Precedents, Consequences, Implications*. Cambridge: Cambridge University Press.

Kosmin, P. J. 2018. *Time and Its Adversaries in the Seleucid Empire*. Cambridge, MA: Harvard University Press.

Krenkel, W. 1970. *Lucilius: Satiren*. Leiden: Brill.

Lachmann, K. 1848. *Die Schriften der römischen Feldmesser*. Vol. 1. Berlin: G. Reimer.

Lange, C. H. 2009. *Res publica constituta: Actium, Apollo, and the Accomplishment of the Triumviral Assignment*. Leiden: Brill.

Last, H. 1953. "The *Tabula Hebana* and Propertius II, 31." *JRS* 43: 27–29.

Leach, E. W. 1988. *The Rhetoric of Space: Literary and Artistic Representations of Landscape in Republican and Augustan Rome*. Princeton, NJ: Princeton University Press.

Lebow, R. N., and B. S. Strauss. 1991. *Hegemonic Rivalries: From Thucydides to the Nuclear Age*. Boulder, CO: Westview Press.

Lee, A. G. 1984. *Ovid: Metamorphoses I*. Chicago, IL: Bolchazy-Carducci.

Lee, H. D. P. 1952. *Aristotle. Meteorologica*. Cambridge, MA: Harvard University Press.

Le Goff, J. 2015. *Must We Divide History into Periods?* Trans. M. B. DeBevoise. New York: Columbia University Press.

Lewis, A.-M. 1984. "Rearrangement of Motif in Latin Translation: The Emergence of a Roman *Phaenomena*." In *Studies in Latin Literature and Roman History* 4, ed. C. Deroux, 210–233. Brussels: Latomus.

———. 1989. "The Popularity of the *Phaenomena* of Aratus: A Reevaluation." In *Studies in Latin Literature and Roman History* 6, ed. C. Deroux, 94–118. Brussels: Latomus.

Lewis, R. G. 1991. "Sulla's Autobiography: Scope and Economy." *Athenaeum* 79: 509–519.

Lightfoot, J. 2007. *The Sibylline Oracles: With Introduction, Translation, and Commentary on the First and Second Books.* Oxford: Oxford University Press.

Lintott, A. W. 1972. "Imperial Expansion and Moral Decline in the Roman Republic." *Historia* 21: 626–638.

Littlewood, R. J. 2006. *A Commentary on Ovid: Fasti Book VI.* Oxford: Oxford University Press.

Long, A. A. 2006. "The Stoics on World-Conflagration and Everlasting Recurrence." In *From Epicurus to Epictetus: Studies in Hellenistic and Roman Philosophy*, 256–282. Oxford: Oxford University Press.

Long, A. A., and D. N. Sedley. 1987. *The Hellenistic Philosophers.* Cambridge: Cambridge University Press.

Long, J. H. 2005. "Culture Heroes." In *Encyclopedia of Religion*, vol. 3, ed. Lindsay Jones, 2090–2093. 2nd ed. Detroit: Thomson Gale.

Longo Auricchio, F., and A. Tepidino Guerra. 1981. "Aspetti e problemi della dissidenza epicurea." *CErc* 11: 25–40.

Lowrie, M. 2002. "Horace, Cicero, and Augustus, or The Poet Statesman at *Epistles* 2.1.256." In *Traditions and Contexts in the Poetry of Horace*, ed. T. Woodman and D. Feeney, 158–171. Cambridge: Cambridge University Press.

Lucas, E. C. 1989. "The Origin of Daniel's Four Empires Schema Reexamined." *Tyndale Bulletin* 40: 185–202.

Luce, J. V. 2006. "Heracles and Hydraulics." *Hermathena* 181: 25–39.

Luce, T. J. 1977. *Livy: The Composition of His History.* Princeton, NJ: Princeton University Press.

Luchte, J. 2009. *Pythagoras and the Doctrine of Transmigration.* London: Continuum.

Luck, G. 1979. "Notes on Propertius." *AJP* 100: 73–93.

Lugli, G. 1964. *Foro Romano, Palatino.* Rome: G. Bardi.

———. 1970. *Itinerario di Roma antica.* Milan: Periodici scientifici.

Lukacher, N. 1998. *Time-Fetishes: The Secret History of Eternal Recurrence.* Durham, NC: Duke University Press.

Luke, T. S. 2014. *Ushering in a New Republic: Theologies of Arrival at Rome in the First Century BCE.* Ann Arbor: University of Michigan Press.

Lyne, R. O. A. M. 1978. "The Neoteric Poets." *CQ* 28: 167–187.

———. 1998. "Propertius and Tibullus: Early Exchanges." *CQ* 48: 519–544.

228 | Bibliography

MacGregor, A. 2005. "Was Manilius Really a Stoic?" *ICS* 30: 41–65.

Machinist, P. 2019. "Periodization in Biblical Historiography." In *Historical Consciousness and the Use of the Past in the Ancient World*, ed. J. Baines, H. van der Blom, Y. S. Chen, and T. Rood, 215–237. Bristol, CT: Equinox.

Maltby, R. 2002. *Tibullus: Elegies*. Cambridge: Francis Cairns.

Mankin, D. 1995. *Horace: Epodes*. Cambridge: Cambridge University Press.

Mansfeld, J., and O. Primavesi. 2011. *Die Vorsokratiker: Ausgewählt, übersetzt und erläutert*. Stuttgart: Philipp Reclam.

Martin, J. 1956. *Histoire du texte des Phenomenes d'Aratos*. Paris: C. Klincksieck.

Martin, L. H. 1991. "Fate, Futurity, and Historical Consciousness in Western Antiquity." *Historical Reflections/Reflexions Historiques* 17: 151–169.

Maticic, D. A. 2022. "Hercules, Cacus, and the Poetics of Drains in *Aeneid* 8 and Propertius 4.9." In *The Impact of the Roman Empire on Landscapes*, ed. M. Horster and N. Hachler, 339–352. Leiden: Brill.

Mattingly, H. 1934. "Virgil's Golden Age: Sixth *Aeneid* and Fourth *Eclogue*." *CR* 48: 161–165.

Mayor, A. 2000. *The First Fossil Hunters: Paleontology in Greek and Roman Times*. Princeton, NJ: Princeton University Press.

McConnell, J. R., et al. 2020. "Extreme Climate after Massive Eruption of Alaska's Okmok Volcano in 43 BCE and Effects on the Late Roman Republic and Ptolemaic Kingdom." *PNAS* 117.27: 15443–15449.

McDiarmid, J. B. 1940. "Theophrastus on the Eternity of the World." *TAPA* 71: 239–247.

McGushin, P. 1992. *Sallust: The Histories*. Oxford: Oxford University Press.

McKay, A. G. 1998. "Non enarrabile textum? The Shield of Aeneas and the Triple Triumph of 29 BC." In *Vergil's Aeneid: Augustan Epic and Political Context*, ed. H.-P. Stahl, 199–221. London: Duckworth.

McKeown, J. C. 1998. *Ovid: Amores*. Leeds: Francis Cairns.

Merkelbach, R. 1961. "Aeneas in Cumae." *MH* 18: 83–99.

Michelfeit, J. 1965. "Zum Aufbau des Ersten Buches des Lucilius." *Hermes* 93: 113–128.

Miles, G. B. 1995. *Livy: Reconstructing Early Rome*. Ithaca, NY: Cornell University Press.

Miles, R. 1980. "The *Epodes* of Horace." ML thesis, University of Newcastle upon Tyne.

Miller, J. F. 2000. "Triumphus in Palatio." *AJP* 121: 409–422.

———. 2004. "Ovid and Augustan Apollo." *Hermathena* 177/178: 165–180.

———. 2009. *Apollo, Augustus, and the Poets*. Cambridge: Cambridge University Press.

Mitchell, F. 2021. "Labor V: The Augean Stables." In *Oxford Handbook of Heracles*, ed. D. Ogden, 80–94. Oxford: Oxford University Press.

Momigliano, A. 1941. Review of A. N. Sherwin-White, *The Roman Citizenship*. *JRS* 31: 158–165.

Bibliography | 229

———. 1966. "Time in Ancient Historiography." *History and Theory* 6: 1–23.

Morris, I. 1997. "Periodization and the Heroes: Inventing a Dark Age." In *Inventing Ancient Culture: Historicism, Periodization, and the Ancient World*, ed. M. Golden and P. Toohey, 96–131. New York: Routledge.

Mosca, B. 1937. "Satira filosofica e politica nelle 'Menipee' di Varrone." *ASNP* (series 2) 6.1–2: 41–77.

Murgatroyd, P. 1980. *Tibullus: Elegies I.* Pietermaritzburg: University of Natal Press.

———. 1994. *Tibullus: Elegies II.* Oxford: Clarendon Press.

Myerowitz, M. 1985. *Ovid's Games of Love.* Detroit: Wayne State University Press.

Neudecker, R. 2015. "Archives, Books, and Sacred Space in Rome." In König, Oikonomopoulou, and Woolf 2015: 312–331.

Newman, J. K. 1997. *Augustan Propertius: The Recapitulation of a Genre.* New York: Hildesheim.

Nielsen, I. 2013. "Creating Imperial Architecture." In *A Companion to Roman Architecture*, ed. R. B. Ulrich and C. K. Quenemoen, 45–62. Malden, MA: Blackwell.

Nisbet, R. G. M. 1978. "Virgil's Fourth Eclogue: Easterners and Westerners." *BICS* 25: 59–78.

Nisbet, R. G. M., and M. Hubbard. 1970. *A Commentary on Horace: Odes, Book 1.* Oxford: Clarendon Press.

Noonan, J. D. 1986. "Myth, Humor, and the Sequence of Thought in Catullus 95." *CJ* 81: 299–304.

Ogden, D, ed. 2021. *Oxford Handbook of Heracles.* Oxford: Oxford University Press.

Oksanish, J. M. 2019. *Vitruvian Man: Rome under Construction.* Oxford: Oxford University Press.

Oliensis, E. 1995. "Life after Publication: Horace, *Epistles* 1.20." *Arethusa* 28: 209–224.

Osgood, J. 2006. *Caesar's Legacy: Civil War and the Emergence of the Roman Empire.* Cambridge: Cambridge University Press.

Palmer, R. E. A. 1974. *Roman Religion and Roman Empire.* Philadelphia: University of Pennsylvania Press.

Pandey, N. 2013. "Caesar's Comet, the Julian Star, and the Invention of Augustus." *TAPA* 143: 405–449.

Parker, H. N. 2007. *The Birthday Book.* Chicago: University of Chicago Press.

Pasco-Pranger, M. 2006. *Founding the Year: Ovid's* Fasti *and the Poetics of the Roman Calendar.* Leiden: Brill.

Paven, P. 2014. "Plutarch the Antiquarian." In *A Companion to Plutarch*, ed. M. Beck, 235–248. Malden, MA: Blackwell.

Pedroni, L. 1999. "*Saecula* e *ludi saeculares* sulle monete repubblicane: Nuovi elementi per un'ipotesi dimenticata." *RIN* 100: 93–112.

Peirano, I. 2012. *The Rhetoric of the Roman Fake: Latin Pseudepigrapha in Context.* Cambridge: Cambridge University Press.

230 | Bibliography

Perkell, C. 2002. "The Golden Age and Its Contradictions in the Poetry of Vergil." *Vergilius* 48: 3–39.

Perrin, B. 1916. *Plutarch. Lives*, vol. IV: *Alcibiades and Coriolanus. Lysander and Sulla.* Cambridge, MA: Harvard University Press.

Pertusi, A. 1955. *Scholia vetera in Hesiodi Opera et Dies.* Milan: Vita e pensiero.

Petrain, D. 2015. "Visual Supplementation and Metonymy in the Roman Public Library." In König, Oikonomopoulou, and Woolf 2015, 332–346.

Pighi, I. G. B. 1941. *De ludis saecularibus populi romani quiritium libri sex.* Milan: Vita e Pensiero.

Poe, J. P. 1984. "The Secular Games, the Aventine, and the Pomerium in the Campus Martius." *CA* 3: 57–81.

Polt, C. B. 2013. "Allusive Translation and Chronological Paradox in Varro of Atax's *Argonautae.*" *AJP* 134.4: 603–636.

Powell, L. 2015. *Marcus Agrippa: Right-Hand Man of Caesar Augustus.* West Yorkshire: Pen and Sword Military.

Primavesi, O. 2006. "Empedokles in Florentiner Aristoteles-Scholien." *ZPE* 157: 27–40.

———. 2008. "Empedocles: Physical and Mythical Divinity." In *Oxford Handbook of Presocratic Philosophy*, ed. P. Curd and D. W. Graham, 250–283. Oxford: Oxford University Press.

Purcell, N. 1995. "Forum Romanum (the Republican Period)." *LTUR* vol. 2, 325–336.

———. 2003. "Becoming Historical: The Roman Case." In *Myth, History, and Culture in Republican Rome*, ed. D. Braund and C. Gill, 12–40. Exeter: University of Exeter Press.

Putnam, M. C. J. 1973. *Tibullus: A Commentary.* Norman: University of Oklahoma Press.

———. 1986. *Artifices of Eternity: Horace's Fourth Book of Odes.* Ithaca, NY: Cornell University Press.

Quenemoen, C. K. 2006. "The Portico of the Danaids: A New Reconstruction." *AJA* 110: 229–250.

Rackham, H. 1932. *The Politics, with an English Translation.* London: Heinemann.

Ramage, E. S. 1991. "Sulla's Propaganda: The Collapse of the Cinnan Republic." *Klio* 73: 93–121.

Ramsey, J. T. 2015. *Sallust, Fragments of the Histories. Letters to Caesar.* Cambridge, MA: Harvard University Press.

Rashed, M. 2001. *Die Überlieferungsgeschichte der aristotelischen Schrift De generatione et corruptione.* Serta Graeca 12. Wiesbaden: Reichart.

Rauk, J. 1997. "Time and History in Catullus 1." *CW* 90: 319–332.

Rawson, E. 1979. "L. Cornelius Sisenna and the Early First Century B.C." *CQ* 29: 327–346.

———. 1985. *Intellectual Life in the Late Roman Republic.* London: Duckworth.

Rea, J. 2007. *Legendary Rome.* London: Duckworth.

Reckford, K. J. 1972. "Phaethon, Hippolytus, and Aphrodite." *TAPA* 103: 405–432.

Reinhold, M. 1933. *Marcus Agrippa: A Biography*. Geneva, NY: W. F. Humphrey.

Renda, C. 2020. "Di *aetas* in *aetas*: Considerazioni sulla storiografia di Seneca Padre e Floro." In *Seneca the Elder and His Rediscovered 'Historiae ab initio bellorum civilium,'* ed. M.C. Scappaticcio, 315–328. Berlin: de Gruyter.

Richmond, J. 1981. "Doubtful Works Ascribed to Ovid." *ANRW* 2.31.4, 2744–2783.

Riedweg, C. 2005. *Pythagoras: His Life, Teaching, and Influence*. Trans. S. Rendall. Ithaca, NY: Cornell University Press.

Riggsby, A. M. 2006. *Caesar in Gaul and Rome: War in Words*. Austin: University of Texas Press.

Riposati, B. 1939. *M. Terenti Varronis De vita populi romani*. Milan: Vita e Pensiero.

Rissanen, M. 2015. "Wolf Portents in Ancient Rome." *Athenaeum* 103: 123–139.

Roccos, L. J. 1989. "Apollo Palatinus: The Augustan Apollo on the Sorrento Base." *AJA* 93: 571–588.

Roller, M. 2015. "The Difference an Emperor Makes: Notes on the Reception of the Republican Senate in the Imperial Age." *CRJ* 7: 11–30.

———. 2018. *Models from the Past in Roman Culture: A World of Exempla*. Cambridge: Cambridge University Press.

Rood, T. 2016. "Horoscopes of Empires: Future Ruins from Thucydides to Macaulay." In *Knowing Future Time in and through Greek Historiography*, ed. A. Lianeri, 339–360. Berlin: de Gruyter.

Rosati, G. 2009. "The Latin Reception of Hesiod." In *Brill's Companion to Hesiod*, ed. F Montanari, C. Tsagalis, and A. Rengakos, 343–374. Brill: Leiden.

Rose, H. J. 1942. *The Eclogues of Vergil*. Berkeley: University of California Press.

Rosenblitt, J. A. 2019. *Rome after Sulla*. London: Bloomsbury.

Rosenmeyer, T. G. 1957. "Hesiod and Historiography (*Erga* 106–201)." *Hermes* 85: 257–285.

Rüpke, J. 2011. *The Roman Calendar from Numa to Constantine: Time, History, and the Fasti*. Trans. D. M. B. Richardson. London: Blackwell.

Rutherford, R. 2007. "Poetics and Literary Criticism." In *The Cambridge Companion to Horace*, ed. S. Harrison, 248–261. Cambridge: Cambridge University Press.

Salles, R. 2005. "Ekpyrosis and the Goodness of God in Cleanthes." *Phronesis* 50: 56–78.

Santangelo, F. 2007. *Sulla, the Elites, and the Empire: A Study of Roman Policies in Italy and the Greek East*. Leiden: Brill.

———. 2013. *Divination, Prediction, and the End of the Roman Republic*. Cambridge: Cambridge University Press.

Saunders, T. J. 2001. "Dicaearchus' Historical Anthropology." In *Dicaearchus of Messana: Text, Translation, and Discussion*, ed. W. W. Fortenbraugh and E.

232 | Bibliography

Schütrumpf, 237–254. Rutgers University Studies in Classical Humanities 10. New Brunswick, NJ: Rutgers University Press.

Saylor, C. F. 1975. "The Theme of Planlessness in Terence's *Eunuchus*." *TAPA* 105: 297–311.

Scappaticcio, M. C. 2020. *Seneca the Elder and His Rediscovered 'Historiae ab initio bellorum civilium': New Perspectives on Early-Imperial Roman Historiography*. Berlin: de Gruyter.

Scheid, J. 1998. "Déchiffrer des monnaies: Réflexion sur la représentation figurée des Jeux séculaires." In *Images romaines. Actes de la table ronde organisée à l'École Normale Supérieure (24–26 octobre 1996)*, ed. C. Auvray-Assayas, 13–35. Paris: Presses de l'École Normale Supérieure.

Schettino, M. T. 2014. "The Use of Historical Sources." In *A Companion to Plutarch*, ed. M. Beck, 417–436. Malden, MA: Blackwell.

Schiesaro, A. 1994. "The Palingenesis of *De rerum natura*." *CCJ* 40: 81–107.

———. 2019. "Varro and Lucretius on the End of the World." *RFIC* 147.2: 352–357.

———. 2021. "Lucretius *On the Nature of Things*: Eschatology in an Age of Anxiety." In *Eschatology in Antiquity: Forms and Functions*, ed. H. Marlow, K. Pollmann, and H. Van Noorden, 280–293. New York: Routledge.

Schultz, C. E. 2006. "Juno Sospita and Roman Insecurity in the Social War." In *Religion in Republican Italy*, ed. C. E. Schultz and P. B. Harvey, 207–227. *YCS* 33. Cambridge: Cambridge University Press.

Sedley, D. 1989. "The Proems of Empedocles and Lucretius." *GRBS* 30: 269–296.

Shackleton-Bailey, D. R. 1956. *Propertiana*. Cambridge: Cambridge University Press.

Sherwin-White, A. N. 1998. *The Letters of Pliny: A Historical and Social Commentary*. Oxford: Clarendon Press.

Shipley, F. W. 1933. *Agrippa's Building Activities in Rome*. St. Louis, MO: Washington University Press.

Short, W. M. 2016. "Spatial Metaphors of Time in Roman Culture." *CW* 109: 381–412.

Skinner, M. B. 1987. "Cornelius Nepos and Xenomedes of Ceos: A Callimachean Allusion in Catullus 1." *LCM* 12: 22.

———, ed. 2007a. *A Companion to Catullus*. Oxford: Blackwell.

———. 2007b. "Authorial Arrangement of the Collection." In Skinner 2007a, 35–53.

Skutsch, O. 1985. *The Annals of Quintus Ennius*. Oxford: Oxford University Press.

Slater, N. 2014. "Speaking Verse to Power: Circulation of Oral and Written Critique in the *Lives of the Caesars*." In *Between Orality and Literacy: Communication and Adaptation in Antiquity*, ed. R. Scodel, 289–308. Leiden: Brill.

Smith, C. J. 2009. "Sulla's *Memoirs*." In *The Lost Memoirs of Augustus*, ed. C. J. Smith and A. Powell, 65–85. Swansea: Classical Press of Wales.

Bibliography | 233

———. 2014. *The Etruscans: A Very Short Introduction.* Oxford: Oxford University Press.

Smith, C. J., and A. Powell, eds. 2009. *The Lost Memoirs of Augustus and the Development of Roman Autobiography.* Swansea: Classical Press of Wales.

Smith, K. F. 1979. *The Elegies of Albius Tibullus.* New York: Arno.

Smith, M. F. 1993. *Diogenes of Oenoanda: The Epicurean Inscription.* Naples: Bibliopolis.

Solmsen, F. 1951. "Epicurus and Cosmological Heresies." *AJP* 72: 1–23.

Solodow, J. B. 1987. "On Catullus 95." *CP* 82: 141–145.

Star, C. 2021. *Apocalypse and Golden Age: The End of the World in Greek and Roman Thought.* Baltimore, MD: Johns Hopkins University Press.

Starr, R. J. 2010. *"Cui dono lepidum novum libellum? Corneli, tibi:* Cornelius Nepos and Catullus 1." *New England Classical Journal* 37: 255–265.

———. 2012. "Catullus 14 and Catullus 1: Gift Books, Booksellers, and Poetic Statement." *Studies in Latin Literature and Roman History* 16: 114–125.

Steudel, M. 1992. *Die literaturparodie in Ovids Ars Amatoria.* New York: Hildesheim.

Stewart, R. 1998. *Public Office in Early Rome: Ritual Procedure and Political Practice.* Ann Arbor: University of Michigan Press.

Strauss, W., and N. Howe. 1997. *The Fourth Turning: What the Cycles of History Tell Us About America's Next Rendezvous with Destiny.* New York: Crown.

Strunz, S., and O. Braeckel. 2020. "Did Volcano Eruptions Alter the Trajectories of the Roman Republic and the Ptolemaic Kingdom? Moving beyond Black-Box Determinism." *PNAS* 117.51: 32207–32208.

Sulimani, I. 2011. *Diodorus' Mythistory and the Pagan Mission: Historiography and Culture Heroes in the First Pentad of the Bibliotheke.* Leiden: Brill.

Swoboda, A. 1964. *Operum reliquiae P. Nigidii Figuli.* Amsterdam: Hakkert.

Tarn, W. W. 1932. "Alexander Helios and the Golden Age." *JRS* 22: 135–160.

Tarrant, R. 2007. "Horace and Roman Literary History." In *The Cambridge Companion to Horace,* ed. S. Harrison, 63–76. Cambridge: Cambridge University Press.

Taylor, L. R. 1934. "New Light on the History of the Secular Games." *AJP* 55: 101–120.

Taylor, M. E. 1962. "Horace: *Laudator temporis acti*?" *AJP* 83: 23–43.

Thein, A. G. 2002. "Sulla's Public Image and the Politics of Civic Renewal." PhD diss., University of Pennsylvania.

Thompson, D. 1981. "The Meetings of the Roman Senate on the Palatine." *AJA* 85: 335–339.

Toohey, P. 1984. "Politics, Prejudice, and Trojan Genealogies: Varro, Hyginus, and Horace." *Arethusa* 17: 5–28.

Tracy, J. 2014. *Lucan's Egyptian Civil War.* Cambridge: Cambridge University Press.

Trompf, G. W. 1979. *The Idea of Historical Recurrence in Western Thought.* Berkeley: University of California Press.

Tsitsiou-Chelidoni, C. 2013. "Horace on the Role of the Poetry's Audience in the Literary Process." *Trends in Classics* 5: 341–375.

234 | Bibliography

Tucci, P. L. 2005. "'Where high Moneta leads her steps sublime': The 'Tabularium' and the Temple of Juno Moneta." *JRA* 18: 6–33.

——. 2015. "Flavian Libraries in the City of Rome." In König, Oikonomopoulou, and Woolf 2015: 277–311.

Turfa, J. M. 2006. "Etruscan Religion at the Watershed." In *Religion in Republican Italy*, ed. C. E. Schultz and P. B. Harvey, 62–89. *YCS* 33. Cambridge: Cambridge University Press.

——. 2012. *Divining the Etruscan World: The Brontoscopic Calendar and Religious Practice.* Cambridge: Cambridge University Press.

——, ed. 2013a. *The Etruscan World.* New York: Routledge.

——. 2013b. "Etruscan Religion." In *The Handbook of Religions in Ancient Europe*, ed. L. Bredholt Christensen, O. Hammer, and D. A. Warburton, 139–155. Bristol, CT: Acumen.

Valgiglio, E. 1975. "L'autobiografia di Silla nelle biografie di Plutarco." *Studi Urbinati* 49.1: 245–281.

Valvo, A. 1988. *La "Profezia di Vegoia": Proprietà fondiaria e aruspicina in Etruria nel I secolo a.C.* Rome: Istituto italiano per la storia antica.

Van den Berg, C. S. 2014. *The World of Tacitus'* Dialogus de Oratoribus: *Aesthetics and Empire in Ancient Rome.* Cambridge: Cambridge University Press.

——. 2021. *The politics and poetics of Cicero's 'Brutus': The Invention of Literary History.* Cambridge: Cambridge University Press.

Van der Meer, L. B. 2011. *Etrusco Ritu: Case Studies in Etruscan Ritual Behavior.* Walpole, MA: Peeters.

Van der Sluijs, M. A. 2006. "Phaethon and the Great Year." *Apeiron* 39: 57–90.

Van Noorden, H. 2015. *Playing Hesiod: The "Myth of the Races" in Classical Antiquity.* Cambridge: Cambridge University Press.

Van Son, D. W. L. 1963. "The Disturbances in Etruria during the Second Punic War." *Mnemosyne* 16: 267–274.

Verdenius, W. J. 1985. *A Commentary on Hesiod, Works and Days vv. 1–382.* Leiden.

Vernant, J.-P. 1960. "Le mythe hésiodique des races: Essai d'analyse structural." *Revue de l'Histoire des Religions* 157: 21–54.

Versnel, H. S. 1994. *Inconsistencies in Greek and Roman Religion*, vol. 2: *Transition and Reversal in Myth and Ritual.* Leiden: Brill.

Vessey, D. W. T. 1981. "Elegy Eternal: Ovid, 'Amores' I.15." *Latomus* 40: 607–617.

Vittinghoff, F. 1964. "Zum geschichtliche Selbstverständnis der Spätantike." *HZ* 198: 529–574.

Volk, K. 2015. "The World of the Latin Aratea." In *Cosmologies et cosmogonies dans la litterature antique*, ed. P. Derron, 253–289. Vandoeuvres: Fondation Hardt.

——. 2016. "Roman Pythagoras." In *Roman Reflections: Studies in Latin Philosophy*, ed. K. Volk and G. D. Williams, 33–49. Oxford: Oxford University Press.

Vollenweider, M.-L. 1958/1959. "Der Traum des Sulla Felix." *SNR* 39: 22–34.

Wagenvoort, H. 1956. *Studies in Roman Literature, Culture, and Religion.* Leiden: Brill.

Bibliography | 235

Wallace-Hadrill, A. 1982. "The Golden Age and Sin in Augustan Ideology." *Past & Present* 95: 19–36.

———. 2008. *Rome's Cultural Revolution*. Cambridge: Cambridge University Press.

Walton, F. R. 1965. "A Neglected Historical Text." *Historia* 14: 236–251.

Warmington, E. H. 1935. *Remains of Old Latin*, vol. 1: *Ennius*. Cambridge, MA: Harvard University Press.

Warren, J. 2000. "Epicurean Immortality." *Oxford Studies in Ancient Philosophy* 18: 231–261.

———. 2001. "Lucretian Palingenesis Recycled." *CQ* 51: 499–508.

———. 2004. "Ancient Atomists on the Plurality of World." *CQ* 54: 354–365.

Weinstock, S. 1971. *Divus Julius*. Oxford: Clarendon Press.

Weiss, P. 1973. "Die 'Säkularspiele' der Republik—eine annalistische Fiktion? Ein Beitrag zum Verständnis der kaiserzeitlichen Ludi saeculares." *MdI, Roemische Abteilung* 80: 205–217.

Welch, T. S. 2005. *The Elegiac Cityscape: Propertius and the Meaning of Roman monuments*. Columbus: Ohio State University Press.

West, M. L. 1978. *Hesiod: Works and Days*. Oxford: Clarendon Press.

Wheeler, S. 2000. *Narrative Dynamics in Ovid's* Metamorphoses. Tubingen.

White, Hayden. 1973. *Metahistory: The Historical Imagination in Nineteenth-Century Europe*. Baltimore, MD: Johns Hopkins University Press.

———. 1980. "The Value of Narrativity in the Representation of Reality." *Critical Inquiry* 7: 5–27.

———. 1987. *The Content of the Form: Narrative Discourse and Historical Representation*. Baltimore, MD: Johns Hopkins University Press.

White, H. 1913. *Appian's Roman History; with an English Translation*. London: Heinemann.

White, P. 1993. *Promised Verse: Poets in the Society of Augustan Rome*. Cambridge, MA: Harvard University Press.

Whitrow, G. J. 1988. *Time in History*. Oxford: Oxford University Press.

Wiedemann, T. 1989. *Adults and Children in the Roman Empire*. New Haven: Yale University Press.

Williams, G. 1972. *Horace*. Oxford: Clarendon Press.

Wiseman, T. P. 2013. "The Palatine, from Evander to Elagabalus." *JRS* 103: 234–268.

———. 2019. *The House of Augustus: A Historical Detective Story*. Princeton, NJ: Princeton University Press.

Zanker, A. T. 2010. "Late Horatian Lyric and the Virgilian Golden Age." *AJP* 131: 495–516.

———. 2017. "The Golden Age." In *A Handbook to the Reception of Classical Mythology*, ed. V. Zajko and H. Hoyle, 193–211. Hoboken, NJ: Wiley.

Zanker, P. 1990. *The Power of Images in the Age of Augustus*. Trans. A. Shapiro. Ann Arbor: University of Michigan Press.

236 | Bibliography

Zerubavel, E. 2003. *Time Maps: Collective Memory and the Social Shape of the Past*. Chicago: University of Chicago Press.

Zetzel, J. E. G., ed. 1995. Cicero, *De re publica: Selections*. Cambridge: Cambridge University Press.

———. 2016. "Philosophy Is in the Streets." In *Roman Reflections: Studies in Latin Philosophy*, ed. K. Volk and G. D. Williams, 50–62. Oxford: Oxford University Press.

General Index

abortion
  in Ovid, 103
  popularity of, 103
Academic school of philosophy, 41,
  47, 54, 60, 69, 102, 198n86
Accius, 153
Acropolis, 53
Aegyptus (mythical figure), 145
Aeneas, 103
Aeschylus, in Horace's genealogy of
  drama, 139
Aesop, 155
Age
  Atomic, 8, 11
  Augustan (see Augustan Age)
  Eighth (of ten) in the Etruscan
    Chronicles, 28–31
  of Apollo, 41, 132
  of Saecularity, 168
  Sullan, 17
Agrippa, Marcus Vipsanius, 112–115,
  120
  emulates Hercules Augean labors,
    112–114
Alcaeus, 158
Alexandria
  embassy from, 161
  scholars of, 137
anacyclosis, 2, 4, 110

Antaeus, 64
Antimachus of Colophon, 144, 154
Antiochus of Ascalon, 198n86
Antipater of Thessalonica, his
  ironic Golden Age, 87–88
antiquarians, euhemerist, 100
Antoninus Liberalis, 185n72
Antony, 110, 115
Apollo and Diana, eclipse Jupiter
  and Juno under Augustus, 133
Ara Numinis Augusti, 129
Aratus
  Justice in, 85–86, 121
  primary influence on the end of
    Catullus 64, 85
  replaced Hesiod as Roman poets'
    source for the Metallic Ages,
    85
Archilochus, 143, 157
Arellius Fuscus, 110
Argo and the Argonauts, 90, 153
Aristion (Athenian tyrant), 53
Aristophanes, in Horace's genealogy
  of satire, 138–139
Aristotle, 54
  and the Great Year, 58–59
  cyclic catastrophes, 57–58
  on first discoverers, 96
Asclepiades (doctor), 102

238 | General Index

Ateius Capito, 125, 152, 159
Athena's robe, 111
Athens, sack of, 18
atomists, 44
August (month), 6
Augustan Age, 115–117
   Augustus' own account in the *Res Gestae*, 117
   Horace's account in *Ode* 4.15, 117–122
   prospective, in the *Aeneid*, 116
Augustan and Julian calendars, 128–130
   Augustan epoch, 130
Augustan principate
   as second childhood of Rome, 167
   difficult relationship with the Republic, 10
Augustus
   as man of the *saeculum*, 121
   as *pontifex maximus*, 131, 134
   death and honors, 6–7
   decorates his villa with giant bones, 64
   doubts about his birthdate and horoscope, 130
   house of, 79
   mortality threatens renewed civil war, 68, 115–116
   not the epicenter of Roman saecular discourse, 169
Avernus, Lake, 114

Balbus (interlocutor of Cicero), 106–107
Bibliotheca Palatina, 131, 156–161
   allowed testing of poet's *primus inventor* claims, 157
   as a spur to literary production, 158–159
   construction an act of literary historicization, 157

contained portraits of Germanicus and Drusus, 160
controlled by the *princeps*, 157–159
Greek and Latin sections embarrassingly disproportionate in size?, 161
   separate or not?, 160–161
librarians of, 158–159
must have included contemporary Greek literature, 157
presence on the shelves controlled and prestigious, 160
slave workers, some Greek, some Latin, 161
used for meetings of the Senate, 161
Bocchus, king of Mauretania, 18
body-state analogy, 2
bones of primeval giants found, 63–64
Bronze Age, in Hesiod, 84
bucolic poetry, full of learned allusions, 94

Cadmus, 145
Caecina, 38
Callimachus, 158
   as model for Roman poets, 141–142, 148
   last canonical Greek poet for them, 157
Calvus
   and Catullus, 143–144
   excluded from Ovid's genealogy of elegy, 140
   included in Propertius' genealogy of elegy, 138
Campus Martius, 124
canons of literature, 135–136
   visibly present in the Bibliotheca, 157

General Index | 239

Capitoline Hill, 79
  eclipsed by the Palatine under
    Augustus, 132–133
  Sulla's rebuilding of, 23, 25–26
Capitoline temple, erection of, 4
Capricorn (zodiac), 130
Carneades, 40, 102
Carthaginians, 77
cataclysmic change, 40, 46
  at fixed intervals (Aristotle), 57
  civilizational collapse without
    physical cataclysm (Aristotle),
    57–58
  global *vs.* localized, 57
  idea brought to Rome by Greek
    philosophers, 69
  Pliny the Younger and Vesuvius,
    48–49
Catalepton 9, 111
Catilinarian conspiracy, 132
Catiline, 108–109
Cato the Elder, 40, 106, 137
Catullus
  and bad poets, 143–144
  and Calvus, 143–144
  and Horace on poetic
    immortality, 150–151
  anxieties about poetic
    immortality, 154
  as neoteric poet, 142–145,
    148–149
  excluded from Ovid's genealogy
    of elegy, 140
  included in Propertius' genealogy
    of elegy, 138
Cecrops, 145
Celsus, *De Medicina*, 101–102
Censorinus
  and Etruscan *saeculum* doctrine,
    17, 29–33
    difficult source relation with
      Varro, 32

  on the two systems for
    calculating the Ludi
    Saeculares, 123
Cerambus, 52
Ceres, as *primus inventor*, 97
Chaldean seer, 20, 22
chariot out of control simile, 64
child, Messianic, 90, 95
chiliastic movements, 6
Chimaera, 107
Christianity, rise of, 6
Christian use of periodization, 165
chronicle, as form of history, 1
Chrysippus, 47–48
Chytroi festival, 53
Cicero
  and four ages of the Roman state,
    167
  and saecular narratives, 106–107
  and three ages of Roman history,
    72–73, 81
  apologizes for his untraditional
    spending, 73
  Aratea, 86
  as neoteric poet, 145
  Brutus, 163
    as evolutionary literary history
      of oratory, 136–137, 140,
      147, 155, 162
    teleological, leading up to
      Cicero himself, 136, 140
  corresponded with Posidonius,
    48
  depicted by himself and others as
    man of the *saeculum*?, 109–110
  history of the Academic school of
    philosophy, 102
  presents himself as a second
    Romulus?, 201n7
  writes narrative technical history
    of literature, 135
Cilicia, 20

240 | General Index

Cinna the poet, 144–145, 150
Cinna the politician, 21
 one of three Cornelii fated to
  rule Rome, 108
Circus Flaminius, 26
Ciris, 111
civilization, fragility of, 69
Claudius, Emperor, 114
Cleanthes, 47
Cleopatra, 115
Cloaca Maxima, Agrippa cleans and
 sails through, 112–115
coins. *See also* numismatic evidence
 Hercules and the Nemean Lion,
  27
 Janus and a ship, 23, 87
 Sulla's gold, 24
Cole, Thomas, "The Course of
 Empire," 2
comets and shooting stars, 104
 comet marks Caesar's
  assassination (*sidus Iulium*), 49,
  117
Comitium, Sulla's repaving of, 24
conflagration, Stoic universal, 25,
 46–47
construction projects, Agrippa
 emulates Sulla, 112
contamination, in Roman comedy,
 139
Corinna, 103
Cornelii, three fated to rule Rome,
 108
cosmetics and women's fashion, 79
cosmic cycle, Empedocles',
 92–94
Crassus, captive soldiers of, 77
Cratinus, in Horace's genealogy of
 satire, 138–139
Cronus, life under, 85
culture hero
 as a concept, 5, 9–10, 83, 95–96
 Grattius has four of them, 198n67

Hercules as, 27
 often propel a metakosmesis, 11
 Prometheus as, 10
 Sulla as, 27
cultus vs. simplicitas/rusticitas, 79–80
Curia Cornelia, 24
Curia Hostilia, replaced, 24, 79
Curio (orator), 137
Cynthia (Propertius' beloved), 75,
 77

Danaus, 145
Daniel, Biblical Book of, 164
Democritus, and palingenesis, 44
deterministic physics of the Stoics,
 46
Deucalion, 96, 98
 and Pyrrha, 41, 103, 168
Dicaearchus, 48, 59–60
Dionysius Exiguus, 165
Diphilus, 139
Dis, 124
Drusus and Germanicus, portraits
 in the Bibliotheca, 160

ekpyrosis, 7, 54
Empedocles, 92–94
 as prototype for later saecular
  discourse, 93
 death by leaping into Etna, 94
 influence on Roman authors,
  94
end of the world, possible, 62–63
Ennius, 41, 139, 157
 as second Homer, 148
 excluded from the history of
  satire by Horace, 138
 immortal poet, 153
 translated Euhemerus, 96
Epaphroditos, 37
Epicureanism, on palingenesis, 40,
 44–45
Epicurus, as *primus inventor*, 97

General Index | 241

eras
 Era Vulgaris, 165
 of Hellenistic kings, 22
 Sullan era beginning 85/84 BCE,
  22
erotic wall-art, 75–76
eschatology, Christian and Jewish,
 165
Esquiline, 26
eternity of God
 and matter (Stoic), 46
 problems with, 106
Etruscan culture, 48
 mixed Roman attitudes towards,
  36–37
 Romans with Etruscan ancestry,
  38
Etruscan divination, 17, 20–21
 Etruscan Chronicles, 30–31
 saecula eight or ten in number,
  32–33
 saecula marked by prodigies and
  portents, 32
 saeculum doctrine, 10–11, 22, 28–29
euhemerism, 98
 Cicero's on Romulus, 81
Euhemerus, 96
Eupolis, in Horace's genealogy of
 satire, 138–139
Evander, 67–68, 131
evolutionary model of literary
 history, 136–137
exiles, history of famous, 103–104
expulsion of the philosophers from
 Rome, 40

Fasti (calendar), 6
Fasti Ostienses, 22
Faustus and Fausta, Sulla's children,
 37
Feeney, Denis, 4
Felix, Sulla's title on his statue and
 coins, 23–24

Fenestella, 165–166, 168
fish, poems used to wrap them, 144,
 162
fishponds, development of, 12
floods
 destroyed Attica, 56
 Deucalion and Pyrrha's, 9, 11,
  74–75
  as metakosmetic episode, 50
  contemporary visual depictions
   scant, 53
  in Horace, 51
  in Manilius, 54
  in Ovid, 50–53
   anticipates post-human
    world, 63
  in Plato, 56–57
  in Propertius, 132
  Lucretius' doubts, 61
 multiple cataclysmic
  in Cicero, 62
  in Lucretius, with other
   cataclysms, 61
  in Plato, 56
 Ogyges's, 11
 Tiber, 113–114
Forum Romanum, Sulla's
 rebuilding of, 23–26
Four Elements, in Empedocles,
 92–93
fragility of civilization, 68–69
Furius Bibaculus, 145–146
future, ancient concepts of, 10

Gaius Caesar (Augustus' heir),
 120
Gallus, in Propertius' and Ovid's
 genealogies of elegy, 138
genealogical model of literary
 history, 137–140
Germanicus, *Aratea*, 86
Germanicus and Drusus, portraits
 in the Bibliotheca, 160

242 | General Index

Golden Age
  alternative version, localized in
    Latium, 23, 67–68, 86–87,
    132
  Dicaearchus and, 59–60
  future second one, in Vergil's
    4th Eclogue, 89–92, 115
  in Hesiod, 84
  in Horace, 115
  in Ovid's Pythagoras myth, 65
  in Posidonius, 48
  in Tibullus, 76, 99–100
  ironic or parodic, 80, 87–88
  Neronian, 163
Gracchi, 36
Grattius, 104
Great Year, cosmic cycle, 58–59
Greek poets
  matched one to one with later
    Roman poets, 158
  temporal rather than geographic
    distinction, 157–158

harvest, failure of, natural process
  or moral punishment?, 105
Helenus, 103
Hellenistic kings as models, 5, 130
Hellenistic poets as models, 141, 145
Hellenization of Rome and Italy,
  libraries and, 159
Hercules, 26–27
  Agrippa emulates by cleaning
    Cloaca Maxima, 112–114
  as problem-solving culture hero
    in Varro, 113
  statue alluding to the Augean
    Stables, 202n22
  Twelve Labors, 113
Heroic Age
  in Hesiod, 84
  in Vergil's 4th Eclogue, 90
  omitted by Cicero, 86

Hesiod, 143. *See also* Metallic Ages
  and Age theory, 4, 7
  and cosmic cyclicality, 163
  unimportant to Roman poets
    before Vergil, 85
  works effectively immortal in
    Ovid, 153
Hippocentaur, 107
historiography, distinguished from
  chronicle, 1
history
  "one damned thing after
    another," 1
  Varro's three divisions, 101,
    103–104
Homer, 41, 143
  chronology of, 81–82
  Ennius as second, 148
Horace
  Carmen Saeculare, performance of,
    159
  complex use of moral decline
    theme, 77–78
  his genealogical model of literary
    history, 138
  changes from *Epistle* 1.20 to 2.1,
    149
  his lyric encomium to Augustus,
    Ode 4.15, 117–122
  connections with *Ode* 3.6,
    121–122
  connections with the *Carmen
    Saeculare*, 122–123
  on old *vs.* new literature,
    147–148
  rejects the Metallic Ages for a
    Golden Augustan Age, 88
  writes narrative technical history
    of literature, 135, 147–150,
    162
hostile politics, 37
Hyginus (librarian), 156

General Index | 243

Icarius, as *primus inventor*, 97
immortality, poetic, 141–142, 146,
  149–150
    threatened by changing tastes,
      151–152, 154
    and popular envy, 152, 155
in saecula saeculorum prayer formula,
  165
inscriptional evidence, 22
intellectual progress, in Cicero,
  80–82
Iron Age
    in Hesiod, 84
    in Ovid's Pythagoras myth, 65
    in Tibullus, 76, 99–100
Isles of the Blessed, 67

Janus
    and saecularity, 87
    and Saturn in the Golden Age of
      Latium, 68, 86–87
    welcomes Saturn to Latium, 23
Jason ("the Aesonian leader"), 152
Jewish use of periodization,
  163–165
Jugurtha, 18
Julius Aquila, 38
Julius Caesar, 104
    apotheosis of, 49
    assassination heralds a new
      saeculum, 49–50, 64, 108
    calendar reforms, 4
    commentarii avoid periodization for
      lapsarianism, 71–72
    planned a massive library, 156
Jupiter, and the flood, 52
Justice (goddess)
    in Aratus, 85–86
    withdraws from humans as the
      ages progress, 85–86

Kosmin, Paul J., 5

Lactantius, 167
Laelius (interlocutor of Cicero), 72
lapsarian model of moral decline,
  70, 95, 105, 167
lapsarian moments, 169
Laverna, Sulla's omen at, 19–21
leader, divinely chosen, 27
legitimating ideology, novel, 37
Lentulus Sura, 108
    one of three Cornelii fated to
      rule Rome?, 108
Lepidus, 109
Lesbia (Catullus' beloved), 75
Libra (zodiac), 130
libraries. *See also* Bibliotheca
    Pollio's, 161
    private and public, 156
Libya, 64
literary history
    evolutionary model, 136–137
    genealogical model, 137–140
    some authors mix the two models,
      140
literature, why artists in different
    genres are often contemporary, 166
Livia, in Ovid, 78–79
Livius Andronicus, 148
Livy, history avoids periodization
    for lapsarianism, 71–72
Love and Strife, in Empedocles,
  92–93
Lucceius, 110
Lucilius (Roman satirist)
    in Horace's genealogy of satire,
      138–139, 148–149
Lucius Caesar (Augustus' heir), 120,
  126
Lucretius
    vs. Manilius on geological
      saecularity, 104–106
    works effectively immortal in
      Ovid, 153

244 | General Index

Lucullus, 19
Ludi Saeculares, 7, 49
  competing timelines for
    celebrations, 123
  epigraphic evidence for
    celebration in 17 BCE,
    123
    doubts about previous
      celebrations, 123
  experience of, 127–128, 132
  interval recalculated from 100 to
    110 years, 7, 45, 123
  lustral function of, 127
  never seen before, never to be
    seen again, 126–127
  Ovid describes the performance
    of Horace's *Carmen Saeculare*,
    126
  surprisingly omitted in the 40s
    BCE, 110
Ludi Tarentini, 124
Luke, Trevor, 5
Luscius, 139
Lycaon, 51

Maecenas, 38
Manilius *vs.* Lucretius on geological
  saecularity, 104–106
Manius Curius, 190n5
Manlius Vulso, 72
Marcellus (Augustus' heir), 120
Marius, 18, 21
material evidence for Etruscan
  saecular doctrine, 34
Mauretanians, 64
memoirs
  Agrippa's, 114
  Augustus', 49, 117
  Sulla's, 18–22
    a source for Fenestella?, 166
    a source for Plutarch in several
      lives, 175n18
    composed until death, 18

dedicated to Lucullus, 19
defensive attitude of, 22
fragments show interest in
  supernatural, 21
room for digressions in, 21
Menander, 139
Messalla Corvinus, 42–43
  as man of the *saeculum* in Pseudo-
    Vergil, 111
Messallinus, 134
Messianic texts, 163–164
metakosmesis, 13, 33–34, 45–46,
  48–54, 71, 95–96
  never seen as imminent by Stoics,
    48
  often propelled by a culture hero,
    11
  Sulla expands rhetorical range of,
    46
Metallic Ages
  in Aratus, 85–86
  in Catullus 64, 90–91
  in Cicero's translation of Aratus,
    86
  in Dicaearchus, 59–60
  in Empedocles, 93–94
  in Germanicus, 86
  in Hesiod, 12, 83–86, 164
    imagines a possible sixth
      post-iron age, 84–85
    not a simple downward
      progression, 84
    uses races, not ages, 84
  in Horace, 67–68, 77–78
  in Ovid, *Metamorphoses* 15, 42,
    86–87
  in Propertius (unserious), 76
  in Tibullus, 99–100
  in Vergil
    Aeneid 8, 67–68
    Eclogue 4, 83, 88–95
  myth facilitated innovative ideas
    on periodization, 83–84

General Index | 245

mythology, 83, 107
repeated in reverse in Vergil's
4th Eclogue, 90–91
metempsychosis, 41–43, 54, 168
in [Tibullus], 42–43
Milky Way, origin of, 54
Mithridates, 18, 109
monologue of a locked door, 74
moral decline, narratives of, 70, 82
lapsarian model, 70–71, 95
requires a simplified history, 71
mortality, poetic, neoteric fear of,
149
Mucius Scaevola, Q. (poet), 145
Muses, 148

Naevius, 139, 148
naming conventions, novel, 37
narrative
cosmic, 9
historical, shapes of, 2
Nebuchadnezzar, 164
Nemean Lion, 27
Nemesis (Tibullus' beloved), 77
Neoclassicism, 8
Neopythagoreanism, 41
neoteric poets, 141–146, 155
definition of neoteric disputed,
141
Horace's closeness to, 151
works mostly lost, 150
Nepos, Cornelius
constructs a chronology of
literature, 136
dedicatee of Catullus, 142–144
hoping to be included in his
canon?, 143
Nicolaus of Damascus, 166, 168
Nigidius Figulus, 38, 41, 132
Numa, 42
numismatic evidence, 22–23, 114,
128
Nux, Ovidian or not?, 102–103

Olympiad, as time unit, 32
omens and prodigies
often accompany metakosmesis, 11
Sulla's, 19–21
Oracula Sibyllina, 164
Orbilius, 146
Orestes and Pylades, 78
Orion, 64
Orobazus, Chaldean seer, 20
Orphic eschatology, 132
Osiris, as *primus inventor*, 97
Otus, 64
Ovid
anxieties about poetic
immortality, 151–155
begs admission to the Bibliotheca
for his books, 160
constructs canons of literature,
135–136
cultus vs. simplicitas/rusticitas, 79–80
his genealogical model of literary
history, 138
emphasizes his similarity to
Gallus, 140
his ironic Golden Age, 87–88
ignores the Capitoline in his tour
of Rome in *Tristia* 3.1, 133
use of Livia as moral *exemplum*,
78–79
use of saecular discourse for
moral exemplarity, 78–79

Palatine complex, 131, 159
emblematic of *cultus* in Ovid, 132
palingenesis, 7, 40, 43–45, 54, 168
Lucretius' objections to, 44
with 440-year interval (Varro),
45, 126–127
Pan, as *primus inventor*, 97
Pandora, 84
paraclausithyron, 74
Parthenius, 141, 213n76
pearls, popularity of, 166

246 | General Index

pendulum model of the Metallic Ages, 92
perfection, and the evolutionary model of literary history, 136–137
periodization, 2–3
  and literary history, 136
  arbitrariness of, 3
  as intellectual tool, 12
  eases connections to the future and past, 10–11, 39, 130–131
  exploded after Sulla, 36–37
  first significant instance in Sulla, 17, 28–29
  in [Vergil]'s *Ciris* and *Catalepton* 9, 111
  in Horace
    Epistle 2.1, 147–150
    Ode 4.15, 120
  not natural for Romans in the Republic, 168
  progress *vs.* decline not a simple dichotomy, 83
  qualitative, largely absent in first decades after Sulla, 38
  rarer than expected in ancient Rome, 3–4
  rejected by Caesar, 110–111
  rejected by Cicero, 110
  saecularity, a version of it, 9
Peripatetic school of philosophy, 41, 47, 54, 60, 69
Phaedrus the fabulist, 155
Phaethon and his fiery ride, 9, 41, 96, 168
  as metakosmetic episode, 50
  contemporary visual evidence, 53
  in Manilius, 54
  in Ovid, 50, 53–54
  mocked by Lucretius, 61–62
Philippi, 63, 64, 68
Philo of Larisa, 198n86
philosophy, Greek, in Rome, 40–69

Phocaeans, 67
Phoebus Apollo, 122
physics, Epicurean, 43–44
Piso Frugi, 71
Plato, 54, 80
  and the Great Year, 58–59
  cyclic catastrophes in the later dialogues, 55–57
  in the *Aeneid*, 42
  Myth of Er, 41
Plautus, 97
  and the genealogical model of literary history, 139
Pliny the Elder, on an error of Fenestella, 166
Pliny the Younger, and the eruption of Vesuvius, 48–49
Plutarch
  and Etruscan *saeculum* doctrine, 17, 28–29, 32–33
    lack of technical detail, 33
    no decline from one age to another, 33
  and Varro on the horoscopes of Augustus and Rome, 130, 207n90
  may have used Sulla's memoirs as a source, 22, 32
  quoted, 19–21, 28–29
poetic fame, from objective merit or popularity?, 154
Pollio, Asinius, 90, 156
Polybius, 4, 60
  anacyclosis, 110
pomerium, enlargement of, 26
Pompeius Macer, 156
Pompey the Great
  as emulator of Sulla, 201n5
  as man of the *saeculum* in Cicero?, 109
  competitors' envy a blemish of the age, 201n6
Pontius the Samnite, 190n7

Porticus Octaviae, 156
Posidonius, 47–48, 182n42
post-human world, anticipated by
  Thucydides, 63
post-Roman world anticipated,
  62–69
  in Horace's *Epodes*, 67–68
  in Vergil's *Georgics*, 63–66
  obliquely
    by Propertius, describing Veii,
      66
    by Scipio Africanus, mourning
      Carthage, 66–67
post-Trojan world depicted
  in Horace, 65–66
  in Ovid, 65
Praxiteles, 155
Priapus, 76
primus inventor, "first discoverer," 95,
  107. *See also* culture hero
  may be good or bad, 96
  of agriculture, 100
  of erotic wall art, 96
  of flattery and parasitism,
    96–97
  of hours and sundials, 97
  of laws and order, 100
  of ships, 97
  of swords, 99
  of yoking oxen, 99
  Sulla as, 37–38
  theme, 166
Proculus, 80
prodigies. *See* omens and prodigies
professionalization of knowledge in
  Rome, 101
progress narratives, 80–82
Prometheus, 10, 52, 84
  as *primus inventor*, 97–99
  first connected with the Golden
    Age by Ovid, 98
propaganda, Sullan and Imperial,
  27

Propertius, 79
  his genealogical model of literary
    history, 138
  in Ovid's genealogy of elegy, 138
  on those who do not fit the spirit
    of the age, 73–76
proscriptions, Sulla's, 18
Proserpina, 124
provincial readers, neoterics
  despise, Horace desires, 150–151
pumice, metapoetic, 211n48
purificatory rites, 128
Pythagoras, 103
  and Numa, 180n14
  had beans for relatives, 180n3
  history of his metempsychoses,
    43
  in Ovid, *Metamorphoses* 15, 42,
    64–65
  statue of torn down, 24
Pythagoreanism, 40–43. *See also*
  metempsychosis
  in the *Aeneid*, 42

Quintilian, writes narrative
  technical history of literature,
  135
Quintus Sextius, 42

rabies, ancient remedies for, 104
Regulus, 77–79
Revelations, Biblical Book of, 165
rhetoric of civilizational collapse, 70
Romanticism, 8
Rome, future demise of, 168
Romulus, 167
  and Remus, 131
  apotheosis of, 80–81
  bones of, 67
rostra, Sulla's rebuilding of, 23–24

Sabines, 75
Sabine women, 79

248 | General Index

saecular model, Vergil's combines Etruscan and Empedoclean models, 93

saeculum
  a term with special significance for Catullus, 144–145
  allows a variety of shapes for history, 2, 4, 11
  cycles of, finite *vs.* infinite, 168
  definitions, 5
  geological saecularity, 104–106
  lexical range of
    cosmic, 7
    interval of the *Ludi Saeculares* recalculated from 100 to 110 years, 7
    length of a human life, 6–7
  man of the, 95, 168
  progress narratives *vs.* decline narratives, 80–82
  saecular discourse and saecularity, 5, 8–9
  changes in the Augustan Age, 115–116, 162
  source in Etruscan divination, 17
  synonyms for (*aetas, aevum, tempus*), 7
    Velleius Paterculus uses all four of them, 166

saeculum Augustum, 6, 169

saeculum Sullanum, 24

Sallust
  avoids periodization for lapsarianism, 71–72, 190n9
  on the three Cornelii fated to rule Rome, 108–109

Samnites, 19

Saturn
  and the Golden Age of Latium, 67–68, 86–88, 100, 132
  on coinage, 23
  seen as a human being, 100

Saturnalia, 143

Scipio Africanus the Younger (interlocutor of Cicero), 80–81

Second Coming, 165

Second Temple Judaism, 164

Secular Games. *See* Ludi Saeculares

Seneca the Elder, and the four ages (*aetates*) of the Roman state, 167–168

Seneca the Younger, and the Neronian Golden Age, 163

Sertorius, 64

Servius Tullius, 26

Sibylline Books, 89–90, 159
  edited under Augustus, 134
  epigraphic evidence for celebration in 17 BCE, 123
  in Horace's *Carmen Saeculare*, 122–123
  loss of, 25
  predicted that three Cornelii would rule Rome, 108–109
  some preserved in Phlegon, 205n61
  transferred from Capitoline to Palatine by Augustus, 134

Silver Age, in Hesiod, 84

skepticism, Cicero's, 106–107

Socrates, 80, 102
  multiple reborn Socrateses, 44

Solon, Sulla as Solon-esque Lawgiver, 26

soothsayers and seers, Roman mockery of, 178n91

Sosii, booksellers, 151

statue of Sulla, gilded equestrian, 23–24

Stoic cosmology, 46

Stoicism, 41. *See also* ekpyrosis

Sulla, Lucius Cornelius, 17–39. *See also* memoirs, Sulla's
  as "*iste Romulus*," 26

career
   building program, 23–26
      emulated by Agrippa, 112
   consulship, 18
   dictatorship, 18–19
   epigraphic evidence for, 19
   expansion of the Senate, 24
   marches on Rome, 18, 20
   outline, 18
   proscriptions, 24
   reforms dismantled in his
      lifetime, 22
   retirement, 18, 108
golden hair, 19
image management, 19, 22
immense significance of, 5
infamy of, 108
inserted himself into the
   Etruscan system as man of the
   saeculum, 33–34
numismatic evidence for, 19
one of three Cornelii fated to
   rule Rome, 108
wedded Etruscan *saeculum* to
   Roman politics, 168
Sulmo, 26
swords and ploughshares, 64

Tabularium, 25–26
Tacitus
   Dialogus de Oratoribus, 163
   writes narrative technical history
      of literature, 135
Tanusius Geminus, 63–64
Tarquinia, votive pit at Pian di
   Civita, 34
Tarquins, expulsion of, 167
Tarquitius Priscus, 38
Tarutius, 207n90
taste, popular, fickleness of,
   141–142, 146
Tatius, 75, 79

technical histories, 101, 104, 107
   as a new temporal mode, 84
   of literature, 135–139
      may be narrative or allusive/
         implicit, 135
   rise of technical scholars in the
      Augustan Age, 130–131
teleology, and the evolutionary
   model of literary history, 136–137
temples and shrines
   of Apollo Palatinus, 79, 108,
      131–133, 156, 159
   of Bellona, 21
   of Hercules Custos, 26
   of Hercules Sullanus, 26
   of Jupiter Optimus Maximus, 133
      burning of, 25
   of Libertas, 156
   of Olympian Zeus at Athens, 25
   of Veiovis, 26
   of Vesta, 131
   of Zeus at Olympia, 113
Terence, and the genealogical model
   of literary history, 139
Thebes, 61
Theogenes (seer), 130
Theophilus of Antioch, 185n71
Theophrastus, on first discoverers, 96
theoxeny, 90
   in the Hesiodic *Catalogue of Women*,
      94n49
Theseus and Pirithous, 78
Thespis, in Horace's genealogy of
   drama, 139
Tiberian Age of Roman literature,
   165–168
Tiberius, 160
   in Ovid, will continue the
      Augustan Golden Age, 116
   not honored with a named age,
      6–7
   turns the Golden Age to Iron, 88

250 | General Index

Tibullus
  as anti-Propertius figure, 76–77
  excluded from Propertius'
    genealogy of elegy, 140
  in Ovid's genealogy of elegy,
    138
  on those who do not fit the spirit
    of the age, 76–77
Tibur, 26
time, sociology of, 3
Toynbee, Arnold J., 1
translatio imperii motif, 164
trees, shade-producing *vs.* fruit-
  producing, 103
Triton, 52
Trojan War, set in Hesiod's Heroic
  Age, 84, 102
Trompf, G. W., 4
Troy, 61
trumpet
  omen of, 20–21, 28–29, 45
  votive, folded, 34
Tuscae Historiae, 31–32
Twelve Tables, 148

Valerius Antias, 123–125
Valerius Cato, 145
Valerius Publicola, P., 123
Varro of Atax
  excluded from Ovid's genealogy
    of elegy, 140
  included in Propertius' genealogy
    of elegy, 138
  Ovid questions his epic's
    immortality, 152–153
Varro of Reate
  and Dicaearchus, 60
  and Etruscan *saeculum* doctrine,
    32–33, 45
  as source of Censorinus, 29–33
  doubtful credibility of, 32
  his three divisions of history, 101,
    103–104

Julius Caesar's choice to run his
    planned library, 156
  mocks end of the world stories,
    62
  on palingenesis, 45
  on the scheduling of the Ludi
    Saeculares, 124
  synchronized the horoscopes of
    Augustus and Rome, 130,
    207n90
vegetarianism, 41
Vegoia, Prophecy of, 34–36
Velleius (interlocutor of Cicero),
  106
Velleius Paterculus, 166, 168
Vergil
  and cosmic cyclicality, 163
  Eclogue 4
    alludes to other versions of the
      Metallic Ages, 94
    his ages different from the
      Etruscans' and Sulla's, 92
    Metallic Ages in, 88–95
    Western (Hesiodic) and
      Eastern (Messianic)
      influences, 89
  Etruscan ancestry, 38
  not the epicenter of Roman
    saecular discourse, 169
  works will last as long as Rome in
    Ovid, 153–154
Verrius Flaccus, 124
Vesuvius, 48–49
Victorianism, 8
Vitruvius, and the evolutionary
  model of literary history, 137, 162
Volusius of Hatra, 144
Vulcanius (or Vulcatius), 49, 117

wars and battles
  Actium, Battle of, 133
  Colline Gate, Battle of the, 19
  First Punic War, 77

General Index | 251

Jugurthine War, 18
Mithridatic War, 18, 109
Naulochus, Battle of, 133
Social War, 18–21, 36
Third Punic War, 71, 167
Trojan, 84, 102
weapons and meat-eating, Bronze
    Age in Aratus, Iron in Cicero, 86
White, Hayden, 1–2

XVviri, 25, 134
    calculated schedule for the Ludi
        Saeculares, 123–124

Zeno, 46–47
Zerubavel, Eviatar, 3
Zeuxis, 155
Zmyrna (Cinna), 144, 150, 154
zoogony, 93

Index Locorum

[Aeschylus], *Prometheus Bound*
  442–506: 98
  502: 173n26
Ammianus Marcellinus
  30.4.12: 184n62
Anonymous, *Phoenix*
  11–14: 184n66
Antipater of Thessalonica
  Anth. Pal. 5.31: 87–88
[Apollodorus], *Bibliotheca*
  1.7.2: 187n89
  2.5: 202n20
Appian
  Bellum Civile
    1.97: 175n33
  Punica
    132: 66
Aratus, *Phaenomena*
  96–136: 85–86, 88
Aristocles
  SVF 1.98 = Long and Sedley 46G:
    182n32
Aristotle
  De Caelo
    270b16ff.: 188n106
    270b19–21: 58
  Metaphysics
    1074a38ff.: 188n106
    1074b10ff.: 58

  Meteorologica
    1074b10: 188n106
    339b19ff.: 188n106
    345a: 187n88
    352a: 57, 59
  Politics
    1264a3ff.: 58, 188n106
    1269a: 58
    1269a5ff.: 188n106
    1329b24ff.: 188n106
Athenaeus
  15.92e: 175n27
Augustine, quoting Varro,
  De Civitate Dei
    22.28: 181n25, 205n68
Augustus
  memoirs
    Frs. 1–2 Cornell: 49
  Res Gestae Divi Augusti
    8.5: 117

Callimachus
  Aetia
    1 = fr. 7.13–14 Pfeiffer:
      142
  Iambi
    2 192.1–3: 198n71
  Incerti operis
    Fr. 493: 198n71

254 | Index Locorum

Cassius Dio
  49.43.1: 202n15
  53.1.3: 156
  54.17: 201n3
  56.25.5: 130
Catullus
  1–14: 210n33
  1: 142, 144–145, 149–150
  1.10: 152
  14: 142–145, 149
  14.23: 210n28
  36: 210n28
  43: 210n31
  64: 85–86, 196n49,
    212n59
  64.291: 184n63
  64.382–408: 91
  66.48ff.: 197n61
  67: 191n21
  95: 142, 144, 149–150,
    154
Celsus, *De Medicina*
  1.proem.54, 69: 199n85
  1.11: 102
  2.12.2: 102
Censorinus, *De Die Natali*
  17.2: 181n17
  17.3–5: 123
  17.5–6: 29–31
  17.6: 172n18
  17.7–11: 172n15
  17.8: 124
  17.10: 205n53
  18.11: 59
  21: 199n84
  21.6: 177n69
Cicero
  Academica
    2.125: 44
  Ad Atticum
    2.1.2: 182n40
    7.2: 141
    8.11.2.8: 179n97

    9.7.3: 201n5
    9.7.3.11: 179n97
    9.10.6.8: 179n97
  Ad Familiares
    5.12: 110
    9.4.1: 156
    13.4.1: 179n97
    13.5.2: 179n97
  Brutus
    70–71: 136–137
  De Amicitia
    5: 192n32
    24: 192n32
  De Consulatu Suo: 109–110
  De Divinatione
    1.1: 194n19
    1.71: 173n1
    1.111: 62
    1.112: 188n113
    2.17: 200n100
  De Domo Sua
    43: 179n97
    79: 179n97
  De Finibus Bonorum et Malorum
    3.6.23: 62
  De Haruspicum Responsis
    9.18: 179n100
    18: 179n97
  De Natura Deorum
    1.7: 199n86
    1.11: 204n44
    1.21: 106
    1.43: 198n65
    2.5: 107
    2.51: 187n104
    3.54: 194n19
  De Officiis
    2.16–17: 59, 188n108
    2.75: 190n7
  De Re Publica
    1.45: 201n11
    1.69: 201n11
    2.2: 106

2.3: 167
2.4: 81
2.18–19: 80–82
2.21: 215n17
2.45: 201n11
3.29: 72–73, 201n12
3.34: 110, 167
6.9.23: 62
De Senectute
33: 216n22
55: 190n5
De Temporibus Suis: 110
Fragments
8 Courtney: 191n19
20 Ewbank (*Aratea*): 86
In Catilinam
2.11: 200n99
3.19–21: 109
Marius: 145
Orator
161: 209n14
Paradoxa Stoicorum
6.46: 179n97
42–50: 73, 190n5
Philippic Orations
9.13: 175n35
Pro Balbo
15: 201n6
Pro Lege Manilia
27–48: 109
Pro Murena
49: 179n97
Timaeus
1: 42
Tusculan Disputations
2.23 (translating Aeschylus):
173n26, 198n70
3.45: 209n14
5.7: 173n26, 194n19,
198n70
Verrine Orations
2.1.43: 179n97
2.3.21: 200n99

Cinna
Fr. 6 Hollis: 145, 210n37
Fr. 13 Hollis: 209n24
Fr. 14 Hollis: 145, 210n37
Cleanthes
SVF 1.510 = Long and Sedley 46L:
182n33
Columella
8.16: 173n30
10.67: 184n62

Dicaearchus
Fr. 40 Mirhady: 181n18
Fr. 53–56b Fortenbaugh and
Schütrumpf: 59–60n109
Fr. 78 Fortenbaugh and
Schütrumpf: 59, 188n108
Diodorus Siculus
4.13.3: 202n20
4.22.2: 114
5.23.2: 187n88
32.24: 66
Diogenes Laertius
8.4–5: 43

Eusebius, *Evangelical Preparation*
15.14.12: 182n32

Fenestella
F19 Cornell: 201n3
F25 Cornell: 166, 178n95, 215n13
Furius Bibaculus
Fr. 83 Hollis: 145–146

Gellius
3.3.3–5: 197n60
13.14.3–4: 176n50
Germanicus, *Aratea*: 86
554–562: 186n79
558–560: 130
Grattius, *Cynegetica*
69: 203n28
399–400: 104, 200n92

256 | Index Locorum

Hesiod, *Works and Days*: 4
   106–201: 84–85
Homer, *Iliad*
   6.448–449: 66, 189n137
Horace
   Ars Poetica
      69–72: 212n54
      275–284: 138
      345–346: 151
      465: 196n45–46
   Carmen Saeculare: 89, 122–123,
      204n49
      67: 206n75
   Epistulae
      1.2.43: 192n31
      1.3.8: 192n31
      1.3.15–20: 213n72
      1.12.20: 196n46
      1.20: 149, 151, 153
      2.1: 147–150, 154–158
      2.1.28–29: 213n76
      2.1.52: 180n7
      2.1.159: 192n31
      2.1.216–218: 214n81
      2.2.91–101: 158
      2.2.92–94: 213n71
      2.2.94: 161
   Epodes
      15.21: 180n3
      16: 67–68, 192n29
      16.9: 192n30
      16.65: 204n48
   Odes
      1.1.35–36: 157
      1.2.1–20: 50–51, 65,
         185n70
      1.2.6: 204n48
      1.3: 173n26, 197n62
      1.32: 211n74
      1.35: 77
      1.35.34–35: 204n44
      3.3.40–42: 65
      3.5: 77–78
      3.6: 121–122, 204n47

   3.6.45–48: 192n29
   3.24: 183n47
   3.24.25: 78
   3.30: 150–152, 154
   4.2.37–40: 88
   4.6.29–44: 204n49
   4.6.37–38: 133
   4.6.41–44: 127
   4.6.42: 204n48
   4.11.25: 184n63
   4.15: 78, 88, 92, 115, 117–123,
      192n29
   4.15.17: 132
   Satires
      1.4.1–6: 138
      1.10.67–71: 149
      2.6.63: 180n3
Hyginus, *Fabulae*
   2.29.1.5: 186n79
   30.7.1: 202n20
   154: 185n71
   274–277: 198n68

Inscriptions
   ILS 112: 206n85
   OGI 458.I.4–10: 206n79
   OGI 458.II.30–77: 206n80

Juvenal
   15.30: 184n62

Lactantius
   7.15.14: 167
Livy, *Ab Urbe Condita*
   Praefatio: 72
   1.19.3: 190n10
   2.1.2: 171n7
   2.14.1: 190n10, 204n44
   3.20.5: 190n11
   5.49–55: 189n139
   7.14.6: 190n10
   10.23: 191n16
   26.22.2: 142
   26.22.15: 191n11

28.12.12: 190n10
28.20.7: 66
34.51.5: 190n10
39.6–7: 71–72
39.22.2: 127
Lucan
1.651–657: 184n66
10.110: 191n17
Lucilius (Roman satirist)
F 284 Warmington:
184n62
Lucillius (Greek epigrammatist),
Greek Anthology
11.131: 184n66
11.214: 184n66
Lucretius, *De Rerum Natura*
1.124: 180n7
1.716–829: 94
2.1113: 192n33
2.1150–1174: 104–106
3.670–678: 44
3.843–862: 44
5.8: 198n65
5.96: 185n74
5.324–415: 61–62
5.335–337: 181n22
5.771–1457: 197n63
5.821–836: 200n94
5.828–836, 1273–1280,
1412–1418: 212n54

Manilius, *Astronomica*
1.46: 142
1.513–517: 104
1.718–804: 54
1.816: 104
2.507–509: 130
2.583–593: 192n32
4.546–551: 130
4.773–777: 130
4.821–839: 54
Martial
5.10.8: 192n33
5.53: 184n66

Nemesius
309.5–311.2 = *SVF* 2.625 = Long
and Sedley 52C1: 181n29
Nepos, Cornelius
F1 and F4 Cornell: 143
F2a–d Cornell: 199n81
Nicolaus of Damascus
FGrHist 90 F77: 215n14
Nigidius Figulus
F67 Swoboda: 179n99, 180n9,
207n98
Nonnus, *Dionysiaca*
Book 6: 184n65

Oracula Sibyllina
Book 3: 164
Ovid
Amores
1.8.39–44: 193n39
1.15: 135, 151–154, 157
1.15.23–24: 185n74
2.3.3: 197n61
2.11.1: 197n62
2.13–14: 103
Ars Amatoria
1.241: 204n44
1.672: 193n39
2.277: 87
3.101–128: 79–80, 207n102
3.118: 191n23
3.119–120: 189n146
3.329–348: 135–136
Epistulae ex Ponto
1.3: 103
1.3.83: 209n20
2.6: 78
3.1: 78–79
Fasti
1.191: 195n21
1.193–258: 86–87
1.229–240: 175n26,
189n144
3.153: 180n3
4.107: 197n63

258 | Index Locorum

Heroides
    1.47–58: 65
Ibis
    544: 186n76
Medicamina Faciei Femineae
    11: 191n23
    11–12: 193n39
    11–24: 79
Metamorphoses
    1.78ff: 198n73
    1.125–347: 191n20
    1.188ff.: 206n73
    1.200–415: 51–52
    1.246–249: 188n121
    1.299–300: 65, 186n85
    1.349: 63
    1.363–364: 98–99
    1.747–2.400: 53, 132
    2.26: 173n25
    2.319–322: 187n87
    2.649: 209n20
    7.353–356: 52, 185n71
    7.392: 198n75
    8.97: 185n73
    15.96: 65, 180n13
    15.158–164: 65
    15.158–175: 180n4
    15.261: 65, 180n13
    15.446: 103, 180n13
    15.834–836: 116–117
    15.871–879: 151–152
Tristia
    2.25–26: 126
    2.415–416: 200n88
    2.521–528: 192n25
    3.1: 133
    3.1.59–68: 160
    3.14: 198n68
    4.3.65: 184n63
    4.10: 138, 151–152, 154
    5.9: 78
Ovid (?), *Nux*
    1.11: 102–103

Phaedrus, *Fabulae*
    4.15–16: 198n74
    5.prol.: 155
    App. 5.1: 98, 173n26
Philodemus
    Epigrams
        31: 195n24
    On Signs
        Fr. 4 (De Lacy): 64
Phlegon, *De Macrobiis*
    5.2: 205n61
Pindar, *Olympian Odes*
    10.28–30: 202n21
Piso Frugi
    F38 Cornell: 190n3
    F40 Cornell: 71
Plato
    Critias
        109d–112a: 56
    Laws
        677: 55–56
    Protagoras
        320c–322a: 198n71
    Statesman: 195n33
    Timaeus
        39d: 58
        41a–b: 182n35
Plautus
    Asinaria
        10–12: 208n12
    Boeotia: 97
    Casina
        31–34: 208n12
    Mercator
        9–10: 208n12
    Trinummus
        18–21: 208n12
Pliny the Elder, *Historia Naturalis*
    2.53: 53, 188n113
    2.94: 49
    7.16: 64
    7.52–56: 181n27
    7.112: 182n41

Index Locorum | 259

7.148: 203n30
7.187: 178n95
7.209: 198n68
9.123: 215n13
10.172: 200n89
13.88: 179n97
17.244: 71
34.26: 22
35.10: 156
35.26: 203n35
36.45: 176n43
36.104: 202n15
36.189: 178n95
37.11: 178n95
Pliny the Younger, *Epistles*
6.20: 48–49
Plutarch
  Life of Caesar
    69.5: 49
  Life of Demetrius
    2.2: 178n83
  Life of Gaius Gracchus
    11.1: 189n138
  Life of Pyrrhus
    1: 185n71
  Life of Romulus
    12: 207n90
  Life of Sertorius
    8.1–9.2: 189n141
    9.6–7: 63–64
  Life of Sulla
    5.5–6: 20
    6.5–7: 174n8
    6.7: 19, 174n11
    7.3: 20–21
    7.3–5: 28–29
    7.6: 174n13
    14: 53
    21.4: 177n68
    26: 178n95
    35.1: 176n57
    36: 176n52
    37.1: 173n1, 177n68

On Common Misconceptions
  1075D: 182n33
Pollio, *Historiae*
  fr. 7: 142
Polybius
  6.5.5–6: 60
  6.51.4: 2
  31.25.3–8: 71
  39.6: 66
Porphyrio, *ad Horatii Artem*
  Poeticam
    67–68: 114, 203n34
Porphyry, *Vita Pythagorae*
  19: 181n18
Posidonius
  Fr. 49 Edelstein and Kidd:
    183n44
  Fr. 53 Edelstein and Kidd:
    183n46
  Fr. 284 Edelstein and Kidd:
    183n45
Propertius
  1.4.7: 194n19
  1.16: 74, 191n21
  1.17.13: 197n62
  2.6: 96
  2.6.27–36: 75–76
  2.12.1–4: 197n56
  2.25: 74–75, 79
  2.25.37–38: 76
  2.31/32: 74–75, 132
  2.31/32.15–16: 186n78
  2.31/32.47–48: 75
  2.33.27–30: 198n66
  2.34: 138, 191n22
  2.34.51–54: 195n24
  3.9.49: 189n146
  3.13: 192n26
  4.1.1–2: 189n146
  4.3.19: 198n76
  4.9: 203n26
  4.10: 66
Prophecy of Vegoia: 34–36

260 | Index Locorum

Pseudo-Acron, *ad Horatii Carmen Saeculare*
  8: 124
Pseudo-Justin, *De Resurrectione*
  6: 44
Pseudo-Ovid, *Consolatio ad Liviam*
  45: 192n33
Pseudo-Theocritus, *Idyll* 25: 113
Pythagoras
  Fr. 40–42 FS: 188n107

Quintilian, *Institutio Oratoria*
  8.3.32: 179n97
  8.6.32: 179n97
  10.1.124: 181n22

Sallust
  Catiline
    6–13: 190n4
    11: 178n95
    47: 108
  Histories
    Fr. 1.49 (Ramsey): 176n51
    Fr. 1.87–90 (Ramsey): 189n141
    Fr. 3.49 (Ramsey): 64
    Fr. 9: 190n4
  Jugurtha
    41: 190n4
Sappho
  Fr. 207: 198n71
Scaevola, Q. Mucius
  Fr. 91H: 145
Seneca the Elder
  Controversiae
    2.4.13: 203n35
    3.7: 212n63
    7: 201n9
  Histories
    F2: 167n16
Seneca the Younger
  Apocolocyntosis
    7.5.3: 114, 203n33
  De brevitate vitae
    13.6: 178n95, 215n12

De Ira
  1.20.4: 179n97
Epistulae Morales
  108.30–31: 215n12
Sententiae Vaticanae
  14: 44
Servius
  ad Aen. 6.72: 208n114
  ad Aen. 6.73: 179n97
  ad Bucol. 4.10: 179n99
  ad Ecl. 6.41: 184n66
  ad Ecl. 9.46: 178n83, 204n41
Statius, *Silvae* 4.6.85–88:
  176n58
Stoicorum Veterum Fragmenta
  1.98 (Aristocles): 182n32
  2.625 (Nemesianus):
    181n29
Strabo 13.1.54: 178n95
Suda 1337: 179n100
Suetonius
  Caligula
    11.1: 187n90
  De Grammaticis et Rhetoribus
    9.6: 145–146
    11, 13: 179n97
    20: 156, 198n68
  Divus Augustus
    7.2: 207n94
    29: 160, 213n69
    31.1: 201n3, 208n113
    72.3: 64
    94.5: 207n99
    94.12: 130
    100.2–3: 172n12
  Divus Claudius
    21.2: 205n64
  Divus Julius
    44.2: 156
    56.7: 156
  Tiberius
    59: 195n22
    73.2: 216n18

Tabula Hebana: 214n86
Tacitus, *Annales*
  4.35: 142
Tanusius Geminus
  Fr. 1 Cornell: 63–64
Terence
  Adelphoe
    6–14: 138
  Andria
    19: 138
  Eunuchus
    246–264: 96–97
    27–34: 138
Thucydides
  1.10: 63
  1.22.4: 173n27
Tibullus
  1.2.69: 199n80
  1.3: 199n78
  1.3.49: 208n116
  1.4: 197n55
  1.4.57: 76
  1.7.19: 197n62
  1.7.29ff.: 197n64
  1.9.49–50: 184n66
  1.10: 99–100
  2.1: 99–100
  2.3: 76, 99–100
  2.4.17–18: 195n24
  2.5.9–10: 134, 208n113
  2.5.26–30: 189n146
[Tibullus]
  3.4.25–26: 194n19
  3.7.18–23: 195n24
  Panegyric to Messalla
    4.1.11: 198n66
    4.1.190–211: 42–43,
      42n16

Valerius Cato
  Frs. 84–86 Hollis: 146
Valerius Maximus
  9.14: 181n27

Varro of Atax, *Argonautae*
  fr. 11 Courtney: 184n63
Varro of Reate
  De Gente Populi Romani: 126
    IV: 45
  De Lingua Latina
    6.11: 177n78
  De Re Rustica
    3.1.3: 199n84
  Menippean Satires
    Bimarcus, Fr. 21 Cèbe: 113, 203n25
    Eumenides: 196n46
    Kosmotoryne: 62
Velleius Paterculus
  2.61.3: 175n34
Vergil
  Aeneid
    1.283: 204n50, 206n75
    1.283–291: 203n37
    6.65–70: 205n65
    6.162ff.: 186n78
    6.791–794: 205n65
    6.792–793: 203n37
    8.193–305: 203n26
    8.306–369: 67–68
    8.314ff.: 194n17
    8.526: 186n79
    8.627: 203n37
    9.605: 186n77
    9.609: 142
  Eclogues
    4: 83, 85, 88–95, 115–116, 164,
      168
    4.4–5: 134
    4.10: 179n99, 207n98
    6.41–42: 184n62
  Georgics
    1.32–35: 130
    1.61–62: 184n62
    1.63: 186n77
    1.121ff.: 208n116
    1.466–468: 187n87
    1.466–514: 64

262 | Index Locorum

Vergil (*Continued*)
 1.468: 104
 1.468–514: 116
 1.469–488: 185n70
 1.489–497: 63
 1.493–497: 200n97
 1.501: 185n70
[Vergil]
 Catalepton 9: 111
 Ciris: 111
 Culex
  128: 184n63

Vitruvius, *De Architectura*
 2.pr.5: 199n82
 2.1: 197n63
 7.pr.1–10: 137
 8.pref.: 196n46

Zeno (Stoic philosopher)
 Alexander Lycopolis 19.2–4 = Long
  and Sedley 46I: 182n33
Zosimus
 2.5: 125–126
 2.6: 205n66